All Faithful People

All Faithful People

Change and Continuity in Middletown's Religion

Theodore Caplow

Howard M. Bahr

Bruce A. Chadwick

and

Dwight W. Hoover

Laurence A. Martin

Joseph B. Tamney

Margaret Holmes Williamson

UNIVERSITY OF MINNESOTA PRESS

Minneapolis

Based on research
of the Middletown III Project, 1976-1981,
under a grant from
the National Science Foundation.

Excerpts from MIDDLETOWN and MIDDLETOWN IN
TRANSITION by Robert S. and Helen M. Lynd are reprinted
by permission of Harcourt Brace Jovanovich, Inc. and Constable
Publishers; copyright 1929, 1937 by Harcourt Brace Jovanovich,
Inc.; copyright 1957, 1965 by Robert S. and Helen M. Lynd.

Library of Congress Cataloging in Publication Data

Caplow, Theodore.
    All faithful people.

    Bibliography: p.
    Includes indexes.
    1. Christianity—Indiana—Muncie. 2. Muncie
(Ind.)—Religious life and customs. I. Bahr,
Howard M. II. Chadwick, Bruce A. III. Title.
BR 560.M86C36 1983   306'.6'0977265   82-24759
ISBN 0-8166-1230-7

Table of Contents

Preface

This is the second volume to report the results of the Middletown III study, which Howard Bahr, Bruce Chadwick, and I have conducted in Muncie, Indiana, since 1976. We have tried to prolong and amplify the study of social change that Robert and Helen Lynd began there almost 60 years ago when they investigated the changes that had occurred in that community between 1890 and 1924 in work, family life, education, leisure, religion, and community activities. Following the polite custom of urban sociology, they gave Muncie the pseudonym Middletown, borrowed from a village a few miles away from the city. The name seemed symbolically fitting. The results of the first Lynd study, published in 1929 as *Middletown*, attracted much wider attention than the authors had expected; the book remains in print to this day. Ten years later, they restudied Middletown to see what changes had been wrought by the intervening decade of prosperity and depression. The results of that study were issued in 1937 as *Middletown in Transition;* we call it Middletown II.

Forty years later, we arrived in Muncie to begin work on Middletown III, using the same method as the Lynds had and, when possible, asking identical questions. From 1976 to 1978, we maintained a field office in Middletown and lived there (in rotation) with our families. New questions and leads have continued to present themselves since that time, and these have sent us back from time to time to pursue additional inquiries. Even as I write this, in the spring of 1982, Professors Bahr and Chadwick are just about to start a new survey of leisure activities in Middletown. Meanwhile,

Middletown's fame as a specimen community has continued to spread, encouraged by local interest and participation. In 1981, the Center for Middletown Studies was established under local auspices to serve as a permanent repository for the voluminous information that has been accumulating. In 1982, the remarkable series of documentaries produced by Peter Davis under the collective title of *Middletown* was shown on the Public Broadcasting System. The films depicted concrete human situations in each of the Lynds' cultural categories (such as a political campaign, preparations for a wedding, a crisis in a family business). As a commentary on that series, Ben Wattenberg directed another television documentary, called *Middletown Revisited,* which summarized the results of the Middletown III study and detailed some changes in Middletown between 1978 and 1982. Indeed, so much attention has recently been lavished on Middletown that some reviewers have reasonably wondered whether its claim to be typical has not been tainted by the celebrity it enjoys for its typicality. We are sensitive to this criticism, but our encounters with Middletown people suggest that, although most of them are aware of the studies and films, their interest remains exceedingly mild. The first volume of this series, *Middletown Families: Fifty Years of Change and Continuity,* published by the University of Minnesota Press in 1982, elicited a grand total of three letters to local newspapers.

Besides *Middletown Families,* more than 20 papers have been published to report the findings of the Middletown III study. A list of these follows the Bibliography. In addition to the contributors to *All Faithful People,* the authors of these reports include John Hewitt, Otis D. Duncan, C. Bradford Chappell, Geoffrey K. Leigh, Grace M. Marvin, Penelope C. Austin, Alexander E. Bracken, William S. Johnson, Thomas M. Guterbock, Lawrence A. Young, David M. Margolick, and Kathleen Bateman.

We again acknowledge our indebtedness to the advisory council of distinguished scholars to whom the project staff turned for advice and guidance in 1977 and 1978. The council was composed of Otis D. Duncan, chairman, and of Jeffrey K. Hadden, Reuben Hill, Charles Hyneman, Alex Inkeles, Sheldon Stryker, and Wilbert E. Moore.

Among the many residents of Muncie and Delaware County,

Indiana, to whom we are grateful for advice, hospitality, and practical assistance, these people stand out: Whitney Gordon, Dr. Philip Ball, David C. Tambo, Ray R. Suput, Hurley Goodall, Lester Hewitt, Alexander Bracken, Sr., John Pruis, Mayor Robert Cunningham, Larry Dyer, and the late Colonel Robert H. Myers, who made his local knowledge available to us as he had done for the Lynds long ago. Another local informant, the Reverend Laurence A. Martin, pastor of Muncie's First United Presbyterian Church, did us the honor of contributing to this volume along with Dwight W. Hoover, professor of history, and Joseph B. Tamney, professor of sociology, at Ball State University, both long-time residents of Muncie whose personal experiences reinforce their scholarly conclusions.

The extraordinarily talented and zealous research staff that carried out the fieldwork included in Muncie Geoffrey Leigh, Bradford Chappell, Penelope Austin, Alice-Lynn Ryssman, Daniel Hayden, Judy Wright, Debra Martin, Ellen Casky, Julie Hourclé, Mark Boarman, Linda Kessler, Debra Ensch, Thomas Wolforth, Cindy Stanley, Linda Holm, Esther Ball, Jan Hendrix, Linda Horton, and Dottie Murk; in Charlottesville, Carmen Matarazza, Robert Kelleher, John Mahoney, Calvin Stover, Donna Jost, John Albright, Bruce Morrow, Carl Pascale, Jr., and Patricia Passuth; in Provo, Utah, Lawrence Young. The secretarial staff was directed by Cleva G. Maggio in Charlottesville. Lorraine Cote also worked there, while Ruth Poll Barlow was in Provo and Ellen Casky and Debra Ensch in Muncie.

The project was generously supported by the National Science Foundation with a grant to the University of Virginia (NSF SOC 75-13580) that was several times renewed between 1976 and 1981 and another grant (NSF SES 79-18528) that enabled us to retabulate the original enumerations of Middletown's population in the eight decennial censuses from 1910 to 1980 in a standard form that facilitates the examination of trends. We are grateful to the three successive directors of the National Science Foundation's sociology program, Donald R. Ploch, Roland J. Liebert, and James J. Zuiches, who supported the project, and also to Martin B. Hickman, dean of the College of Social Sciences at Brigham Young University, who provided research support for Middletown III from that institution.

When this manuscript was in final preparation, we were saddened by the death of Dr. Helen Merrell Lynd at the age of 85. It was Dr. Lynd, the surviving author of the original Middletown studies, who made Middletown III possible by giving us access to the files of Middletown I and II, deposited under seal in the Library of Congress.

All Faithful People is a jointly authored book and not a collection of contributed papers and, because we have collectively reviewed and corrected each other's contributions, the chapters are not separately attributed to their principal authors. But, for the convenience of readers, they are listed here: I am primarily responsible for Chapters 1, 4, and 14; Bahr for Chapters 5, 7, and 11; Chadwick for Chapters 3, 8, and 10; Chadwick and Bahr for Chapter 12; Hoover for Chapter 2; Martin for Chapter 13; Tamney for Chapter 6; and Williamson for Chapter 9.

Like its predecessor, *Middletown Families,* this volume is about change and continuity in a single American community, which was selected for its lack of outstanding peculiarities. The findings of Middletown III about family and religion have attracted unusual public attention in the media because they show more continuity in these fundamental institutions than had been promised by the myth that social change is now more rapid and destructive than ever before. The facts, we believe, show something quite different: that modernization, the principal engine of recent social change, has been slowing down in the United States during the past half-century and that this deceleration has allowed some features of American culture to remain virtually unchanged. But the surprising continuities in religion that we report in this book ought not to obscure the equally important changes described here (for example, the great increase of religious tolerance that has occurred in Middletown without any diminution of religious zeal).

Theodore Caplow

Charlottesville, Virginia

All Faithful People

Chapter 1

Religion in Middletown

This is a book about change and continuity in the religious life of one American community during the 20th century. Toward the end of the 1970s, we went back to the small midwestern city that Robert and Helen Lynd had studied in the 1920s and again in the 1930s to see what the intervening decades had done to its social institutions.[1] The Lynds called the place Middletown, a name they borrowed from a village near the city. It was and is the practice in community studies to assign a collective pseudonym to the place studied; many of these have become famous: Yankee City, Elmtown, Plainville, Southerntown, Eastern City, Crestwood Heights, and Park Forest, among others. But Middletown is the most famous of all, perhaps because of its location so close to the center of American culture. The most striking feature of Middletown is that it contains nothing extraordinary. When the Lynds went there, it was primarily industrial; engine parts, glass bottles, and woven wire were its best-known products; it was also a trade center for the surrounding agricultural counties. Its population was mostly white, mostly native born, mostly Protestant. It had no "outstanding peculiarities or acute local problems" and was just far enough from Indianapolis, Indiana, and Dayton, Ohio, to be able to resist their influence.

The children the Lunds observed almost 60 years ago are now elderly people or they are dead. Middletown's population has tripled, from about 40,000 to about 120,000 in the city and its suburbs. Most of the factories that were operating during the 1920s are still open but some have been closed, and those that remain are approaching obsolescence. The little teachers' college has mushroomed into a state university that is now the community's largest employer. The population is not quite as homogeneous as it used to be: there are proportionately more blacks (12 percent) and more Catholics (22 percent) now than there were during the Lynds' study. Despite these changes, Middletown seems to us to have preserved the identity and atmosphere the Lynds described in the 1920s and the 1930s (Lynd and Lynd 1929, 1937).

It is easier for us to grasp change than continuity because change forces itself on our attention and continuity does not. At Wright Field near Dayton, 75 miles east of Middletown, a modified version of the Curtis JN-4D "Jenny" was still being used for training purposes when the Lynds began their study. The plane weighed 1400 pounds and cost $5,000. It had a maximum speed of 75 miles per hour and a range of nearly 200 miles. By 1976, when we began the restudy of Middletown, the F-111 was being used; it weighed 40,000 pounds, cost $5,000,000, and could exceed a speed of 2,000 miles per hour. The contrast between the frail contraption of cloth, wicker, and wire and the huge gleaming tube of exotic metal is almost absurd. They seem not to have been devised by the same race.

If technology provides us with the thrill of rapid change, social institutions can do the same. In 1924, the federal government was represented in Middletown by a handful of postal employees and a U.S. marshal, based in Indianapolis, who occasionally visited. In the 10 years prior to 1976, 29 agencies of the federal government operated more than 90 separate programs fo social improvement and control in Middletown and spent nearly $700 million on them. At least half of Middletown's families, the rich as well as the poor, depend on direct payments from the federal government for a substantial part of their incomes. The change from an autonomous, private economy to one largely controlled by the national state is as spectacular in its way as the contrast between the JN-4D and the F-111. Such leaps are part of daily experience throughout the contemporary world, even in places like Middletown where the great surge of modernization took place during the 19th century and the *rate* of modernization has recently slowed down (Bahr, Caplow, and Leigh 1980).

The skyrocketing changes may dazzle us so much that we cannot see the continuities that go along with them. Indeed, it is possible to imagine dazzling changes where nothing has changed at all. When experts do this, there are certain rhetorical tricks they find useful. For example, they may compare a present situation accurately observed with a past situation imaginatively constructed out of whole cloth—like that American past when everyone went to church and the rules of morality were universally respected. Another device is to manufacture a picture of the present out of scraps of surmise and wisps of anxiety. "Organized religion," says a minister addressing a civic club in Texas, "is sadly weak. Churches are plagued by crippling problems. Membership and Sunday school enrollments are down seriously" (Shoman 1980, 28). Statistically this is nonsense, but it has a persuasive ring, and to someone in a declining denomination it may sound like the literal truth.

American religion is too broad a phenomenon for comprehensive observation. That is why, in this book, we have taken the opportunity to examine the changes in religious practices and beliefs that have taken place in a single community for which, by great good fortune, we have an accurate, highly detailed description of religious life 60 years ago to compare with the description drawn from surveys conducted between 1977 and 1981. After we have made our comparisons and assessed the changes and continuities in Middletown's religion, it will become reasonable to ask whether Middletown's collective experience resembles the national experience, for it is to understand the national experience that we study Middletown. None of us had any personal ties to that hospitable midwestern community when we went there, but, because it was so carefully described by our great predecessors two generations ago, it is now uniquely informative about the main trends in American society. The Lynds, of course, never claimed that Middletown represented the United States or even the Midwest, and we will follow their good example in this as in other things. A trend or pattern discovered in Middletown cannot be ascribed to the whole country without some chain of inference, but we will try as we go along to construct such chains where they can be subjected to reasonable tests. If we find, for example, that men and women are more alike in their religious behavior in today's Middletown than they used to be, we may fairly ask whether the change is unique to Middletown and look for national data that may shed light on that question. In some instances, we can stretch the chain of inference a little farther. For example, we have figures for church attendance in Middletown from 1890 to the present and comparable data for the entire country from 1948 to 1980. If the trend from 1948 to 1980 has been the same in Middletown and in the country as a whole, we are authorized to consider the possibility, which we cannot prove, that the trends may have been similar before 1948, too. But all this comes later in our story, when we begin to match statistical series.

Tocqueville's Formula

It was Alexis de Tocqueville, that uncannily acute observer of the nation in its youth, who first described the American system of religion and ventured to explain it in *Democracy in America,* first published in 1835. He asked himself why the division of Christianity into "innumerable sects" and the total separation of the clergy from politics had reinforced, instead of diminished, the influence of religion and the link between religion and morality. He wondered, too, why Americans were so much more religious than Europeans when religion in America entirely lacked the official support that it enjoyed in every European country during the 19th century.

"One may suppose", he wrote, "that a certain number of Americans, in the worship they offer to God, are following their habits rather than their convictions. . . . Nonetheless America is still the place where the Christian religion has kept the greatest real power over men's souls. . . . The religious atmosphere of the country was the first thing that struck me on arrival in the United States. The longer I stayed in the country, the more conscious I became of the important political consequences resulting from this novel situation.

". . . I wondered how it could come about that by diminishing the apparent power of religion one increased its real strength and I thought it not impossible to discover the reason" (Tocqueville [1835] 1969, 295-96).

Tocqueville's explanation was that the fragmentation of American religion prevented it from developing any alliance with the state. A religion could only be destroyed, he thought, by its involvement in the shifting currents of politics or by its confrontation with another religion. American religion was protected from the latter danger by its sectarian fragmentation and from the former by the indigenous doctrine that church and state should be entirely separate.

To this Tocqueville added a straightforward Durkheimian model of individual motivation (although he wrote it before Durkheim was born). An egalitarian society encourages self-interest and love of pleasure to the point of demoralization unless the selfish strivings of individuals are limited by norms of duty imposed from the outside. But in a democratic egalitarian society such as the United States, the government lacks the moral authority to impose such norms. The citizens cling to religion because it provides the restraints on their own behavior that are necessary for their happiness.

Tocqueville observed that all the American denominations preached the same morality and held the same conception of civic duty. "There is an innumerable multitude of sects in the United States. They are all different in the worship they offer to the Creator, but all agree concerning the duties of men to one another" (Tocqueville [1835] 1969, 290).

As a practicing Catholic, Tocqueville sought out and made friends with Catholic priests in his travels. He was fascinated to discover that Catholicism, which in Europe was then considered the bulwark of absolutism and social hierarchy, supported democratic liberties in America with as much fervor as any of the Protestant denominations and that the Catholic clergy in the United States, like their Protestant colleagues, stood aloof from politics, took no part in government, and drew a sharp line between religious and secular issues.

Almost 150 years later, Tocqueville's description is still partially applicable to the condition of religion in Middletown. The sects, if not innumerable, are very numerous. We counted 24 denominations in 1980 that support church buildings and salaried ministers. About 35 more denominations are represented in various ways, and there are many independent churches as well. For the most part, they hold common views about private and public morality, supporting, in the private sphere, monogamous marriage, family solidarity, the Ten Commandments, private charity, self-control, self-improvement, dutifulness, and patience under suffering and, in the public sphere, patriotism, the authority of the law, democracy, and human rights. They are less unanimous in their opinion on those specific issues in which the separation between religion and politics has been breached, either by the rise of social activism within denominations or by the expansion of governmental activity into the domain formerly reserved to religion. Middletown's denominations do not agree about abortion, parochial education, the equality of the sexes, or the obligation to perform military service. But, aside from such politicized issues, there is little difference to be noted between the moral positions of Catholics and Quakers, Presbyterians and Nazarenes, Methodists and Jews.

When the Lynds observed the churches of Middletown in 1924, the abstention of the clergy from politics was as complete as it had been in Tocqueville's time, although the ministers of business-class congregations might occasionally have echoed from the pulpit the sentiments of their golf partners about labor unions or referred in passing to "godless Bolshevism." When the Lynds came back to Middletown 10 years later in the midst of the Great Depression, they were themselves much more committed to social activism than they had been before and they found it deplorable that only a few Middletown ministers had increased their political involvement in response to the depression. The sermon topics of 1935 were interchangeable with those of a decade before and had almost nothing to say about current events. The Ministerial Association had no program for dealing with economic hard times. The Lynds were distressed to see that, with one or two exceptions, the Protestant churches of Middletown were taking no position at all on "internationalism, disarmament, pacifism, labor organization, social planning in the interest of the masses and the redistribution on wealth, civil liberty, the amendment of the Constitution, socialized medicine, and birth control" (Lynd and Lynd 1937, 312). And the Catholics and the Jews were even more remote from public issues than the Protestants.

The Lynds saw less virtue in this separation than had Tocqueville. They thought that the churches ought to be more actively coping with social change and lamented that "Middletown's churches appear to be forever bartering the opportunity for leadership in the area of change for the right to continue a shadowy leadership in the changeless, as the church defines the latter" (311). They also deplored, as Tocqueville had once applauded, "the encouragement of patriotism by the churches" (312).

During the 1960s, a few of Middletown's churches developed an active interest in public events. The clergy led the movement; their congregations followed at a distance and with apparent reluctance. A line of fracture developed between "worldly" and "other worldly" factions within the churches affected by the change. These internal conflicts were particularly sharp in the denominations the Lynds had identified as "business class," especially the Presbyterians and the Methodists. Working-class denominations such as the Southern Baptists, the Adventists, and the Assemblies of God were untouched by the problem and thrived between 1960 and 1980, while the Presbyterians and the Methodists declined in membership for the first time in living memory. The Catholics and the Lutherans, wracked by the same issues, barely held their own in membership as their church attendance and ritual participation declined.

Meanwhile, the wall of separation between church and state was breached with enthusiasm by the federal judiciary until, in the words of Chief Justice Warren Burger, it became "a blurred, indistinct, and variable barrier." The U.S. Supreme Court decided at various times in the 1970s that transporting parochial students to and from school at public expense is constitutional but transporting them on field trips is unconstitutional, that the loan of a public school's textbooks to a parochial school is constitutional but the loan of audiovisual material is unconstitutional, that a state may provide guidance counseling for parochial students in a mobile unit but not on their school grounds, and so on and so forth until no one could tell what the principle of separation meant in a particular case without resorting to litigation. The Catholics of Middletown, who by 1980 sent most of their children to the parochial school, found themselves permanently involved in politics over the question of school aid, while at the same time the abortion issue joined Catholics and Protestant fundamentalists in an unprecedented alliance. By 1980, the pattern that Tocqueville so much admired—the innumerable sects, their support of a common morality, and their total abstention from politics—had been somewhat damaged by these developments. But it was by no means destroyed. Most of Middletown's churches were still apolitical most of the time, and most of them still agreed about the duties of people in their dealings with one another. Indeed, they had found some new areas of agreement.

The Middletown Spirit

The values that Middletown held in 1935 are summarized—or parodied—in Chapter 12 of *Middletown in Transition*, "The Middletown Spirit," a litany of the platitudes that were current in Middletown around 1935.[2] One section of it deals with religion. Wrote the Lynds (1937, 416-17):

By and large, Middletown believes:

That Christianity is the final form of religion and all other religions are inferior to it.

But that what you believe is not so important as the kind of person you are.

That nobody would want to live in a community without churches, and everybody should, therefore, support the churches.

That churchgoing is sometimes a kind of nuisance, one of the things you do as a duty, but that the habit of churchgoing is a good thing and makes people better.

That there isn't much difference any longer between the different Protestant denominations.

But that Protestantism is superior to Catholicism.

That having a Pope is un-American and a Catholic should not be elected President of the United States.

That Jesus is the Son of God and what he said is true for all time.

That Jesus was the most perfect man who ever lived.

That God exists and runs the universe.

That there is a "hereafter." "It is unthinkable that people should just die and that be the end."

That God cannot be expected to intercede in the small things of life, but that through faith and prayer one may rely upon His assistance in the most important concerns of life.

That preachers are rather impractical people who wouldn't be likely to make really good in business.

That I wouldn't want my son to go into the ministry.

That preachers should stick to religion and not try to talk about business, public affairs, and other things "they don't know anything about."

When the faint vein of satire that runs through this text is disregarded, these elements can be discerned in it: a simplified, straightforward, and highly ecumenical version of Christian theology; a chauvinistic contempt for non-Christian religions and for Catholicism by Protestants; a view of church activity as onerous but worthwhile; and a respectful disparagement of ministers.

If the Lynds were accurate in their recording of this litany—and we know that they had fine ears for the voices around them—then what we hear in today's Middletown shows a surprising evolution. To sum it up hastily (we will return to the details in later chapters), Middletown Protestants follow the same theology now as then, but (1) they are no longer contemptuous of Catholics or of non-Christians, (2) they express considerable respect for ministers as a class, and (3) they are now more inclined to regard churchgoing as a pleasure than as a chore.

With respect to doctrine, the faint differences between Protestant denominations have become fainter in the past few decades, and the gulf between Protestants and Catholics is now more easily bridged. Middletown people nowadays think nothing at all of attending services or taking communion at a church of some other denomination. Most of Middletown's Protestants have Catholic friends and attend Catholic services without embarrassment. Catholics, for their part, no longer regard the inside of a Protestant church as a dark, heretical place. Indeed, for some churchgoers, the essential line of division is no longer drawn between Protestants and Catholics but between the sacramental and the evangelical denominations, but this distinction is not absolute either. There has been a charismatic revival among Catholics, Episcopalians, and Lutherans, and some Methodist services have a very sacramental tone.

Denominational Geography

Column 1 of Appendix Table 1-1 shows the denominational affiliations of a composite sample of Middletown adults; the affiliations were compiled from the responses to our several surveys that asked for the respondents' religious affiliations. As previously noted, about 60 denominations (Tocqueville's "innumerable sects") are represented in this one small city, but the summary data show considerable concentration. Methodists, Baptists, Catholics, and Presbyterians account for over half of the total population; the remainder is widely dispersed. In order to get a picture of the distribution, we have grouped the smaller denominations as follows: Pentecostal denominations, conservative denominations, special-creed denominations, Unitarians, and non-Christians. This is not a very satisfactory taxonomy, but we have not been able to devise a better one. The Pentecostal churches are rather informally organized; they insist on the literal interpretation of the Bible and attach importance to charismatic practices. The conservative denominations, like the Brethern and the Disciples of Christ, are more formally organized; they interpret scripture literally but follow a strict liturgy in their services. Each of the several denominations uncomfortably lumped together as "special-creed Christians" has some unique doctrine that sets it apart from other Christians. The Unitarian group includes Universalists and Deists. The few non-Christians are mostly Jews; there are a handful of Muslims and Buddhists, and a few members of exotic cults.

The next step is to compare Middletown's religious distribution with that of the entire United States. Questions about religion are not included on the national census, but there have been numerous national surveys that provide good estimates. Column 2 of Table 1-1, taken from a 1978 survey by the National Opinion Research Center, shows such a national distribution. We see at once that Middletown has fewer Catholics, fewer Baptists, and more Methodists than the country has as a whole.

So far as we can discover, no single community in the United States conforms closely to the national distribution for the simple reason that American denominations are regional entities. Except for Episcopalians, who are present in small numbers everywhere, each major denomination is concentrated in its own province.

"The Appalachian Mountains," wrote Richard Niebuhr in 1929 (1968, 187), "drew the first dividing boundary between American denominations, the Mason and Dixon Line bisected the two unequal portions which resulted and added churches of the North and South to churches of the East and West." Thus, the Baptist province occupies nearly the whole area below the 37th parallel between the Atlantic and the Rockies; the Upper Midwest is a Lutheran territory; Catholics are predominant in the Northeast, around the Great Lakes, and in the Southwest; Jews are concentrated in New York; and Mormons are even more heavily concentrated in Utah. Describing this distribution, Marty (1979, 87) identified Middletown's region as part of:

the Methodist empire, "the North of the South and the South of the North," the legacy of the circuit rider and evangelist who crossed the Appalachians and dashed west for 50 years as far as Kansas. This belt is not solid. The middle and border states simply had too many competing voices to permit a single dominance. But Methodism, far more diffused throughout the country, still could rely on this area. In the years when Methodists were united in support of specific causes like temperance, this was a belt that could be counted on. The religious proclamation there might have been stamped as more liberal than was the Baptist version. The seminaries permitted more critical study of the Bible than did the Southern Baptist counterparts. Nevertheless, Methodism created a churchly culture of significant potency in determining the mores of an area.

Unlike the Baptists, the Methodists do not comprise a majority of the total population in any significant part of their empire. But east, west, and north of Middletown, there is no sizable community within 200 miles where Methodists are not well represented.

Another way Middletown differs from the United States as a whole is that it has little to show us about what Greeley calls "religion as an ethnic phenomenon" (Greeley 1972a). Middletown has so small a proportion of recent immigrants and their children that the boundaries of ethnic groups are blurred to forgetfulness. Even in 1890, less than 5 percent of the city's population were foreign-born; by 1980, less than 1 percent were. Its Lutheran congregations can no longer be identified as Swedish Lutheran or German Lutheran. The Catholic church is not Irish Catholic or Polish Catholic. The English, Scotch-Irish, and German names borne by the majority of the population do not predict which church they attend.

Although every church in Middletown ostensibly welcomed black members by 1980, and many did so with real conviction, 11 o'clock on Sunday morning is still, in the familiar phrase, the most segregated hour of the week, a condition that owes as much to the reluctance of blacks to leave their own cohesive churches as to the unspoken reluctance of whites to accord them full fellowship. But because the religion of Middletown's black citizens is being separately and extensively investigated by our colleagues Rutledge Dennis and Vivian Gordon, we will have relatively little to say about it in this volume.

The Methods of the Study

The Middletown III study, of which this report on Middletown's religion is a part, was designed as a replication of the study of Middletown carried out by Robert and Helen Lynd in 1924 and 1925 and reported in *Middletown* (1929), which was the first socio-logical work to become a best-seller in the United States. It went through six printings the year it was published, and it has never been out of print. More than half a century after its original publication a paperback edition of *Middletown* is still finding new readers.

The Lynds enjoyed the rare gift of a timeless sociological style. Hardly anything they wrote in the 1920s strikes the contemporary reader as old-fashioned or out-of-date. When we used questions from their 1924 questionnaires in our own surveys, we discovered with surprise that most of them required no revision at all in order to be acceptable to contemporary respondents. How the Lynds accomplished this, we cannot tell. Most survey questionnaires are hopelessly out of date within 10 years.

Middletown was much more than a description of Muncie, Indiana, in 1924. It was a grandly designed study of social change organized around half a dozen key concepts such as—using modern labels—stratification, inequality, modernization, value consensus and dissensus, and disynchronous change. These concepts had al-ready appeared in the sociological literature, especially in the great 1918 study of Polish immigration to America by Thomas and Znaniecki (1958) and in a series of brilliant studies of Chicago's subcommunities by the students of Robert E. Park.[3] But the Lynds handled these ideas so deftly that even now the systematic study of social change has not moved much beyond the point to which they brought it.

They were the first sociologists to grasp the necessity of study-ing social change as a movement from one precise point in time to another. In order to provide a base period for the 1924-1925 study, they did a retrospective survey of 1890 Middletown using diaries, letters, newspapers, official records, and what would now be called oral-history interviews.

The scientific study of social change is intrinsically difficult in that it often requires us to compare the present—about which we know too much—with the past—about which we know too little. Myths are made by trimming the people and events of a bygone era to match our present visions of progress or decay. When the vision changes, the facts must also change. The temptation to mythologize is personal as well as collective. What parents describe to their children the treatment they received from their own parents without some mythologizing?

Memory is particularly fallible about the collective values and attitudes of the past. Were Middletown's factory workers more concerned with their jobs and their prospects in 1890 than in 1924; were children more obedient to their parents; were religious beliefs assailed by fewer doubts? The answers to such questions that can be developed from oral-history interviews are nearly worthless, partially because of imperfect memory but mostly because the respondents did not have the means to make accurate observations back in the base period. The partial reconstruction of past values and attitudes from documentary sources is sometimes feasible when the right documents are available. In their reconstruction of 1890, the Lynds relied heavily on a few good diaries, which provided an illuminating if highly selective view of archaic Middletown; and they also used newspaper clippings, sermons, commercial reports, organizational advertisements, and even fiction to flesh out their description.

Occasionally they fell victim to the temptation of inferring the attitudes of the vanished audience from the exhortations addressed to them, but they were not deceived that way very often. Their reconstruction of 1890 Middletown was grounded on verifiable demographic, economic, and cultural data. The Lynds were approriately reticent, for want of reliable information, about the trends in religious commitment, inequality, occupational satisfaction, marital happiness, and other elusive indicators from 1890 to 1924. Consequently, their picture of the critical era that witnessed Middletown's metamorphosis from an agrarian to an industrial community is full of gaps. For example, we cannot tell, after close examination of the Lynds' data, whether Middletown showed more or less consensus about major social values in 1890 than in 1924. Even an unlimited investment of time and effort could probably not recover that information from the surviving documents. If the reconstruction of the subjective aspects of the past is so difficult for Middletown—a small city about which more is known than about any other city in the world—it must be nearly impossible for any larger community.

The extraordinary difficulty of ascertaining trends in collective attitudes and values when we start with the present and work back to the past does not discourage journalists and politicians and scholars from doing it. They find all sorts of encouraging trends when progress is in style and all sorts of grave symptoms when social problems are in fashion. Of such stuff are sociological myths made, like the myth of the crumbling American family. The myths embody the mood of an era but tell us nothing useful about social change. Since the study of social change seems to us to be the raison d'être of sociology—as it was for Comte, Tocqueville, Marx, Spencer, Durkheim, Weber, Pareto, Thomas, Park, and the Lynds, among others—it is distressing to realize how little we actually know about social change in modern communities after all the attention that has been lavished on the topic. The Lynds, it seems to us, had the right idea more than 50 years ago when they combined hard data on demography, employment, housing, school attendance, magazine circulation, and a hundred other indicators with what they could discover about attitudes and values to elicit the trends from 1890 to 1924. That is probably why *Middletown* continues to find new readers today.

The Lynds had an even better idea when they decided to go back to Middletown in 1935 to see what changes had been wrought by a decade of prosperity and depression and to use the extensive data they had collected in 1924-1925 as a base from which to measure those changes. In the experimental sciences (physics and chemistry, for example), replication is the cornerstone of scientific procedure. In the social sciences, it is more often praised[4] than practiced. The Lynds introduced replication into the sociological study of communities when they went back to Middletown in 1935 to gather information about the various sectors of community life and to compare the new information with the information they had gathered according to the same rubric 10 years before. Although the second study was not on the scale of the original study, *Middletown in Transition* (1937) is probably the best source we have about the impact of the Great Depression on American society. Although the Lynds had specifically warned against the incautious application of their findings to other cities or to Americal life in general, their findings obviously *were* applicable to some extent to spheres beyond Middletown. "Despite some local and sectional peculiarities," said a *New York Times* reviewer when the book appeared, "Middletown is the country in miniature, almost the world in miniature" (Dufus 1937).

This notable work ought to have established replication as the standard procedure in the study of social change, but it did not. Community studies drifted off in other directions, some suggested by other aspects of the Middletown study, and for a long time there were no more replications on any significant scale. A. B. Hollingshead, who studied Elmtown, another midwestern community, during the 1940s, visited the place for a few weeks 30 years later and wrote a fascinating but cursory supplement to *Elmtown's Youth* (1961, 1975). Two graduate students went back at different times to the congenial Boston slum that Whyte described in *Street Corner Society* (1943) and wrote up their findings (Boelen 1970), and Whyte himself kept in touch with subsequent developments there (Whyte 1955). Yankee City, comprehensively studied by Lloyd Warner and his associates in the 1930s,[5] was studied again 30 years later by Thernstrom (1964) with the object of revising the idyllic picture of the community's past drawn by the original study. Thernstrom's restudy, however, touched on only part, and the weakest part, of Warner's vast community survey and cannot be considered a replication of it.

The innovative method of community study suggested by *Middletown in Transition* was not fully imitated until 1976, when we went to Middletown to begin the replication we call Middletown III. Gathering data for Middletown III took between 50 and 60 person-months in the field, about the same as the effort devoted to Middletown I more than half a century ago.

Despite our confidence in replication as a method, at the outset we did not fully understand the importance of matching the survey data gathered in the 1920s with comparable data from the 1970s and of centering the new study on those topics for which the old study gave us the opportunity to measure trends with some accuracy. As we went along, we realized how rare and precious it is to have a long-term social trend firmly grounded at both ends, and we focused our efforts accordingly. Like our predecessors, we made extensive use of participant and detached observation and of documentary materials of all kinds: diaries, maps, photographs, newspapers, letters, minutes, advertisements, speeches, circulars, case histories, court records, programs, greeting cards, and other samplings from the vast mountain of paper a contemporary community produces. Like the Lynds, we attended church services and political meetings, picnics and graduations, weddings and funerals, private parties and public ceremonies. Four of us brought children to Middletown and sent them to the local public schools, where in their fashion the children made useful observations. We were able, as the Lynds were not, to draw upon the experience and knowledge of scholars on the faculty of the state university that has grown up in Middletown since the Lynds' time. Two of the state university faculty members, Dwight Hoover and Joseph Tamney, contributed to the present volume; another contributor, Laurence Martin, is the pastor of one of Middletown's leading churches. Others, who will be mentioned in due course, have been extremely helpful.

Although we regard replication as the best method of studying social change, we hasten to admit that a sociological replication can never be an exact repetition of the original study. The principal difference in method between Middletown I and Middletown III is that the latter depended much more on formal interview and questionnaire surveys and much less on unstructured interviews. The reasons behind this change in approach were compelling. First, the present population of Middletown is twice as large (three times as large when the suburbs are included) as it was in the 1920s, and the structure of the community is correspondingly more complex. Second, although the Lynds conducted only three formal surveys as part of their study, the findings of those surveys turned out to be the most valuable part of their work for our purposes, and it is likely that survey findings will be the part of our work most useful to future investigators. Third, the technique of the social survey has been greatly improved in recent decades.

Between 1977 and 1979, we conducted 14 separate surveys as part of the Middletown III project—9 by written questionnaire and

5 by interview. The present volume draws principally upon the 1977 housewives' survey, a careful repetition of a 1924 interview survey conducted by the Lynds; the 1978 survey of religious attitudes and practices, a mail questionnaire; the 1977 high school survey, a questionnaire administered to the entire population of Middletown's public high schools that was very similar to the questionnaire the Lynds administered to the high school population of 1924; the 1978 questionnaire survey of Middletown ministers; a 1979 interview survey about Middletown's celebration of the previous Christmas; and a small interview survey of ministers undertaken in 1981.

The nine other surveys undertaken by the Middletown III team do not deal extensively with religion. However, those having to do with family dynamics, neighboring, the occupations of women, the occupations of men, and the local activities of the federal government have furnished background information for this volume.

Survey data are not as colorful and deeply textured as information obtained by participant observation or in-depth interviewing but they are much more reliable, and those of us who have made extensive use of surveys in the study of social change could not be persuaded to dispense with them in favor of any other method of investigation. The survey method is particularly suited to the study of religious beliefs and practices under contemporary American conditions, since most adults construe their own beliefs and practices as voluntary and are happy to talk about them.

We will have more to say in a later chapter about how religious voluntarism has developed in Middletown. The major denominations no longer coerce or threaten the wavering faithful. Husbands and wives need not copy each other in their religion; it is common for one to attend church regularly while the other stays permanently away. They may belong to different denominations without attracting censure from either set of fellow communicants. There is no disgrace attached to leaving one church for another or to doing it more than once. The pious are not mocked by unbelievers, and the unbelievers are not scorned by the pious.

Although in the 1920s duty was the principal motive for church attendance, most of the people who attended church regularly in the 1970s said that they did so for the pleasure of it while most of those who stayed away regularly did not apologize for their absence. Most people in Middletown are willing to describe their religious experience to a stranger, and they do so without embarrassment. Those who are "born again" are proud of it, but those who have sloughed off their faith are rather pleased with themselves, too. The net result of these attitudes is that surveys of religious behavior are much less troublesome to carry out than surveys of family behavior, where guilt and shame lurk at every turn; or of occupational behavior, in which the respondent must often recount his or her own failures; or of financial or sexual activities, about which there are many motives for secrecy.

Previous Surveys

The Lynds' high school survey and their housewives' survey, both done in 1924, were the first sociological surveys of religious belief and practice in the United States as far as we have been able to discover. In 1943, Cantril reported the results of a question on religious affiliation included in two public opinion polls in 1939 and 1940 that made it possible to show the interrelationship of religious affiliation (Catholic, Protestant, nonmember) with income and education by region (Cantril 1943). In 1944, Bultena undertook a "census survey" of Madison, Wisconsin, to obtain information on denominational membership, church attendance, and some status indicators from nearly 25,000 respondents (Bultena 1949). He discovered that church membership was not correlated with occupational status, educational achievement, or housing values—a major discovery for its time—and that church attendance varied greatly by denomination—a finding that would be confirmed repeatedly by later studies.

Then, beginning in 1952 and continuing until 1970, a series of major surveys described every aspect of the religious beliefs and practices of Americans in such detail that little remained to be discovered. The only aspect of religious life on which these surveys were not informative was long-term change, on which we focus in this volume.

The first of these surveys was undertaken in 1952 by the Columbia Bureau of Applied Social Research for the National Council of the Protestant Episcopal Church. An aggregate sample of nearly 2,000 bishops, priests, and lay people returned questionnaires.

The study was designed to investigate the relationship between the church involvement of clergy and laity and their attitudes on various secular issues. It was commissioned by a division of the denomination's national headquarters working to increase the involvement of the church in social issues and was intended to gauge the response of their constituency to this effort. The first published report of this survey (Glock, Ringer, and Babbie, 1967) did not appear until 15 years after the surveys were conducted, but the results were widely known to people working in this field before they appeared in print.

Church involvement was measured along several dimensions. The ritual, organizational, and intellectual dimensions of involvement were found to be highly correlated but to have little, if any, bearing on the attitudes parishioners took on various social issues, (Tables 66 and 68). In general, the clergy was much more desirous of involving the church in current social issues than the laity was, but there was little, if any, relationship between the clergy's attitudes on social issues and those of the congregations (Table 69).

With respect to church involvement, a number of interesting and previously unsuspected patterns were found. For example, young married persons of both sexes reported the least amount of church involvement. In general, parishioners with incomplete family ties were most involved in the church. Both church and family appeared to provide effective protection against anomie, and the family and church appeared to be mutually substitutable to some extent.

The next broad-ranging survey was undertaken in 1957 by the National Council of Churches of Christ, with a sample of more than 12,000 respondents drawn from five Protestant denominations: Congregationalists, Disciples of Christ, Presbyterians, Baptists, and Lutherans. The secondary analysis by Demerath (1965), published after a considerable delay, was focused on the single question of how an individual's social status affects his or her religion. Demerath organized his analysis around the familiar dichotomy of church and sect introduced by Ernst Troeltsch (1932) and subsequently used by many investigators. Demerath seems to have found that there was some relationship between social status and religious involvement in each denomination but that the relationship varied among denominations.

A major survey that emphasized styles of religious participation was carried out by Fukuyama (1961) with a sample of about 4,000 members of 12 Congregational Christian churches in seven cities, supplemented by 79 interviews. Fukuyama reorganized Glock's four dimensions of religion as follows: cognitive for knowledge, cultic for religious practices, creedal for belief, and devotional for feelings. He constructed indexes to measure them separately. Taking differences of 10 percent or more as significant, his tables seem to show that women in this denomination scored higher on the devotional and creedal dimensions than men, that middle-aged people scored higher on the cultic dimension than those younger or older, that devotion increases with age, that knowledge and religious practice increase with education, that devotion decreases with education and socioeconomic status, and that religious knowledge increases with socioeconomic status.

A particularly impressive survey of religion was undertaken in Detroit in 1958 as part of the series of Detroit Area Studies (conducted in 1952, 1953, 1954, 1955, 1956) under the direction of Harry Sharp at the University of Michigan. An initial sample of 750 yielded a response of 87 percent, and the same high rate is reported for a special sample of the ministers of churches attended by the lay sample. Lenski's subsequent (1961) analysis of the data divides the population into five major groups: white Protestants, white Catholics, negro Protestants, Jews, miscellaneous, and no preference. Thus, the study is uninformative about denominational differences but has a great deal to tell about Protestant-Catholic-Jewish differences and the effects of race on religion.

In much the same way that Demerath showed the correlations between religious and secular items to vary from one Protestant denomination to another, Lenski showed that they varied from one major ethnic-religious group to another. For example, among Catholics and nonsouthern white Protestants, the church attendance of the immigrant generation was low and their children attended more; among Jews, the synagogue attendance of the immigrant generation was high and their children attended less.

The Protestant clergy, both white and black, was more anti-

Catholic and less anti-Semitic than the Protestant laity; the Catholic clergy was no more or less tolerant than parishioners.

One of the themes introduced by the Detroit survey — the inter-relationship between religious commitment and ethnic prejudice — became the central concern of a compound survey conducted by the Survey Research Center at Berkeley under the sponsorship of the Anti-Defamation League. The initial sample was selected in 1962 from a list of Protestant and Catholic congregations in four counties in and around San Francisco. The sample responded to a mail inquiry. Eighteen months later, a similar form was used by the National Opinion Research Center to interview a national sample of about 2,000 respondents. Although the results of this second survey do not seem to have been published, statistics drawn from it appear here and there in the published reports of the San Francisco survey. In 1968, these surveys were supple-mented by a survey of parish ministers from the nine largest Protestant denominations in California, again by mail questionnaire. The results have been published in a series of volumes (Glock and Stark 1965, 1966; Stark and Glock 1968; Stark et al. 1971).

The central hypothesis of this impressive group of studies is that anti-Semitic attitudes held by American Christians are partially attributable to theological doctrines holding the ancient Jews responsible for the crucifixion and encouraging the transfer of that responsibility to modern Jews. The case for that hypothesis is made very forcefully in *Christian Beliefs and Anti-Semitism* (Glock and Stark 1966). It appears to fit denominations better than individuals and the laity better than the clergy. When Pro-testant denominations were arrayed on a continuum of orthodoxy, from Unitarians at the extreme left to fundamentalist sects at the extreme right, there was a spectacular increase from the left to the right end of the spectrum in the proportion of respondents blaming the ancient Jews for the crucifixion and agreeing with such state-ments as "The Jews can never be forgiven for what they did to Jesus until they accept him as the True Savior" and "The reason the Jews have so much trouble is because God is punishing them for rejecting Jesus." When the same respondents were asked to agree or to disagree with various expressions of secular anti-Semitism, the gradient was weaker but still clearly discernible. And the clergy in the 1968 sample, although much less inclined to anti-Semitism than their parishioners, also showed a denominational gradient. Besides the data bearing on the study's central hypothesis, these reports summarize a huge volume of information about the religious beliefs and practices of American Protestants and Catholics in the 1960s and the complex but generally close relationships among the "dimensions" of religiosity, now increased to five (Stark and Glock 1968) and labeled belief, practice, experience, knowledge, and consequences.

A 1964 survey by Campbell and Fukuyama (1970) relied on a large, curiously stratified sample of more than 8,000 respondents belonging to the United Church of Christ. This was the first major survey to focus on long-term change, although change viewed from a single moment in time. The stated purpose of studying this high-status denomination was to see whether traces could be found of a transformation that would eventually secularize it out of existence (Campbell and Fukuyama 1970, 16). Although the survey gathered much useful information on the relation of such factors as age, sex, education, social class, race, and rural-urban location to church participation, it arrived at no definite conclusions with respect to secularization.

Another survey of the same era (Schroeder and Obenhaus 1964) told us a great deal about the fabric of religious belief in one midwestern county, where about 3,000 respondents living in four different types of settlements were interviewed by sociologists with theological training. The relation of religious beliefs and practices in Corn County with such background factors as sex, occupation, marital status, and intellectual ability and the interrelation of the several dimensions of religious experience are set forth in fascinating detail in Schroeder and Obenhaus's report.

Toward the end of the 1960s, two separate and unrelated surveys of Lutherans were undertaken at nearly the same time. Kirsten (1970) and his associates interviewed 886 lay respondents in four Lutheran denominations in the Detroit area, obtained questionnaires from 241 clergymen of the same denominations, and surveyed a comparison sample of 1,095 college students of all faiths. The study, which was supported by several Lutheran bodies, is notable for its explicit demonstration that the denominations studied occupy the same relative positions on the political scale from liberal to conservative as on the religious scale from liberal to orthodox. Clergymen were more conservative politically than lay-people and their responses varied much more by denomination. Orthodoxy was not found to be correlated with racial prejudice among laypeople. Clergy and laity showed extreme divergences, not only with regard to anti-Semitism, but also on a wide range of moral, secular, and theological issues. The four Lutheran denominations spanned about as wide a range of orthodoxy as the dozen or so denominations arrayed by Glock and Stark in various studies. In the two more orthodox Lutheran branches, the clergy was much more orthodox than the laity; in the two liberal branches, it was more orthodox than the laity on theological issues but more liberal on secular issues.

A nearly concurrent survey of Lutherans was carried out by Strommen, Brekke, Underwager, and Johnson (1972), who administered a very long questionnaire to a representative national sample of about 5,000 Lutherans between the ages of 15 and 65 years in three of the four branches covered by the study just described (the Wisconsin Synod was omitted). The survey was explicitly designed to challenge Glock and Stark's findings on the religious roots of ethnic prejudice. Among Lutherans, the investigators found that ethnic prejudice was *not* related to the "need for religious absolutism" and some similar variables. Age, occupation, education, sex, region, and congregational size were found to have relatively little influence on beliefs and practices. Sharp differences were again found between clergy and laity on major items of Lutheran belief and practice and in secular attitudes as well. This study, which paid considerable attention to generational differences, found nothing that could be called a generation gap but did uncover some intergenerational tensions.

The foregoing inventory of major surveys is by no means complete. (Several other large-scale surveys less closely related to our present purposes were carried out during the same period, and there were numerous minor ones.[6]) Our brief descriptions of these studies can yield little idea of the wealth of detailed information about American religion that has thus far been made available. Only a few of these studies, however, had much to say about long-term social change. In 1966, Earle, Knudsen, and Shriver (1976) undertook a partial replication of the study of Gastonia by Liston Pope (1942) a generation before, and the new study included an interview survey of some 400 respondents of both races drawn from the general population. It was, however, so narrowly focused on the linkage between religious involvement and unionism as to be relatively uninformative about other trends within the church, particularly since the respondents' attitudes about union issues were only slightly influenced by their religious situations.

In sum, although a great deal is now known about American religion, not very much is known about its long-term trends. The only useful source of information about trends in religious beliefs and practices over an appreciable span of time that was available when we went to work in Middletown was George Gallup's 1976 report, *Religion in America.*[7] The high points of that report deserve to be summarized here.

The question "Do you believe in God or a universal spirit?" was asked in 1948, 1968, and 1975. The proportions responding positively were 94 percent, 98 percent, and 94 percent, respectively. There was no net change over the 27-year period.[8] The same question was asked at the same three points of time in Benelux, where the proportion answering affirmatively did not vary significantly from 80 percent; in France, where a slight increase from 66 to 72 percent was recorded; and in Scandinavia, where there was a significant decrease from 81 to 65 percent. The United States still appears to be, as it was in Tocqueville's time, more religious than any country of Western Europe, on the basis of not only the foregoing question but also the follow-up question asked in 1965: "Do you believe that this God or universal spirit observes your actions and rewards or punishes you for them?" To this more pointed question, 68 percent of the Americans sampled answered affirmatively compared to 34 percent of the British, 37 percent of the French, and 36 percent of the West German respondents. But belief in an observing God who rewards and punishes actions is even higher in Latin America, sub-Saharan Africa, and the Far East than in the United States. Survey data do not provide much support for the hypotheses of universal secularization.

With respect to the belief in life after death, the proportions of American samples saying that they believed in life after death was 68 percent in 1948, 73 percent in 1968, and 69 percent in 1975 — again, no trend is apparent. Again, these findings contrast sharply with survey results for the Western European countries sampled at the same three points in time. All of them—France, the United Kingdom, Benelux, and Scandinavia—showed significant declines in the proportion of the samples believing in immortality, and all were significantly lower than the United States by 1975.

Various Gallup polls provide information about the church attendance of the general American populations as far back as 1958 and through splicing to earlier and not entirely comparable surveys, all the way back to 1939. Figure 1-1 shows the trend graphically.

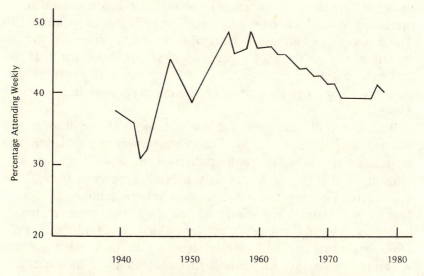

Figure 1-1. Church attendance in an average week, United States, 1939-1977. (Based on Cantril 1951, 699-700; Gallup 1972, 643-44, 902, 1222, 1252; and Gallup Poll Index 1978, 22.)

These figures cannot be broken down for the earlier years, but for more recent years the data are excellent. The decline from 1964 to 1975 upon analysis turns out to reflect a decline in Catholic church attendance in the aftermath of the Vatican II Council, from above 70 percent to about 55 percent of all communicants attending in an average week. During the same period, Protestant church attendance remained nearly level at just under 40 percent.

For Protestants, at least, there is no evidence of any recent decline in religious observance in the United States. The decline of religious observance among Catholics was appreciable but seems now to have leveled off, leaving American Catholics with a much higher rate of church attendance than Protestants and a much higher rate than Catholics in most other countries (Gallup Opinion Index, 1978).

The proportion of the U.S. population who claimed no religious preference in the 1977-1978 surveys was 6 percent, a figure impossible to reconcile with the waning of religion so often mentioned as a contemporary social trend. That illusion can itself be measured as a trend. Over the years, the Gallup surveys have included the question "At the present time, do you think religion as a whole is increasing its influence on American life or losing its influence?" The proportion of all respondents who said that religion was losing its influence rose from 14 percent in 1957 to 75 percent in 1970 and then began to fall again. By 1976 it was back down to 45 percent, rising to 48 percent in 1978 (Gallup Opinion Index 1978-1980, 27).

When we look at Figure 1-2, we can see how the illusion developed. Figure 1-2, the ratio of church members to population, is, so far as we know, the only published statistical series about religion in the United States that goes back beyond 1939. The general trend is unmistakable. Church membership increased three-fold between the Revolution and the Civil War, then remained nearly unchanged until 1890, then increased threefold again until 1960, and then declined slightly. It was that slight decline plus widespread ignorance of the past that generated the illusion of an organizational crisis in the churches.

But with the solitary exception of church membership, we do not have any usable statistical information at all about the United States that takes us back before World War II. Church membership by itself is not very informative, since it appears from our Middletown data that the relationship between church attendance and church membership was quite different in 1890 than it is today, people then being much more likely to attend regularly a church to which they did not belong.

The particular usefulness of the Middletown data is that it gives us a reasonably complete picture of religious belief and practice in 1924 and a few usable statistical series going back as far as 1890.

Percent	0	10	20	30	40	50	60	70
1650			14%					
1700			12%					
1776		8%						
1800		7%						
1810		9%						
1820			11%					
1830			13%					
1840			14%					
1850			16%					
1860				23%				
1870			18%					
1880			20%					
1890			22%					
1900					36%			
1910						43%		
1920						43%		
1930						47%		
1940						49%		
1950							57%	
1960								64%
1967								64%
1970								62%
1974								62%
1978								61%

Figure 1-2. Ratio of church members to population in America. (from Backman 1976, xv; Backman's sources for the percentages shown in his graph are the various selected volumes of the annual *Yearbook of American Churches,* including the 1933 edition. Membership figures after 1970 were not included in Backman's published charts and derive from *Yearbook of American and Canadian Churches, 1976* [p. 229], and *Yearbook of American and Canadian Churches, 1979* [p. 226].)

These glimmers of light shine far in the statistical darkness that otherwise conceals the religious lives of our grandfathers. The other advantage of the Middletown data is that they allow us to examine the pattern of religious activities, beliefs, and personal characteristics at two points in time separated by more than 50 years. By putting this one specimen sliced off the huge bulk of America under high magnification, we hope to make some useful discoveries about how religion has responded to changing social conditions.

The Problem of Bias

No field of human activity is more disputatious than organized religion, not even politics. Differences of religious opinion cannot be resolved by empirical evidence or by formal reasoning, and in matters of faith the willingness to compromise is not as praiseworthy as it is in politics or trade.

In theory, the sociology of religion stands aloof from the controversies of religion and considers religious phenomena with scientific detachment, measuring them with instruments that are not affected by the preferences of the scientific observer. In practice, it is not easy to maintain this desirable impartiality, and it is even possible to discover antireligion and proreligion factions among the sociologists of religion.

The antireligion sociologists of religion (1) do not accept religious experience as intrinsically valid, regarding it either as an illusion or as a sociopsychological device, (2) perceive a contradiction between the rationality of science and the irrationality of religion, and (3) anticipate the decline and ultimate disappearance of religion. Scholars of the proreligion faction hold nearly opposite views. They (1) interpret religious experience as an interaction between human persons and an external reality, (2) understand science and religion to be dealing quite compatibly with different aspects of experience, and (3) do not regard the decline of religion as inevitable or even probable.

Since the appearance of scientific sociology in the 19th century, the antireligion faction has been the more influential. Andrew Greeley, a prominent member of the proreligion faction, has argued that "the conventional wisdom of a religious crisis" depends on two assumptions that most sociologists have accepted without question: that society evolves in a predetermined direction and that *Gemeinschaft* is progressively replaced by *Gesellschaft* (Greeley 1972a, chapter 2).

As it happened, none of the scholars who had the most influence on the development of modern sociology — Spencer, Marx, Durkheim, Weber, and Simmel — was particularly open to religious experience. For Spencer, it reflected a primitive stage of social development. Durkheim's attitude toward religion is well expressed by his comment in *Le Suicide* that "religion modifies the inclination to suicide only to the extent that it prevents men from thinking freely" ([1897] 1975, 373-64). In his culminant work on the elementary forms of religious life, he purposed to show that God is only society in disguise: "The reality which mythologies have represented under so many different forms, but which is the universal and eternal objective cause of these sensations *sui generis* out of which religious experience is made, is society" ([1912] 1965, 465). Georg Simmel paid so little attention to religion in his sociological writings that it is difficult to discern his views. Karl Marx, as everyone knows, thought that religion was a trick of the ruling class and that it was, in any case, historically doomed by the inevitable progress of reason, the same inevitable progress of reason that appeared to conservatives like Spencer and to liberals like Durkheim. "The religious world," Marx wrote in *Das Kapital* ([1867] 1952, 35), "is but the reflex of the real world . . . [which will] only then finally vanish when the practical relations of everyday life offer to man none but perfectly intelligible and reasonable relations with regard to his fellowmen and to nature."

In 1904, Max Weber (1958) undertook to refute Marx's opinion that religious beliefs were merely a by-product of economic relations by showing how Protestant beliefs had influenced economic relationships in the crucial case of European capitalism. In his later work on comparative religion, Weber ([1922] 1963) examined the interplay between religious beliefs and social structures in various cultures. Unlike Durkheim, he did not explicitly deny the validity of religious experience, but neither did he affirm it.

The idea that religion is a vestigial institution destined to decline and eventually to disappear persists among some contemporary sociologists, but the idea itself is a vestige of theoretical positions they no longer held. The 19th-century confidence in the eventual triumph of reason in human affairs has long since passed. Modern sociologists, if they believe at all in historical inevitability, are more likely to predict catastrophe than unending progress. Nevertheless, the dim view of religion that positivism held in its heyday lingers on among the spiritual heirs of Durkheim and Weber.

Meanwhile, in Eastern Europe and Latin America, there are signs of religious revival among the spiritual heirs of Marx and Lenin. How seriously these signs should be taken it is difficult to say. Marxism-Leninism, as practiced in the Soviet Union, can be analyzed as though it were a religion. It has rituals and hymns, a body of dogma, sacred texts, saints, and relics. Maoism in its heyday was even more liturgical in its worship of party, state, and heroic leader, as were Naziism in its time and a number of other political cults in the contemporary world. As Robert Bellah (1967) noted, there is even an attenuated form of political cult in the United States, which he named the civil religion. Whether these movements should be considered religious or quasi-religious is entirely a matter of definition. Since religion is a polythetic classification capable of multiple definitions, there is no way to resolve the question out of hand. If religion is the means whereby men and women come to terms with the ultimate reality—life and death, pleasure and pain, self and others, time and eternity—it is doubtful whether the political cults really address these dilemmas. An orthodox historical materialist might say that the dilemmas were meaningless; a fascist might say they were unimportant. These are matters almost impossible to resolve objectively. For our present purposes, it is sufficient to note that political cults do not seem to be complete substitutes for transcendental religions. The efforts of centralized states to suppress religion have not been completely successful, and there is no reason to suppose that a political cult, like the American civil religion, that is not backed by force has much effect on religion of the ordinary kind.

The Pilgrimage to Middletown

The Lynds went to Middletown in 1924 to study the crisis of the Protestant churches in a typical American community (every generation perceives a crisis in the churches). The expansion of that original study into a comprehensive community survey occurred while they were doing their fieldwork. Indeed, the sponsors of the project in the Institute for Social and Religious Research were astonished to discover the new direction it had taken. We do not know how and why this transformation took place, but the vast amount of information the Lynds collected about religion suggests that the topic retained its primacy for them in 1924 and 1925. By contrast, they gave only cursory attention to religion in their 1935 study.

Robert Lynd was trained to be a Presbyterian minister but had already turned away from organized religion when he began to observe Middletown's churches in 1924, according to one of his principal informants who was still living in Middletown when we arrived there. The two Middletown books were read, correctly or incorrectly, as exposés of grass-roots Protestantism. By contrast, most of the investigators involved in the Middletown III project are active in the church. There is a sense, therefore, in which our replication is not faithful to the original study. We are inclined to characterize religion in Middletown by those elements of it that appear valid to us; the Lynds, however, were inclined to emphasize those elements that appeared questionable to them.

With a bias that differs so fundamentally from that of the Lynds, we run a considerable risk of misreading the comparison between their data and our own. But there is not very much we can do about it except to caution the reader — and ourselves.

The Measurement of Secularization

Secularization is supposed to be an irreversible process accompanying modernization. It is thought of as continuous, starting from an unspecified point in the past, somewhere between 1600 and 1900, and proceeding irresistibly into the future.

According to Peter Berger (1967, 107-8):

By secularization we mean the process by which sectors of society and culture are removed from the domination of religious institutions and symbols . . . as there is a secularization of society and culture, so is there a secularization of consciousness. Put simply, this means that the modern west has produced an increasing number of individuals who look upon the world and their own lives without the benefit of religious interpretation.

Berger proposed that secularization varies for different groups of the population and different parts of the world, having more effect on men than on women, on the middle-aged than on the young or the old, in the city than in the country, on industrial workers than on shopkeepers, on Protestants than on Catholics, and so forth. In Europe, he suggested only marginal populations and individuals have resisted secularization, while in America the churches have kept their central position "only by becoming highly secularized themselves." We will consider presently what this might mean.

In another work, Berger (1970, 5-6) described the "demise of the supernatural" in terms, he said, of the "available evidence."

Whatever the situation may have been in the past, *today* the supernatural as a meaningful reality is absent or remote from the horizons of everyday life of large numbers, very probably of the majority, of people in modern societies, who seem to manage to get along without it quite well. This means that those to whom the supernatural is still, or again, a meaningful reality find themselves in the status of a minority. . . .

It was this interpretation of the "available evidence" that first started us thinking that secularization might be a myth rather than a historical process, since we have abundant survey evidence that the supernatural *is* present as a meaningful reality to a majority of the people in modern societies.

If Berger, trained both as a sociologist and a theologian, could be so badly mistaken about the facts of religion in the observable contemporary world, is it not possible that he and less critical colleagues are equally mistaken about the facts of religion in those vanished eras from which secularization started? The theorists of secularization have generally relied on their instinctive knowledge of the past in tracing the curve from the religious past to the irreligious present. Not many of them have delved into the archives to look for statistical indicators of religious activity and belief in the 17th century or, for that matter, in the 19th. Such indicators may be fallible and cannot be expected to tell us the whole story. But, if there has been a massive long-term trend of secularization, it must certainly be reflected somewhere in the vast, patchy records of modern history.

If secularization is a shrinkage of the religious sector in relation to other sectors of society, as most definitions imply, then it ought to produce some or all of the following indications: (1) a decline in the number of churches per capita of the population, (2) a decline in the proportion of the population attending church services, (3) a decline in the proportion of rites of passage held under religious auspices (for example, declining ratios of religious to civil marriages and of religious to secular funerals), (4) a decline in religious endogamy, (5) a decline in the proportion of the labor force engaged in religious activity, (6) a decline in the proportion of income devoted to the support of religion, (7) a decline in the ratio of religious to nonreligious literature, (8) a decline in the attention given to religion in the mass media, (9) a drift toward less emotional forms of participation in religious services, (10) a dwindling of new sects and of new movements in existing churches, and (11) an increase in attention paid to secular topics in sermons and liturgy.

As it happens, we have fairly reliable information from Middletown about most of these 11 indicators going back more than 50 years and in some instances more than 90 years. For the entire United States, as previously noted, there is one series that goes back much farther.

As we will presently show, none of these series offers much support for the hypothesis of secularization. The longest and most significant series of all—church membership in America—has somehow gotten itself backward and shows a long-term rise in church membership. There have been some fluctuations along the way but never a significant downward trend. This notable and inconvenient fact must somehow be circumvented in order to discuss secularization, and there are two different ways of doing it.

It can be argued that church membership has little or nothing to do with church attendance and other religious practices. There is no evidence to support this argument. Every quantitative study that has touched on the subject has found a close relationship between church membership and other religious practices.

It can be proposed that the subjective meaning of church membership has changed over time so that, for example, while the fact of belonging to a church implied a deep religious commitment in the early 19th century, it no longer does so. But there is no evidence for this proposition either. The majority of contemporary church members say that they pray privately, think about heaven, experience God as a personal presence, believe in the fundamental tenets of Christianity, and judge their own conduct by religious standards. Even if the total membership of the early 19th century churches had consisted of persons outstanding for their piety, they would have been a smaller proportion of the population than persons of similar disposition are today.

My friend and colleague Jeffrey Hadden has proposed a different concept of secularization that calls for other indicators. Hadden (1980, 101) wrote:

The impact of secularization in modern societies is an historical fact of inestimable significance. At the same time, conceiving of secularization as an inevitable unilinear erosion of religious influence in culture, leading to the eventual demise of religious organizations, is an ill-conceived idea that is overdue for a quiet burial.

Alternatively *secularization should be viewed as merely a process which has broken the historical link between church and state.*

A break in the link between church and state should be reflected by indications such as these: (1) a declining level of political activity by organized religious groups (including lobbying and campaigning by religious groups and office holding by members of the clergy, (2) diminished interest in the religious credentials of candidates and office holders, (3) less legislation and litigation about religious matters and less regulation of religious organizations by government, and (4) the removal of religious symbols from the ceremonies and insignia of the state and of patriotic symbols from the ceremonies and insignia of the church. Not all of these indicators, when arranged as statistical series, run in the same direction. We will examine their trends in a later chapter, but it is evident at first glance that they are not going to support the hypothesis that religion and the state have been moving farther apart in the United States during recent years.

We are not the first students of religion to describe secularization as a myth. Andrew Greeley did so a decade ago in an admirable book called *Unsecular Man* (1972b), in which he showed that the statistical data simply do not indicate any decline of religion in the United States and that, considered in absolute terms, the level of religious belief and participation in this country is extraordinariy high. He quoted with approval Swanson's demonstration that interest and participation in religion are substantially higher than participation in politics, that people have about as much religious as political knowledge, and that people are somewhat more likely to participate in religious than in political activity (Swanson 1968). But, though Greeley was able to show that American society around 1970 was not very secularized, the statistical indicators available to him went back only about 15 years and proved only that there had been little change during that brief period. Without quantitative data, the temptation to derive trends by constructing an imaginary past is nearly irresistible, and Greeley, having neatly dissected the myth of secularization, yielded to the temptation long enough to propose some trends of his own: that religious symbols now require more interpretation than they did formerly, that religion is now more of a personal choice, and that the choice is now more likely to be made in isolation. These trends are plausible but entirely speculative, and we will have reason, after reviewing the Middletown data, to relegate them to the same heap as secularization.

Mind you, we do not say there have been no changes in organized religion during the past half-century. That would be absurd. Much of this volume is given over to the religious changes that have been occurring in Middletown and in the wider society around it. Liturgies have changed, attitudes have changed, and whole bodies of doctrine have changed radically. The sexual morality preached in Middletown's churches in 1980 is quite different from what it was in 1960, let alone 1900. A mass in one of Middletown's Catholic churches nowadays—celebrated in English with the priest facing the congregation and the kiss of peace exchanged afterward—bears little resemblance to the stately Latin ritual of 1960. The same Presbyterians and Lutherans who speak in tongues nowadays would not have spoken to anyone who defended the practice a few years ago. The Episcopal Church has women priests and a new prayer book. The YMCA no longer has any religious importance, but the Jehovah's Witnesses do. Where every church was once explicitly segregated by race, all are now integrated in theory and many are in fact. There are people in Middletown who practice witchcraft seriously and others who shave their heads and meditate on reincarnation. There are enough new things under the sun in Middletown's religion to amaze and delight a curious observer. But we have not been able to find much trace of the great massive trend that was supposed to be carrying us irresistibly out of an age of faith into an age of practical reason. What has happened instead—the persistence and renewal of religion in a changing society—is much more interesting than the secularization that never occurred.

Chapter 2

From Simpson Chapel to Grace Baptist

The Lynds' view of religion in Middletown is best illustrated by these quotations from their second book.

The predicament of institutions like the church and school which may seek to alter Middletown's dominant values is further heightened by the pervasive instrumentalism that characterizes Middletown's culture. The instrumentalism is the hidden side of the bright banner of Progress under which this culture lives (Lynd and Lynd 1937, 316).

Said a leading minister speaking to Kiwanis: "In the old days, people went to preachers for consolation, information, and inspiration. They still come to us for consolation, but go to the newspapers for information and inspiration." This expresses succinctly the apparent role of religion in Middletown as an emotionally stabilizing agent, relinquishing to other agencies leadership in the defining of values (Lynd and Lynd 1937, 318).

Robert Lynd was a graduate of Union Theological Seminary, and before he became a social researcher he had intended to be a Presbyterian minister.[1] The sponsor of the community study of Middletown was the Institute of Social and Religious Research, a branch of the Interchurch World Movement, which was originally the Presbyterian Board of Home Missions. The primary interest of the Institute of Social and Religious Research in supporting the Lynds was to determine the changing condition of religion in the United States. By studying Middletown, the Lynds could show how religion had fared in at least one community.

The Lynds structured their study of religion around the role of the minister, the function of the church, the correlation of religious practices with social class, and the impact of industrialization on religious beliefs in Middletown. They found that the role of the minister was to reinforce the property-centered values of an industrial society and to put his imprimatur on the Magic Middletown creed. The Lynds concluded that ministers were overworked and lacked the time to read and to study in order to overcome deficiencies in their intellectual training. The churches, according to the Lynds, served to reinforce class boundaries in the community and to rationalize the social system. They did not curb the excesses of the developing industrial society. Finally, the Lynds concluded that industrialization was leading to increased secularization, that each succeeding generation was less religious than the previous one, and that the business class was more secularized than the working class. The religious zeal of the working class was taken by the Lynds as confirmation of their implicit thesis, in Richard Jensen's (1979, 316) words, that "religion was an obsolescent survival of premodern culture."

Despite the Lynds' conclusions, some of their own evidence seems to show that perhaps religion in Middletown in 1924-1925 was stronger than they believed. Looking at the content of sermons, they examined the "long abstracts sent in by ministers and appearing each Monday morning in the press, from one to six appearing each week . . ." (Lynd and Lynd 1929, 371, n. 1) as well as interviews and staff reports. The fact that the Middletown newspapers gave this much space to religion when compared to the "disappointingly meager" (Lynd and Lynd 1929, 371, n. 1) coverage they gave it during the base year of 1890 might have led the Lynds to question whether the importance of religion really was waning in Middletown, but it did not.

For lack of data, some of their judgments concerning the past tended to be subjective. For example, they counted 21 revivals reported in the Middletown newspaper in 1924; among them was a revival at the largest Protestant church, High Street Methodist Church, that caused much excitement (Lynd and Lynd 1929, 378-80). Then the Lynds asserted that "revivals were more frequent in 1890—one gathers, even more frequent than today —" without any supporting data (Lynd and Lynd 1929, 378). But given the fact that there were only 12 Protestant churches in Middletown in 1889 and that 2 of these, the First Universalist and Grace Episcopal, did not hold revivals, there could have been no more than about 10 revivals in 1890 (*Emerson's Directory* 1889, 274-75). As Chapter 6 shows, they also undercounted the 1924 revivals.

The Lynds acknowledged that in some respects Middletown was less irreligious in 1924 than in 1890. They quoted part of a 1890 speech to the Ethical Society by a local doctor who had challenged belief in the hereafter, and they then commented that such public challenges to orthodoxy were not heard in Middletown during the 1920s (Lynd and Lynd 1929, 321). They also noted that, in 1900, a description of a Sunday cockfight sponsored by the iron and glass workers appeared in the next day's newspaper without any unfavorable comment and that trade unions met regularly on Sunday morning during the same year (Lynd and Lynd 1929, 341).

When the Lynds restudied Middletown in 1935, they devoted much less space to religion—one chapter instead of four—but once again conveyed their conviction about the irrelevance of the institution to modern life. "There is no area in Middletown's life, save religion, where symbol is more admittedly and patently divorced from reality than in government . . ." (Lynd and Lynd 1937, 322). They did note that two denominations had constructed new stone churches to replace "rusty brick buildings" dating back to gas boom days (these were the First Baptist Church built in 1929 and High Street Methodist built in 1930) (Lynd and Lynd 1937, 296). Three other churches, among them a second Catholic church, St. Mary's, had begun new buildings but, with the onset of the Great Depression, had to stop construction and to hold services in the finished basements. Despite this evidence of institutional growth, the Lynds believed that religion in Middletown was continuing to fade.

Richard Jensen has argued that the Lynds found a new theory to account for the continuation of religion while they were carrying out their second study. Still clinging to the idea that religion was irrelevant to modern industrial society, they "suddenly realized," according to Jensen (1979, 316), "that the irrelevance of religion was in fact highly functional and necessary for the individual to cope with society." This realization placed them squarely on the horns of a dilemma. On the one hand, modernization diminished religion; on the other, religion cushioned the impact of modernization upon those being modernized. In one context, religion was superfluous; in another, it was essential.

Models of Change

There is another model for the history of religion in America besides progressive decline. Religious history may follow a cycle — an alternation of awakenings and stagnation — wherein religious enthusiasm waxes and wanes. Such indeed was the argument of William G. McLaughlin (1978), who described four great awakenings in American history: the first from 1730 to 1760, the second from 1800 to 1830, the third from 1890 to 1920, and the fourth from 1960 to 1990. Despite the unlikely coincidence that all awakenings last 30 years, the McLaughlin model might explain the Lynds' impression that religious fervor was less obvious in Middletown during the 1920s than it had been during the 1890s.

Another possibility is that religious institutions have been growing in strength in America during both the 19th and 20th centuries. This would correspond with the data of succeeding censuses that record a steady increase in aggregate church membership. In that model, the growth of one denomination runs its course but is duplicated by the growth of other denominations at later times, while new sects continue to appear and to develop into denominations. The visible signs of this transformation are the replacement of the casual meeting place in a home or public building with a frame sanctuary that in turn gives way to a brick church and later to a stone church. Still another possibility is that no regular trend can be detected, that religion follows an idiosyncratic pattern of change.

What we propose to do in this short history of religion in Middletown is to trace the appearance of religious groups in the town, their early history, their appeal to individuals and groups, their development, and their changes in location, mission, and attitudes. This discussion will be both ecological and theological.

Religion in a Pioneer Community

Religion in early Middletown was home centered. High Street Methodist claims the deepest roots of any church in the community, in keeping with the tradition that Indiana was a Methodist state and Middletown was a Methodist town. The Methodists established the Western Conference in 1800 to carry the gospel via circuit riders to the trans-Appalachian West. The first Methodist church in Indiana was established in 1807, and by 1924 the state of Indiana had become part of the Illinois Conference (Herrick and Sweet 1917, 2-3).

Five years later, the first Methodist minister appeared in Middletown, two years after the town's founding. His name was Charles Downey, and he preached in private homes and in the original log courthouse. He was succeeded in 1830 by the Reverend Thomas J. Babcock, who, in the words of the official church history, "captured the town in toto, or nearly so" (*High Street Church History*, p. 1). When the Indiana Conference was organized in 1832 (*High Street Church History;* Herrick and Sweet 1917, 3), Middletown became a stop on the New Castle circuit. Four years later, the community rated a circuit of its own, and in 1839 the first church was built. This church was very small, 30 feet by 45 feet, but adequate for the membership of 30. The land for the church at Washington and Elm had been donated by Goldsmith Gilbert and his wife (*High Street Church History*, p. 1). Gilbert, the founder of Middletown, had also donated land for the courthouse and other civic facilities. Although the history of High Street Church records that the Gilberts were loyal Methodists, the record is unclear as to whether they gave the land to the church because of their religious faith or because of their desire to promote the town. Still, they were the first of many prominent Middletown citizens who were members of this church.

Two other denominations came to Middletown during the 1830s; the Baptists in 1835 and the Presbyterians in 1838. The Baptists held services in private homes or in public buildings until 1859. The Presbyterians began plans to build a church in 1839, the same year that the first Methodist church was finished, but they did not complete their building until 1843 (Middletown's evening newspaper, June 16, 1979).

The order of the founding of churches in Middletown was not typical of frontier communities. The Presbyterians were not committed to missionary activity among the unchurched: "The records indicate that their missionaries and ministers went to the frontier looking primarily for Presbyterians and only in a few instances attempting to form new churches with previously non-Presbyterian members" (Miyakawa 1964, 29). On the other hand, the Baptists shared with the Methodists the missionary enthusiasm of a dissenting sect from the Atlantic seaboard. The Baptists' sectarian tendencies—like the Methodists—intimate fellowship, rigorous discipline, absence of universalism and cosmopolitanism, strong fraternal life, lay participation and leadership, withdrawal from the world and hostility to high culture[2] —proved attractive to the people who migrated to pioneer communities. But the Baptists concentrated more on rural areas, believing towns to be sinful and threatening: "As elsewhere in the early West, Indiana Baptists were weak in the larger towns and consequently the missionaries had to take the initiative" (Miyakawa 1964, 153).

The early Presbyterian and Baptist groups had few members. James Shields, who visited Middletown's County in 1835, found an almost dead Presbyterian church that very much wanted a minister (Rudolph 1963, 1-3). The historian of the First Presbyterian Church in Middletown, however, chose to date its foundation from March 1838, ignoring the evidence of Shields. According to his version, members of this newly founded church journeyed the next month to Blountsville, where they met the Reverend Robert Irwin, a supply minister sent by the Oxford (Ohio) Presbytery to preach in rural Stoney Creek Church. Irwin agreed to accompany the delegation back to Middletown and to preach a sermon in the courthouse at 11 o'clock one Thursday morning. He so impressed the local Presbyterians that he was invited back in July to organize a church, and in October he was assigned by the Oxford Presbytery to preach half-time in Middletown and half-time in churches in the neighboring area. Services then were held in the courthouse on Sunday, and weekday services took place in any home available (Thomas 1938, 12-15; Middletown's evening newspaper, June 16, 1979).

The congregation originally consisted of nine members, including two doctors, Samuel Anthony and George Ganst. A year later, the congregation decided to build a church. Thomas Kirby donated three lots at Walnut and Charles extending to Mulberry, presently the site of Middletown's leading department store, for the church building. The church secured additional land at Adams and Cherry, the present location of the Friends' Church, for a cemetery. A 40-foot-square church of frame construction was completed in May 1846 (Thomas 1938, 17-18).

The completion of the new church home did not symbolize instant growth or harmony. Three years after the new church opened, the Middletown Presbytery relieved Irwin of his post amidst charges and recriminations. Irwin accounted for his difficulties in the community in these memorable words: "Often we are charged with holding the most absurd doctrines; that we believed in the damnation of infants; that we were mere formalists knowing nothing about experiential religion; and that we charged five dollars always for a funeral service" (Thomas 1938, 22).

The Presbyterian pulpit remained empty for four years before another minister ventured to assume it. John Boyd, a graduate of Union Theological Seminary, visited Middletown by chance in the summer of 1853 and took the pastoral post upon request despite his awareness of the factions in the church (Thomas 1938, 24-25).

Religion and Early Urban Growth

When Middletown was incorporated in 1854, with a population of approximately 900, there were two churches in the town, the Methodist and the Presbyterian. Both churches had been instituted by a few interested persons of some standing in the community; they had held services in private homes or at the courthouse until they were able to build small frame buildings used exclusively for worship services on land donated by patrons, and they had made do with itinerant ministers until they were able to support full-time ones. In other respects, they differed considerably. The Methodists were still a sect dedicated to informal religion, while the Presbyterians were more formal (witness the complaint of Irwin). With the pastorate of Boyd, the Presbyterians commanded the services of a minister trained in one of the foremost seminaries of the day. Both churches claimed members from among the leading families of the frontier community.

It is difficult to determine the proportion of the population of Middletown that belonged to these first two churches. Both groups worshiped in new churches by the end of the decade: the Methodists completed Simpson Chapel in 1856 (*High Street Church*

History, p. 3), and the Presbyterians built a new church, "the largest and finest church edifice in Middletown," in 1860 (Thomas 1938, 27). Each church, the former at Jackson and Mulberry and the latter at Walnut and Charles, was larger than its predecessor. The Methodists claimed that they had 352 members out of a total population of 1500 in 1856 (*High Street Church History,* p. 3). Both the membership and the population estimates are probably exaggerated. The Presbyterians made no such claim but announced that their new church, which cost between $6,000 and $7,000, would seat 200. Simpson Chapel cost only $4,647, so it probably had less capacity; if the Methodists had as many members as they claimed, they might not have fit into the new church.

The two pioneer churches were joined by a third in the 1850s. The Baptists date the beginning of their services in Middletown from 1835, but they did not organize a formal congregation until 1858 when, led by the Reverend G. Williams, they met in the courthouse to found the First Baptist Church. Three years later, their newly built church was ready at Jefferson and Jackson streets. The Baptists claim that this church was the first one in the community to be built of brick (Middletown's evening newspaper, May 19, 1979).

The same decade witnessed the first appearance of non-Protestant groups: Catholics and Jews. Middletown has never had a sizable foreign-born population, but the census of 1860 showed the highest proportion, 9 percent, at any time in the community's history.[3] The largest proportion of immigrants were Irish, but a considerable number were Jews from Alsace-Lorraine in France. Although neither the Catholic church nor the Jewish temple became an ethnic church per se, they approached that model more closely than other Middletown religious groups.

The first mass was said in 1853 at the log home of Patrick Tuhey (an Irish Catholic whose descendants became prominent Democrats in Middletown during the 20th century) at Jackson and Jefferson streets (Middletown's evening newspaper, June 23, 1979). The Tuhey home lot later became the site of the First Baptist Church and still later of the public library. The Catholic congregation grew slowly until 1870, when it had 45 members and a resident priest. In 1873, the first Catholic church was built of limestone and brick at Charles and Hackley streets, with seats for

200 people (Middletown's evening newspaper, June 23, 1979). This church, St. Lawrence's, has not moved since the first building was erected, although a new building and elementary school replaced the old structure in 1893.

The Jewish presence in Middletown was inconspicuous. Services were first held in homes in 1855 by a congregation of 19 members, but not until 1891 did they move into a rented building, the Delaware Masonic Lodge. The Beth-El congregation continued to meet in rented buildings, at High and Adams streets and on East Main Street, until 1922, when it built a brick structure at Jackson and Council streets that still remains (Middletown's evening newspaper, May 5, 1979).

In 1860, Middletown had many fewer churches than the rest of the county. According to the census of that year, the county had 1 Baptist church, 1 Baptist-Tunker church, 14 Methodist churches, 3 Presbyterian churches, and 1 Universalist church (U.S. Bureau of the Census, 1866). Only three denominations—Methodist, Presbyterian, and Universalist—had churches in Middletown.

The Universalists, who later joined the Unitarians, had quite different origins than their Unitarian cobelievers. Unitarianism was an elite movement of New England Congregationalists. The Universalists were a lower-class denomination.

As a lower-class denomination, the Universalists competed with the Methodists and Wesleyan-oriented Free-Will Baptists for the allegiance of the common people. While the Universalists were concentrated initially in New England, they moved into the newer settlements of the West with such success that by 1850 they had more than twice as many churches as the Unitarians (Hudson 1973, 162).

The Universalists of Middletown organized a congregation in 1859 and built their church at Jackson and Madison streets the following year. The first Universalists, led by Samuel I. Watson, who had come to Middletown from Ohio in 1855, met in the home of Dr. S. O. Budd two blocks from where the church was to be built. The church, when finished, had the highest steeple in town, a distinction deliberately sought (Mitchell 1974, 1-2). Its basement sheltered the Central Academy in 1868, the forerunner of Central High School, and it loaned its space free to other religious groups, such as the Campbellites and the Quakers, who were struggling to organize (Mitchell 1974, 7).

The Protestant churches' pattern of growth continued from 1860 to 1890. Nine new churches were added to the five churches of 1860—Simpson Chapel, the First Presbyterian Church, the First Baptist Church, the First Universalist Church, and St. Lawrence's. They were the Jackson Street Christian Church (now Hazelwood) (1868), Bethel African Methodist Episcopal (1868), the Calvary Baptist Church (1872), the Methodist Protestant (now Main Street) (1872), the Grace Episcopal Church (1881), the Friends' Memorial (1876), the First Evangelical Lutheran (1889), and two more—the Church of God and the Congregational Church—for which the founding dates are unknown.[4] All save the last two still survive. Since the vanished churches are not mentioned in Thomas B. Helm's history of the county (1881), they were probably formed after the book was published. Two churches that did survive, Bethel African Methodist Episcopal and Calvary Baptist, had black congregations.

The story of these newer churches is instructive. In several instances, the real founder was a woman; the Jackson Street Christian Church is an example. The Disciples of Christ began as a frontier sect that attracted members from the "New Light" Christians of Barton Stone, the Free-Will Baptists, and, particularly, the Campbellites. The founder of the Campbellites was Alexander Campbell, a Baptist who opposed infant baptism, predestination, and missions. He started a paper, the *Christian Baptist,* in 1823 and attracted many followers, especially Baptists who were well educated and close to Unitarianism (Cady 1942, 65-69; Miyakawa 1964, 150, 157).

The Campbellites had moved into Indiana by 1829 and taken over Silver Creek Church, the oldest Baptist church in the state (Garrison and De Groot 1948, 218). In 1848, a Campbellite elder from Daleville named Benjamin Franklin visisted Middletown and preached in the county seminary; he continued to visit thereafter in order to baptize members and to keep the faith alive. A Middletown woman, Emily Adamson, gathered believers and held meetings in her home from 1865 on, although she was ostracized by at least one neighbor for her beliefs. The Campbellites persisted. A part-time minister who was also a physician, Dr. George W. Thompson, began to hold services in 1868, the year from which the Campbellites mark their founding. They met in homes and then in

Wallings Hall, close to the courthouse, for two more years before building a church at Jackson and Council streets (Middletown's evening newspaper, June 9, 1979).

The Friends had a similar beginning. Although the Quakers came to eastern Indiana in early territorial days, they did not form a meeting in Middletown until the mid-1870s. The person responsible was Mary Goddard, the wife of a local merchant. She arranged for a Quaker preacher to come to Middletown in 1875 to speak in Simpson Chapel. This sermon led to an invitation to preach at the First Presbyterian Church and to use it for future meetings. The Friends also met at the Goddard home, where they organized themselves formally with 18 charter members in 1876. The Friends met in Wallings Hall, just as the Campbellites had, then in a small frame building on Washington Street, and then in another near the courthouse before building their own small meeting house at Mulberry and Wall in 1880 (Middletown's Sunday newspaper, February 2, 1908; Middletown's evening newspaper, May 12, 1979).

Grace Episcopal Church, founded in 1881, began in somewhat the same way. Although an Episcopal priest held services in Middletown in the Presbyterian church as early as 1859, a mission was not organized until 1875. Mrs. J. A. Heinsohn proposed the idea, and the first meeting was held in the Kirby House, Middletown's best hotel, which was owned by Mrs. Heinsohn's husband. The mission became official in 1878, and Grace Episcopal became a parish in 1881. The church started with a modest frame structure on North Walnut Street costing only $650, but before the year was out the church moved to another site at Adams and Mulberry purchased with a bequest (Haimbaugh 1924, 349-50, Middletown's evening newspaper, June 30, 1979).

The Evangelical Lutheran Church was founded by a minister, the Reverend Benjamin C. Bowman, in 1889. Services were first held in the Friends' Meeting House at Mulberry and Seymour and then later in the "Corn Crib Church" of the Universalists before the construction of a permanent building at Howard and Liberty streets in 1890 (Middletown's evening newspaper, July 7, 1979). The congregation remained there for 65 years; it changed its name to the Holy Trinity Lutheran Church in 1920 (*Churches of Delaware County, 1976*, 1976, 75).

Middletown Churches during the Gas Boom Era

Most of Middletown's churches in 1890, the Lynds' base year, were clustered around the downtown district, separated from each other by only a few blocks. The two black churches located about 10 blocks east of downtown, the Catholic church near downtown, and two ephemeral churches south of downtown—the Church of God at Chestnut and Third and the Congregational Church at 825 South Walnut—were the exceptions. Pulpit sharing was a feature of the initial stages of growth, and the physical proximity of the churches in 1890 made them seem close in spirit as well. Early congregations often met in a host church until they could manage to finance a building of their own, and that building was often a frame church taken over from a congregation that had graduated to a brick structure.

Even though several of the congregations—the Methodists, Baptists, Universalists, and Christians—began as frontier sects, they had become more than respectable by the gas boom days. Prominent citizens who were members of Simpson Chapel (soon to become High Street Methodist) included C. M. Kimbrough (industrialist and father of the noted author Emily Kimbrough), Dr. G. W. H. Kemper (prominent local physician and historian), and William McNaughton (proprietor of the leading department store in Middletown, the forerunner of the Ball stores). Among the members of Grace Episcopal were Julius A. Heinsohn (proprietor of the Kirby House, son-in-law of the church's founder, and organizer of the Natural Gas Company), Marcus Claypool (banker, mining-company organizer, and prominent farmer), John Kirby (the founder of Kirby-Wood Lumber Company), and George F. McCulloch (local entrepreneur and streetcar magnate). After they became a denomination, the Quakers boasted of Joseph Goddard, the town's leading wholesale merchant. The Universalists had Adam Wolf, a prominent local businessman, and four of the five Ball brothers, the ruling members of the X family celebrated and criticized in *Middletown in Transition* (1937) (*High Street Church History*, pp. 3-5; Herrick and Sweet 1917, 144-48; Bohlander 1979, 4-5; Mitchell 1974, 34-42).

The distribution of the community's social and economic elite among several denominations and the churches' downtown locations suggest that the churches of 1890 were not sharply segregated by class. With the exception of St. Lawrence's Catholic Church and the two black churches and the possible further exception of the Church of God and the Congregational Church, none was located in a working-class neighborhood. There were no churches near the big factories owned by the Ball brothers, Indiana Steel and Wire, or Indiana Bridge. The church nearest the factories was the Methodist Protestant Church, but it stood in a prosperous residential district closer to downtown than to the factories. The absence of churches in working-class neighborhoods and the business-class leadership of the downtown churches make the identification of any church as working-class problematical, although there may have been some still meeting in homes, which would not have been recorded in the city directories of the time.

Asking respondents about their parents' church attendance around 1890, the Lynds found that approximately half of the parents attended church regularly in 1890 and that 53 out of a sample of 123 working-class housewives reported that their parents had gone to church three or four times a month in 1890 (Lynd and Lynd 1929, 350). Since there were no working-class churches per se, those parents who lived in Middletown must have attended the mainline churches.

In 1890, Middletown had a population of 11,345 and the total county population was 30,131 (U.S. Bureau of the Census, 1890). The town had 14 of the county's 53 churches (*Emerson's Directory* 1889, 273-75; U.S. House of Representatives 1891, 150-805) but only 2 of its 20 Methodist churches (U.S. House of Representatives 1891, 509). The total number of church members in the county identified by the 1890 census was 6,722 (U.S. House of Representatives 1891, 150-805), and most of the church members belonged to three denominations: Methodists, 2,761; United Brethren in Christ, 1,161; and Disciples of Christ, 979 (U.S. House of Representatives 1891, 346, 509, 782). There were no United Brethren of Christ churches in Middletown and only one Disciples of Christ church, on Jackson Street, and so few members of those denominations could have been counted in town. The 1890 census does tell us the membership of those Middletown churches that were the sole representatives of their denomination in the county: African Methodist Episcopal, 49;

Presbyterian, 256; Universalist, 250; Roman Catholic, 445; and Protestant Episcopal, 70 (U.S. House of Representatives 1891, 238, 546, 652, 722, 805). These five churches together reported only 1,070 members, about 10 percent of Middletown's population. Could the remaining nine churches have enrolled another 4,000 persons, thus bringing the community's total to the 50 percent figure estimated by the Lynds?

If any church accounted for a large share of the difference, it should have been High Street Methodist, the new church built and renamed in 1889 to replace Simpson Chapel. According to the official history of the Methodist Conference, "The churches in Madison and Delaware Counties, where the population had doubled within ten years, failed to gain in proportion. In fact, there was but one church in these counties [in the North Indiana Conference] whose membership had increased worthy of mention, and that was High Street, [Middletown]" (Herrick and Sweet 1917, 148). This expansion occurred in the pastorate of the Reverend C. U. Wade, who began preaching in 1886 and increased the membership by almost 60 percent in three years, thus necessitating the construction of a new brick building (Herrick and Sweet 1917, 146; *High Street Church History*, p. 5). Yet, that increase brought the membership of High Street Methodist to only 858 (Herrick and Sweet 1917, 146; *High Street Church History*, p. 5).

The dynamic ministry of Wade made a significant impression in Middletown, beginning a decade of religious awakening within the national pattern of religious experience. William G. McLaughlin has maintained that the third great awakening in America ran from 1890 to 1920 and that it was attempted earlier (in 1875 through 1885 by Dwight L. Moody) but reached its zenith with the evangelism of Billy Sunday (McLaughlin 1978, 141, 145-47). McLaughlin (1978, 2) argued that:

Great Awakenings (and the revivals that are part of them) are the results, not of depressions, wars, or epidemics, but of critical disjunctions in our self-understanding. They are not brief outbursts of mass emotionalism by one group or another but profound cultural transformations affecting all Americans and extending over a generation or more.

If so, the Lynds base year of 1890 may have marked the beginning of a period of intense religious interest.[5]

Religion in an Industrial City

In any case, the decade after 1890 witnessed a flurry of revivals and church building in Middletown. One striking example was the construction of High Street Methodist Church. The new church was described in the conference history as "the most commodious and beautiful building in the conference" (Herrick and Sweet 1917, 146). On its dedication day, June 2, 1889, the congregation raised $10,000 in the morning and evening services, enough to pay off all the remaining debt (*High Street Church History*, p. 5). More than any other church in Middletown, High Street encouraged the formation of congregations in the new suburbs and the growing industrial areas. These new churches helped expand the total number of churches from 14 to 33 as the population grew from 11,345 to 20,942 in the decade of the 1890s (U.S. Bureau of the Census 1900; *Emerson's Directory* 1899, 174-76).

Five new churches were satellites of High Street. Avondale Methodist was founded in 1891 in a working-class area at Tenth and Sampson. The next was Whiteley Methodist Episcopal established in 1892 near a newly built foundry in a northeast neighborhood, which later became black. High Street also sponsored a black church, Trinity Methodist, begun in 1895 at 918 East First Street, a black neighborhood then and since. Madison Street Methodist opened its doors the same year near the Ball brothers' plant on the southern outskirts of town. Normal City (now College Avenue) Methodist was encouraged to form a congregation in 1900 in the area named after Eastern Indiana Normal College (now the state university) (*High Street Church History*, p. 5; *Churches of Delaware County 1976* 1976, 8, 79, 120, 126; Van Meter 1979, 6-8).

High Street Methodist aided these satellites in a variety of ways, contributing money as well as furniture, rugs, and hymnbooks to the congregations. The ministers of High Street took an active role. Wade called the 16 charter members of Avondale together and his assistant, George A. Wilson, led that congregation for a time. Something similar happened in Whiteley, where Wilson taught the church school around which the congregation formed. Later, the conference helped by assigning ministers to the new churches. One minister served Avondale and Whiteley in 1895, another went to Madison Street and Whiteley in 1897; and a third preached at Normal City and Whiteley in 1903 (*High Street Church History*, p. 5; *Churches of Delaware County, 1976* 1976, 8, 79, 120, 126; Van Meter 1979, 6-8; Herrick and Sweet 1917, 310-11). All of the new Methodist churches had to struggle during the depression of the mid-1890s. Avondale waited until 1898 to complete its building and Madison Street until 1899.

No other church matched High Street's vigor in stimulating denominational growth, but the First Baptist Church did sponsor the Congerville Baptist Church, begun in an old school building in a working-class district at the southern edge of town in 1893. Four years later, the church moved to an even more remote site and became the Seventeenth Street Baptist Church. Its former building became the new home of the United Brethren Church (*Churches of Delaware County, 1976* 1976, 112).

The formation of a satellite church by Jackson Street Christian was discussed as early as 1889 by members who thought that the original congregation was too large and should be divided. Those who broke off met in the old Baptist church at Jefferson and Jackson before securing a place to build farther from downtown on West Howard Street. This became the Central Christian Church. The new endeavor proved unsuccessful, and the members of Central Christian moved back to Jackson Street in 1912 (Middletown's evening newspaper, June 9, 1979). Another church established with the aid of Jackson Street Christian was the Second Christian Church in Congerville. It had disappeared by 1908.[6] The First Christian Church was more successful; it began in 1892 in a public building called Blue Ribbon Hall and later built at Elm and North (Kemper 1908, 455).

The First Presbyterian Church sponsored a satellite church in 1891 at the request of members on the west side in Normal City. It was set up in a frame building at Adams and Martin with furnishings from First Presbyterian: "We were given the pews, pulpit, and the pulpit chairs—the organ—a massive two-manual reed instrument which required a pumper to assist the organist, the 12-light ceiling gas chandeliers, the red wool carpet and the bell" (Thomas 1938, 127). This church, Westminster Presbyterian, was closed in 1903, and the members moved back to First Presbyterian.

Thus, part of the religious activity of the 1890s was the establishment of satellite churches of mainline denominations in working-class and suburban districts; this was most successful for the Methodists but less so for the Baptists, Christians, and Presbyterians. In all, 10 satellite churches were founded between 1890 and 1900, while 9 new denominations entered the town in the same decade. Among these were the Christian Scientists, who first came to Middletown in 1892; the congregation organized in 1899 and met in private homes or rented space until its first church, a two-story building on West Charles Street close to downtown, was completed in 1912 (*Churches of Delaware County, 1976* 1976, 55; Middletown's evening newspaper, July 14, 1979). Other new denominations were the English Lutherans, St. Paul's German Church, the First Brethren (Dunkards), and the United Brethren. Less familiar denominations appearing at about the same time were the Christian Salvation Church, the Wesleyan Methodist Church, and the Spiritual Temple (*Emerson's Directory* 1899-1900, 774-76). These churches followed the same pattern as those established earlier; the congregation formed and met in private homes before renting a public building or buying a secondhand church building. For example, the First Brethren Church, an offshoot from the German Baptists, purchased a former Christian church in 1898.

The first decade of the 20th century in Middletown seemed to belong to the United Brethren. Originally a Moravian sect that became German, the United Brethren in Christ came to America in 1789. In many ways close to the Methodists, the Brethren did not become part of that denomination because of the Methodists' unwillingness to allow services to be held in German (Wilmore 1925, 15, 645). The Brethren came to Indiana as early as 1808 and had a church in Middletown's county near Selma by 1854, but they did not move into Middletown until 1900. (The United Brethren in Christ are not to be confused with the First Brethren Church, which was German Baptist and did not grow.) The first church they organized in Middletown was Industry United Brethren in 1900, the second was Riverside United Brethren in 1903, the third was Normal City United Brethren in 1905, and the fourth was St. Mark's United Brethren (now Fountain Square United Methodist) in 1910 (Kemper 1908, 475-76; *Churches of Delaware County, 1976* 1976, 59, 76, 91, 103).

Since the United Brethren were close to the Methodists in their theology and were attractive to Hoosiers (Indiana ranked third behind Ohio and New York in the number of United Brethren churches) (Wilmore 1925, 647), their penetration from the surrounding countryside can be understood as an advancement of Methodism in Middletown. What was different about the Brethren was their preference for locations away from the center of town, either in working-class neighborhoods such as Industry or St. Mark's or in business-class neighborhoods such as Riverside and Normal City. Three began in private homes; the fourth, Normal City, took over the "little white church" abandoned by the Westminster Presbyterians who had moved back to the First Presbyterian Church. Each eventually built a church; two were frame structures later replaced by brick ones; the others were constructed of brick at the start. Industry enjoyed the patronage of Edmund B. Ball, one of the original Ball brothers, perhaps because of its proximity to the glass plant. Ball was on the board of trustees and donated an acre of land for a church and a parsonage in 1920, although he himself was a member of the First Universalist Church (Wilmore 1925, 306-8; *Churches of Delaware County, 1976* 1976, 59, 76, 91, 103).

The Arrival of Fundamentalists and Pentecostals

The newer groups coming into Middletown after 1910 were less closely related to the Methodists, although their backgrounds were not dissimilar. These incipient denominations had their roots in the post-Civil War Holiness movement that affected Methodism and in the English and American millenarianism that in 1919, took on the name of fundamentalism (Sandeen 1970, 246). The millenarian movement in 19th-century England proclaimed the imminent second coming of Christ as proven by a prophetic chronology, the restoration of the Jews, and a secret rapture of church members (Sandeen 1970, 20-41). Although the original proponents of this theology were members and ministers of well-known denominations, their American followers eventually shed their old affiliations and created new sects.

Among such groups were the Church of God, founded by Daniel S. Warner, who had been an elder in the Churches of God in North America, a revival sect from the frontier. In 1881, Warner left that sect to lead his own movement. By 1917, the Church of God had a general ministerial assembly (Handy 1977, 296). Similarly, a Canadian Presbyterian, Albert Benjamin Simpson, was instrumental in the formation of the Christian and Millenary Alliance in New York in 1887. Beginning as a nondenominational fellowship, the group emphasized Holiness and divine healing and organized urban missions (Handy 1977, 296). Another church in this tradition was the Nazarene Church, which was first organized in Los Angeles by a Methodist minister named Phineas Bresee, "who left his church to carry the Holiness message to young and poor"; the Nazarenes emerged as conservatives, revivalists, and perfectionists (Handy 1977, 296-97).

Although these churches were fundamentalist or millenarian, they were not Pentecostal and did not celebrate speaking in tongues. Much of the religious impetus for the Pentecostal churches came from California and an unplanned series of revival meetings conducted in Los Angeles in 1906 by a black minister with a Baptist and Holiness background. These meetings influenced the formation of such Pentecostal churches as the Church of God (Cleveland, Tennessee) in 1906, the Church of God in Christ (which was to become the largest of the black Pentecostal churches) in 1907, and the Assemblies of God, founded in Hot Springs, Arkansas, in 1914 (which placed great emphasis upon the person of Jesus) (Handy 1977, 298-99).

It is difficult to ascertain exactly when these fundamentalist and Pentecostal groups entered Middletown. The Christian and Missionary Alliance came during the early 1920s and settled on East Howard Street. Cowing Drive Wesleyan Church began much earlier, in 1904, after a Holiness revival in Whiteley. It became the International Apostolic Holiness Church in 1907 and then the First Pilgrim Holiness Church in 1925. The Glad Tidings Assembly of God began with a tent meeting at Eighth and High in 1919. The first Church of God (Anderson) began with a prayer meeting in an old store at Walnut and Eighteenth in 1909. The Second Church of God, Southside, began in 1926 in a building purchased from the Congerville Church of Christ. The First Church of the Nazarene began as the Five Point Nazarene Mission in the early 1920s and in 1927 was followed by the Southside Church of the Nazarene, which was organized on the far southside of Middletown by the First Church (*Churches of Delaware County, 1976* 1976, 21, 31, 66, 93, 116, 117; *Emerson's Directory* 1924, 1198-99). These were not the only Holiness and Pentecostal churches in Middletown at the time. *Emerson's Directory* for 1925-1926 also lists the Apostolic Faith Assembly, the High Street Assembly of God, the Full Gospel Tabernacle, the Triumph Holiness Church, the Union Home Mission, and the United Christian Light of Hope (*Emerson's Directory* 1925, 18-20).

These new denominations differed from the older denominations in several ways. They resembled the Methodists of a century earlier in their belief in perfectability, the simple life, and personal holiness. The Pentecostals were distinguished by their yearning to be touched by the Spirit and to speak in tongues. They replaced the older denominations in their relinquished buildings and competed with them for converts in working-class neighborhoods through evangelical techniques. But they, too, in time began to progress from a frame church to a brick church and eventually, if possible, to a stone church.

Revivalism

The older denominations had reached a kind of watershed by the early 20th century. Their growth had become less dependent upon revivals and more on natural increase and Christian education. Revivalism seemed somewhat unbecoming to these second- or third-generation denominationalists. The First Universalist Church, for example, refused to participate in the Billy Sunday Crusade when invited by the Ministerial Association in 1908, although, interestingly enough, the congregation decided to join in supporting a special tabernacle for revival purposes in 1913 despite the opposition of its minister (Mitchell 1974, 45-46, 58). The First Universalist Church and the High Street Methodist Church depended much more upon their Sunday schools to attract members. Against his better judgment, F. C. Ball, superintendent of the Sunday school at First Universalist, was persuaded to allow the church to compete with 18 others in a 1913 contest to see which could add the most members. To his surprise, First Universalist won (Mitchell 1974, 56-57). The history of High Street records the peak of Sunday school attendance in 1919, with an average of 967 students per Sunday for the year (*High Street Church History*, p. 7).

The older denominations were moving in the direction of formalism. Friends' Memorial, built in 1908, was made of stone and had stained glass windows with silver-plated tablets dedicated to the railway men who donated them (Middletown's Sunday newspaper, February 2, 1908). In 1913, the First Universalist Church became St. John's Universalist Church at the urging of the minister, Dr. E. G. Mason. When E. B. Ball and Margaret Ball, of the second generation of that family, joined, they were baptized — the first time that ceremony was used in the church. The Reverend Mason, according to the church history, advocated the name change in order to emulate the Episcopal and Catholic churches (Mitchell 1974, 55-59); the baptismal ceremony may have reflected a similar ambition. Meanwhile, the First Presbyterian Church continued its tradition of appointing highly trained ministers. The minister appointed in 1921, Reverend Neeley, was a graduate of Princeton and McCormick Theological Seminary and had been a professor at the American University in Beirut (Thomas 1938, 72-72-73).

Although his fellow Princeton graduate Robert Lynd might have been expected to gravitate toward the First Presbyterian Church, the focus of Lynd's attention in 1924 was on High Street Methodist. Although six revivals were conducted by local ministers that year in Middletown, the one Lynd chose to describe was High Street's (Lynd and Lynd 1929, 378-81). This decision almost scuttled the research project, according to Mrs. Lynd (1980, 1):

At times the Institute [of Social and Religious Research] wanted to drop it. One reason they disliked the manuscript [of *Middletown*] was that they said it was savage on religion. There is an account of a Methodist revival that they particularly disliked. Later, the Methodists in Muncie built a new church, and felt Bob's was the best account there had ever been of a revival service, and in the cornerstone of the church placed a copy of the Bible, and of the Methodist creed, and of *Middletown*.

Still, the Lynds averred that the revival as a religious form was dying in the mainline churches and noted that the "ministers of several leading churches opposed revival services because they drew energy away from other religious activities" (Lynd and Lynd 1929, 381).

Despite their slackening enthusiasm for revivals in the older churches, the improvement of facilities continued. The satellite churches of the 1890s were now entering the brick-church stage. In 1910, Seventeenth Street Baptist moved into a new building on Walnut Street and changed its name to Walnut Street Baptist; the sanctuary of Avondale Methodist was remodeled and enlarged in 1921; and Madison Street Methodist finished its brick building in time for services in 1926 (*Churches of Delaware County, 1976* 1976, 8, 79, 112). Thus did these churches proclaim their respectability and permanence.

The upgrading of facilities took various forms. One older, mainline church moved without building a new church; instead, it moved its existing frame-and-stucco church and expanded it. Grace Episcopal Church trundled its old building a few blocks from Adams and Mulberry to Adams and Madison in 1922 and has remained there every since (Middletown's evening newspaper, June 30, 1979).

Although the reliability of their data on church membership and attendance is questionable, when the Lynds were in Middletown, the ratio of churches to population was approximately the same as it was in 1890.[7] Given the considerable improvement and enlargement of the older churches that had taken place, the average seating capacity surely exceeded that of 1890.

Growth during Hard Times

When Robert Lynd returned to Middletown in 1935:

The first indication of change in Middletown's religious institutions since 1925 struck one almost as one got off the train. In the heart of the downtown section of the city two imposing new stone churches have replaced rusty brick buildings that dated back to the gas-boom days of the 1880's (Lynd and Lynd 1937, 296).

The two new stone churches Lynd described are easy to identify: they are the First Baptist Church at Adams and Jefferson, a few blocks from its earlier location, finished in 1929; and the High Street Methodist Church, a new building at the same location but on an expanded acreage, put up in 1930 (*Churches of Delaware County, 1976* 1976, 50, 74; *High Street Church History*, pp. 9-10). Both structures were impressive in 1935 and remain so today.

The High Street church, in particular, was a notable achievement. The congregation asked the minister, Dr. Claude King, to tour Europe and to study church architecture. He brought back pictures of Gothic cathedrals, some of which served as models for the Methodists' new church. The building cost $445,000, of which $210,000 had to be borrowed. This obligation constituted more than half of the total debt of the entire North Indiana Conference for the next 10 years (*Churches of Delaware County, 1976* 1976, 50, 74; *High Street Church History*, pp. 9-10; Norwood 1957, 112), but the result was what the builders had planned. High Street Methodist dominated the town architecturally.

A third stone church was begun downtown in 1932. This was the First Church of Christ Scientist, dedicated in 1937.

A new Catholic church, St. Mary's, marked the extension of Catholicism across the river into the newly developed and prosperous northwest district. Although instituted in 1930, the parish was unable to finish its church during the Great Depression and used a basement for services. In 1948, St. Mary's purchased one of the estates of the Kitselman family (the Y family of *Middletown in Transition*), where an imposing stone structure was completed in 1965 (*Churches of Delaware County, 1976* 1976, 8; Middletown's evening newspaper, June 23, 1979). The social respectability of Catholicism grew with its numbers. In 1925, the Lynds noted a ratio of 1 Catholic to 15 Protestants (Lynd and Lynd 1929, 332); by 1978, there were 2 Catholics for each 15 Protestants. The Lynds (1937, 315) remarked in *Middletown in Transition* that "the Catholic Church pursued in 1935 the same quiet, resolute, inconspicuous course as in 1925. It is not involved in local politics or any public aspects of Middletown's life." Today, the Catholic churches are involved in both; many Catholics run for public office, and priests are actively engaged in civic affairs.

The mainline denominations erected other new churches in the outer ring of the city during the 1930s. Riverside United Brethren built a new brick building on its old site in 1930; Normal City Methodist had moved a few blocks and biult an impressive brick structure the year before to become College Avenue Methodist Church. Normal City's old building became the home of a satellite of the Jackson Street Christian Church, Normal City Christian Church (*Churches of Delaware County, 1976* 1976, 23, 103,

127). These three congregations increased in size as the college grew and new homes sprang up around them.

The theologically conservative churches grew, too. A second Lutheran church came to Middletown in 1936, Grace Lutheran Church of the conservative Missouri Synod. A number of families called a pastor and met in the YMCA for two years before building a frame church in 1940 on Reserve Street in the northwest section (Middletown's evening newspaper, July 7, 1979). The Church of God Tabernacle began services in Riley Elementary School and later built a church on North Walnut Street and changed its name to Northside Church of God (*Churches of Delaware County, 1976* 1976, 93). These moves into middle-class neighborhoods were not to be the last.

A New Wave of Churches

During the 1950s, the migration of factory workers from the southern Appalachian region increased significantly. The migrants, mostly from Tennessee, clustered around United Baptist churches, which resembled those they had known at home. By 1970, the migrants amounted to about 8 percent of Middletown's population (Jones 1978, 267).

The First United Baptist Church, founded in 1936, was the mother church of seven others: five in the 1950s and two in the 1960s. All of these were located in the southeastern part of Middletown in poor or working-class neighborhoods, although they were not neighborhood churches. Named after churches in Appalachia, each except the first began as a consequence of dissension within another United Baptist church. Each went through the same stages of growth, meeting first in private homes, then moving to a storefront, and then acquiring a building of its own (Jones 1978, 210-30). Characteristically sectarian, the United Baptists resemble the 19th-century primitive Baptist groups. These independent congregations shun the world and have unpaid or low-paid ministers who must work at other jobs in order to survive. Their members are Sabbatarian, premillennial, and emotional and yet not free-will Baptists. However, as the migrant workers in these congregations became more skilled, more settled, and hence more prosperous, some of the churches changed their character.

Such was the case with the first migrant church by 1957: "Twenty-one years after its founding this church was no longer a United Baptist church, but rather a Southern Baptist church which espoused freewill, social community action, and numerous changes in ritual—in other words it had gone modern" (Jones 1978, 257). But not all the Baptist groups went in that direction: some kept their earlier mold, competing with the new fundamentalist churches that came to town or the older ones that expanded. By 1950, *Polk's City Directory* (1950, x, 10-11) listed four Holiness, four Pentecostal, two Seventh Day Adventist, and four Nazarene churches.[8] One of the Churches of God was the Cleveland Assembly, which had begun in Tennessee and attracted many of the migrants from that state. The growth of fundamentalist churches, however, did not quite keep pace with the growth of the population.

Moving Out

Besides the growth of the United Baptist churches and their fundamentalist relatives, the 1950s were marked by the continued outward expansion of the city, particularly to the northwest and the far south, stimulated by the postwar growth of the state teachers' college and by the development of shopping plazas in each of those districts. As more families moved into the new developments on opposite sides of the city, a question arose for the downtown churches. Should they—First Baptist, First Church of Christian Science, High Street Methodist, First Presbyterian, Grace Episcopal, St. John's Universalist Church (renamed First Universalist Church in 1954), Friends' Memorial, Jackson Street Christian, and Temple Beth-El—follow their members to the new residential areas? Not only were the old downtown churches challenged, so were the satellite churches that these churches had formed in the 1890's—Congerville Baptist, Madison Street, and Avondale Methodist—and whose members had also become more affluent and had moved farther south, leaving their old neighborhoods to less prosperous successors.

If the downtown churches did not move, would the experience of the 1890s be repeated as established denominations created satellites in the new suburbs, or would newer, fundamentalist groups in transition from sect to denomination preempt the opportunity for expansion as they had done in the 1920s? The older churches had considerable investments in their relatively new buildings. High Street, for example, had not paid off its building debt by 1948 (Norwood 1957, 126). Moreover, its symbolic position at the center of the city was not to be readily surrendered.

Nonetheless, some of the older churches moved. The first was Jackson Street Christian, which, as previously noted, relocated in 1952 to a former estate of the Y family and took the name of the estate, Hazelwood, for its own (*Churches of Delaware County, 1976* 1976, 73). The house became an educational building and the carriage house the minister's home. Eventually, a new stone church was built. First Presbyterian moved to Riverside, only a few blocks from Hazelwood and the state university, three years later (*Churches of Delaware County, 1976* 1976, 57). The new edifice, though constructed of brick instead of stone, was impressive enough to earn the sobriquet "Our Lady of the Cadillacs." The move seemed to strengthen the attractiveness of this church for the professionals and managers moving into Middletown to work in the industries taken over by larger, national firms. By the end of the 1970s, First Presbyterian could claim to be the most influential church in town.

The next to move was First Universalist (renamed Unitarian-Universalist in 1961 when the two national groups merged) (Handy 1977, 337). In 1963, the church decided to rebuild, and it surveyed the residential pattern of its members. The results showed that 63 percent lived in the northwest quadrant, 14 percent in the northeast, 13 percent in the southwest, and 10 percent in the southeast (Mitchell 1974, 178). A plot of land was selected in the northwest, and a church was begun with the aid of a $15,000 grant from Ball Brothers (Mitchell 1974, 203-20). Located in a wooded area still outside the city limits today but now surrounded by houses, the First Unitarian-Universalist Church can still claim at least one member of the Ball family as a member.

Although the churches that moved prospered, those that remained did not appear to suffer. In the 1960s, Friends' Memorial discussed moving to the outskirts of town but rejected the idea, instead building an educational center connected to the church. In January 1978, a gas explosion ruined the interior of High Street

Methodist. Refusing the option to move, the congregation voted to remain and to refurbish the sanctuary at a cost of $4 million. It repeated the Sunday pledge ceremony of 90 years earlier, which had paid for the brick building that preceded the ruined stone one, and raised most of the necessary funds in one day.

In order to survive, the downtown churches, like the downtown stores, had to accommodate the automobile. Either they built parking lots on land they owned or found nearby lots they could use for Sunday and evening services.

Not all the downtown congregations had memberships as stable as Friends' Memorial, High Street Methodist, and Grace Episcopal. Main Street Methodist had begun as the First Methodist Protestant Church in 1872 in what was to become a fashionable residential section. (The Methodist Protestant Church began in 1828 after a schism in the Methodist Episcopal denomination over the question of congregational autonomy) (Handy 1977, 404). Its brick church, located near the site of the original building, was completed in 1911. In 1939, the church returned to the larger Methodist fellowship when the Methodist Protestants merged with the Southern and Northern Methodists (Handy 1977, 404; *Churches of Delaware County, 1976* 1976, 80; Norwood 1957, 43). Meanwhile, the neighborhood had decayed, with large dilapidated houses divided into rooms and apartments and with a high crime rate. By late 1960, the membership of the church had changed so much that it was defined by its pastor, the Reverend Garrett Phillips, as a "servant church, serving many who no one else would accept" (*Churches of Delaware County, 1976* 1976, 80).

The churches founded in the suburban ring in the 1890s faced similar problems and took similar actions. Such was the case with Congerville Baptist Church, begun in 1893, which had moved to Walnut Street in 1910 to become Walnut Street Baptist. When the character of its lower-middle-class residential neighborhood changed, the church decided to move into a new neighborhood. The new church, Shawnee Heights Baptist, built in 1972, is outside the city limits south of town in a relatively expensive housing development (*Churches of Delaware County, 1976* 1976, 112).

Madison Street Methodist, founded at almost the same time as Congerville Baptist and located closeby, chose to stay. Occupying a brick church built in 1926, it found itself in the 1960s and

1970s in a commercial strip of gasoline stations and fast-food restaurants. Its pastor estimates that more than half of the present congregation commutes, and he attempts to minister to them as well as to the socially disadvantaged people who live nearby in the original parish (*Churches of Delaware County, 1976* 1976, 79).

The Latest Revival

According to McLaughlin, the 1960s saw a new wave of religious enthusiasm in the United States that challenged the older churches, even those that were already fundamentalist.

The Fourth Great Awakening began in the 1960s but its birth was obscured by the belief that Kennedy's program marked a revival of Liberalism in politics, even though many of his advisors shared Reinhold Niebuhr's neo-orthodox view of human nature and destiny. Niebuhr's pessimistic view of rationalism and idealism was only a partial answer to the old consensus (McLaughlin 1978, 193).

The new fervor, like the old millenarianism, began in a nondenominational way and attracted many people in older denominations, some of whom remained in their churches home and joined new groups while others withdrew to form splinter congregations or changed denominations. The movement was Pentecostal, seeking the direct manifestation of the Holy Spirit for speaking in tongues and healing. It included such groups as the Full Gospel Businessman's Fellowship, begun in 1951 in California (Handy 1977, 397), and charismatic movements in several mainline denominations, especially among Catholics and Episcopalians.

The movement came to Middletown in the 1960s and 1970s and attracted followers, including many high-income managers and professionals. This further blurred the class lines in the churches and made the sorting of churches into working-class and business-class even more difficult than it had been before. The prediction of the Lynds and many other students of religion that increased education and scientific knowledge would threaten the more fundamental and conservative versions of religion has not been fulfilled.

Instead, the newest churches continued to grow and extended into more prestigious residential areas. An example was Halteman Village Baptist Church, built in one of the most expensive northwest subdivisions. The developer had donated a lot for a church in 1959 with the object of making the development more attractive for families. But, unlike the earlier subdivisions that attracted satellites from downtown churches, the Halteman Village Baptist Church became associated with the theologically conservative Southern Baptist Convention. Moreover, it revived the old Middletown pattern of helping to establish satellite churches. Of the four satellites—Creekwood, Gaston, Yorktown, and North Delaware— two are in suburban developments, one is in a nearby town, and only one, Creekwood Baptist Church (founded in 1965), is in a working-class neighborhood.

The penetration of suburban areas by the Southern Baptists was not an isolated event but a harbinger of things to come. The most rapidly growing church of the 1970s was Grace Baptist Church, which advertises itself as independent, fundamental, and evangelistic and has attracted both working-class and business-class members to its fold. It operates Heritage Hall, the only private high school in the community. Grace Baptist, like Halteman Village Baptist, is a suburban church located beyond the western boundaries of the city.

In 1967, when Collins Glenn came to Middletown to assume the pulpit of Grace Baptist, the church had an average attendance of 85 persons; it now has a tabernacle where attendance averages 1200 at Sunday services. The church has a fleet of buses and an aggressive sales program to attract new members.

These were not the only fundamentalist churches to move into "better" locations. In 1948, the Normal City Church of God built a white frame church at Riverside and Tillotson, then regarded as the far west side. In 1967, it moved a mile north into a recently developed area next to a junior high school and built a handsome stone church (*Churches of Delaware County, 1976* 1976, 93).

About the same time, doctrinal dissension within the older churches led to a number of schisms. St. Andrew's Presbyterian Church was organized by 22 ex-members of the First Presbyterian Church in 1962, and it duplicated the history of earlier churches by meeting first in a garage, later in the local elementary school, and then building a church on the northern outskirts in 1964 (*Churches of Delaware County, 1976* 1976, 106). Theologically conservative, the church counts executives of local corporations and an ex-president of the state university among its members.

Five years after the founding of St. Andrew's, another group of dissatisfied Presbyterians founded Westminster Presbyterian Church, the most conservative Presbyterian church in town and affiliated with the Reform Presbyterians. In a reversal of the historical succession, Westminster Presbyterian bought the old frame building vacated by the Northside Church of God when it moved to a new building (*Churches of Delaware County, 1976* 1976, 129).

The Presbyterians were not the only mainline denomination to proliferate. In 1962, another Baptist church affiliated with the American Baptist Convention was founded in the northwest section by the missionary efforts of the First Baptist Church and the Walnut Street Baptist Church (*Churches of Delaware County, 1976* 1976, 102). Its history much resembled that of another satellite church, Congerville Baptist, founded in 1893.

In 1966, a third Lutheran church, the Lutheran Church of the Cross, appeared on North Wheeling close to Halteman Village. The church was formed as a mission congregation by the Ohio Synod of the American Lutheran Church (*Churches of Delaware County, 1976* 1976, 78). It has the same national connection as the Holy Trinity Lutheran Church.

The third Catholic church, St. Francis of Assisi, is more liberal than its predecessors. Begun as the Newman Center at the state university in 1939, St. Francis became a separate parish in 1972 (Middletown's evening newspaper, June 23, 1979). With a large student membership, St. Francis has the reputation of being heavily involved in such social issues as peace, world hunger, and racial justice.

Conclusion

By the late 1970s, Middletown was much less Methodist than it had been in the 1890s. A directory published in 1976 listed 145 churches, of which 19 were Baptist, 14 Methodist (including the Evangelical United Brethren who merged with the Methodists in 1968), 8 Nazarene, and 8 Churches of God[9] (*Churches of Delaware County, 1976* 1976). There is still only 1 Episcopal church, 1 Unitarian-Universalist church, and 1 Friends' church. Given that a number of the Baptist churches, particularly the migrant churches, are small, Methodism is probably still the largest denomination in Middletown but not by a wide margin.

The growing religious heterogeneity of the community accounts in part for the increase of facilities available to the faithful. By 1976, there was approximately one church for every 550 persons. This represents a considerable growth over 810 persons per church in 1890 and 798 in 1925.

During the 1890s, serious thinkers in Middletown could attack organized religion and working-class groups could schedule union meetings or cockfights on Sunday, but the business-class leaders of the community would not endorse such sentiments or behavior[10] (Lynd and Lynd 1929, 321). Religious observance was necessary in order to socialize a rough, rapidly industrializing community. Hence, businesspeople and community leaders aided the churches even when they themselves were not believers, and the churches encouraged the growth of other churches by sharing resources or facilities. The town officials permitted the use of public buildings, including the courthouse, for religious services. The point was to improve the town, to impose social order.

The founding of churches in Middletown during the 19th century assumed a pattern that would appear again later during periods of increased religious activity. In the Middletown experience, congregations were founded by local initiative rather than by missionary efforts from outside. A private citizen, often a woman, wishing to worship in a particular denominational atmosphere would organize a group of persons of like persuasion. A minister of the faith would be invited into the community to stimulate interest and, if sufficiently successful, to occupy a pulpit.

Volunteer efforts such as this, it is true, were often aided by denominational agencies. Dioceses encouraged Grace Episcopal and St. Lawrence's; High Street Methodist provided both monetary and spiritual encouragement to the satellite Methodist churches of the 1890s. Still, the impetus came from the local group of believers who wished to be helped and who asked for assistance.

Middletown churches continued to proliferate during the 20th century in much the same way, however with significant modifications. Some new churches were not composed of local residents without a church connection but were formed by believers already in a church but dissatisfied with its doctrines or practices. Such a group might form a new congregation or join another congregation with congenial beliefs. The first experience is illustrated by St. Andrew's Presbyterian Church; the second by the growth of St. Francis of Assisi, which was originally a mission for state university students. The same process occurred in the history of the United Baptists, who were aided by a surplus of ministers and the family ties of the secessionists.

The religious enthusiasm manifest in schisms and the founding of new congregations was not restricted to any one segment of the religious spectrum. It was common to liberal and conservative churches, to mainline denominations and Pentecostal sects. Middletown people have always expected religious institutions to meet their needs. Begun perhaps by community leaders to improve social control in a frontier community, Middletown's churches became the firm possessions of those who worshiped in them.

By 1920 social order had improved. Despite the passage of Prohibition, the rate for social-order crimes in Middletown was lower than it had been for years (Hewitt and Hoover 1980, Table 2). However, at the same time, the growth of the media, particularly the expansion of newspapers to include more national news, the advent of radio, and the elevation of the movies to respectability, had changed attitudes about sex and sin. The newer sects coming into town took on a fundamentalist cast in opposition to the older denominations, which placed their reliance on education and Christian nurture. The educated and affluent struggled with the problem of reconciling modernism and religion. There was much questioning of faith, but enough remained so that considerable energy and resources were invested in expanding the very churches that contained those most prone to doubt. In Middletown, as elsewhere in the United States, "sincere religiosity has been persistently misinterpreted" (Nash 1970, 147).

By the 1970s, the question of reconciling religious belief and modernism had receded. It was then taken for granted that the religious and technological perspectives were separate but not necessarily incompatible. As Lawrence Veysey has said, "The average church member is a computer expert who lives in Atlanta and attends a Southern Baptist Church." No longer was it true, if it had ever been true, that speaking in tongues was confined to those with calloused hands.

Chapter 3

Changes in
Religious Observance

An early Sunday morning finds Middletown remarkably quiet, but by 9 o'clock cars carrying families to church jam the streets, almost like the rush to work on a weekday. Church parking lots are crowded most of the morning. Around noon, churchgoing clothes are changed for more casual dress as the traffic flow shifts from places of worship to the shopping and entertainment centers. For many Middletown residents, shopping, going to a movie, or having a meal at the Middletown Mall is a Sunday afternoon ritual as fixed as church attendance. Even though the shopping centers thrive on Sunday afternoons, a fair number of families still attend afternoon and evening church services.

If one were to infer current religious observance in Middletown from superficial observations, the conclusion would be that most Middletown citizens attend church services on Sunday morning and, having fulfilled their obligation to worship, then spend the rest of the day in recreation. Shopping, seeing movies, dining out, pleasure driving, picnicking, boating, playing golf, and playing tennis are popular Sunday-afternoon activities. However, such observations are notoriously inaccurate, and so this chapter will document, with careful observation, church records, census data, and self-reported beliefs and activities, religious observance in Middletown today and compare it to that in earlier eras.

As it has already been pointed out in Chapter 1, the Lynds saw contradictory trends in religious behavior in Middletown during the 1920s and later during the 1930s. There were some indications that religion was declining, but other indications suggested the contrary.

Church Attendance

The 1920s witnessed a growing competition between religion and recreation for dominance on Sunday. The Lynds saw the church slowly but surely relinquishing the Sabbath to recreational pursuits. Sunday afternoon in particular was becoming defined as a time for play rather than for worship: "A number of churches held Sunday School in the long Sunday afternoons of 1890, but today the afternoon is usually swept clear of services" (Lynd and Lynd 1929, 341). Six Protestant ministers were asked in 1924 whether their churches offered any Sunday afternoon or evening programs. Three replied that they offered none, while the others said that they had no regular services but did conduct special programs such as Sunday school at the orphan's home, singing at the hospital, and home prayer groups on an irregular schedule. The Lynds' believed that Sunday afternoon church attendance was fading: "With this generation the 'Sabbath' of 1890 is increasingly secularized into the 'Sunday holiday'" (Lynd and Lynd 1929, 343).

The trend toward Sunday recreation was even more evident in 1935. More automobiles and improved roads invited Sunday motoring, country clubs were open for golf and tennis, riding clubs held Sunday rides, shooting clubs sponsored Sunday meets, and city parks were used for baseball and football. The city had not yet begun to sponsor organized ball leagues on the Sabbath, but the municipal swimming pool was open, and it was expected that Sunday baseball and football programs would soon follow.

City-sponsored athletic leagues now play on Sunday, and Sunday recreation flourishes but not, apparently, at the expense of church participation. Although the heaviest flurry of church activity in contemporary Middletown occurs between 9:30 A.M. and noon, one is struck by the variety of church schedules. Prayer breakfasts are held as early as 7:30 A.M. Sunday morning. Worship services and church schools fill the morning. Carry-in dinners after morning services have become regular events in many churches.

There are also religious recreations that compete with secular recreations on Sunday afternoons: slide shows of missionary programs, religious films, and occasional special worship services. Gospel concerts, "singspirations," films, and plays are scheduled on Sunday evenings, along with regular sermons. There are several gospel groups who make the rounds of Middletown's churches presenting song and sometimes testimony; the United Family Gospel Singers, the Sons of God, and the Heavenly Travelers were among those active during 1979 and 1980. Films such as *Gospel Road,* produced by Billy Graham, in which Johnny Cash and June Carter tell the story of Jesus in music are shown repeatedly.

The abandonment of Sunday to secular recreation that the Lynds anticipated has not yet occurred. The religious services of various kinds held throughout the day are, on the whole, well attended.

In addition, most churches sponsor some weekday activities, such as skating parties, watermelon feeds, fund-raising projects, and men-only or women-only services and revivals. The observed frequency of contemporary church attendance suggests that the decline in religious observance the Lynds reported in the 1920s and 1930s and expected to continue has reversed itself. Today, church services in Middletown are more numerous than they were two generations ago and better attended.

To show this pattern, we will start by reexamining the Lynds' data about religious attendance in 1890 and 1924 and comparing them to our own data for the late 1970s. The wives of a sample of 164 Middletown families were interviewed for the 1924 study. The sample included 124 working-class and 40 business-class families, all native-born whites, with husband and wife living together and with one or more children between 6 and 18 years old at home. The wives reported their current church attendance as well as that of their husbands and children and tried to recall the church attendance of their parents around 1890. For convenience of inspection and in order to permit comparison with data from other sources, we have condensed the Lynds' six attendance categories into four: *regular,* attends religious services four times a month or more; *intermittent,* attends one to three times a month; *occasional,* attends less often than once a month; and *never,* never attends religious services.

Appendix Table 3-1 shows the church attendance reported by business- and working-class women in Middletown for themselves and their husbands in 1924 and for their fathers and mothers around 1890. The table has interesting implications, some of which were not discussed by the Lynds. Assuming that the respondents' recall of their parents churchgoing habits was reasonably accurate, there had been a significant decline in regular church attendance from 1890 to 1924 affecting both men and women and both social classes. The decline was greater in the working class, where there had been a sharp increase in the proportion *never* attending religious services, from a little more than a third in 1890 to about two-thirds in 1924. By 1924, most of Middletown's working-class adults seemed to have entirely given up the habit of church-going. Only 20 percent of them reported regular attendance compared to approximately 50 percent of the working-class wives' parents from the previous generation.

Although the working-class adults stayed home from church, they did insist that their children attend. Sixty-three percent of the children in the working-class families of the 1924 sample attended Sunday school regularly, and only 12 percent never attended. This level of attendance was not quite as high as that of the business-class children (80 percent), but it was stirking compared to their parents' avoidance of church. In the typical working-class family of 1924, the parents stayed away from church on Sunday but sent their children to Sunday school. For these people, most of them recent rural migrants to the city, churchgoing meant social climbing and a display of respectability more than piety.

The business-class wives and husbands of 1924 were more than twice as likely to attend religious services regularly as their working-class counterparts and much less likely to stay away from church altogether. The proportion of business-class men who never attended church in 1924 was slightly less than the proportion of their fathers-in-law who had stayed away from church around 1890, although business-class wives showed a moderate increase in nonattendance compared to their mothers.

The several surveys we conducted in Middletown in 1977 and 1978 have enabled us to bring these trends up-to-date. Appendix Table 3-2, based on the Lynds' survey of 183 housewives in 1924, the retrospective information they gave about their parents' habits around 1890, and our comparable interviews with 333 housewives in 1978, shows several interesting things about married women in white Middletown families over an interval of about nine decades. First, the downward trend of church attendance from 1890 to 1924 reversed itself some time between 1935 and 1978. Nearly half of the 1978 respondents reported attending religious services regularly (at least four times a month), more than twice the proportion so reporting in 1924 and not much lower than the proportion who did so in 1890. At the other end of the distribution, only 17 percent of the 1978 respondents said that they *never* attended religious services, less than a third of the corresponding proportion in 1924 and significantly lower than 1890 as well. But, since one reason for the higher attendance reported in 1978 was the inclusion of relatively more business-class wives in the sample, it is important to examine the churchgoing behavior of working-class and business-class families separately.

Social Class and Church Attendance

In 1890 and 1924, as Appendix Table 3-1 shows, Middletown's two social classes differed sharply in their pattern of church attendance. Two-thirds of working-class adults stayed away from church in 1924, while most business-class adults attended. The data from five Middletown surveys conducted in 1977 and 1978 were combined in Appendix Table 3-3 to show the current church attendance of business-class and working-class men and women. In 1977-1978, business-class and working-class families are still distinguishable in their church attendance, although the gap has narrowed by about half. Business-class persons of both sexes have a significantly higher rate of regular attendance and a significantly lower incidence of nonattendance than working-class persons. When we examine the relationship between socioeconomic status and religiosity in terms of continuous variables such as income and education instead of class membership, small but significant correlations are obtained.

Sex and Church Attendance

There is an anomaly in the Lynds' data about the church attendance of men and women that calls for explanation. The rates of attendance reported for husbands and wives in 1924 were virtually identical. This equal participation did not square either with the Lynds' subjective impression of predominantly female congregations or with a questionnaire survey of average weekly attendance at religious services that they administered to all the ministers of Middletown in November 1924. The adjusted account of average weekly attendance based on the ministers' reports showed the attendance at Sunday morning services to have been 61 percent female and 39 percent male. This is a substantial difference and suggests that, although the rates of attendance of husbands and wives in intact families were practically identical, women in other family situations and other stages of the life cycle attended church services significantly more often than men in those situations. Aside from the fact that more single, divorced, or widowed women than men attended church in 1924, men more often than women were prevented from attending church because they worked on Sundays. A number of the manufacturing and assembly plants and businesses providing services to the public operated seven days a week, and a considerable number of men, as well as a few women, worked every Sunday.

Appendix Table 3-4 shows the distribution of church attendance by sex based on the five recent surveys. Women still attend church more than men, but the differences are now smaller than those observed in 1924 and 1935. What our investigations saw while attending various Middletown churches in 1977 and 1979 was a prevailing pattern of family worship. There were usually a few more women than men in the congregations, but the differences were not impressive.

Age and Church Attendance

The Lynds did not present quantitative data about the relationship between age and church attendance, but they mentioned in several places that church participation increased with age. Their description of working-class churches in 1935 noted "the same preponderance of gray-haired persons . . ." (Lynd and Lynd 1937, 298) as in 1924, and a business-class respondent is quoted as saying, "Not many people under thirty-five go to church—none that we know. It's mostly just the same older crowd that keeps on going" (Lynd and Lynd 1937, 305). When Robert Lynd revisited Middletown's churches in 1935, "The audiences seem older than formerly and, especially in the business-class churches, persons between fifteen and twenty-five years of age seem fewer, although this is only an impression" (Lynd and Lynd 1937, 297).

In Appendix Table 3-5, we show 1977-1978 church attendance by age. The figures confirm that church involvement becomes greater with age; middle-aged and older people had higher rates of attendance. Regular attendance and intermittent attendance increase for each increment of age, while occasional and never decrease; the relationship is statistically significant. Although church congregations are older than the general population, younger adults are by no means absent. Approximately 30 percent of Middletown adults under 35 attend regularly (that is, weekly) and another 10 percent attend at least monthly.

The Lynds, in 1935, thought that young people were drifting away from church. A high-school teacher with a reputation for being close to his students was cited as "rude evidence" of this trend: "Children are growing farther and farther from religion," he said (Lynd and Lynd 1937, 304). But adolescents in Middletown today attend church about as often as their parents. Thirty-two percent of the high school students surveyed in 1977 attended church regularly, which was close to the rate for their parents; 13 percent intermittently; and 37 percent occasionally. Only 17 percent said they never attended.

The Middletown Youth Study Group conducted a survey of Middletown ministers in 1937 (Fuller 1937) as part of a nationwide study of American youth coordinated by the American Council on Education. The ministers' responses to the questions "What changes have you noted in the past few years with regard to the attendance of youth at church and other religious services? And how do you explain these changes?" revealed contradictory perceptions of young people's church attendance during that era. Thirty-six percent of the ministers agreed with the Lynds that the attendance of adolescents at their churches had decreased. For example:

There has been a falling away in the attendance of youth due: (1) to the fact that adults do not attend; (2) teachers do not attend; (3) preachers have failed to sense their needs; (4) criticized too much for non-attendance; and (5) a reaction against being made to attend during childhood and early youth (Fuller 1937, 92-93).

But about the same proportion of ministers (32 percent) thought they saw a trend of increasing church participation among young people. For example:

I will have been here two years this May. The year 1936-37 has been marked by the attendance of young people. There is an increase of 100% this year due, I believe, to our revival meeting and a definite program of work for youth. 75% of our Epworth League now remains for Sunday evening services. We have a very marked increase in attendance of youth within the past 6 years, because:

1. Church has become more youth-minded.
2. More devoted and better trained adult leadership.
3. Better equipped buildings.
4. More consideration given youth in the planning and execution of the churches' programs (Fuller 1937, 92-93).

The remaining third of the ministers perceived some fluctuation in adolescent church attendance but no clear trend.

The findings of this 1937 survey conducted 2 years after the fieldwork for *Middletown in Transition* do not support the Lynds' impression that Middletown's churches were being abandoned by the young. We do not know, alas, what trends prevailed during the ensuing 40 years, but in the late 1970s the religious interest and participation of young adults were fairly high. Over two-thirds of the students at Middletown's university listed a denominational preference when they registered in the fall of 1978, which is comparable to the proportion of the general U.S. population who do so. We do not have information about how frequently college students attend religious services, but heavy enrollment in religion classes indicates serious interest. Colleges and universities in the surrounding area report a similar experience. The dean of the Religion Department at a private college close to Middletown remarked in 1978 that "ten years ago our religion classes were small. Today, they are second in enrollment to biology" (Middletown's evening newspaper, February 25, 1978). That same year, a large university in Middletown's state reported that its Old and New Testament classes were filled to capacity (Middletown's evening newspaper, February 25, 1978).

From the accounts of 1977-1978 church attendance obtained in our surveys, the pattern seems to be for young people to join and to attend church about as often as their parents, which is quite often indeed. When they marry and establish their own families, their church attendance declines for a while and then slowly but consistently increases again as they grow older.

Reasons for Church Attendance

One factor that helps to explain the high rate of church attendance observed in Middletown in 1978 is the systematic promotion of attendance by the local churches. Seminars and workshops teaching ministers how to increase membership and participation in their churches are held periodically by a number of denominations. For example, in January 1979, a three-night seminar on the principles of church growth was conducted by the Middletown District of the United Methodist Church. Over 300 ministers and lay persons were told how to help their churches achieve their "potential growth and outreach" (Middletown's evening newspaper, January 20, 1979).

Revivals are still held in the city and in the surrounding county, especially during the summer. They are intended to revive commitments to local churches as well as to "bring new souls to Christ."

Revivals were common in 1924. The Lynds counted 21 that year, 6 conducted by local ministers and 15 by imported evangelists (Lynd and Lynd 1929, 378), although as we show in Chapter 6, they seem to have miscounted them. A dozen years later, according to *Middletown in Transition*, there was a "meager sprinkling of revivals in the individual working-class churches during the depression. . . . But on the whole, if the number of revivals is any index of religious interest in the depression, there has been a marked recession" (Lynd and Lynd 1937, 303). At the same time, the "business-class churches were slowly giving up the revival idea" (Lynd and Lynd 1937, 302). The Lynds were not sure why interest in revivals had declined but thought that it might have been because of the organizers' insistence on receiving cash contributions from the participants during the depression, when people had little money to give. The fading enthusiasm for revivals was also seen by the Lynds as part of a general decline in religious observance.

Whatever the reasons for the decline of revivals in the 1930s, the revival spirit has gained new life in the interim. During the late 1970s, a column called *Church Notes* in the local newspaper announced at least one revival nearly every week during the year and more in the summer months. Most were sponsored by the fundamentalist denominations—the Pentecostals, Baptists, and Nazarenes. A visiting preacher was usually featured along with one or more gospel music groups. But even those denominations that never sponsored revivals brought visiting preachers to Middletown in order to stimulate interest and increase church attendance. (See Chapter 6).

Campaigns to increase church attendance are often elaborate. For example, during April 1977, one Baptist church attempted to increase its attendance by means of a contest with a church in a neighboring city. Four special services were held during the month in connection with the contest. On the first Sunday, a 200-foot banana split was made in the churchyard and eaten by the congregation, with appropriate publicity. On Palm Sunday the congregation flew kites, and on Easter Sunday another special program was presented. A "bus appreciation Sunday" concluded the month, and youngsters who rode the bus to church were taken to McDonald's afterward for hamburgers (Middletown's evening newspaper, April 18, 1977).

Some insight into the persistence of churchgoing is afforded by people's reports about why they attend or stay away from church. The most important reasons for attending mentioned by married women in 1924 were reiterated in 1978: (1) churchgoing is habitual for them and their families, (2) they enjoy the services, and (3) they attend for their children's sake. The reference to these themes in the 1924 and 1978 surveys are very similar in tone. "We were all raised to go to church. It helps you in bringing up a family to do right—and that's hard enough anyway in these days" [1924]. "It is a habit. It is important to the children. I was raised in the church and enjoy it" [1978].

But content analysis of the reasons given for church attendance reveals some shift in the motivational patterns between 1924 and 1978. In 1924, as Appendix Table 3-6 shows, habit was the most common motive for church attendance. In 1978, there were significantly fewer people who said they went to church primarily out of habit. When they do attend church, Middletown people seem now to attend for more positive reasons. Spiritual renewal, instruction, inner peace, and Christian fellowship were repeatedly mentioned as benefits. Compared to the 1924 respondents, the 1978 respondents mentioned benefits to their children somewhat more often and social and business motives somewhat less often. The reasons given for attending or avoiding church indicate that in Middletown the influence of habit or blind faith has been partially replaced by a conviction that religious observance is enjoyable.

The reasons given for *not* attending church for 1924 and 1978 are more similar than the reasons for attending. Appendix Table 3-7 shows the six reasons given most often for staying away from church; the 1924 and 1978 lists show no statistical differences. Fatigue was a factor for many people. (The 1924 comments are from Lynd and Lynd 1929, 362-65).

I would pick up and go to church but I just don't—I'm too tired mostly. My husband's a member of the Methodist Church and he don't like to work Sundays but he just has to keep his job [1924].

I don't attend because I need Sundays to sleep in [1978].

By the time I get the children ready, it's too late to start and I'm too tired. He works hard all week and rests Sunday. I approve of church all right but just can't scrape up time and energy to go [1924].

Sundays are our time alone. The children go to church. My husband works long hours and is tired on Sunday [1978].

Other families are habitual nonattenders in the same casual way that some of their neighbors are habitual attenders.

Both he and I are tied down all week and need to get out Sundays. I feel it's better to keep the family all together than for me to go to church Sunday morning and my husband to be home alone [1924].

Sunday is the only day for the family alone. We both work, including some Saturdays. But the church is a great teacher of children [1978].

A few people left a particular church in silent resistance to a tithe or a forced contribution.

It cost too much and we just didn't get much out of it. People talk about tithing, but what's a tithe to some ain't a tithe to others. It's all right always to give to others, but when you see other people shiftless and you're saving and scrimping, why ought you to give to them when they get in trouble through not having saved [1924].

Laziness. Plus couldn't keep up wtith tithing and when the church commented about it, it turned us off [1978].

I believe in bringing up a child in going to church; it gets him in with a good class of people. We don't have a close church connection any longer, though, because once we couldn't pay our regular contribution, they dropped us from the roll [1924].

We left the church when asked for a tithe and we were threatened to be dropped from the membership list [1978].

This theme occasionally appears in letters to the editor in Middletown's newspapers. For example:

I stopped going to church. Everytime I looked up someone was "passing the hat". It would take lots of money to give all they asked for. . . . I would advise everyone to read "Elmer Gantry" by Sinclair Lewis. That tells exactly what my opinion is about the high-toned ministers and evangelists reaching out their little "paws" for every cent they can rake in, building big rich churches, riding in their Cadillacs, wearing their expensive clothes (Middletown's evening newspaper, May 20, 1977).

Only 6 percent of the 1924 respondents and 13 percent of the 1978 respondents gave ideological reasons for staying away from church. Again, the responses to the two surveys 54 years apart are very similar in tone (Lynd and Lynd 1929, 365).

After I married, I drifted away from church. Then I began to decide I didn't WANT to attend anyway. There are too many people in church that worship the almighty dollar—too many mean people that oughtn't to be there [1924].

We are not attending because the church has let down the young people. The people are too socially-affluent oriented [1978].

Other Religious Observance

Religious observance involves more than attending traditional Sunday or weeknight services. A sample of those Middletown church members who occasionally or regularly attend church services reported their outside religious observances. The results are presented in Appendix Table 3-8. Half of the sample participated in at least one of these outside observances.

Televised services, sometimes called the Electronic Church, are very popular. Local as well as nationally prominent ministers conduct television services every Sunday. The Electronic Church attracts many elderly people who lack transportation to their own churches or whose health makes attending difficult. The popularity of the Electronic Church is suggested by the 1979 application of a group sponsored by the Full Gospel Businessmen's Fellowship of Middletown for a license to telecast religious programs 24 hours a day, seven days a week (Middletown's evening newspaper, May 22, 1979).

Eighteen percent of the sample participated in scripture study groups in private homes and 13 percent in home prayer groups. These religious observances represent a restoration of customs that had nearly disappeared in the Lynds' time. The Lynds (1928, 338) reported that "the early custom of using the home for meeting of 'prayer bands' and 'cottage prayer meetings' survives today chiefly in the outlying working-class neighborhoods." But now significant numbers of people gather together in homes throughout the community for religious training and worship.

Gospel-music concerts are held periodically, especially at Christmas and Easter, and are attended by 18 percent of the population.

Several of the major denominations have established retreat centers where members go for weekends of discussion, meditation, and worship. Twelve percent of the sample had some recent retreat experience. For example, the Center for Peace and Life Studies, located 17 miles from Middletown, is a 52-acre retreat center with a community building, seven camp cabins, and two family homes. According to the director, a Catholic priest, the center offers several weeks of family camps; personal, family, and community retreats; and weekend retreats on topics ranging from world peace to simple living (Middletown's evening newspaper, June 24, 1978).

The number of people participating in home churches, coffee-house ministries, and religious communes is small, but these alternative modes of organized worship are found in Middletown also.

The Lynds inferred some decline of religion in Middletown from 1890 to 1924 from a decrease in the proportion of marriages performed by clergymen, 85 percent in 1890 and 63 percent in 1924 (Lynd and Lynd 1929, 112). The resurgence of religious observance suggested by our survey data on church attendance is at least partially confirmed by a concurrent rise in the proportion of religious weddings. In 1975, 79 percent of Middletown's marriages were performed by ministers of religion. This is another piece of evidence that the declining trend in religious observance noted by the Lynds during the 1920s has since reversed so that today's religious pattern is closer in some ways to 1890 than to 1924.

Church Membership

The significant place that formal religion now occupies in the lives of Middletowners is illustrated by their account of the voluntary associations, including churches, to which they belong. Appendix Table 3-9 shows the percentage of married men and women who belonged to churches, social clubs, lodges, labor unions, and other voluntary associations in 1978. Nearly 75% of the married women belonged to a church and nearly 60 percent were active in it. Nearly the same proportion belonged to social clubs, but membership in other types of voluntary associations was considerably lower. Sixty-one percent of the husbands belonged to a church, 45 percent to unions, and 29 percent to lodges. Wives and husbands were sharply differentiated with respect to every type of voluntary association, with women more active in churches and social clubs and much less active in unions and lodges.

Financial Contributions

Some Christian denominations, on the authority of the Bible, call on each member family to tithe, that is, to contribute 10 percent of its income to the church. In a sample of 100 working-class families, the Lynds found only one family paying a full tithe, and they seemed to suggest, although they did not say, that the rate of contribution was declining in 1924.

Financial support of the churches appears in Middletown at all levels, from the spontaneous giving of the traditional tithe on the part of a few ardent church members, through the stage of giving "because I wouldn't like to live in a land without churches" or because it is "expected," to not giving at all. In the face of increasing financial demands of the individual churches and their denominational boards, "giving of one's substance to the Lord" is meeting with greater competition as community-wide charity is becoming secularized and the outward dominance of the church in the community is declining. Meanwhile, according to statements by the ministers and by the treasurers of two business-class churches, the increasing money needs of the churches and their denominations and the declining dominance of the "message" of the church with many Middletown people are increasing the relative prominence of the money tie between a church and its members as compared with a generation ago (Lynd and Lynd 1929, 358).

But 54 years later, we found that 70 percent of the married couples in one of our samples contributed to a church in 1978, as did 62 percent of another sample that included both married and single adults. The average percentages of family income contributed to churches by working-class families in 1924 and 1978 are shown in Appendix Table 3-10. The competition of secular charities has not intensified since 1924; working-class families contributed 0.7 percent of their income to such charities in 1924 and only 0.8 percent in 1978. Today's working-class families, in contrast, contribute much more to organized religion. The relative contribution of the median-income working-class family doubled from 1924 to 1978; from 1.6 percent to 3.3 percent of family income. Although only one working-class family in the 1924 sample paid a full tithe, 4.5 percent of the working-class families in the 1978 sample did so. The Lynds did not report the contributions of business-class families in 1924; such families' rate of contribution in 1978 did not differ significantly from that of working-class families.

Churches in Middletown today utilize rather sophisticated fund-raising techniques—pledges, computerized statements, fund-raising occasions, and credit-card facilities—to encourage the generosity of their members. But churches used similar practices in the 1920s and 1930s, too. The Lynds (1937, 296) reported that one major church in the early 1930s published the "honor roll" each year listing those who had paid their pledges in full. As reported earlier, the pressure to contribute is sometimes ineffective. A few people in the 1924 sample and in our 1978 sample were sufficiently offended by what they perceived as excessive pressure to leave a church entirely. Although fund-raising devices undoubtedly contribute to the prosperity of Middletown churches, it is the religious commitment of church members that moves them to allocate their money for this purpose rather than for other satisfactions.

Chapter 4

Changes in
Religious Sentiment

The Lynds (1929, 232-39) attached particular importance to answers given by the married women they interviewed to the following three questions.

A. What are the thoughts and plans that give you courage to go on when thoroughly discouraged?
B. How often have you thought of Heaven during the past month in this connection?
C. What difference would it make in your daily life if you became convinced that there was no loving God caring for you?

Persistent Responses

We repeated these questions in our 1978 survey of 333 married women living with their husbands and children. Of the 73 working-class women who answered question A in 1924, 27 percent said that it was their religion that gave them courage and 23 percent referred to their families; the remaining responses were widely scattered. Of the 98 working-class women who responded to the same question in 1978, 27 percent referred to their religion, 24 percent to their families, and 6 percent mentioned both; the remaining responses were scattered among the same themes recorded by the Lynds. The stability of the percentages is matched by a persistence of tone. The following verbatim responses of working-class wives are from both 1924 (Lynd and Lynd 1929, 323-31) and 1978. We doubt whether readers would be able to tell them apart without the dates.

I used to cry when I was discouraged, but that didn't help any. Now I just get down on my knees and pray and that gives me strength [1924].

I rely on the Bible scriptures; there are a lot of promises [1978].

When I'm discouraged, I just read the Bible and think of the coming of the Kingdom [1924].

I know there's a plan for my life. My Heavenly Father is in control. I don't need to worry. If I have a relaxed mental attitude, things will work out according to His plan [1978].

I pray and think of God. I've lots of faith in prayer. My baby was awfully sick and almost died; a lady came and prayed and the folks in church went up and knelt around the altar, and the baby got well and is better than ever. The doctor says it was prayer and nothing else did it [1924].

I guess God, really. I think about the beautiful things around me and how there must be a God. My religious beliefs are confused, but when things get really bad, I pray [1978].

Of the working-class women who answered question B in 1924, 46 percent said "often or every day" and 31 percent said they "never or almost never" gave heaven a thought. Of the working-class women who answered the same question in 1978, 35 percent said "often or daily" but only 17 percent said "never or almost never."

In answer to question C, "What difference would it make in your daily life if you became convinced that there is no loving God caring for you?" 13 percent of the Lynds' working-class respondents rejected the proposition as unthinkable and 58 percent "were so emphatic as to say that life would be intolerable or utterly changed" (1929, 323-31). When we put the same question to working-class women in 1978, 17 percent of them rejected it as unthinkable and 51 percent said that life would be intolerable or utterly changed.

It is a sin not to believe in God and His care and anyone who doesn't is just stubborn [1924].

I don't believe that would happen. Nothing could convince me of that. God is and always will be [1978].

Nobody could make me believe there isn't a God [1924].

This, to me, is too stupid to even relate to [1978].

I could never become so bitter over things as to doubt God [1924].

I couldn't be convinced. I *know* there is! [1978].

Eleven percent of the working-class housewives responding in 1924 said that it would make no particular difference to them; 9 percent said so in 1978.

A comparison of business-class women's 1924 and 1978 responses to these questions is less satisfactory. The Lynds' sample of business-class women was very small to begin with and showed more resistance to these particular questions. Of the 19 business-class women responding to question C in 1924, a majority said that they would be affected little or not at all if they lost their belief in a loving God; several implied that they had already lost it. The small size of the sample precludes taking these results too seriously.

Ten percent of the business-class women responding to question C in 1978 found the proposition unthinkable, 47 percent said that their lives would be intolerable or utterly changed, 22 percent said that it would make some difference, and 21 percent said that it would make no difference, most of the last saying or implying they did not then believe in a loving God and a few asserting their emotional self-sufficiency. The religious commitment implied by these responses is slightly less than that of the working-class women surveyed in 1978 but vastly greater than what the Lynds reported for their tiny sample of business-class women in 1924.

It is possible, of course, that respondents to the 1978 survey were simply giving us what they thought were the expected and socially approved answers to our questions. Certainly this occurred in some cases. On the other hand, we would not expect business-class women to respond more conventionally than working-class respondents. The former are more comfortable with unconventional ideas and more accustomed to expressing them. There is even less reason to suppose that insincere conformity is more common in 1978 than it was in 1924, since Middletown is more tolerant of dissident opinions now than it was 60 years ago. But what really persuades us to take the religious commitment of business-class women more or less at face value is their language, which does not sound like the parroting of conventional themes. Here are some of their responses to the question "What differences would it make in your daily life if you became convinced that there is no loving God caring for you?"

I'm afraid I'd become more concerned about acquiring material things, less concerned about people, and my business dealings would be less according to Hoyle.

I would be gone. My whole premise would be torn apart. I couldn't deal with that.

I'd be afraid to even get up in the morning. I can't really imagine that. No one could convince me that there wasn't a loving God caring for me.

I'd cut my wrists if no one above loved me as I am. I would be miserable.

You might as well give up and die; if you don't believe in God, you're lost.

I would wonder what the purpose of trying to teach the children right from wrong would be. I would wonder what was going to become of all of us. It would make all the difference, change all the priorities and motivations.

That the religious attitudes of business-class women and working-class women have moved closer together over the past half-century is not wholly unexpected. Other Middletown III surveys seem to show that in many of their attitudes and habits the business-class women in 1978 were closer to the working-class women of 1924 than to the business-class women of 1924 (Caplow et al. 1982).

What about the difference between men and women? As it happened, the Lynds never interviewed adult men about their religious feelings, although they did ask high school boys about their adherence to the formal tenets of Christianity. (We will discuss those responses later.) For 1924, there is now no way of telling how similar the religious sentiments of husbands and wives may have been, although the Lynds had the impression that women were more fervent about religion than men were. In the 1978 religion survey, we did take the opportunity of putting question C, "What difference would it make in your daily life if you became convinced that there was no loving God caring for you?" to a sample of men. The men's responses, as far as we could judge, were indistinguishable from the women's.

If I became convinced of that, I would become the most miserable man around because worldly life happiness only lasts for a short period of time.

I feel that God helps me to face trouble with confidence and accept joys and success with a light amount of humbleness — without that life would not be worth living.

My moral quality would change. I probably would cheat on my taxes, cut corners, and not be so caring for others.

There is a God. No one can convince me otherwise.

The Common Creed

It is mildly surprising to discover so little difference between social classes and between men and women in these subjective manifestations of religion. It is even more surprising that a fairly unified belief system emerges from the responses of a population scattered among many denominations whose official beliefs on such matters as salvation and free will differ sharply one from another. The religious experiences reported by members of all of Middletown's Protestant denominations—and some non-Protestants, too—in response to questions A, B, and C run in opposition to the religious dogmas that are the raisons d'être of Middletown's separate denominations, neither affirming nor contradicting them. The themes most often repeated are the following. (1) Prayer is internally efficacious; it strengthens the sufferer to endure or to surmount his or her suffering. (2) Prayer is externally efficacious; it can avert danger and cure the sick. (3) Bible reading is internally efficacious in the same manner as prayer. (4) The Bible guarantees the eventual safety of those who read and believe it. (5) Jesus takes care of those who have made a commitment to Him. (6) Morality of any kind is predicated on the existence of God. (7) God provides all of life's meaning and hope. (8) The presence of God, when directly experienced, is not challengeable by argument. (9) Personal immortality is promised by God and therefore is certain although not clearly visualizable. These nine themes (it might be more accurate to call them attitudes) seem to provide the basic pattern for Middletown's dominant religion as described by its believers in 1924 and again in 1978.

There are some curious features to this experiential religion. It is not founded on formal proofs, and it requires none. Each element—God, Jesus, the Bible, the church, heaven, morality—is linked to and supported by the others. One or more elements can be dropped out of the pattern without destroying it. The Unitarians seem to live the same experience without accepting the divinity of Jesus, and there is a whole population of devout Christians in Middletown who make a point of having nothing to do with the church. But each omission weakens the pattern, and it probably is not possible to deny God or to reject the Bible or to repudiate common morality without ceasing to be a practicing Christian, as Middletown understands that label.

Middletown's experiential religion is difficult to summarize in words because it is more emotional than verbal and because it has only a tenuous connection with the formal doctrines of the denominations active in the community. The reports of their religious experience that Middletown people gave us seldom contained any clues about whether the speaker was a Lutheran or a Baptist, a Jehovah's Witness or a Catholic.

To the question "How often have you thought of heaven during the past month?" 35 percent of the working-class women and 29 percent of the business-class women who answered the question in 1978 said "often or daily." Seventeen percent of the former and 24 percent of the latter said "never or not at all." Most of the rest gave exact figures ranging from once to 25 times. In other words, more than three-quarters of the women in the sample had been thinking of heaven recently and could tell us with fair precision when and in what circumstances those thoughts had occurred. But the thoughts they reported were curiously general. There was little imagery and less dogma in our interview reports. The typical experience was diffuse and emotional. For example: "I think of heaven when I say my prayers. I don't consciously think of it. It's there. I wonder what it will be like. It makes me feel closer to my parents and grandparents, who are deceased."

The character of these responses is nothing new. What the Lynds heard in their interview sounded much the same, but, since they guessed that Middletown people around 1890 must have held much more concrete images of heaven and hell, they inferred that the belief in an afterlife was being gradually eroded by secularization. During the ensuing half-century, there has been no detectable erosion of the belief in an afterlife, but that does not mean that it may not have occurred earlier. We simply do not know whether people in Middletown in the 19th century thought of heaven and hell as geographic places and made empirical statements about them. That habit, if it ever existed, was gone by the time the Lynds came on the scene, and what we hear today is that most people in Middletown believe in personal immortality with varying degrees of conviction but that these beliefs are not, for the most part, deduced from formal dogmas of the church or defended by authority or natural reason. There is surprisingly little discussion of heaven and hell in Middletown's churches, and arguments about immortality are not often heard around the dinner table. Immortality is perceived not as a public issue but as a facet of personal experience. Other elements of religious experience are viewed in much the same way. Although theological positions and arguments are occasionally expounded by the local clergy, they roll off the minds of the laity without leaving any perceptible trace. Faith in Middletown is supported in a general way by religious institutions, but it is validated only by each believer's interpretation of his or her own experience. By accident more than design, Middletown's religion has evolved toward the most extreme Protestantism imaginable, and its common creed rests largely upon personal revelations.

This common creed has very little connection with the theological positions that originally set the Protestant denominations apart from one another, as the Lynds discovered in their time. They summarized the common creed in three statements included in the survey on "various public questions" that they administered to Middletown high school students. The proportion of Middletown high school students who agreed with each statement in 1924 and the proportion of Middletown high school students who agreed with the same statement in 1977 are shown in Table 4-1.

Table 4-1
Percentages of High School Students Responding Affirmatively to
Three Statements on Religion, 1924 and 1977

Statement	1924	1977
"The Bible is a sufficient guide to all the problems of modern life."	74	53
"Jesus Christ was different from every other man who ever lived in being entirely perfect."	83	67
"The purpose of religion is to prepare people for the hereafter."	60	56

Sources: Lynd and Lynd, 1929, 316-19; Middletown III high school survey, 1977.

A sizable majority of the respondents marked each of these statements as "true" in 1924. A smaller majority agreed with each statement in 1977, but it was still a majority.

These majorities are impressive by themselves, and they become even more impressive when we examine the three statements more closely. Like most items on attitude scales, they can be variously interpreted. As it is worded, the first statement invites disagreement by people who regard the Bible as a guide for spiritual life and not as a manual for secular problems. Similarly, the characterization of Jesus as "entirely perfect" in the second statement strikes a false note for those Christians who see Him as sharing the human burden of sin and imperfection. Although the third statement is aimed at tapping belief in the existence of an afterlife, it could surely be rejected by any believer for whom preparation for the hereafter is one of the purposes of religion but not *the* purpose. And, as a sociological generalization, it might be quite acceptable to a skeptic.

In other words, the percentages of agreement elicited by these statements are not exact measures; they could have been shifted upward or downward by small changes of wording. The differences between the percentage responses obtained in the 1924 survey and in the 1977 survey are not exact measures either; we must not presume that the words used had exactly the same nuances at both points in time. However, even if these numbers are not very precise, they are nonetheless informative. Comparing the two sets of responses, we see at once that the main points of the common creed are the same now as they were then.

Though Middletown's contemporary adolescents accept the same creed as their grandparents, they make different inferences from it. When we repeated three other statements from the 1924 questionnaire in our 1977 survey, the distribution of responses was not the same as in the earlier survey (Table 4-2).

As these figures suggest, Middletown's Christians have become

Table 4-2
Percentages of High School Students Responding Affirmatively
to Three Statements on Religion, 1924 and 1977

Statement	1924	1977
"Christianity is the one true religion and all people should be converted to it."	94	41
"It is wrong to go to the movies on Sunday."	33	8
"The theory of evolution offers a more accurate account of the origin and history of mankind than that offered by a literal interpretation of the first chapters of the Bible."	28	50

Sources: Lynd and Lynd 1929, 316-19; Middletown III high school survey, 1977.

much less chauvinistic, less punitive, and less antiscientific. Indeed, the two sides in the war between science and religion have drawn so close together that people in Middletown who want the scriptural account of creation to be taught in the public schools label it an "alternative model" and the supporters of Darwinian evolution describe that theory as "the simple truth."

Changes in Religious Attitudes

It is equally plain that Middletown's religion is much less censorious than it used to be. That only a small minority now disapproves of Sunday moviegoing has no special importance, but it does illustrate the virtual disappearance of the antithesis between religion and pleasure that used to be taken for granted and that made Sunday moviegoing wrong not because movies were sinful but because they gave pleasure on the Lord's Day. Middletown, of course, was never Puritan New England. Cockfights and baseball games were regularly scheduled on Sundays in the 1890s; golf was competing with Sunday morning services in the 1920s. Nevertheless, the Puritan tendency to equate virtue with suffering and sin with pleasure was still strong in Middletown when the Lynds were there. It is now so greatly diminished that sermons against Sunday recreation are seldom heard even in the most hard-shell churches. Those same churches have kept their aversion to drinking and gambling, but their taboo on dancing has virtually disappeared.

It is difficult, perhaps impossible, to say whether the weakening of the ancient antinomy between virtuous austerity and wicked gratification is best accounted for by changing attitudes toward eroticism or whether eroticism benefits from a general reevaluation of pleasure as innocent. The high school boys who adhere to the basic tenets of Christian doctrine read *Playboy* more than any other magazine. The high school girls who go regularly to the Planned Parenthood clinic to draw their ration of federally funded oral contraceptives are likely to agree that "the Bible is a sufficient guide to all the problems of modern life." There are certainly people in Middletown today who regard themselves as sinful because of their sexual practices, but that pattern of self-condemnation is no longer widespread. The same tolerance is extended to others. Middletown's pious people are extraordinarily hesitant nowadays to condemn relatives and neighbors who divorce and remarry their partners in adultery or even those who set up housekeeping with homosexual partners. The toleration of premarital fornication has almost the standing of a positive norm. Shotgun weddings are as extinct in today's Middletown as lynchings. A Middletown father has neither a duty nor a right to protect his daughter's virginity, and one who attempted to do so in any aggressive way would probably be suspected of unnatural cravings.

The most interesting of these shifts, at least to us, is that in 1924, 94 percent of the high school students agreed that "Christianity is the one true religion and all people should be converted to it"—virtually all of the Christians or nominal Christians in the population. In 1977, only 41 percent still held that missionary opinion, although church affiliations and church attendance were somewhat higher among the adolescents of 1977 than among those of 1924.

When we compare the responses given to the three creedal questions by boys and girls in 1924 and in 1977, the results look like Table 4-3.

Table 4-3
Percentages of High School Students Responding Affirmatively
to Three Statements on Religion, 1924 and 1977, by Sex

Statement	1924		1977	
	Males	Females	Males	Females
"The Bible is a sufficient guide to all the problems of modern life."	69	77	49	51
"Jesus Christ is different from every other man who ever lived in being entirely perfect."	82	84	64	72
"The purpose of religion is to prepare people for the hereafter."	57	62	54	53

Sources: Lynd and Lynd 1929, 316-19; Middletown III high school survey, 1977.

The comparison is not spectacularly informative, since the differences in religious conviction between the sexes were small in 1924 and remained small in 1977.

We cannot compare any differences there might have been between the religious convictions of business-class and working-class adolescents in 1924 with those we found in 1977 because the Lynds did not break down the responses to their high school survey by social class. For 1977, the proportion of high school students of each social class agreeing to the three creedal statements is shown in Table 4-4. The slight variations that appear in the responses to particular items are insignificant. Middletown's two

Table 4-4
Percentages of High School Students Responding Affirmatively
to Three Statements on Religion, 1977, by Social Class

Statement	Business Class	Working Class
"The Bible is a sufficient guide to all the problems of modern life."	46	53
"Jesus Christ was different from every other man who ever lived in being entirely perfect."	70	66
"The purpose of religion is to prepare people for the hereafter."	49	55

Source: Middletown III high school survey, 1977.

social classes, like Middletown's two sexes, share the same creed. What about the two races? (See Table 4-5.) The differences between white and black high school students do turn out to be significant: more of the black adolescents adhere to the common creed. Indeed, on two of the three statements, the black adolescents of 1977 showed a higher level of belief than the white adolescents of 1924.

It is equally interesting to break down responses to the other

Table 4-5
Percentages of High School Students Responding Affirmatively
to Three Statements on Religion, 1977, by Race and Sex

Statement	Whites		Blacks	
	Male	Female	Male	Female
"The Bible is a sufficient guide to all the problems of modern life."	49	50	71	82
"Jesus Christ was different from every other man who ever lived in being entirely perfect."	65	69	72	78
"The purpose of religion is to prepare people for the hereafter."	58	51	75	66

Source: Middletown III high school survey, 1977.

survey statements about religion according to sex, social class, and race. In 1924, more girls than boys insisted on the "one true religion" and thought it wrong to go to the movies on Sunday. By 1977, there was no difference at all. We have elsewhere (Bahr 1980) reported the general diminution of differences in behavior between boys and girls over the same interval of time.

Between business-class and working-class adolescents, there was no appreciable difference in 1977 in the proportion of those claiming to have the "one true religion," but the few respondents who still regarded Sunday moviegoing as wrong were drawn almost entirely from the working-class. The breakdown by race again shows black respondents to be significantly more traditional in their attitudes than white respondents. Fifty-six percent of them accepted the characterization of Christianity as the one true religion, compared to 41 percent of their white schoolmates. Fourteen percent favored the prohibition of Sunday moviegoing, compared to 8 percent of the white respondents.

No matter how we divide the high school population, we cannot turn up a group whose religious chauvinism comes anywhere near the level that was normal in 1924. To put the matter in perspective, about half of the Middletown adolescents who belong to and attend a church and who believe in Jesus, the Bible, and the hereafter do not claim any universal validity for the Christian beliefs they hold and have no zeal for the conversion of non-Christians. Such a situation may never before have existed in the long history of Christianity. This extraordinary ecumenicism is not limited to adolescents. In our 1978 survey of the religious beliefs and practices of Middletown adults, 67 percent of the respondents thought that the public schools should teach about all world religions, and those who attended church regularly were no less likely to think so than those who attended church occasionally or not at all.

In a liberal perspective, these findings are almost too good to be true. On the one hand, Middletown people are extraordinarily attached to their faith; on the other hand, they are reluctant to impose it on others or even to assert that it ought to be imposed. Religious fervor no longer goes hand in hand with missionary zeal, and the reason may be that Middletown people are not aware of having a common creed and holding it strongly. Their division into numerous denominations conceals from them the extent to which they agree, and their stereotyped misreading of social change persuades them that religion is weaker than it is. Devout Christians in Middletown, like happily married couples there, regard themselves as exceptional: surrounded by people just like themselves, they think they stand quite alone. This almost universal illusion explains, at least in part, why Middletown people are so reluctant to lay down the law or to expound the prophets for the benefit of their neighbors. In this sense, there is less community in Middletown today than there was in 1924 or in 1890, when it was customary for respectable people to perceive themselves as participating in a moral consensus. It is possible to regard the loss of this moral unanimity as a kind of decadence, but it is equally plausible to argue that the manners and morals of Middletown have been improved by it.

Neither the religious fervor nor the new religious tolerance is imaginary. The acceptance of the fundamental tenets of Christianity by the nearly half of Middletown's adult population who attend church regularly is extremely high: 84 percent say they have no doubt about God's existence; 86 percent have no doubt about the divinity of Jesus; 97 percent believe that the Bible is inspired. Ninety-one percent of the churchgoers say they pray often when alone, and nearly all of them compose their own prayers in addition to using those they have been taught. Religious fasting and meditation are widely practiced in Middletown but not much talked about, and so they pass almost unnoticed.

When we divide the sample who responded to our survey on religion into men and women and into those above 40 and under 40 years old, we find surprisingly weak differences by sex and age, although the differences found are consistent with the conventional opinion that women are more religious than men and older people more religious than younger people. Of the women over 40, 70 percent had no doubts about the existence of God, compared to 65 percent of the younger women; and 60 percent of the older men had no doubts, compared to 53 percent of the younger men. Seventy-two percent of the older women and 65 percent of the younger women had no doubts about the divinity of Jesus; 58 percent of the older men and 53 percent of the younger men had no such doubts. Eighty-three percent of the older women and

90 percent of the younger women accepted the Bible as a divinely inspired book; so did 86 percent of the older men and 79 percent of the younger.

When the sample is taken as a whole, 69 percent had no doubts about the existence of God, 68 percent had no doubts about the divinity of Jesus, and 91 percent accepted the Bible as inspired. Yet, when these same respondents were asked about the teaching of religion in the public schools, only 19 percent wanted only Christianity to be taught and 64 percent were sure that they wanted to include other religions.

The minority who were not tolerant of non-Christian religions or even of Christian denominations other than their own were so clearly in the minority that they were hesitant about announcing their views. Religious authority speaks with a muted voice in today's Middletown. It does not order people to church to save their souls or to confound the heathen; instead, it attracts them there with promises of solace and enjoyment. As we noted elsewhere in this chapter, women who participated in the housewives' survey of 1924 were asked why they went to church (when they did so) or why they stayed away (when they did that). When we compared the responses of Middletown housewives in 1978 to the question "Why do you attend (or not attend) religious services?" to the responses the same question elicited in 1924, we discovered a change from religion as obedience to religion as pleasure.

When we examine the two sets of verbatim answers, the initial impression suggests continuity, not change. The language is the same; the cadences sound similar; the same key words appear in both sets of responses. Both in 1924 and 1978, some people attended church only for the sake of their children and others stayed away because Sunday was the only day for the family to be together. Continuity, not change, is what stands out in these responses, a continuity one would never glimpse by looking at the 1978 responses alone. Similarly, for many Catholics, in 1978 as in 1924 (Lynd and Lynd 1929, 360-69), being a Catholic was a sufficient explanation for churchgoing.

We're Catholic and go regularly [1924].

We've been Catholic all our lives. It would be difficult to state precise benefits. We'd never give it up [1978].

I and the children are Catholics and go regularly. He's a Baptist who works seven days a week and don't feel like church [1924].

There's not a strong unity between my husband and me about this. He is Catholic and wouldn't want to go to any other church [1978].

Still, within the continuous and persistent pattern, as we have noted all along, important trends can be identified. When we count the number of people who gave each kind of response in 1924 and in 1978, we do find an unmistakable shift from religion as obedience to religion as pleasure.

Belief and Practice

Of the 58 women in the 1924 survey who gave their reasons for attending church on a regular basis, 27 attended obediently, regarding it as "an unquestioned custom which needs no explanation," "something to be done without debate" or that "has never presented itself as a problem" or as something to be done "as a matter of principle" (Lynd and Lynd 1929, 360-66). Twenty-two other respondents mentioned distinct values that they found in the service, and the remainder had miscellaneous reasons for attendance, of which the most important was some benefit for their children.

Obedience, then, accounted for 45 percent of the 1924 responses and pleasure for 38 percent. In response to the same question in 1978, 208 women gave their reasons for going to church. This time the score was 51 percent for pleasure and 28 percent for obedience. The difference is not earthshaking, but the trend it reflects appears to be real, particularly when we examine the responses more closely. In 1924, Middletown housewives said that the church did them good, that they felt better for it, that they had more respect for themselves when they attended. In 1977, the key word was "enjoy."

I enjoy the music and the peaceful feeling about me. The minister gives interesting talks. Sometimes I need a moral uplifting.

I always get something out of the church service. It relieves me in a way and I enjoy seeing people. I sing in the choir and enjoy participating in the service.

I think it does a person good, to restore your faith in life, to lift your spirits. It's just kind of like taking a good hot bath.

It is consistent with this new emphasis that the pressure exerted by children on parents and by parents on children to attend church or to participate in other church activities has been much reduced. In 1924, 28 percent of the respondents to the high school survey listed "being an active church member" as one of the two qualities most valued in a father, and 25 percent mentioned it as one of the two qualities most desirable in a mother. In 1977, fewer than 10 percent listed active membership as a desirable trait in either parent. The proportion of adolescents who reported that they quarreled with their parents about attending religious services declined correspondingly (Bahr 1980, 44).

Just as many of the people who attend church regularly do it for enjoyment and not out of moral compulsion, so many of those who stay away do so, not on principle, but because they dislike something about the services of a particular church or prefer some other activity on Sunday morning. Militant atheism, the Lynds noticed, was rarer in 1924 than it had been in 1890; it is practically unknown in Middletown today. The level of belief and even of religious practice among those who never go to church is impressive; 40 percent of them expressed no doubts about the existence of God, 37 percent voiced no doubts about the divinity of Jesus, and 72 percent said that they accept the Bible as inspired. Forty percent claimed that they pray often when alone and nearly all of these said that they compose their own prayers in addition to using those they were taught as children or learned as churchgoers.

It appears at first anomalous that nearly twice as many of the nonchurchgoers accepted the Bible as inspired as were sure of the existence of God, but Middletown's religious beliefs are not arrayed in syllogistic order. The common Christian creed described earlier in this chapter is so closely woven into the community's culture that nonbelievers also use it as their point of departure. The denial of God or Jesus is a standard experience in the Protestant theogony. Indeed, an account of the experience of denial is part of the testimony expected from those who yield to the evangelistic exhortation to accept Jesus and to be born again. The rejection of the Bible, even retrospectively, has no place in the story.

The unchurched Christian, then, is a familiar figure in Middletown.

He or she often boasts of leading a "good Christian life" without the "hypocrisy" of church participation.

Really I'm a religious believer. I just don't practice. I don't believe you have to attend church to live a good life. God is everywhere. You don't have to go to the church to find Him.

We believe that you don't have to go to church to believe in God. It's how you live in your daily life that matters.

I feel myself that if you love God, you can worship just as well at home. And a lot of people in church are hypocrites.

If active forms of skepticism are rare in Middletown, religious indifference is not. The forms it takes can be glimpsed in the responses we obtained to another remarkably evocative question of the Lynds: "What are the thoughts and plans that give you courage to go on when you are thoroughly discouraged?" From the moderately pious majority, this question often elicited a purely religious response in 1978, as it had in 1924.

Jesus Christ is my Savior and Redeemer. He died to make me whole and all of us can trust him with our own lives even when discouraged.

I don't think I'm ever thoroughly discouraged. I have the deep and abiding love of a caring God.

I know there is a plan for my life. My Heavenly Father is in control. I don't need to worry. If I have a relaxed mental attitude things will work out according to His plan.

Other women referred to God and to their immediate families in the same breath, giving them equal importance and taking a close connection between them for granted.

I think I have to go on because I have the children and they need me. My husband needs me. I know there is a God that helps me.

I think about my children growing up and I can't fall apart and break down and leave them alone. And God's helping me to a better day.

If I help myself God will give, and my husband gives me moral support.

Women who were a little more indifferent to religion mentioned the family alone as their source of comfort in times of trouble.

I believe in the people who are closest to me. I believe in the future based on the way events in the past have turned out when things were not going so well.

I want to stay a vital person to my husband and children. When I was sick I came to realize the important thing is not to be loved but to love. I wanted to get well for them. It was a learning experience.

Gary and I have a strong marriage and will take care of each other.

I put my family above everything else in this world. No matter how bad things are in this world, I know my family still needs me.

There were only a handful of women in this sample of married women living with husbands and children who did not mention either religion or their families as a principal source of emotional support, and these respondents characteristically substituted a belief in themselves, their own strengths, and their own virtues.

I draw upon my inner strength. There are ups and downs and cycles. Sooner or later it's going to come back to the good cycle. I can take care of most situations and cope with them.

I believe in myself. I can keep striving to do better. Sometimes it pays off and sometimes it doesn't. But generally I can value that striving.

This theme of moral self-sufficiency was sometimes combined with references to husbands and children and other relatives as sources of support but never in this survey with any reference to God or Jesus or prayer. There appears to be a continuum of attitudes whereby, at one extreme, the pious place all their trust in heaven; those who are a little less pious rely on heaven and their families; and those who are even less pious find meaning in their lives through their families alone. At the secular end of the scale, belief in oneself becomes the sole article of faith.

For believers and nonbelievers alike, Middletown's religion is personal and emotional and remarkably free of theological dilemmas. Middletown's Protestant churchgoers take personal revelation for granted but never worry at all about the conflicting authority of personal and scriptural revelations. Some believe fervently in free will and others talk of predestination, but these opposing views never seem to clash. Many Christians in Middletown address their prayers only to Jesus and others only to God and others to Father, Son, and Holy Spirit; but an argument about Trinitarianism, if it ever occurred, would be considered peculiar. The issues that are debated in Middletown's churches are peripheral to theology: liturgical reform, the ordination of women, legalized abortion, homosexuality, pornography. Each of these issues involves some confrontation between religious liberalism and religious orthodoxy, but none of them bears directly on essential questions of faith. They merely enlarge a confrontation originating in the political domain between liberals bent on enforcing equality between men and women, whites and nonwhites, parents and children, clergy and laity, heterosexuals and homosexuals, citizens and aliens, and conservatives who want to preserve some of the traditional inequalities.

If we had only our 1978 data for Middletown to refer to, it would be tempting to describe the "privatization of religion" in resistance to the pressure of bureaucratization in government, industry, and mass communications. It would be equally tempting to explain how the promulgation of egalitarian doctrine as governmental policy in the late 1960s and through he 1970s challenged religious orthodoxy to the point of breaching the traditional separation between religion and politics in Middletown.

The Message from the Pulpit

The hypothesis of privatization is particularly attractive because it seems to explain the unexpected strength of religious and family institutions in Middletown — and of the connection between them — as a form of future shock, a flight away from trends in the larger society, rather than as a mere persistence of old habits. But in this instance, as in so many others, we are restrained in our effort to trace the grand outlines of social change by the Lynds' observations of Middletown in 1924 and the retrospective information they gathered for 1890. One relevant passage is worth quoting at length.

A study of sermon titles shows them concerned with much the same themes today as a generation ago. All sermon subjects mentioned in the local press during 1890, a total of eighty, and all announced in the press during the two sample months of April and October, 1924, a total of 193, were classified by titles according to general emphasis—Biblical, theological, practical ethics, and so on—but the titles were, in most cases, so vague that the classification was felt to be of little value; no change since 1890 was apparent.

The prevalence of sermon subjects too general to afford an adequate clew to their content, "Not a Taste," "Three Men," "Pinch Hitters," "Law and Liberty," and so on, in a period when the general discourse is tending to disappear elsewhere may be in itself a significant indication of their character.

And even the more definite sermon subjects suggest a type of diffuse treatment which, while still found in other public addresses today, is less dominant than in the nineties. Today, as in 1890, the subjects run week after week: "The Journey to Canaan," "The Sorrow of Jesus," "Sunday Observance," "Why Jesus Went to Church," "Play Square with God," "Jesus as Son of God," "Will Jesus be at the Feast?" "The Importance of Faith," "The Call of the Universe," "The Seven Joys of a Christian," and so on (Lynd and Lynd 1929, 372-73).

We did something similar in the 1978 ministers' survey by asking each respondent for the title of his most recent sermon. Here is a random sample of the titles: "I Believe in the Cross," "Christ, Our Comfort," "Remember Who You Are: A Father's Day Blessing," "Peace for the Troubled Heart," "What Is a New Testament Church?" "Discouragement — The Devil's Dagger," "Two Kinds of Fear," "The Task of the Sower," "What Makes a Church Great?" "One in the Spirit," and "The Faith Factor."

Each minister was asked for a short summary of the sermon's content. the summaries abundantly illustrate the continued prevalence of a "type of diffuse treatment" in sermons. Thus, the message of the sermon on "The Task of the Sower" was "to continue implanting God, for there is a harvest." The message of "Remember Who You Are: A Father's Day Blessing" was "youth must be taught and led to the discovery of who they are, to courage, respect for God and a balanced awareness of good and evil in the world."

Of the 102 sermons for which summaries were provided, only 2 seemed to refer to secular issues, one on "human sexuality" and the other on "a Christian approach to politics." But the first of these turned out to emphasize the familiar theme of "judge not that ye be not judged," and the second went no further than to say that "we live within the moral tension of having to bear witness to God's rule over all systems, while making responsible moral choices about particular issues and leaders."

Most Middletown sermons are moral homilies or general exhortations to faith. When they do touch on social or theological issues, they do so only obliquely.

Here are three examples, recorded on a Sunday morning in the spring of 1981.

I know how sick with longing grows the heart that ponders what the world would be like if all the inventions of man and all the energies He has released were dedicated to the highest good of all. But faith demands that we believe it will be so one day and that Man will see built on earth the Eternal City. We may not see it from this side. But we may, from the unseen, be allowed to go on helping to build it on earth. For myself I will not look for some coming of Christ in oriental splendor, or in some way which would contradict all I have learned of Him from the Bible, the saints, and my own meager but precious experiences of His ways with persons. I know there is grandeur in God, and majesty and might. I know He dwells in light inaccessible, and that His being is in one way terrifying. Yet if Jesus is a true picture of God, as I believe, it is His meekness that is terrible and His humility that is awful and His love that is the light I cannot bear. I cannot believe that He who died for love will resort to terror, and that He who knocks at the door of the heart will at a Second Coming break it in. Yet I believe he is always coming.

At the risk of repeating the obvious, I would venture to say that we are still in a state of moral confusion in America today. Our movies reflect it, our television and HBO reflect it, the rate of broken homes and social decay reflect it. We no longer share the common codes of behavior and morality that once united and bound us together as Americans. To correct this some would say that we must return to the old ways, to the good ol' virtues of America as she was. Then we shall once more be great, say these advocates of the golden age of the past. Our strength will be in our recovery of the past. America will prosper once more when she once more becomes "righteous — whatever that was. The *past* is where we must go to mine the treasures of greatness. But there are other voices. And these voices say "no," to those who would return to the past. True, there is much in our country's heritage that must be remembered and valued. But, they warn, there are also things we must leave behind. Times have changed, the world has changed. And so we are also called to change. In fact, one very prominent church historian from Yale has announced that since the 60's we now live in a different epoch in America. We now live in the post-Puritan epoch. To try to *return* to the Puritan epoch would be a mistake. It would be like swimming upstream. History has changed America. And America must allow itself to gracefully accept those changes.

This morning, we do not stand in condemnation of the prophet Elijah — he becomes our teacher. And hopefully, we learn from his experience of second-guessing God in ways that distort his own understanding of God. In looking for God, for instance, in the wind, Elijah indicates his anticipation of a God who can be heard without listening, and serve without any effort. That's the kind of a God he was giving voice to. In looking for a God in the earthquake, Elijah indicates his anticipation of a God who can be known without the risk of faith or the necessity even of believing. And in looking for a God in the fire, Elijah indicated his erroneous anticipation of a God whose judgments can be watched comfortably from afar off, as though God is my God and not your God, and not our Father. God was not in the wind; God was not in the earthquake; God was not in the fire, but the record says He was in the silence which followed this whole process of disillusionment. He came in the still small voice. The only certainty on which we can build our lives is that the being who is behind all of this tremendously unimaginable world of life, that that being comes to us, why, when, how, can only be guesses, because He keeps His own counsel. But of this much we can be sure—as the Christian faith affirms every time people gather to worship, that God's counsel is always good for his creations, for His children. . . . And so faith, and trust must be placed in the place of our meager, short-sighted, human expectations as to how God operates, and it's only to the extent that we have faith and trust in God that God, to us, is allowed by us, to be God.

The religion of the pastors is very much like the religion of their flocks: diffuse, hopeful, absorbed in personal experience and moral self-improvement within the narrow sphere of family and local church. Privatized it may be, but, since it has followed the same style for nearly 90 years, we must hesitate before ascribing the character of this religion to any recent developments in the larger society.

Even the issues of church organization and public morality that obsess the members of some denominations do not occupy an important place in the sermons preached on Sunday mornings or in the private devotions of the faithful. They are encountered elsewhere—in conventions and synods, in the televised services of the Electronic Church, in the auxiliary associations that fill out the church schedule. They are related to Middletown's religion but are not an integral part of it. It is still true, as the Lynds complained more than 50 years ago, that "in other aspects of its life Middletown is involved in change but it values its religious beliefs in part because it is assured that they are unchanging" (Lynd and Lynd 1929, 403).

Chapter 5

Changes in Denominational Identity and Character

Middletown's churches have changed in size and in the nature of their membership since 1924. We will highlight the changes indicated in local records as well as those suggested by the survey data.

Changes in Number and Type of Congregation

According to the Lynds (1937, 297), there were 65 churches in Middletown in 1935. According to the city directories for Middletown published annually since 1931-1932, there were 61 churches in 1931, 93 in 1952, and 160 in 1977.

Some problems arise from using the directories to assess changes in denominational influence in that they omit congregational size. Long-established churches with large buildings and many members are listed in the same way as small, new congregations. Growth or decline in the membership of a church does not affect its listing unless the congregation divides or disappears. When examining successive directories, we have no way of telling whether a congregation has grown or declined.

Despite such limitations, an inspection of the directory lists may provide some useful hints about what has been happening in Middletown churches. By grouping churches according to denominational category, we can discover some indication of trends in the city's "mix" of Protestant churches. A tally of the churches listed in successive directories from 1931 to 1977 reveals that the number of congregations has grown faster than the population.

(See Appendix Table 5-1.) There were 763 people per church in 1931; 746 in 1936; 629 in 1952; 549 in 1960; 473 in 1970; and 500 in 1977.

This increase in the number of churches per capita may reflect higher church attendance (more churches are needed to provide religious services for a given population), or it may only mean that today's congregations are smaller. If so, then worship in Middletown has become more communal (*gemeinschaftlich*) in the sense that worshipers have an opportunity to know each other better. We cannot tell from the directories which of these explanations is correct, but the essential point, we think, is that neither an increase in the aggregate attendance nor a decrease in the average size of congregations is compatible with the notion that religion has been declining in Middletown. Since there are more churches in proportion to the population than there used to be, we can surmise that the long-term trend in religious participation is either stable or rising.

The directories show a small decline in the proportion of Methodist churches and a large increase in the proportion of Baptist and Pentecostal-Evangelical churches between 1931 and 1977. Although the number of Methodist churches doubled, proportion of all congregations that were Methodist declined from 18 percent in 1931 to 14 percent in 1977.

The most striking gains were made by the Baptists. In 1931, they had 13 percent of the city's churches; in 1977, their 38 congregations represented 24 percent. The Pentecostal-Evangelical segment of the city's congregations accounted for just over 1 in 4 of Middletown's churches in 1931-1932, but five years later that fraction had increased to one-third and by 1960 to one-half. Between 1960 and 1977, their relative number decreased, but there were still more congregations of this type than any other in 1977 (38 percent of the total). A modest decline in percentage of churches in the Lutheran/Church of Christ/Brethren category (15 percent of all congregations in 1931, 11 percent in 1977) masks a sharp decline in the representation of the Brethren denominations (such as the Church of the Brethren and the Evangelical United Brethren) and a corresponding increase in the number of Lutheran and Church of Christ congregations. Of the 9 churches in this category in 1931, 7 were Brethren, 1 was Church of Christ,

and 1 Lutheran. Of the 18 churches in this group in 1977, 4 were
Brethren, 5 Lutheran, and 9 Church of Christ.

Many of the Pentecostal-Evangelical congregations have been
short-lived. Present in the 1952 list but missing from the 1960 list
were the Church of the Morning Star, the McCallister Log Cabin
Prayer Chapel, the Rock Built Mission, and the Sunny South
Church of the Christian Fellowship in Christ. Among the most
stable Pentecostal-Evangelical churches, the Nazarenes increased
from 2 congregations in 1931 to 8 in 1977 and the Church of
God/Assembly of God from 3 in 1931 to 13 in 1977.

All of these findings suggest that Middletown has seen a modest
increase in the influence of "southern" Protestantism, especially
Baptist and Pentecostal-Evangelical denominations, and a corresponding decline in the "northern" Protestant denominations
(Methodist, Lutheran/Church of Christ, Brethren, Presbyterian,
Christian, Episcopalian). Taken together, these "northern" Protestants accounted for almost half of Middletown's churches in the
1930s and fewer than a third today.

Of the remaining denominational categories, Catholics and
Universalists-Unitarians had about the same representation in the
1970s as in the 1930s; the special-creed Christians (Quakers, Mormons, Seventh-Day Adventists, Christian Scientists, Jehovah's
Witnesses) doubled the number of their churches as the population
doubled, so that their proportionate share of the city's congregations remained at about 5 percent. There was just one synagogue
in 1977, as there was in 1931.

Denominational Preference

One way to describe the religious composition of a community is
to count and classify its religious organizations. Another way is to
ask individuals about their religious preferences.

All of our surveys contained a question about religious preference, and specific denominational preference was obtained in four
surveys—those on kinship, family roles, neighboring, and adolescent attitudes and behavior.

The denominational preferences of Middletown's adults during
the late 1970s as derived from these surveys are summarized in
Appendix Table 5-2. They were predominantly Christian (84

percent) and Protestant (74 percent). Although there was considerable diversity (more than 60 denominations were reported) the mainline denominations—Methodist, Baptist, Presbyterian, Christian, Episcopalian—accounted for more than half of the denominational preferences, more than two-thirds when we exclude Catholics. The Lutheran/Church of Christ/Brethren churches totaled about 6 percent, and the Pentecostal-Evangelical denominations described by the Lynds (1937, 297) as "marginal groups somewhat deplored by the older denominations" claimed about 10 percent of the population in 1977. The special-creed Christians, such as Quakers, Unitarians, and Mormons, together accounted for 5 percent.

Gender and Denominational Preference

A statement of denominational preference is not equivalent to formal membership and does not necessarily imply that the respondent belongs to or even attends a church of that denomination. Nevertheless, to state a denominational preference is to make a choice among alternative ways of presenting oneself; it is a significant aspect of personal identity.

By many of the standard indicators of religiosity—denominational preference, church membership, church attendance, and personal religious importance—previous research has shown women to be more religious than men. National figures for 1977-1978 based on interview surveys conducted by the Gallup organization show that men are more likely to state no religious preference (8 percent compared to 4 percent of women), more likely to have no religious affiliation (38 percent versus 26 percent), less likely to attend church during an average week (37 percent versus 46 percent), and less likely to say that their religious beliefs are "very important" to them (50 percent versus 65 percent).[1]

Our Middletown surveys revealed two major differences between men and women in religious preference. First, the men were less likely to express any preference: 21 percent of the men, compared to 12 percent of the women, selected the "no preference" response. Second, the men were significantly less likely to select a church in the Presbyterian/Christian/Episcopalian category (6 percent versus 12 percent). For the other categories of religious preference, the

the differences between men and women were negligible. (See Appendix Table 5-2.)

Similar findings emerged when we compared the denominational preferences of adolescent boys and adolescent girls. The percentages of boys and girls selecting given denominations do not differ significantly; the only sizable difference is in the "no preference" category (33 percent of the boys, 25 percent of the girls). Middletown men and boys were less likely to express a denominational preference, but the preferences of those who did were much the same as those of women and girls.[2]

Given the existing differences by gender (Appendix Table 5-2), for every 100 females identifying with a denomination or denominational category, we would find the numbers of males shown in Table 5-3. For most of the Protestant churches in Middletown,

Table 5-3
Religious Preferences of Males (per 100 Females), Middletown, 1976-1977

Religious Preference	Adults	Youths
Methodists	87	86
Baptists	109	77
Roman Catholic	100	107
Protestant (unspecified)	138	133
Presbyterian/Christian/Episcopal	50	67
Pentecostal-Evangelical	70	67
Lutheran/Church of Christ/Brethren	71	100
Special-creed Christians	100	50
No preference	175	132

Sources: Middletown III kinship survey, family role survey, and high school survey, 1977.

this pattern of preference implies a predominance of female worshipers since there are slightly more females than males in the population[3] and since females attend church somewhat more frequently.

Generational Change in Denominational Preference

The kinship survey included the questions "What is (was) your mother's religious preference?" and "What is (was) your father's religious preference?" The distributions of response to these items, compared to the respondents' own preferences, tell us about the persistence of denominational preferences from one generation to the next. The detailed comparison of the preferences of the parents of Middletown adults with those of their children (and other adults now living in Middletown) reveals extraordinary stability. Middletown people in 1976-1977, taken together, reported about the same distribution of denominational preferences for their parents as for themselves. (See Appendix Table 5-4.) The largest change from the older to the younger generation was an average increase from 5 percent to 10 percent for the Pentecostal-Evangelical denominations. There were no other differences to speak of between the denominational preferences of today's adults and those of their parents. Nor, judging from the "no preference" responses, has there been much change in the incidence of religious disaffiliation.

Comparing the denominational preferences of the high school sample with those of the composite sample of Middletown adults, we find that adolescents are twice as likely to claim "no preference" and only about half as likely to include themselves in Middletown's most popular denomination, Methodist. That 29 percent of Middletown's high school students said they had no religious preference does not necessarily suggest that they will be unaffiliated as adults. Some of them, at least, will discover a denominational preference as they grow older, marry, and have children.

The denominational composition of the high school closely paralleled that of the adult population. (The respective categories are all within one or two percentage points, except for the unexplained deficit of Methodists and a four-point difference in "Protestant, unspecified.") On the basis of this similarity and on the assumption that some of the "no preference" responses by adolescents mean "haven't decided which" rather than "opposed to all," we conclude that the three-generation pattern shows a long-term pattern of denominational stability. There is some decline in the predominance of Methodism, and there are hints, when we examine specific denominational categories across the three generations, of declines in the Lutheran type of Protestantism (8 percent to 6 percent to 4 percent as we move from the first to the second to the third generation) and also in "high church" (Presbyterian/Christian/Episcopalian) Protestantism (11 percent to 9 percent to 7 percent).

A mid-depression study of "youth needs and services" in Middle-town sponsored by the American Council on Education and directed by Raymond Fuller included interviews of more than 1,000 graduates and dropouts from the city's high schools in 1936-1937. The interview schedule contained a question on religious preference with four possible responses: Catholic, Protestant, Jewish, and other; interviewers asked for a specific denomination when the answer was Protestant.[4] A comparison of the denominational distribution of Fuller's 1,080 white respondents (Appendix Table 5-5) with our own reveals nearly identical proportions of Methodists and Baptists but relatively more Catholics and Pentecostal-Evangelicals and fewer Lutheran and "high church" Protestants today. Fuller's interview schedule did not allow for "no preference"; therefore, the apparent tenfold increase in "no preference" respondents between 1937 and 1977 is meaningless. A more realistic comparison of the numbers of unaffiliated young people in both samples can be made by combining "Protestants, unspecified" and "no preference" respondents into a single category in both surveys. The combined category accounts for 29 percent of the 1937 respondents and 36 percent of the 1977 respondents, a moderate but statistically significant difference.

Both surveys included questions about frequency of church attendance, and so the percentages of respondents saying that they never attended church can be directly compared. Of the young people interviewed in 1936-1937, 27 percent said they *never* attended church (Fuller 1937, Appendix B, xx); of the high school students who answered the church attendance question in 1977, 20 percent said the same. Thus, the apparent increase in "no preference" is not confirmed by a decline in church attendance. On the contrary, the young people in the 1977 sample were *more* likely to attend church than those studied in 1937. We do not want to make too much of this comparison because the 1937 sample was about 5 years older on the average than the 1977 sample, but it surely provides no evidence for a secularizing trend over this 40-year period.

The denominational preferences of successive generations have so far been discussed in the aggregate. We have not asked what proportion of Middletown adults have religious preferences different from their parents'. The stability of the overall pattern conceals a great deal of interdenominational mobility within families. Many Middletown people have denominational preferences different than their parents', but, as long as the net gain in a denominational category is approximately equal to the net loss, that type of mobility does not show up in aggregate comparisons.

Change in Religious Preference among Individuals

Denominational switching is very common in the United Stated. According to national polls conducted in the mid-1970s, about a sixth of all Catholics are converts and at least a third of active Protestants belong to a denomination in which they were not raised.[5] The denominations with the highest percentage of "stayers" were the Catholics (83 percent), Lutherans (73 percent), and Baptists (70 percent). The propensity for switching was *not* more characteristic of "liberal" than of "conservative" denominations, although there was a tendency for people in the denominations classified as "conservative" to stay within that group of denominations (74 percent) a little more often than "moderate" or "liberal" Protestants stayed within their respective groups of denominations (68 and 64 percent, respectively) (Roof and Hadaway 1977, 409-10). The point, however, is that there is a great deal of interdenominational switching by Christians of all kinds.

Similar patterns of intergenerational mobility in religious preference appear in the 1964 national sample of white adults analyzed by Stark and Glock (1968, 195) and by Mueller (1971)[6] in which the percentage of switchers varied from 12 percent for Catholics to 45 percent for Presbyterians. If denominational mobility in Middletown is anything like the national pattern as revealed in these earlier studies, the apparent stability in the distribution of religious preferences over three generations should be found to mask denominational switching by a large part of the population.

We can test this expectation with our survey data on mother's religion and father's religion as reported by our respondents.[7] Exactly half of the Middletown men in the kinship survey who identified a specific denomination as their mother's or father's preference did not give that same denomination as their own preference. Forty-three percent of the women listing a denominational preference for their mothers gave a different one for themselves, and 45 percent had a preference different from their father's.

Provided that the respondent's parents had a denominational preference, the rate of switching was about the same whether mother's or father's preference was taken as the reference point. However, the apparent equivalence of mother's and father's influence did not hold when the parent had *no* religious preference. Persons whose mothers had *no* preference were significantly more likely to have no preference themselves than persons whose fathers had no preference (63 percent versus 34 percent). (See Appendix Table 5-6.) The transmission of the "no preference" identity is most likely from mothers to sons and least probably from fathers to daughters. Almost all men whose mothers had no preference also had no preference themselves (80 percent, $N = 15$); about half of the women whose mothers had no preference (50 percent, $N = 20$) and the same percentage of men whose fathers had no preference (51 percent, $N = 35$) also had no preference. But fewer than one-fourth (23 percent, $N = 57$) of the women whose fathers had no preference had no preference themselves.

The switching rate does not change very much when we arrange related denominations in categories. Of the respondents whose parents had a religious preference, 42 percent placed themselves not only in a different denomination but in a different category.

The denominations with the highest retention rates are the Catholics (68 or 78 percent, depending on whether mother's or father's preference is the point of origin), Methodists (65 or 67 percent), and special-creed Christians (67 or 81 percent). The Presbyterians, Baptists, and Lutherans have retention rates in the 51-to-57-percent range and have gained about as many members as they have lost in our samples. In contrast, the Pentecostal-Evangelical denominations have moderately high retention rates and have gained many more members than they have lost.

The Middletown adults we questioned in 1976 and 1977 were no more likely than their parents to have no religious preference.[8] It may be that the religious organizations have themselves become more secularized or that the beliefs and behavior of their members are less "conservative," or "orthodox," than formerly. But the data we have on generational change in denominational preference does not establish a secularizing trend in Middletown.

The rates of intergenerational mobility exhibited by Middletown adults are comparable to those found in national studies, with the exception that Catholics in Middletown are somewhat more likely to leave the faith: 86 percent of American Catholics are reported in another study to be "stayers" (Roof and Hadaway 1977, 412), compared to between 68 percent (father's preference) and 78 percent (mother's preference) in Middletown. Part of this difference may be due to the relatively low percentage of Catholics in the Middletown population, which increases the likelihood that Catholics will marry non-Catholics and adopt the denominational preferences of their husbands or wives.

Interdenominational Marriage

Previous research on intermarriage has shown Catholics to be least endogamous, Jews most, and Protestants somewhere in between (Greeley 1970, 949). However, many studies of intermarriage have grouped all Protestants in a single category and defined "inter-marriage" to mean Protestant-Catholic, Protestant-Jewish, or Catholic-Jewish unions, thus accepting marriage between members of different Protestant denominations as religiously endogamous.

Among the few researchers who have compared intermarriage rates for specific denominations are Thomas Monahan and Andrew Greeley. Monahan (1971) reported that the amount of interdenominational marriage is much greater than is generally recognized, and he cited figures from the 1957 Current Population Survey of religion in the United States that show that among white married couples in 1957 about one marriage in five was interdenomina-tional,[9] although he followed the dubious procedure of counting "no religion" responses as a denomination when counting inter-denominational marriages. Among named denominations, inter-marriage was most frequent among Lutherans (26 percent of all marriages) and least frequent among Baptists (21 percent) and Jews (8 percent) (Monahan 1971, 87-88, 90).

Andrew Greeley (1970), interpreting the results of the same 1957 survey, emphasized the predominance of *intra*faith marriages: "Not only are Protestants married to other Protestants, but they are married to Protestants who share the same denominational affiliation. And the ratio of mixed marriages *does not vary much* *across denominational lines."* Greeley went on to compare the national intermarriage rates for 1957 with those from a 1968 national survey of college graduates. Finding virtually no difference, he concluded that during the 1957-to-1968 decade, "the tendency to seek denominational homogeneity in marriage does not seem to have weakened in the slightest" (Greeley 1970, 950).

It may be that a decade is too short a time to identify trends in interfaith marriage. Larry Mumpass's (1970) analysis of Canadian national data on the religions of brides and grooms at the time of marriage reveals a sizable increase in interfaith marriage between 1927 and 1967. In 1927, 6 percent of Canadian brides and grooms were marrying someone of a different religion.[10] By 1967, the percentage had risen to 16 percent.

Bumpass (1970) reported that a cohort analysis of U.S. sample surveys reveals a similar trend. Using data from 1965 National Fertility Survey, he divided white women married once into five-year marriage cohorts by the year they were married and then compared changes in the percentages intermarried. For women married between 1935 and 1939, the percentage intermarried was 5 percent for Protestants and Jews and 12 percent for Catholics. The percentage intermarried gradually increased over the next five cohorts, doubling by the 1960-1965 cohort, in which 11 percent of Protestants, 10 percent of Jews, and 20 percent of Catholics had mixed marriages. Bumpass (1970, 254-55, 258) concluded that the United States, like Canada, has experienced a trend toward interfaith marriage, and he attributed at least part of the increase to a growing similarity among Catholics and Protestants in their ethnic and socioeconomic backgrounds.

Inasmuch as Bumpass's computations place all Protestants into a single category, they take no account of intermarriage between Protestants of different denominations. When we include inter-denominational marriages between Protestants in the total, about one-third of Middletown's marriages are interfaith marriages[11] (Appendix Table 5-7) in the sense that husbands and wives in 1977 gave different denominational preferences. Of course, this omits a considerable number of marriages in which husband and wife belonged to different denominations at the time of marriage but one or both have since changed.

Is interfaith marriage more prevalent now than it was in the past?

Respondents in the kinship survey were asked about the religious preferences of their parents. From the results it appears that somewhat fewer of the parents than of the respondents had mixed marriages.[12] (See Appendix Tables 5-8 and 5-9.) Among the major denominations, Methodists had the lowest rates in both generations. But 1977's "low" rate (26 percent) among Middletown Methodists is higher than any rate in the parental generation.

Divorce

Protestant and Jewish religious authorities are more permissive in their policies toward divorce than Roman Catholic authorities are. The differences in Catholic, Protestant, and Jewish divorce rates that some investigators report are at least partially attributable to doctrinal differences. William Goode (1956, 190-91) found that Catholics experience somewhat more "trauma" in divorce than do Protestants, and a study of divorce in England and Wales interpreted the lower divorce rates of Catholics there to be a result of the stronger "normative barrier" to divorce among Catholics (Thornes and Collard 1979, 39-41). Statistical studies have generally found Catholics to have lower divorce rates than non-Catholics, Jews to have lower divorce rates than Christians, and persons with no religious affiliation to have higher divorce rates than people of any religious affiliation (Bumpass and Sweet 1972).

Among ever-married respondents in the Middletown surveys, the differences between Catholics and active Protestants in the percentage ever divorced were not statistically signifcant. The variation among denominations is quite small; the percentage ever divorced falls between 12 percent and 18 percent in every denomination except Baptist (24 percent). (See Appendix Table 5-10) The Catholics are at the low end of this range (14 percent), but so are persons in the "high church" denominations (12 percent), the special-creed Christians (14 percent), and the Pentecostal-Evangelicals (14 percent).

A significant difference in propensity to divorce separates persons who identify with any denomination from those who have no religious preference or who place themselves in the nebulous category of "Protestant, unspecified." For all Protestant denominations combined, the percentage ever divorced was 16; for

Catholics, as we have said, it was 14; but for those without a denominational preference, it was 26. For marital stability, the important distinction in stability is between the unchurched and those who have a denominational preference.

Elsewhere in this book we discuss the "new tolerance" in Middletown. A blurring of the sharp social boundaries that formerly divided the population into fairly homogeneous segments (business-class and working-class, Protestant and Catholic, upper income and lower income) is apparent in many aspects of community life. We suspect that the smallness of the Catholic-Protestant difference in propensity to divorce that we found in Middletown and that has been reported in other recent surveys[13] is a manifestation of the new tolerance, which seems to extend not only to socioeconomic and religious categories but also to such formerly stigmatized statuses as being divorced. Besides, Middletown has had a high divorce rate for more than 60 years. As we have noted elsewhere, to be a divorced person in Middletown is not at all exceptional.

By 1975, a majority of the adult population (59 percent according to our family roles survey) had experienced one or more divorces in their immediate family, either their own or those of their parents or siblings.

Over this long period of time, people have become accustomed to marital breakups. The dismay about the numerous Middletown divorces noted by the Lynds is not much in evidence anymore. Divorce, like marriage, is a normal part of life, and most people do not expect marriages to last forever (Caplow et al. 1982, 53).

Family Size

Historically, some religious groups have had higher fertility rates than others. These differences seem to be narrowing, but most national surveys continue to show that Catholics have more children than Protestants and that Protestants have more children than Jews. According to the 1965 National Fertility Study, among ever-married women aged 35-to-44, the average number of births for Catholic women was 3.64, compared to 2.92 for Protestant women, 2.76 for women with no religious preference, and 2.13 for Jewish women (Westoff and Ryder 1977, 280-81). Numerous earlier studies reported fertility differences as large as these or larger, with Catholics being consistently the most fertile, Jews the least fertile, and Protestants in between.[14] Concurrent with the decline of the birth rate since 1965 in the United States, Catholic and Protestant rates have converged, meaning that Catholic fertility has declined more rapidly than Protestant fertility (Westoff and Ryder 1977, 282-83). Greeley (1979, 99) cited research that suggests that by the mid-1970s the convergence had progressed to a point where the time-hallowed Catholic advantage in fertility was about to disappear.

Although the difference in fertility between Catholics and Protestants has been a familiar fact of demography since the beginning of that science, fertility differentials among Protestant denominations have been much less conspicuous and have rarely been studied. One study of women students in 44 colleges and universities in 1963-1964 found that the average number of children wanted by those who belonged to Protestant denominations varied only between 3.4 and 3.6, although women with no religious preference desired significantly fewer children.[15] A similar finding had emerged from an earlier (1957) survey of metropolitan wives who had borne a second child during the previous year. The variation in number of children wanted among women belonging to seven Protestant denominational categories was only between 2.8 and 3.1 children; the corresponding figure for Catholic wives was 3.6 and for Jewish wives 2.7[16] (Westoff et al. 1961, 180-82).

On the other hand, an analysis of fertility in Canada that was based on census data revealed some consistent differences among Protestant denominations over a 50-year period, with Mennonites and Mormons showing markedly higher fertility than Pentecostals and Pentecostals showing higher fertility than Anglicans or members of the United Church of Canada (Burch 1966, 179).

On the basis of research in other settings, we anticipated that Catholic women in Middletown would have more children than Protestant women. Moreover, we expected that, if there were differences among the Protestants, women in the more sectarian denominations—the special-creed Christian and the Pentecostal-Evangelical—would show higher fertility. Finally, we anticipated that women without any religious preference would have smaller families than either Protestants or Catholics.

Among ever-married Middletown women who had completed most or all of their childbearing—those aged 35 and over—the average numbers of children were as follows[17] :

Catholic	3.7
Baptist	2.9
No preference	2.9
Pentecostal-Evangelical	2.9
Special-creed Christian	2.9
Presbyterian/Christian/Episcopal	2.8
Protestant (unspecified)	2.5
Lutheran/Church of Christ/Brethren	2.3
Methodist	2.3

Thus, Middletown Catholics, as anticipated, did have larger families than the Protestants. Moreover, the more sectarian Protestants—the special-creed Christians, the Pentecostal-Evangelicals, and the Baptists—had larger families than other Protestants.

When we consider the fertility of women of all ages instead of limiting our inquiry to those who have completed their families, the denominational differences are smaller. For all the women in our kinship and family role surveys who had ever been married (N = 498), the average numbers of children by denomination were:

Catholic	2.7
Baptist	2.7
Pentecostal-Evangelical	2.6
Special-creed Christian	2.6
Presbyterian/Christian/Episcopal	2.5
Protestant (unspecified)	2.4
Lutheran/Church of Christ/Brethren	2.4
No preference	2.3
Methodist	2.0

A comparison of these percentages with the previous set suggests that Catholic-Protestant fertility differences are declining but that Catholic women in Middletown still have relatively large families, as do fundamentalist Protestant women, while Methodists have the smallest families in Middletown.

Social Class

Education, income, and occupation are indicators of social class. Throughout much of the present century, American Catholics lagged behind Protestants on all three indicators. Most of the nation's Catholics are relative newcomers; their forebears arrived as immigrants during the "new" migration, between 1880 and the late 1920s, and had to compete with the more numerous Protestants who had arrived earlier and who already occupied the more desirable positions.

As late as 1961, Lenski's influential book *The Religious Factor* (1961) described the disadvantaged condition of American Catholics. In the same year, Westoff and his associates published an important survey of fertility in metropolitan families that showed that in 1957 Catholics had been underrepresented in professional, managerial, and proprietary occupations; 20 percent of Catholic husbands in Catholic couples were in such occupations, compared to 23 percent in mixed Catholic couples, 32 percent in Protestant couples, and 59 percent in Jewish couples. The same authors found sharp differences in educational attainment, with Jews and Protestants having more education than Catholics (Westoff et al. 1961, 186, 213).

A 1969 survey of another mid-American community, Springfield, Ohio, revealed that Catholics in that community had reached near parity with Protestants in occupational status and income, although they still lagged behind in education (Boling 1973). About the same time, Schuman's (1971, 41) replication of Lenski's Detroit study, from 1966 data, found that white men whose fathers were Catholics were about as likely to be in upper-middle-class occupations as those whose fathers were Protestants (32 percent and 34 percent, respectively).

National surveys conducted in the 1970s and 1980s have shown that in education, income, and occupational achievement Catholics now score as high or higher than Protestants, and this pattern persists when the major minority groups in the population—Protestant blacks and Catholic Hispanics—are not included (Greeley 1979, 92-93). The convergence between Protestants and Catholics that we noted with respect to fertility also seems to have occurred in socioeconomic achievement. The evidence suggests that there has been "an economic, social, educational, and intellectual transformation in American Catholicism, going on for many years but reaching its fulfillment during the 1960s . . . " (Greeley 1979, 95).

If contemporary national patterns are mirrored in Middletown, then Middletown's Catholics should not exhibit lower educational attainment, occupational status, or income than Middletown Protestants. However, we did expect some differences among Middletown's Protestant denominations in social class, for it is well documented that among American Protestants the well educated and the well-to-do are overrepresented in certain denominations, especially the Episcopalians and the Presbyterians, and underrepresented among the Baptists and the Pentecostal-Evangelicals.[18]

To return to the comparison of Catholics and Protestants, Middletown Catholics are at least as well educated as Middletown Protestants. Twenty-six percent of the latter have completed college, but 36 percent of the former. (See Appendix Table 5-10.) Only the "high church" denominations and the Universalists-Unitarians have higher percentages of college graduates than the Catholics.

Corroborative evidence of Catholic educational achievement appears when we consider the poorly educated, for there are some sharp religious differences in the likelihood of being poorly educated. Listed below are the percentages of persons who never completed high school in each denominational group.

Pentecostal-Evangelical	46%
Baptist	36
No preference	33
Protestant, unspecified	30
Special-creed Christians	24
Lutheran/Church of Christ/Brethren	23
Presbyterian/Christian/Episcopal	16
Methodist	14
Catholic	11
Universalist-Unitarian	7
Total	25%

These percentages highlight the educational disadvantages of the "southern-style" Protestants and the new advantage of the Catholics.

Just as education is unequally distributed by religious preference, so is income. In 1976, about one Middletown resident in seven belonged to a family whose total family income was less than $6,000. One-fifth of the special-creed Christians and a like proportion of those without a religious preference had low incomes, as well as 17 percent of Pentecostal-Evangelicals. At the other end of the distribution, the Universalist-Unitarians (7 percent), the

Presbyterian/Christian/Episcopalians (8 percent), and the Catholics (11 percent) had less than their "share" of poor people. The top two income categories in which the respondents could place themselves involved incomes of $20,000 or more. If families with these incomes in 1976 are considered well-to-do, then prosperity is more unevenly distributed by religious preference than poverty. Almost half of the Universalist-Unitarians and the Presbyterian/Christian/Episcopalians had incomes that high, along with a third of the Methodists and a third of the Catholics and only a sixth of the Pentecostal-Evangelicals and a sixth of those without religious preference. (See Appendix Table 5-11.)

Conclusions

Contemporary Middletown, like the Middletown of yesteryear, is a predominantly Protestant community. Today, the influence of "southern" Protestantism—not only the Southern Baptists but the Holiness churches, the Churches of God, the Nazarenes, and the other denominations we have put under the Pentecostal-Evangelical rubric—is stronger than it used to be. The major denominational division in the community is no longer the traditional Catholic-Protestant dichotomy; in many ways, Middletown's Catholics and Protestants are indistinguishable. The major division is now between the "southern" Protestants and the more affluent and better-educated "northern" Protestants and Catholics.

There is no evidence of a declining attachment to organized religion in contemporary Middletown. Nowhere do we see secularization undermining the community's religious institutions. On the contrary, there are relatively more churches than there used to be, and their members attend more zealously than their predecessors did two generations back.

Middletown's adult citizens show nearly the same pattern of denominational preference as their parents did. But, taken individually, a larger minority of them belong to other denominations than their parents did.

Although religious identification is at least as strong now as it was in the Lynds' time, the Christianity of Middletown is less bristling, strident, and sharp edged than it was then. As the increase in interfaith marriages and the easy mobility between denominations suggest, Middletown people are much less likely than they used to be to define their particular brand of Christianity as the *one* solution to everyone's problems.[19] We will discuss the "new tolerance" among Middletown churchgoers again in a subsequent chapter. In demographic characteristics—family size, marital status, education, occupation—Middletown's congregations are more alike than they were 50 years ago. Denominational differences are muted, and religion may be a greater force for community solidarity today than it was when the Lynds said that "militant Protestantism" was used by the Ku Klux Klan to divide the city (Lynd and Lynd 1929, 428).

Chapter 6

Middletown's Rituals, 1924-1980

American religious rituals have not been studied very much. There have been many more studies of church attendance than of church services, perhaps because the social survey method is better suited to the former than to the latter. *Middletown* (Lynd and Lynd 1929) was a happy exception; the Lynds gave more attention to the description of church activities than was usual in community studies. In this chapter, we attempt to update and extend their account of Middletown's rituals. We begin with a discussion of the newest religious activities in Middletown and conclude with an analysis of the oldest and most important ritual, the Sunday church service.

Nonchurch Rituals

The number of Christian rituals carried on outside the churches of Middletown has increased since the Lynds' original study. The only nonchurch rituals to which any importance was attached in *Middletown* were those that took place at home, and these were described as falling into disuse: ". . . it is generally recognized in Middletown that the 'family altar,' the carrying on of daily prayer and Bible reading by the assembled family group, is disappearing" (Lynd and Lynd 1929, 337). This decline was explained by the increased number of occasions that took family members away from home in the evening and on weekends. On a similar note, the Lynds wrote that "the early custom of using the home for meetings of 'prayer bands' and 'cottage prayer meetings'

survives today chiefly in outlying working class neighborhoods"
(Lynd and Lynd 1929, 338).[1]

In 1978, the Middletown III survey of religious beliefs and practices put this question to respondents: "Besides services sponsored
by your church do you ever participate in any of the following
activities?" The question was followed by a list of nine activities.
In this chapter, we will analyze the responses to this question.

In June 1978, questionnaires were sent to a random sample of
1,000 names listed in the Middletown city directory. After two
follow-up letters, 230 completed questionnaires were obtained.
The sample is biased in several obvious ways: it is excessively
female (68 percent), white (95 percent), and educated (17 percent
reported graduate study).

We exclude nonwhites from the analysis because there are not
enough responses from nonwhites to analyze. And, since the question was asked only of those individuals who identified themselves
with a denomination or a church and since most (94 percent) of
those respondents were Christians, we limit our analysis here to
the responses of white Christians.

Half of the white Christians in our sample participated in some
type of religious service away from church, most frequently by
watching televised services at home (25 percent). Seventeen percent took part in home Bible study groups, about the same proportion attended gospel music concerts, 13 percent had gone to
retreat centers and 12 percent belonged to home prayer groups.
A few were familiar with home churches, coffeehouse ministries,
and religious communes.

All in all, nonchurch religious activities seem to be more varied
and more important now than when the Lynds wrote *Middletown.*
This finding raises some further questions: Do these nonchurch
activities complement or replace conventional church services;
What sort of people do they attract?

Church Attendance and Nonchurch Rituals

Appendix Table 6-1 shows the relationship between church attendance and participation in nonchurch rituals. Those who attend

church frequently are most likely to engage in nonchurch rituals. Only 8 percent of those who attended church *more* than once a week refrained from all nonchurch rituals, but nearly half of those who went to church weekly refrained from such participation. This constitutes a striking difference between these similar categories. At the other end of the scale, we found that nearly a fourth of those who *never* went to church took part in nonchurch rituals. Among those who did not attend church regularly (at least once a week), frequency of attendance had only a slight influence on participation in other religious activities.

Accordingly, we divided our respondents into three categories: constant churchgoers (more than once a week), regular churchgoers (once a week), and occasional churchgoers and nonattenders (less than once a week). Appendix Table 6-2 shows participation in nonchurch rituals by these categories. As that table shows, the constant churchgoers were much more likely to participate in home services and to go to gospel music concerts. People in this category seem to have centered their lives on religion so that religious activities enter their private worlds and guide their use of leisure.

Going on retreats is another matter. Here the line is drawn between regular and occasional churchgoers. Those who went on retreats had a serious but not necessarily exclusive commitment to institutional religion.

The audience for televised services is structured still another way. A sizable percentage of those who rarely or never attended church watched televised services. For these people, the Electronic Church seems to be an alternative to the traditional church. The constant churchgoers had no special predilection for televised services; it was the relatively lukewarm churchgoers who showed the greatest interest.

Christian respondents were asked to specify their denominational background.[2] This enabled us to regroup them into four broad categories: Catholic, mainline Protestant, lower-class Protestant, and Pentecostal/others. Their relative participation in nonchurch rituals is shown in Appendix Table 6-3.

In the aggregate, Catholics and mainline Protestants reported much less participation in nonchurch rituals than the other groups. Home prayer, home Bible study, and gospel music concerts are

Pentecostal folkways. The Electronic Church, by contrast, appealed much more to Protestants than to Catholics but about equally to all kinds of Protestants. Attending retreats—restricted to a small minority in any case—was about equally attractive to the four kinds of Christians.

We also examined the relationship between the sex, age, and education of the respondents and their participation in nonchurch rituals. The results are shown in Appendix Tables 6-4 and 6-5. (Like the preceding tables, these refer only to respondents who identified themselves with a church or a denomination.) There is a trivial inverse correlation between education and participation in nonchurch rituals; it reflects a weak curvilinear relationship whereby participation is higher for persons of average educational achievement than for those who have less-than-average or more-than-average education.

Education had more influence on participation in retreats than in any other of the listed activities (tau b = .16). No respondent with less than a high school education took part in this activity, and only three of the high school graduates in the sample had ever gone on a retreat. In the three upper educational levels, nearly a fifth of the respondents had some experience of retreats.

Sex and age had no discernible effect on participation in nonchurch rituals except that women were much more likely (32 percent) than men (11 percent) to watch televised services and older women were much more likely (55 percent) to watch than younger women (28 percent). The relationship is shown in Appendix Table 6-5.

We pursued the matter further by dividing our respondents into those who had and did not have paid employment. Employment status had no effect on the feeble interest of men in televised services, but it did affect the viewing habits of women. Only 28 percent of those with paid employment watched televised services, compared to 43 percent of those without, most of whom were occupied as housewives.

Another potential element in the appeal of televised services is ideology. Television preachers tend to hold conservative attitudes toward the role of women in society and could be expected to attract women with similar attitudes. Another question in the survey was "Leaving aside their tactics, what is your attitude toward the women's liberation movement?" Among women who held favorable attitudes toward or were undecided about women's liberation, only 23 percent said they watched televised services; among women opposed to that movement, 49 percent did so.

Appendix Table 6-6 shows the combined effect of paid employment and attitude toward women's liberation on the likelihood of a respondent's participation in the Electronic Church. The findings suggest that the attitudinal variable is as influential as employment status. Housewives may watch televised services because they have more free time or because television preachers emphasize the importance of the wifely role or, of course, for both reasons.[3]

Despite the risk of running this peripheral inquiry into the ground, we constructed a variable called "cosmopolitanism" that examines the matter further. A high score on cosmopolitanism suggests that the subject enjoys three kinds of "high culture" activities: public television, reading, and travel. To our surprise, there turns out to be a modest correlation between cosmopolitanism—so measured—and watching televised services for both men and women. Moreover, this was the only nonchurch religious ritual related to cosmopolitanism. Cosmopolitanism was not significantly related to participation in the Electronic Church among women unfavorable to women's liberation, but of women favoring women's liberation who also scored high on cosmopolitanism ($N = 29$), 38 percent reported watching televised services. We ascribe this phenomenon to curiosity, for want of a more coherent explanation.

To recapitulate, participation in the Electronic Church—at least for the Protestant women who comprise the bulk of the audience—is not a function of church affiliation or attendance. The appeal of these services has more to do with the social ideology of television preachers and their ability to entertain and to distract their viewers than with the theological principles they profess.

Let us summarize our findings about nonchurch rituals. First, they seem more varied and important than they were in 1924. Second, they are in no way limited to the working class, as they may have been during the Lynds' time. Third, nonchurch rituals seem to support rather than to compete with church services.

Fourth, the appeal of the Electronic Church seems only distantly related to its theology.

Revivals

The Lynds' impression of Middletown's religious services in 1924 "was that of an unalert acceptance, punctuated periodically in the less socially sophisticated churches by bursts of religious energy during a revival" (Lynd and Lynd 1937, 295). The latter served to stir the emotions and to "limber up the church," according to one of their informants (Lynd and Lynd 1929, 278).

The revival movement seemed to the Lynds to be faltering in 1925 and to be dying out in 1935. In *Middletown*, they noted that "revivals were frequent in 1890—one gathers, even more frequent than today . . ." (Lynd and Lynd 1929, 378). In *Middletown in Transition* (1937, 302-3), they wrote that

it is possibly indicative of the apparently negligible effect of the depression as a quickening factor in local religious life that the bottom has dropped out of the revival movement which flourished in 1925. . . . According to a prominent minister: "The business-class churches are slowly giving up the revival idea . . . ." There has been a meager sprinkling of revivals in individual working-class churches during the depression. . . . But, on the whole, if the number of revivals is any index of religious interest in the depression, there has been a marked recession.

The Lynds counted 21 revivals reported in the press during 1924, 15 of which were conducted by imported evangelists (Lynd and Lynd 1929, 378). Elsewhere in this volume, we challenge the Lynds' perception that the frequency and importance of revivals declined between 1890 and 1924. Looking for the trend of revivals in Middletown between 1924 and 1980, we came across some information that makes the supposed decline from 1890 to 1924 even more doubtful. Our own reading of one local paper yielded quite different results for 1924 than the Lynds obtained. We found announcements of 49 revivals, which were held at 38 different churches during that faraway year;[4] like the Lynds, we counted 15 revivals led by imported evangelists. (They were not, by the way, imported from very far. Eight of them came from Indiana, five from adjacent states, one from Syracuse, New York, and one from Morgantown, West Virginia.)

The discrepancy between the Lynds' count of the total number of revivals and ours can probably be blamed on the vagueness of the term; not all churches use the word "revival." We counted any special service lasting at least two days as equivalent to a revival, with the exception of a three-day series of "lectures" held at one church. What we counted as revivals were variously described in the local papers as "revivals," "evangelistic services," and "tent meetings."[5]

The public announcements were not always precise about the duration of a revival, but fair estimates for the 1924 revivals in Middletown are listed in Table 6-7. This tabulation is only approximate, but clearly the 1924 revivals were both frequent and lengthy.

Table 6-7
Duration and Number of Revivals, Middletown, 1924

Duration	Number
Less than seven days	1
A week	5
More than a week	7
At least two weeks	4
Two to three weeks	10
Three weeks or more	6

To obtain similar information for 1980, we studied the church news page in the Saturday edition of the same newspaper 56 years later.[6] In 1980, unlike 1924, there were many paid advertisements by churches on that page, along with a column of church news. In 1980, there were six major revivals sponsored collectively by a number of churches. In 1924, there had been only two revivals sponsored by more than one church, a pair of churches in each case. Some of the major revivals of 1980 cut across denominational lines. One of them, the Albany-DeSoto United Rally for Christ, was interdenominational, involving a whole group of churches in the same locality; another was a camp meeting sponsored by no less than 18 Nazarene churches. These large-scale efforts had no counterparts in 1924.

For 1980 we counted 106 revivals sponsored by 81 different churches. A directory of churches in Middletown's county listed 217 churches. It appears, therefore, that about one-third (37 percent) of the county's churches held revivals in 1980. According to Dwight Hoover, there were 42 churches in the county in 1920; according to the count mentioned above, 37 of them (88 percent) held revivals. We cannot be sure that it is appropriate to compare the Lynds' figure for the city of Middletown with recent figures for Middletown's county, and no doubt the numbers are not to be considered completely accurate for either 1924 or 1980 since churches come and go and we cannot be sure that all revivals were announced in the newspaper. Yet, with these caveats, it is fairly certain that the average duration of revivals declined between 1924 and 1980, as the figures for 1980 suggest (Table 6-8). Where-

Table 6-8
Duration and Number of Revivals, Middletown, 1980

Duration	Number
Two days	10
Three to five days	27
Six days	29
Seven days	13
Eight to ten days	15
Fifteen days	1

as in 1924 the median length of the revivals was about two weeks, in 1980 only a single revival lasted that long and the median length was six days. The 1924 revivals were more demanding; four of them were scheduled to run indefinitely; there was only one less than a week long. In 1980 there were 10 two-day "weekend revivals," a form unknown in 1924. Current revivals, then, take up less time but without necessarily being less enthusiastic.

Fifty-two imported evangelists whose origins are known to us participated in Middletown revivals in 1980. Many more of them came from Tennessee and Kentucky than had been the case in 1924.

What about the Lynds' finding that revivals were a working-class phenomenon? In neither 1924 nor 1980 was there an announcement of a revival in an Episcopalian, a Presbyterian, or a Lutheran church. Meanwhile, the Methodists have almost abandoned the custom. In 1924, 20 out of 48 revivals were theirs; in 1980, only 8 out of 106 were. Present-day revivals are the province of the

Baptist, Nazarene, and independent churches. How far these denominations can be identified as working class is a matter we explore in other chapters.

Retreats

Retreats were almost unknown in Middletown in 1924, but they had become an important feature of the community's religious life by 1980. A retreat is a temporary withdrawal from the world for the purpose of meditation, religious instruction, and prayer. Seven retreats were announced in 1980 by six Middletown churches: St. Mary's Roman Catholic (two, one for women and one for teens; the latter was not called a retreat but an "encounter Christ weekend"), Eden United Church of Christ, High Street United Methodist, Madison Street United Methodist, Friends' Memorial Church, and Eaton First Church of God. Two other events apparently were equivalent to retreats: Hazelwood Christian Church held a two-day "Festival of Friendship," and Corinth United Methodist Church planned a "famine fast" for their youth lasting 30 hours. During the fast, a film on world hunger was shown and the young people studied the scriptures. None of the churches that held a retreat had any official part in a revival. For Catholics and mainline Protestants, the retreat is a somewhat intellectualized substitute for the revival.

Revivals, then, (1) seem to have become less important, since they occur in a smaller percentage of churches and are shorter, (2) are associated with working-class religion, but (3) may be being replaced to some extent by retreats in middle-class churches.

Anthropologist Victor Turner has suggested that people need to supplement the normal experiences of a structured society with the experience of *communitas,* living with others, an event that minimizes the differences among them and dramatizes the sharing of a significant moment in life. He has suggested "the revivalist camp meetings of rural America" as examples of *communitas* (Turner and Turner 1978, 241). It is possible that religious retreats also exemplify *communitas.* That is, both revivals and retreats can be interpreted as community-building rituals. Turner believes such rituals are necessary to restore a sense of community among people whose daily life is competitive and isolating. If this is true, what happens in churches that have neither revivals nor retreats? How do they establish *communitas*? The remainder of this chapter considers the central religious ritual in Middletown, the Sunday church service.

Sunday Church Services

Rituals, wrote Ducey (1977, 84-85), can be interpreted on three symbolic levels:

(1) The exegetical meaning is in the explanation of ritual made by those who participate in it, and contained in the verbal formulas of the ritual itself. (2) The operational meaning is revealed by the motor activity required for the performance of the ritual, and in that aspect of language known as "style." . . . (3) The positional meaning is given by the spatial arrangements of the performance.

In the discussion that follows, we will try to sketch out the exegetical, operational, and spatial meanings attached to the Sunday church service in Middletown.

Content of Sermons

The Lynds noted in 1924 that except in the Catholic and Episcopalian churches "the main auditorium comes to a focus in the platform or pulpit where the preacher stands" (Lynd and Lynd 1929, 336). The most important feature of the Sunday service was the sermon, and so the minister was "first and foremost expected to be a good talker" (Lynd and Lynd 1929, 344, 371, 403).

The Lynds, searching for changes from 1890 to 1924, attempted to classify the 80 sermon topics mentioned in the local press during 1890 and the 193 sermon topics announced in two sample months of 1924 according to general emphasis, for example, theological or practical ethics. They found, however, that the titles in most instances were too vague to permit precise classification. Despite this problem, they discerned no change from 1890 to 1924. In place of classifications, they reproduced verbatim excerpts from 10 sermons selected as the most representative of those heard by the research staff or sent in to the press during the period under study, the churches being otherwise classified as "working class," "business class," "prominent business class," "business and working class," and "Catholic." They added further excerpts from

revival sermons, Sunday school lessons, and young people's meetings and concluded almost derisively that Middletown "values its
religious beliefs in part because it is assured they are unchanging"
and "this emphasis upon the unchanging character of essential
religious beliefs is perhaps not unrelated to a tendency to regard
them not as practical concerns . . ." (Lynd and Lynd 1929,
403-4). They were even harsher about the content of sermons in
Middletown in Transition: "The gap between religion's verbalizing
and Middletown life has become so wide that the entire institution
of religion has tended to be put on the defensive" (Lynd and Lynd
1937, 311).

Elsewhere in this volume we present equivalent excerpts from
1981 sermons, and we can glean some additional information from
a 1972 preelection survey conducted in Middletown that contained
two questions about the content of sermons.[7]

When respondents were asked "How many of the sermons you
hear refer to the next world, heaven and hell?" 26 percent checked
"just about all of the," 16 percent "more than half," 18 percent
"about half," 20 percent "less than half," and 21 percent "hardly
ever or never." When asked "Does your minister (priest) speak out
on public issues such as school integration or taxes or war?" 46
percent of the sample said he did so at least sometimes and 54
percent said rarely or never. As these findings indicate, Middletown
sermons are not all tailored of the same cloth.

Appendix Table 6-9 combines the answers to these questions.
The four corner cells in the table are nearly equal. So, though 15
percent of the respondents heard sermons that frequently referred
to heaven and hell and also heard comments on public issues, 22
percent heard comments on public issues but infrequently heard
about the next world. We found no significant statistical tendency
for sermons to be divided into this-worldly and other-worldly
topics, although there was a slight tendency for sermons that frequently referred to heaven and hell to exclude comments on
public issues. In general, however, the two themes seem to be
mixed randomly.

Respondents were asked whether they considered their church
religiously liberal or conservative: 35 percent said liberal, 39
percent chose conservative, and 25 percent were not sure. (Again,

note the dispersion of churches across the categories.) Slightly more respondents belonging to religiously liberal churches (50 percent) than those affiliated with conservative churches (43 percent) said the sermons dealt with public issues, but the difference was slight. What this suggests is that, although Middletown residents may frequently hear comments on current social issues, these remarks are as likely to be conservative as liberal.

It is possible that the diversity of sermon styles reflects the existence of distinct social classes. Appendix Table 6-10 shows the relation between respondents' education and the topics of the sermons they heard. As the table shows, education is negatively related to the occurrence of sermons that contained references to heaven and hell. The relation to this-worldly references is less clear, but it does seem noteworthy that the most educated heard the most comments on public issues. That those with some college rarely heard such remarks, however, seems inconsistent with the general pattern in the table; we have no explanation for this result.

Ritual and Entertainment

Like other world religions, American Protestantism blends religion and entertainment in its rituals. It did so in 1924 and it does so today. On April 19, 1924, the local newspaper listed the churches' complete Easter programs, including the names of soloists and musical ensembles. For instance, the program at Grace Episcopal listed Miss Dunn singing "Lord Have Mercy upon Us" by Gounod, and on the same day at First Baptist Mrs. Olin Bell played "Spring Song" by Mendelssohn on the organ. On the last Sunday in Advent 1980, the High Street United Methodist Church presented its eleventh annual carol sing "accompanied by an orchestra of more than 50 instruments."

According to Michael L. King (1980, 25), magic, ventriloquism, and puppetry all find their places in contemporary religious services. There is a "Fellowship of Christian Magicians" that claims to represent about a hundred magician-preachers. These developments are reflected in Middletown, of course. The Selma Church of the Nazarene announced in 1980 that the special workers in their crusade would "use puppets, flannel stories, skits and magic in their ministry." In the same year, the First United Presbyterian Church held a "clown worship service, conducted in mime with musical background." But the most unusual addition to a Middletown church service in 1980 was surely the following: "Dr. Wendall Hasen, internationally known bird trainer, will present a special program at 10:30 a.m. Sunday in the First Church of the Nazarene. Tropical and exotic birds gathered from around the world will be featured." The advertisement for this event promised "Unbelievable Feats! Flying Backwards! Sword Swallowing! Plus Much More!"

Ritual Style

In 1924 nearly all Sunday church services featured a sermon by a minister, a Bible reading, a set order of prayers, and the singing of hymns. Among the Catholics, Episcopalians, Presbyterians, and Lutherans, the sermon shared importance with the ceremony of communion—a difference not mentioned by the Lynds, but they did note some other variations from the modal pattern of the Evangelical Protestant churches.

. . . in the Catholic and Christian Science churches the sermon is relatively less important in the Sunday services, with correspondingly greater emphasis on ritual; in these churches there is greater emphasis on ritual; in these churches there is greater emphasis on the religious instruction of the young than in the main group of Protestant churches. Both the Christian Scientists and the small but ardent group of Spiritualists make a strong appeal through their emphasis upon the here and now benefits of religion in health and prosperity. The small Jewish Reformed Temple without a resident Rabbi differs from other religious groups by its nonadherence to the prevailing Christian tradition and a certain austere simplicity in its service of worship (Lynd and Lynd 1929, 402).

But the Lynds did take note of congregational fervor in working-class churches, and in *Middletown in Transition* this grew into a little theory of ritual style.[8] Business-class services in 1935 were described as having an "earnest minister," an audience paying "respectful" attention, sermons that were "mild and dignified," a closing hymn "sung doggedly and rather raggedly by people who do not seem to enjoy hearing themselves sing," and "the final subdued neighborliness of the greetings as the congregation files out" (Lynd and Lynd 1937, 298, 308).

Working-class services were said to be "a more reciprocal experience between leader and congregation," the congregation was less passive, the sermons were "more strenuous" and accompanied by the "yes's" and "that's right's" of the auditors (Lynd and Lynd 1937, 298, 308). They went on to suggest a continuum of enthusiasm roughly — and inversely — linked to social status.

Certain individuals in Middletown privately reject all religious forms, even including the preaching and singing and praying of the Presbyterians and the rituals and prayers of the small group of Episcopalians; and the latter two groups in turn tend to feel that the immersing Baptists and the vocal Methodists are "somehow different" and "less refined" than themselves; while all four tend to be somewhat pained by the ardor of the Seventh Day Adventists and Spiritualists. These last feel that the uptown churches are cold and lack spirituality (Lynd and Lynd 1937, 314).

A Dichotomous Classification of Ritual

We have elsewhere described two types of ritual, holiness and solemn, which support social unity by different mechanisms (Tamney 1965). Holiness rituals produce solidarity by giving participants a direct experience of their mutual similarity. This effect is achieved by minimizing structural differences (for example, by rotation of leaders), public confessions by everyone, and sharing personal problems during the ritual. When the ritual is successful, the participants develop a strong sense of common identity and a shared emotional state. The Pentecostal revival is a holiness ritual.

Solemn rituals are characterized by silence, slowness of action, absence of emotional display, and stylized performances by persons in uniform manipulating sacred objects. These actions express respect for a powerful being. The Catholic mass is a solemn ritual. Although emphasizing some different ritual elements, Von Hildebrand perceived (1943, 68-69) the underlying theme of the Catholic mass to be the consistent expression of reference "in the bodily comportment of the priest, the faithful and the religious, in the standing up during the reading of the Gospels . . . in the bowing of the head during the *Gloria Patri.*" Through such a ritual, which creates feelings of reverence and submission, members realize their oneness indirectly "in Christ." The direct effect of solemn rituals is a sense of dependence on a powerful being.

Ducey (1977, 88) classified rituals in another, not dissimilar way as "mass" and "interaction" rituals. The first type inhibits freedom, the second type encourages it. The mass ritual has distinct clergy roles, whose incumbents wear special clothing to symbolize their power; the clergy alone direct the course of the ritual (Ducey 1977, 108). Ducey's mass type and our solemn type seem to be the same phenomenon. For instance, just as we associate the solemn ritual with reverence (Tamney 1965), Ducey associated mass ritual with awe (1977, 102) and the rejection of mass rituals with the loss of solemnity (1977, 173).

Interaction and holiness rituals, however, seem quite different. Ducey (1977, 9) identified the original form of the Quaker service as an interaction ritual. There is certainly a dramatic difference in real life between a Pentecostal revival and a Quaker meeting.

Ducey, (1977, 87), following Bellah, proposed a theory of religious evolution whereby religion progresses inevitably toward the fuller expression of personal autonomy. According to this theory, the interaction ritual represents an improvement over the mass ritual and exemplifies the historical movement toward autonomy, which is celebrated in various ways in the interaction ritual. Each participant is expected to develop a personal interpretation of the presented symbols; the purpose of the ritual is to discover new shared meanings through the free exchange of these experiences. The outcome of the ritual is determined by the participants collectively; the casual assignment of ritual functions reflects their essential equality: the "role of initiating sacred utterance or action is assigned by the congregation to various of its members at random" (Ducey 1977, 7). The participants in such a ritual may not hold the same theology; they are committed to a process of religious exploration. "Persons who are moved by Interaction ritual are moved by the process of creating meaning with others and not simply by the dramatizations of momentary unanimity" (Ducey 1977, 176).

By freedom or autonomy, Ducey meant both the spontaneous behavior that occurs during the ritual and the freedom of speech and consensual procedure for determining the nature of the ritual. Is it possible that both forms of freedom can be realized in the same cult? To answer this question, we must reconsider how spontaneity figures in ritual performances.

The purest form of spontaneous ritual is what the Turners

(1978, 252) called "existential *communitas.*" Ecstatic rock concerts are a contemporary, or at least recent, example. The participants in ecstatic rituals are detached from "social and historical rootedness" (Myerhoff 1975, 34). Ordinary social structure is suppressed and is replaced by a collective entity based on the shared experience of release (Martin 1979, 113). As was written about an appearance by the Rolling Stones: "All that counted was sound and the murderous mood it made. . . . The words were lost and the song was lost. You were only left with chaos, beautiful anarchy" (Martin 1979, 104). The effectiveness of such rituals depends on the existence of a firm social structure, for *communitas* is a critical comment on such a structure, a temporary rejection of it (Myerhoff 1975, 34). Without the rejected structure, *communitas* would be meaningless. As the negation of a familiar structure, it can celebrate spontaneity and remain meaningful.

Both *communitas* and interaction rituals encourage spontaneity. According to Ducey (1977, 173), "The experience of discovering the sacred in the authenticity of another person's spontaneous contributions . . . appears to be the central meaning of Interaction ritual. . . ." Spontaneous remarks make "contact with unconscious knowledge and desires" (Ducey 1977, 105). Yet, Ducey's model of an interaction type is a service in "a rational rather than an enthusiastic middle-class church . . ." (1977, 163). It included a "talkback" session during which participants critically discussed the just-completed service. "The 'alliance of autonomous egos' is manifested in energetic debate, the attempt to arrive at substantive agreements, and the agreement to disagree" (Ducey 1977, 121). The same church held formal meetings to plan future rituals. This interest in discussion, debate, and participatory democracy is worlds apart from a *communitas* ritual. Although spontaneous behavior is valued in the interaction ritual, it is subordinated to the orderly procedures that permit democratic discussion. What is valued in interaction rituals is not emotional spontaneity so much as the rejection of formal dogma and the acceptance of personal reactions from all levels of consciousness. By contrast, emotional spontaneity is the essence of a *communitas* ritual.

Interaction ritual differs from *communitas* (and mass rituals) in another way. When they discuss the meaning and relevance of religion, the participants in an interaction ritual are encouraged to reveal important aspects of themselves and thus to establish their distinctive individuality, that is, to emphasize their differences from their fellows (Ducey 1977, 179). "The community of Interaction ritual is not based on any assumed likeness of kind. . . . In fact, it assumes just the opposite: that each participant is unique and therefore different from everyone else" (Ducey 1977, 178).

The contrasting effect of a *communitas* ritual is the obedience to individuality. "In its most exaggerated and complete form, Communitas is a loss of self, a fusion of the individual with the group . . ." (Myerhoff 1975, 43). It appears, therefore, that we must recognize at least three different types of religious ritual: (1) the solemn ritual, which expresses submission to a powerful superior entity and uses spatial symbolism to dramatize the separation between the sacred and the profane, (2) the holiness (or *communitas*)[9] ritual, which encourages the merging of individuals into an emotionally spontaneous group, and (3) the interaction ritual, which encourages reasoned expression as a means of achieving a much cooler kind of group solidarity.

The church services the Lynds saw in business-class churches were solemn rituals; what they described as typical working-class services were holiness rituals. They described no interaction rituals, although they did report comments to the effect that "the congregation ought to have more part in the service" (Lynd and Lynd 1929, 381).

Do contemporary church services in Middletown fit this typology?

Questionnaires were mailed out during the spring of 1978 to all members of the clergy listed in a directory compiled by the Christian Ministries of Middletown's county. Information was requested from one person in each church, so that each respondent represented a different church.[10] The sample included only Christian denominations; Jews, Spiritualists, and Moslems were not included.

Appendix Table 6-11 shows the distribution of denominations in the county and the religious affiliation of the ministers who returned questionnaires. After several attempts to improve the response rate, we obtained completed questionnaires from 112 out of the 217 (52 percent) of those listed in the directory.

The unit of analysis was "the main religious service" at each respondent's church.[11] The respondents were asked to describe this ritual by checking as many as they wished of 31 descriptive characteristics. The list of characteristics included most of the information needed to identify a ritual by type, information that could be conveniently obtained by a questionnaire.[12]

Ritual Style in Middletown

If interaction rituals exist in Middletown, they are very rare. In only 6 percent of the 112 churches did lay readers control the preparation of the Sunday service; in another 10 percent the locus of control was unclear because the minister (priest) said the manner of preparation changed from service to service. In only 4 percent of the churches was the sermon customarily given by someone other than a minister or a priest. We did find a "dialogue" in 15 percent of the services, but we know from participant observation that at least in some cases the dialogue is formal and predetermined and not the open exchange of ideas described by Ducey. In our opinion, there does exist some support for the interaction style; even in 1924 the Lynds found such sentiment. Ministers are concerned about increasing congregational participation, but we doubt that this had led, except perhaps among the Quakers, to any full-fledged interaction rituals.

In the quantitative analysis of the 31 descriptive statements, we isolated four dimensions of ritual. One of them clearly distinguishes solemn and holiness rituals. The items forming this dimension and the interrelations among them are presented in Appendix Table 6-12.

The first four items describe the solemn style; the last four the holiness style. That these two subsets are inversely related affirms the validity of these types. All eight items were combined into a single measure of ritual and style. Appendix Table 6-13 shows the distribution of Sunday services along this dimension. The greater frequency of the solemn style is a consequence of response bias in our sample. A more representative sample would show a more equal distribution along the dimension. The point to be emphasized about the distribution shown in Appendix Table 6-13 is the variety of rituals in Middletown. Clearly, it is more realistic, as the Lynds intimated, to think not of a typology but of a continuum.

Chapter 7

Private Devotions

Acts of private devotion are attempts to communicate with the divine. They may or may not result in a perceived encounter with the divine. For purposes of definition, it is enough that the seeker *tries* to communicate or to understand.[1]

Acts of private devotion are enjoined by the Bible, which is believed by 9 out of every 10 Middletown adults to be a divinely inspired book, at least in part.[2] It calls the faithful to prayer: "As for me, I will call upon God; and the Lord shall save me. Evening, and morning, and at noon, will I pray and cry aloud: and He shall hear my voice. . . . Cast thy burden upon the Lord, and He shall sustain thee" (Ps. 55:16-17, 22) and "But thou, when thou prayest, enter into thy closet, and when thou has shut thy door, pray to thy Father which is in secret; and thy Father which seeth in secret shall reward thee openly" (Matt. 6:6). Private acts of devotion performed in one's closet, one's home, or even in one's mind are, as these quotations suggest, essential to the practice of Christianity.

Devotional practice is particularly worthy of study because, unlike knowledge and belief, it involves overt behavior and, unlike ritual, it is rarely performed for nonreligious reasons. Religious devotion is a good indicator of religious commitment because there is little point to the performance of private devotions for other than religious motives (Stark and Glock 1968, 108).

Examples of private devotional acts include Bible reading, prayer, meditation, and fasting. Frequency of personal prayer is the indicator of religious devotion that has been most often used in previous research (Stark and Glock 1968, 109). Prayer, wrote Stark and Glock, is "undoubtedly the primary private ritual expectation of Christian churches."[3] Prayer is universally encouraged by Christian ministers, and it is available to everyone, rich and poor, solitary and crowded, busy and leisured.

Another reason to study private devotions is that there seems to be a logical sequence in the various expressions of religious commitment. John Finney's analysis of that sequence uses data from a survey of religious commitment to suggest that, although a variety of background factors affect the five dimensions of religious commitment he described, ritual practice is logically antecedent to the other four. Knowledge is antecedent to experience, belief, and devotion; experience is antecedent to belief and devotion; and belief is antecedent to devotion. The other dimensions of religious commitment all lead, in one way or another, to private devotions, and these, in turn, strengthen the other forms of commitment.

> . . . private activities, such as prayer and Bible reading, help to legitimate one's religious experience and beliefs. In this context, private devotional activities are behaviors, the purpose of which is to incorporate an understanding of one's religious experiences into religious terminology and symbolism. Devotional activities thus provide evidence that one's beliefs are "true" (Finney 1978, 22-23).

Private devotions seem to be affected less by external, nonreligious factors than some of the other dimensions of religious commitment. One may have ulterior motives for engaging in religious rituals in public; one may acquire religious knowledge without religious experience; one may assert a belief without inner conviction.

Private devotions represent a search for contact with the sacred, a reaching out through prayer, through some denial of the secular or the profane, or through immersion in "the Word." In contrast, the experiential "encounter" conveys a sense of communication achieved, of prayers answered. Thus, the devotional and experiential aspects of religious commitment are reciprocal; they represent two sides of the same communication process.

Devotionalism in Middletown

The Lynds had little to say about the private devotions of Middletown people. Instead, they (1929, 338-39) described the dominant religious beliefs (the broad consensus about the all sufficiency of Christianity, the divinity of Jesus, and the existence of heaven and hell), the ambivalence toward organized religion, and the workings of Middletown's religious organizations. They quoted local ministers to the effect that there had been a decline in home-centered religious devotions such as daily prayer, Bible reading in an assembled family group, and even the verbal blessing of food before meals. The Lynds (1929, 343) concluded that "religious observances appear to be a less spontaneous and pervasive part of the life of the city today . . ." than in the preceding generation.

They approached the topic more closely in *Middletown in Transition*. After observing that outward forms of religious observance were seemingly unchanged by the Great Depression, they asked "whether the depression has affected the inner feeling of Middletown people as regards religion." They answered this question largely in the negative on the basis of comments by local ministers and other informants. They quoted a local physician who said that "there is no wave of religious feeling in [Middletown] in the depression, despite the prediction of the ministerial profession that the depression would bring people closer to God." Not only were Middletown people *not* returning to God, said the Lynds, but there was evidence of a continued decline of religious interest: children were increasingly alienated from organized religion, and the decline of Sabbath observance and the secularization of Middletown's other institutions had continued. Religion in Middletown, they concluded, was "an emotionally stabilizing agent" but not much more (Lynd and Lynd 1937, 301, 303-8, 315-18).

Part of the "Middletown spirit" recorded by the Lynds during the mid-1930s was the belief that, although God might not intercede in relatively unimportant matters, "through faith and prayer one may rely upon His assistance in the most important concerns of life." Reliance on the Almighty was said to be greater among women than men and greater in the working class than the business class.

Middletown people vary widely in the literalness of their belief in prayer. In general, women believe in it more than men and the South Side more than the North Side. While only the women in a South Side church might ordinarily pledge themselves to pray for a piece of legislation, as did one group in the case of the Eighteenth Amendment, in times of great personal or familiar emergency even many businessmen will admit to close friends that they "prayed" over it. "Not," as one of them explained, "that I exactly thought it would make any difference, but my wife was so sick I just wasn't going to leave any stone unturned" (Lynd and Lynd 1937, 417).

The Lynds had no hard evidence that the working class ("south side") was more prayerful than the business class, and their evidence for the greater spirituality of women than men was similarly impressionistic and anecdotal since they had interveiwed only women in their 1924 community survey. However, the idea that women were more religious than men found some support in the results of the 1924 high school surveys. Girls were more likely than boys to agree that "Christianity is the one true religion and all peoples should be converted to it" (92 percent to 83 percent) and that "The Bible is a sufficient guide to all the problems of modern life" (68 percent to 58 percent). There were similar differences in other religious attitudes.

Gender Differences in Religion

That women are generally more religious than men (and more devotional where that has been studied specifically) has been a consistent finding in American surveys. Almost three decades ago, Thomas summarized the existing research literature in these words: "All surveys of religious beliefs and practices indicate that women are more religiously inclined than men." He then corroborated that pattern in his analysis of a 1952 national survey. In that survey, 68 percent of the women in the country had reported that they offered "night prayers," compared to 54 percent of the men, and more than half of the women said that they prayed twice a day or oftener, compared to about one-third of the men (Thomas 1963, 128).

Contemporary surveys continue to show greater female spirituality. According to a national survey conducted by the Gallup organization in 1976, more women than men had "a great deal of confidence" in organized religion (41 percent to 35 percent); women were also more likely to attend church during an average week (46 percent to 37 percent), to say that their religious beliefs were "very important" to them (65 percent to 50 percent), to have had a "born again" experience (39 percent to 28 percent), and to report a "sudden religious insight or awakening" (34 percent to 27 percent) (Gallup Opinion Index, 1977-1978, 13, 17, 27, 43, 54).

Although we cannot be sure that Middletown men of the 1920s and 1930s were less likely than Middletown women to engage in private devotions, the Lynds and their local informants apparently thought this was so. Today in Middletown, men pray less than women do. Twenty-five percent of the men in the 1978 religion survey said they *never* prayed, compared to only 7 percent of the women, although, on the other hand, a somewhat higher proportion of men said that they prayed regularly. Table 7-1 provides a detailed breakdown, by sex, of the responses to the question "Do you every pray privately?"

Table 7-1
Frequency of Private Prayer by Gender, in Middletown, 1978

Response	Men	Women
Never pray	25%	7%
Pray only on very special occasions	25	17
Pray quite often, but not at regular times	19	50
Pray regularly, at least once a week	31	25
	100%	99%
Number of cases (N)	(72)	(151)

Source: Middletown III religion survey, 1978.

But the social-class difference in piety that the Lynds described has not persisted at all. Working-class Middletowners in 1978 were not more given to prayer than business-class Middletowners. In this, as in so many other respects, there seems to have been a convergence of business-class and working-class life-styles. Table 7-2 lists the responses to the same question, broken down by sex and social class. It would seem that there were no substantial differences between the responses of business- and working-class respondents; almost three-fourths of the women in both classes and between one-third and one-half of the men said that they prayed regularly or quite often. Differences that exist indicate more prayer by business-class people, but the differences are slight, and the subsamples are small. The safest conclusion is that class differences in the inclination to pray are insignificant.

Table 7-2
Frequency of Private Prayer, by Social Class and Gender, in Middletown, 1978

Responses	Business Class			Working Class		
	Men	Women	Total	Men	Women	Total
Never pray	29%	9%	17%	21%	8%	11%
Pray only on very special occasions	19	17	18	42	22	26
Pray quite often but not at regular times	21	42	34	5	48	39
Pray regularly, at least once a week	31	31	31	32	22	24
	100%	99%	100%	100%	100%	100%
Number of cases (N)	(42)	(64)	(106)	(19)	(64)	(83)

Source: Middletown III religion survey, 1978.

Another set of data corroborates this finding. In the 1978 community survey, Middletown women were asked what gave them "courage to go on" when they were "thoroughly discouraged." When responses to this question were coded thematically, we discovered that about one-third of both business- and working-class women had mentioned their religious faith as something that gave them courage. Religious themes accounted for 13 percent of all themes mentioned by business-class women and 16 percent of all themes mentioned by working-class women. Further details about the analysis of these responses are given in Appendix Table 7-3.

Let us carry the question of social class and private devotions a little farther by asking whether private prayer in Middletown is influenced by education, family income, or self-ratings of social class.[4] As it turns out, none of these measures is significantly related to private devotions in Middletown. About two-thirds of the respondents at each educational level said that they prayed quite often or regularly. Though those who held advanced degrees were most likely to say they *never* prayed (21 percent), they were also the most likely, along with persons who had completed some college, to say they prayed regularly (33 percent). People who had not completed high school were the least likely to say that they prayed regularly (14 percent). Family income showed no relationship at all to frequency of prayer, and, as can be seen in Appendix Tables 7-4 and 7-5, the frequencies of private prayer were almost identical for people who rated themselves as working-class and as upper-middle-class.

Most of the prayers offered by Middletown people are personal and informal. More than half (55 percent) of the 196 respondents who prayed said that they made up their own prayers. Forty-one percent said that sometimes they made up their own and sometimes used the words of prayers they had been taught. Only a tiny fraction, 4 percent, said their personal prayers were limited to prayers in set language.

If we had to choose a single indicator of devotion, it would be prayer, for it is the only private devotional activity that is practiced by the majority of Middletowners. But the religion survey asked about other kinds of devotional activity as well, including meditating, fasting, and spiritual counseling. Responses to these questions were distributed this way:

"Do you fast?" (N = 221)

Never	59%
Once in a while	34
Frequently	7
	100%

"Do you ever practice meditation?" (N = 227)

No	68%
Yes, almost every day	11
Yes, at least once a week	6
Yes, several times a month	4
Yes, several times a year	7
Yes, frequency not given	4
	100%

"When you feel troubled about a serious thing, which of the following do you usually do?" (N = 228)[5]

I meditate	14%
I pray	56%
I talk with a minister, priest, or spiritual leader	12%

About 4 of every 10 Middletown adults said that they fast, and about 1 of every 3 practiced meditation at least a few times a year. At least 1 in 8, when seriously troubled, sought help from a minister or a spiritual leader, and more than 1 in 2 said they prayed when they were troubled.

Devotion and Discouragement

Another perspective on private devotions in Middletown can be gained from women's reports about how they deal with personal discouragement. The 333 women interviewed in our replication of the Lynds' community survey were asked, "What are the thoughts and plans that give you courage to go on when you are thoroughly discouraged?" Analysis of their answers revealed 17 common themes, 5 of them related to religion. Three of these themes—prayer, scripture reading, and meditation—involved activities that can be defined as devotional practice.

Statements of religious belief were heard much more often in response to this question than reports of devotional practice because the question referred to "thoughts and plans" rather than to practice. Nevertheless, 1 woman in 12 (11 percent of the business-class respondents, 6 percent of the working-class respondents) said that her private devotions gave her the "courage to go on."

Correlates of Devotion

A Summary Index of Devotion

In an effort to summarize our findings on private devotion, we constructed a devotional index based on four questions in the religion survey: the three items on frequency of prayer, fasting, and meditation and the item on devotional behavior when faced with serious personal trouble.

This last question read, "When you feel troubled about a serious thing, which of the following do you usually do?" There followed a list of nine possible responses, and people were asked to check those that fit themselves. The proportions of the sample checking each response are listed in Table 7-6. Sixty-one percent of our sample reported at least one devotional response in time of trouble; 18 percent reported more than one.

In constructing the composite index of personal devotion, we divided the respondents into two groups: those who had and those who had not checked one of the three devotional responses to personal trouble. Similar divisions were made of those who did or did not report prayer, fasting, and meditation. The distributions are shown in Table 7-7.

Next, the devotional index was computed by assigning one point for each of the items on which a person gave the devotional response. For example, someone who said she prayed regularly,

Table 7-6
Usual Responses to Troubled Feelings, Middletown Adults, 1978

Response	Percentage
Try to face the problem myself	68
Pray	56
Talk with a family member	49
Talk with a friend	48
Meditate	14
Talk with a minister, priest, or spiritual leader	12
Talk with a doctor	7
Talk with a professional counselor	5
Try to ignore or forget the problem	4
Number of cases (N)	(228)

Note: The percentages are not additive.

Source: Middletown III religion survey, 1978.

Table 7-7
Percentages Reporting Selected Devotional Responses
to Personal Trouble, Middletown Adults, 1978

Devotional Response	Percentage
Prays regularly or quite often	67
Has at least one devotional response to personal trouble	60
Fasts once in a while or frequently	41
Has practiced meditation	32

Note: The percentages are not additive.

Source: Middletown III religion survey, 1978.

prayed when personally troubled, sometimes fasted, and occasionally practiced meditation would have a devotional index score of four; someone who did none of these things would have a devotional index score of zero. Table 7-8 shows the distribution of

Table 7-8
Distribution by Devotional Index Scores, Middletown Adults, 1978

Index	Level of Devotion	Percentage
0	None	17%
1	Low	18
2	Moderate	30
3	High	24
4	Very high	11
		100%
Number of cases (N)		(230)

Source: Middletown III religion survey, 1978.

respondents by devotional index scores. This index distributes the population much more normally (in the statistical sense) than any of the questions that compose it.[6]

Middletown's religion-centered people are indistinguishable from their neighbors. Women do not score significantly higher on the devotional index than men; and education, self-defined social class, occupation, and family income are not significantly related to devotion. The business class does not seem to be less devotional than the working class, the well educated are not less devotional than the uneducated, and the well-to-do are not less devotional than the poor, despite our expectations. (See Appendix Tables 7-5 and 7-9.)

Two characteristics that *do* seem to make a difference are age and denominational background. Generally speaking, young adults are less devotional than older adults. We cannot say whether this is a function of chronological age or of the values prevailing in a particular generation, but 39 percent of the respondents under age 30 scored low on the devotional index and fewer than 1 in 4 scored at a high or very high level.

Those whose denominational backgrounds were Catholic, Baptist, Pentecostal, Nazarene, or "other Christian" were likely to show a high or very high devotional index; about half of them did so.[7] Those with Methodist, Presbyterian, and Episcopalian backgrounds reported much less devotion, and among the few respondents who had no religious background or preference *no one* scored high on the devotional index.

Devotion and Belief

Middletown people who practice private devotions tend to be religious believers, but many people who say they believe strongly are not devout.[8] Two-thirds of Middletown's adults affirmed that they "really know God exists," and almost the same fraction affirmed that "Jesus is the divine son of God and I have no doubts about it." (See Appendix Table 7-10.) However, only half of these "true believers" were devout (index scores of three or four), and slightly more than a third had low scores of zero or one. In other words, only about half of the believers were devout, but about 90 percent of the devout said that they knew God existed or that they had no doubts about the divinity of Jesus.

Consider this finding in another way: persons who seldom or never engage in private devotions are almost as likely to be believers as nonbelievers, but a devout nonbeliever is a very rare bird.

If most devout people are believers but only about half of the believers are devout, the effect of devotion on belief would seem to be stronger than the effect of belief on devotion. Recall that in Finney's (1978, 23) causal model of the connections among the dimensions of religious commitment, religious beliefs stimulated devotional activities. The reverse linkage, whereby devotional activities stimulate belief, was mentioned in his discussion but not represented in the model itself. Our results suggest that the model might be modified to account for the reinforcement of religious belief by devotional practice.

Devotion and the Relevance of Religion

How do the devout people differ from other residents of Middletown? We asked the respondents in the religion survey how they thought their religious faith influenced their choice of friends, their voting for political candidates, their leisure activities, their treatment of their families, and their performance on their jobs.

Regardless of their level of devotion, there was a consistent order in the respondents' perceptions of how their religion influenced their lives: they saw the most influence in their family lives and the least in their choice of political candidates. As Appendix Table 7-11 shows, there is a very strong relationship between private devotions and the influence attributed to religion in other aspects of life. Devout persons saw their religious faith as having a "great influence" in the way they treated their families (78 percent), how they performed their jobs (67 percent), in how they handled their relationships with friends (57 percent), and in how they spent their leisure time (49 percent). But only 29 percent of them said that they were much influenced by religion in their voting for political candidates.

People who did not practice private devotions were likely to say that their religious faith had *no* influence on these aspects of their lives. Only in family relations did the nondevout perceive some religious influence. One out of four of the nondevout respondents (index scores of zero or one) said that religion had a great influence on the way they treated their families, and almost two out of three thought it had *some* influence.

Thus, the devout people in Middletown view religion as permeating most sectors of their lives. The nondevout see religion as largely irrelevant to work, leisure, friendship, and politics but closely linked to family life.

The following excerpt from an interview with a working-class respondent illustrates the devout attitude toward secular activities in an extreme form.

Well, everybody that goes to church is not a Christian. Everybody that says they're a Christian, is not a Christian. . . . That's the way I figure. That's the way I watch, I watch as well as pray. Well, I can look at a person and just about weigh him out. How he or she, you know, whatever, and talk with them a little bit. Then I can figure out whether he's lying to me or not. And I come close. I don't miss far. And if you trust in the Lord and ask him to lead and guide you and direct your mind, you know, whatever you do will be right. And pleasing in the sight of God, that it will work out, but you've got to have faith, and you have to continue to pray, you just can't pray today and forget it and pray tomorrow and all that. You constantly pray.

You take, for instance, I get bored at my work. Someone has sent up for me to do something, but if they know what to do why send for me? Just stand back and let me figure what to do, just get out of the way, don't tell me what to do, let me figure it out. I get kinda upset, I whisper a little to myself. Some people cusses a lot and I don't cuss. And they say things that I really don't approve of, and it upsets me but I whisper a little prayer while I'm maybe listening to what they're saying, and it helps me and then I'll tell you exactly what's wrong with the machine. And I believe to my soul that the Lord directs my mind. I don't leave a machine. I go in there second shift, and they got all kinds of machines broken down. I get them going in just a few minutes; it has to be the Lord. I got it worked out. I got the machine going when it's been out all day. . . .

If you trust in the Lord and ask him to lead and direct your mind and whatever you're asking, he'll do it. May not come just now, but it will.

Devotion and Community Involvement

It might be supposed that the devout people, being more committed than others to prayer, fasting, and meditation, would be more "other worldly," more concerned with their relationship with God and the supernatural and less involved in the here-and-now and with other people in the community. Or it might be assumed that devout people would be more stable and therefore *more* involved in the community. We were able to test these alternatives by using as measures how many families in the neighborhood the respondents knew personally, how many close friends or relatives they had in Middletown, and how many memberships they maintained in voluntary associations ("clubs, service organizations, unions, school organizations or lodges").[9]

The data seem to show that involvement with friends and neighbors *increases* with devotional activity. The higher the respondent's score on the devotional index, the more neighbors he or she knew ($r = .24$) and the more close friends and relatives he or she had ($r = .21$).[10]

The respondents' scores on the devotional index were not related to number of memberships in voluntary associations they held ($r = .04$), but they were not inversely related either. Devout people were heavily involved in religious organizations and activities but no more or less likely than their nondevout neighbors to belong to other voluntary associations.

Most devout people were regular churchgoers. Among the respondents in the religion survey, 76 percent of those who prayed regularly in private also attended church at least once a week, and only 4 percent said they never attended church. The frequency of private prayer is quite closely related to church attendance, as Table 7-12 shows.

Table 7-12
Frequency of Private Prayer, by Church Attendance, Middletown, 1978

Frequency of Private Prayer	Percentage Attending Church in Past Year
Never	38
Only on very special occasions	42
Quite often but not regularly	77
Regularly, at least weekly	90

Source: Middletown III religion survey, 1978.

Despite the close correlation between devotion and church attendance, there are people in Middletown who pray, meditate, and read the Bible but are quite detached from organized religion. One business-class respondent told us:

We hardly ever go to church. We read the Bible about 20 minutes every evening and discuss take-offs on it. I think our way is more meaningful, but I suppose others would not classify us as very religious. I go to several religious speakers on campus whenever they come. In a way I would consider that a religious service.

The author of a letter to the editor in a Middletown newspaper described himself, in effect, as both devout and anticlerical.

We all have a Bible, I'm sure. I don't need anyone to tell me how to be a Christian. I don't intend to buy their prayers if they don't give them freely. I don't need them. I would advise everyone to read "Elmer Gantry" by Sinclair Lewis. That tells exactly what my opinion is about the high-toned ministers and evangelists reaching out their little "paws" for every cent they can rake in, building big rich churches, riding in their Cadillacs, wearing their expensive clothes. Do they ever help the poor? I ask you.

According to our survey, such persons constitute about a fifth of the devout population and perhaps an eighth of the total adult population. They sounded like this:

I believe that I can worship God at home as well as I could by going to church.

I find organized church too structured. It interferes with my personal religious feelings. It "programs" me.

I am religious and a Christian, but not denominational. I do not believe that I must attend services in a church.

I feel that one does not need a public place to declare his beliefs. If I feel the need to communicate with myself or out loud, I do it in private.

I feel I can be close to God in my own home too—not just in church.

There is some local recognition of the fact that some "religious" people do not attend church. In 1977, a controversial evangelistic campaign was sponsored at Middletown's state university by The Way International. The Way's national leader was quoted in the local newspaper as affirming that "the theology of The Way conflicts with conventional Christian denominations in many respects; therefore, we discourage people who are interested in The Way from participating in conventional denominational services." A year later, the local newspaper described the campaign of Young Life, an evangelistic movement aimed at young people: "Young Life doesn't get into religion: it gets into Christ." The movement was described as affirmative and informal: "It reaches out to young people with the positive, powerful love of Christ without preaching religion. It presents Jesus on a social level, informally, going out to where the kids are."

A November 1977 article on the religious preferences of students at the state university maintained that there was a continuing trend away from preference for organized denominations but an increased concern among the students about "the search for spiritual meaning in life." Three months later, the local newspaper ran a feature article on the national "surge in on-campus religion" that stated:

A campus movement these days centers on a theme of "God is Alive." The surge in religious activities had been documented in a survey of some of the nation's top private colleges. . . . It comes across strong and steady. It indicates the "God is dead" movement that dominated campuses in the late 1960s is dead or dying.

Among persons who identified with a specific denomination, 16 percent of those with devotional index scores of three (high) and 9 percent of those with scores of four (very high) said that they went to church only "several times a year" or "once or twice a year." Nevertheless, devotion is a better predictor of churchgoing than churchgoing of devotion.

Among the devout respondents (scores of three or four) in the religion survey who identified with a denomination, 76 percent attended church weekly or more often. Of the respondents in the same survey who attended church weekly or more often, 61 percent were devout. The same pattern appears more dramatically in the area of private prayer and church attendance. Seventy-six percent of those who prayed privately every week also attended church every week, but only 46 percent of those who attended church every week prayed privately every week.

Devotion and Happiness

Does religion make people happy? From the responses we received to the question in the housewives' survey "What difference would it make in your daily life if you became convinced that there is no loving God caring for you?" it appears that most Middletown women see faith as a means to happiness, or peace of mind, or mental health or as an affirmative and actualizing approach to life. Typically, they said that without the protection of faith their lives would be depressed, miserable, unendurable, meaningless, terrible, or frightening. "I'd be afraid to even get up in the morning," said a business-class housewife. Another woman said calmly, "If I didn't believe in an afterlife, there would be no direction or purpose to living; this life stinks."

The popular belief in a direct connection between religious faith and personal happiness has been reported many times before but has not often been corroborated by researchers. When put to the statistical test, the advantages religious people enjoy in happiness or quality of life turn out to be modest. For example, McCready and Greeley's (1976, 99-103, 107) analysis of a national survey of "ultimate values" showed that persons classified as "hopeful" were far happier than those classified as "pessimistic" but that "religious optimists" were "secular optimists." In their summary of the effects of beliefs on social behavior, McCready and Greeley (1976, 127) affirmed that people's ultimate values, which include their religious values, have *some* effect on social attitudes. The link, however, is complex, and the direct effects are relatively modest.

The relationship between ultimate values and social attitudes is complex and indirect. . . . Only a modest fourteen percent of the variance in trust is explained by the model . . . but we did not expect very large correlations. . . . Ultimate values, world view, basic beliefs, whatever we call these things, they do influence practical ethical decisions. Those who, for whatever reasons, reject the idea that human life is without meaning and purpose are likely to be happier people.

The modest relationship between ultimate values and perceptions of personal happiness is paralleled for at least two other dimensions of religiosity, the experiential and the devotional. One study of the relationship between the religious experience and "self-actualization" of college students concluded "that high and low self-actualizers alike have religious experiences and that such experiences cannot inherently be viewed as either symptoms of pathology or evidence of positive mental health." (Larsen 1979, 39, 44, 46-47).

Eric Cohen (1977) argued persuasively that Christians should not necessarily expect mental health (or self-actualization or happiness) to accompany "holiness."[11] He maintained that, although personal holiness must eventually lead to happiness (in the metaphysical long run), in the short run there is not much connection between holiness and mental health, and what correlations appear should be weak.

It may be true that being in good mental and physical health might facilitate movement toward God but so might suffering. . . . Man's movement toward holiness ultimately moves him toward a healthier position, yet we need to realize as Christians that God's methods of making us holy may involve rather drastic means. We may need to go through experiences of tremendous stress and anxiety before true dependence upon God and true holiness become possibilities for us. We may experience psychological disorder and pathology along the road to holiness and wholeness. . . .

. . . holiness ultimately yields wholeness and soundness of mind, but . . . our experience of holiness as a progressive reality does not always involve a condition of mental stability and health. . . . This relationship is neither one of full identity nor full independence, but it is rather correlational (positive) and does involve some degree of causality. The degree of correlation is small in light of interactional possibilities, but nevertheless we would generally expect that holiness would coincide and work to facilitate a condition of mental health. Exceptions to this are prevalent (thus the small correlation), but nevertheless they are exceptions (Cohen 1977, 289-90).

The relationship between devotionalism and happiness in our religion survey follows this formula: it is positive but weak. Those who prayed regularly were twice as likely as other people in the sample to describe themselves as "very happy" (32 percent versus 18 percent). Even so, the relationship between frequency of prayer and personal happiness does not reach statistical significance.

The correlation between the devotional index and happiness was a negligible .05; the correlations with marital happiness were even lower. Middletown's devout people are not appreciably happier than their nondevout neighbors.

Conclusion

Contemporary Middletown, as we have said elsewhere, is surprisingly pious, even when the prayers and observances that are parts of regular church services are discounted. Two-thirds of its people pray "regularly" or "quite often" in private. Half of them pray when troubled, and almost half of them sometimes fast.

Chapter 8

Catholics and Protestants

Catholics constituted a rather small minority in the Middletown of the 1920s; there was only 1 Catholic for every 15 Protestants. Catholicism has grown considerably in Middletown during the past 50 years, and today there is 1 Catholic for every 6 Protestants. Catholic authorities indicate that most of the growth has resulted from the immigration of Catholics to the community, rather than from the conversion of Protestants or the unchurched: "There are just lots and lots of Catholics who have moved into the community."

Middletown is divided east and west into two Catholic parishes of roughly equal geographical area. One has approximately 1,000 families and the other about half that number. There is also a parish associated with the state university; it serves 3,000 Catholic students and about 450 families who have chosen to affiliate with the University Church rather than one of the neighborhood churches. Middletown, however, is still a predominantly Protestant community. The 1978 phone directory listed 134 Protestant churches. The entire spectrum of Protestant denominations from traditional Episcopalians to fundamental Pentecostals can be seen in Middletown. The houses of worship include majestic edifices with stained glass windows, modest one- or two-story chapels, and converted office buildings and storefronts.

In the midst of the Catholics and Protestants, a few non-Christian groups struggle to survive in Middletown; they account for about 5 percent of the adult population. Aside from the small Jewish community, the non-Christians are concentrated among the students and faculty at the state university who are adherents of Buddhism, Hare Krishna, Scientology, Transcendental Meditation, and the Unification Church.

Catholics in Middletown attend church more sedulously than do Protestants. As indicated in Table 8-1, in comparison to Protestants, Catholics in 1978 reported significantly higher levels of church attendance.

Table 8-1
Church Attendance of Catholics and Protestants in Middletown, 1978

Church Attendance	Catholics (N = 138)	Protestants (N = 729)
Weekly	59%	37%
At least monthly	12	14
Several times a year	12	17
Special occasions	10	15
Not at all	7	17
Total	100%	100%

Sources: Middletown III men's occupational survey, women's occupational survey, religion survey, community survey, and government services survey, 1978.

Although Catholics attended more frequently, Protestants were significantly more involved in church activities. Twenty-six percent of the Protestants reported that they held office in their churches, but only 4 percent of the Catholics did. Protestant churches offer many more opportunities than Catholic churches for lay people to engage in church activities and to lead religious services.

About the same proportions of Catholics and Protestants donated money to their churches during 1978 (70 percent of the Catholics and 82 percent of the Protestants), but Protestants gave more. Almost a third of the Protestants contributed a tithe (10 percent) of their income to the church, while not a single Catholic did so. This difference is not surprising in light of a difference in Catholic and Protestant expectations about contributions. Although Protestants in almost every denomination are exhorted to pay a tithe, Catholic priests in Middletown report that their parishioners are asked to give 5 percent of their incomes to the church and another 5 percent to secular charities.

Catholics seem to have a more intense experience of personal worship. Significantly more Catholics, 89 percent, reported that they prayed in private every day, compared to 69 percent of the Protestants. There was, however, no significant difference in the relative numbers of those who meditated or contemplated their relationship to God.

We asked the respondents to react to three statements of Christian orthodoxy: the existence of God, the divinity of Jesus, and the authority of the Bible. Seventy-three percent of the Catholics and 70 percent of the Protestants had no doubts about the existence of God. Forty-four percent of the Protestants and 39 percent of the Catholics said they believed the Bible to be the word of God. Middletown's Catholics and Protestants do not appear to differ significantly in theology.

We were interested in determining whether people feel that their religious faith affects their daily lives. The proportions reporting that religion "greatly influenced" their choice of friends, treatment of their families, work performance, leisure-time activities, and support of political candidates are shown in Table 8-2.

Table 8-2
Percentages of Catholics and Protestants "Greatly Influenced"
by Their Religion, Middletown, 1978

Activity	Catholics (N = 26)	Protestants (N = 136)
How I treat my family	55	60
How I perform my job	45	41
The friends I have	28	36
What I do in my leisure time	22	29
The political candidates I support	6	13

Source: Middletown III religion survey, 1978.

The majority of both Protestants and Catholics reported that their religious beliefs and practices "greatly influenced" how they treated their families. Many reported that religion affected their job performance. About a third said that religion greatly influenced their choice of leisure-time activities. The small differences between the responses of Catholics and Protestants are not statistically significant.

In sum, the religious attitudes and practices of Protestants and Catholics in Middletown are strikingly similar. They share common beliefs about God, Jesus Christ, and the Bible. Both groups feel that religion has a real impact on their personal lives. Catholics attend religious services a bit more often than Protestants, but the difference is less than it used to be. Both Catholics and Protestants provide the financial support their religious leaders ask for. It takes a fine screen to distinguish Catholics from Protestants in contemporary Middletown.

The New Tolerance

Catholicism was mentioned infrequently in the Lynds' description of 1924 Middletown, but the strong anti-Catholic sentiments of that time were apparent. The Ku Klux Klan came to Middletown just after World War I; by 1924, it had a large following among men from both social classes. The Klan was bitterly hostile toward Catholics.

. . . Tales against the Catholics ran like wildfire through the city. In a sermon on "The Godliness of America" the minister of a thriving working class church earnestly passed on to his flock this story:

"They say the Pope isn't wanted in Italy. France has been approached and she doesn't want him. The Balkans say no. Russia—'not on your life!'. England, Germany, Switzerland, Japan—all refuse; and they say the Catholics are building a great cathedral in our national capital at Washington, which is to become his home." Then as though half-ashamed at relaying this gossip, the minister added, "I don't know this; it's just talk, but that's what they say" (Lynd and Lynd 1929, 482).

The Klan distributed such anti-Catholic literature as a pamphlet entitled "Confessions of Helen Jackson, An Escaped Nun." Speakers proclaimed that the Klan must continue to march until the Catholics tore down the "prison walls" around their convents and nunneries.

Catholic parochial schools were targets of the same movement. The Lynds quoted part of a speech by a lawyer from the state capital attending a Klan rally in Middletown: "Lincoln said that no nation can exist half slave and half free. My friends, this nation cannot exist with half its children in the great American free schools and the other half being taught a different thing in the parochial schools" (Lynd and Lynd 1929, 483).

The Mother's Council, sponsored by Middletown's large churches, had replaced the PTA in Middletown in 1924. It brought mothers together to discuss the education of their children. According to one of its members, quoted by the Lynds, the best thing the council did during the early 1920s was to bring Catholic and Protestant mothers together in an effort to overcome anti-Catholic prejudice. The informant sadly reported that even this modest success was almost spoiled when a "minister's wife bitterly attacked the Catholic attitude towards Bible study in the schools" (Lynd and Lynd 1929, 293).

Older Catholics in Middletown still recall that during the 1920s and even into the 1930s their priests were subject to considerable abuse. They were pelted with tomatoes and jeered, and more than one cross was burned on the parish lawn.

Middletown's Protestant majority no longer exhibits much anti-Catholic prejudice. According to one of the parish priests:

It's very positive. There are elements of prejudice, of course. For the most part, I would say exceptionally good . . . I think there's a broader base of understanding on the part of people that are not Catholic, more so today than twenty years ago. Catholics of twenty years ago in Middletown were considered kind of a minority. As you know this was kind of a hotbed for the Klan and all the prejudice and all that came out of that.

There are a lot of groups which traditionally have been opposed to the Catholic church and they continue to do so. You hear a lot of negative things being said by some churches about the Catholic church, but I don't involve myself in the discussion, nor do we share that approach. It's here, I mean that's all I'm saying, is that it's here. There is some antagonism and interestingly enough most of the antagonism is from the very fundamentalist churches, it's not from the major part of the community. With the mainline churches we have no problem at all.

Serious criticism of the Catholic church or its representatives has disappeared for the most part except for an occasional fundamentalist sermon. Catholic priests are encouraged to participate in the County Ministerial Alliance. Most of them belong to it, and one served as president a few years ago.

The new amity between Protestants and Catholics was clearly reflected in our religion survey, in which we asked respondents actively affiliated with a Protestant denomination whether they associated with Catholics and whether they had participated in Catholic services (Table 8-3). Most Protestants had attended a service of one kind or another in a Catholic church, more than half had attended a mass, and an appreciable number had even taken communion. Almost half had contributed money to a Catholic charity. Clearly, unlike Middletowners 50 years ago, contemporary Middletown Protestants do not perceive Catholicism as evil or anti-American.

Table 8-3
Protestants' Participation in Catholic Services and Association with Catholics, 1978

Activity	Percentage of Protestants ($N = 133$)
Attended a Catholic mass	59
Attended a Catholic wedding or christening	71
Taken communion in a Catholic church	11
Contributed to a Catholic charity	42
Dated a Catholic	47
Had a Catholic as a close friend	87
Married a Catholic	5

Source: Middletown III religion survey, 1978.

A large majority of the Protestant respondents, 87 percent, had had a Catholic as a close friend. Nearly half had dated Catholics during their courtship years, and a few had married Catholics.

Only 20 active Catholics were included in the religion survey, and they responded to similar questions about their participation in Protestant activities. Although the comments must be analyzed with caution because of the small number in the sample, they do provide some insight into the Catholic experience in Middletown. All but 2 of the Catholics had participated in a Protestant service; the same number had attended a Protestant wedding or christening. Five had taken communion in a Protestant church, and 15 had contributed money to a Protestant charity. It appears that Catholics in Middletown feel welcome at Protestant services; presumably, this had not been the case during the 1920s.

Catholic respondents reported extensive social interaction with Protestants. All but 1 had had a close Protestant friend. Most had dated Protestants, and 10 of the 20 had married Protestants!

Although a few fundamentalist Protestant ministers may still rail against Catholicism, most Middletown Protestants accept their Catholic neighbors, go to church with them, invite them to their own churches, and, in general, treat them no differently than fellow Protestants. The Catholic minority is even more accepting of Protestants.

Family Life

According to Andrew Greeley (1977), sociological researchers have given little attention to whether unique family behavior patterns persist among Protestants, Catholics, and Jews in the United States. He reviewed several studies and concluded that Catholics marry later, divorce less, and have larger families than do Protestants. In Middletown, however, the differences between Catholics and Protestants in age at marriage and divorce are statistically insignificant. Average family size in the sample is very similar: Catholic families, 2.0 children, and Protestant families, 1.9 children; surprisingly, however, 41 percent of the Catholics interviewed had no children, compared to only 31 percent of the Protestants. The Catholics were slightly younger than the Protestants. The Catholics accounting for that difference, but young Catholic couples do seem to be having small families. At the other end of the scale, 24 percent of the Catholics but only 17 percent of the Protestants had four or more children.

Greeley (1977, 188-89) noted the same phenomenon: ". . . the larger Catholic family size is limited to those women between thirty-five and forty-five; under thirty-five Catholic married women may be having fewer children than Protestant women." Liu and Pallone (1970, 8-9) also reported that Catholic fertility declined during the later 1960s and early 1970s, and they offered a speculative explanation.

Perhaps the most important implication in the decline in fertility, however, is that the emphasis in family life among American Catholics seems to be shifting from parenthood coupled with total sacrifice of self-interest for the welfare of the children—under the benign smile of the Holy Mother, the Church, ever ready to proscribe the limitation of family—to conjugal love and/or companionship between a man and a woman—a family system characterized of industrially advanced societies.

Catholic families have long been stereotyped as patriarchal, with the husband as head of the household and the wife at home, but Greeley (1977, 187-88) recently discovered that ". . . the overwhelming minority of all the Catholic ethnic groups approve of working wives." When we asked Middletown husbands and wives who had the final say in family decisions, we heard very similar answers from Catholics and Protestants: 49 percent of the Protestants and 43 percent of the Catholics said "husband mostly" or "husband always"; 41 percent of both Catholics and Protestants said that authority was equally shared in their families.

Two measures of marital satisfaction were included in the surveys we conducted in 1978. Respondents were asked to rate the happiness of their marriages and also to rate their satisfaction with their mates. The ratings of marital happiness were very high and marginally higher among Protestants (Table 8-4). About half of all marriages were rated as "very happy"; most of the remainder as "pretty happy." The ratings of Protestant and Catholic respondents showed similar distributions.

Table 8-4
Marital Happiness, Middletown, 1978

Marital Happiness	Catholics (N = 78)	Protestants (N = 462)
Very happy	46%	53%
Pretty happy	38	37
Not too happy	12	8
Pretty or very unhappy	4	2
Total	100%	100%

Sources: Middletown III men's and women's occupational surveys, religion survey, community survey, and government services survey, 1978.

When we asked respondents about their satisfaction with family life, both Protestants and Catholics reported considerable satisfaction, but Protestants were significantly more satisfied (Table 8-5).

Table 8-5
Family Life Satisfaction of Catholics and Protestants, Middletown, 1978

Satisfaction with Family Life	Catholics (N = 26)	Protestants (N = 14)
A great deal	46%	65%
Quite a bit	42	22
Some, a little, none	13	13
Total	101%	100%

Source: Middletown III religion survey, 1978.

Greeley (1977, 212), in the excellent book on the American Catholic we have quoted several times already, concluded that ". . . Catholic ethnics are still different in the fundamental matter of family structure and they are likely to continue to be different. There is, therefore, bound to be some tension between Catholics and others." In Middletown we found Catholic-Protestant differences in family life to be too slight to generate much tension between Catholics and their neighbors, although Protestants did seem to be a bit happier.

The Protestant Ethic

Considerable research has been carried out over the past five decades comparing Protestants and Catholics with respect to educational achievement, occupational status, and income. Some of this research has tested the theory that Protestants are more likely than Catholics to have successful careers because of the "Protestant ethic." Max Weber (1958) in his classic work *The Protestant Ethic and the Spirit of Capitalism* originally published in 1904 suggested that Protestant beliefs facilitated the growth of capitalism, although he said it less emphatically than is sometimes supposed. The important Protestant beliefs that are reputed to encourage capitalism are (1) the belief that hard work is virtuous, (2) the belief that economic judgments should be made on rational grounds and not according to tradition or sentiment, and (3) the belief that worldly prosperity is a mark of God's favor. The belief in the virtue of work can be illustrated by the words of Martin Luther, a principal figure in the Protestant Reformation (quoted by Lenski 1961, 93).

Your work is a very sacred matter. God delights in it, and through it he wants to bestow his blessing on you. This praise of work should be inscribed on all your tools, on the forehead and the face that sweats from toiling. For the world does not consider labor a blessing. Therefore it flees and hates it . . . but the pious who fear the Lord, labor with a ready and cheerful heart; for they know God's commandment and will. Thus a pious farmer sees this verse written on his wagon and plow, a cobbler sees it on his leather and awl, a laborer sees it on wood and iron; "Happy shalt thou be, and it shall be well with thee".

In the Catholic perspective of Luther's time, work was a necessary evil, the penalty for Adam's fall in the Garden of Eden.

According to the Protestant ethic, wealth was not to be squandered on comfort or pleasure but was to be invested and reinvested in profitable enterprises. Early modern Catholicism still condemned the lending of money at interest as usury on the grounds that the lender would prosper from another's misfortune.

Those investigators who have attributed achievement orientation to the Protestant ethic have assumed that there are variations in the degree to which different Protestant denominations hold Calvinist attitudes toward work and wealth but have expected Protestants in general to be more achievement oriented than Catholics and Protestants with respect to educational achievement, occupational status, and family income.

An early study along these lines was conducted by Cantril (1943), who analyzed data collected in two national surveys in 1939 and 1940 from more than 13,000 respondents in the United States. Cantril found a slightly higher level of educational achievement among Protestants; 15 percent of the Protestants in his sample but only 7 percent of the Catholics had graduated from college. The percentages of high school graduates in the sample were very similar, however: 33 percent of the Catholics and 34 percent of the Protestants.

Cantril controlled for education and compared respondents' incomes. He discovered that at all educational levels Protestants enjoyed higher incomes. Although the differences were modest, they were consistent with the expectation that Protestants would achieve more than Catholics.

Another early study was conducted in Madison, Wisconsin, where information was collected from nearly 25,000 respondents in 1944 (Bultena 1949). Seventeen percent of the Protestants worked in professional occupations but only 9 percent of the Catholics. At the other end of the scale, the difference was smaller; 50 percent of the Catholics and 45 percent of the Protestants were "laborers." Protestants reported an average housing value of $3,355, compared to $3,151 for Catholics. Although these differences were slight, they were interpreted as supporting the hypothesis.

In March 1957, the U.S. Bureau of the Census collected information about religious affiliation and other matters from more than 35,000 households in the United States. This large study provided a great deal of information about the educational and occupational characteristics of Catholics and Protestants in the United States during the 1950s. Protestants in the sample had a median educational achievement of 11.3 years, compared to 10.4 years for Catholics. Labor-force participation was nearly identical for the two populations (81 percent of males over 14 years old were in the labor force during the spring of 1957), and their occupational distributions were also very similar: 11 percent of the Protestants and 9 percent of the Catholics were in professional occupations, 14 percent of the Protestants and 13 percent of the Catholics were managers, and so on.

Catholic men reported a bit more income for 1956 than Protestant men: $3,956 versus $3,728. Goldstein (1969) suspected that Protestant concentration in the South and in rural areas was responsible for the unexpectedly favorable showing of Catholics. He controlled for region and found that Protestant men in urban areas had slightly higher incomes than did their Catholic neighbors. Because the differences were so small and so strongly affected by regional and urban location, Goldstein predicted that they would soon disappear.

The best-known study involving the Protestant ethic is probably Gerhard Lenski's *The Religious Factor* (1961). Lenski interviewed 650 people in the Detroit metropolitan area during the spring of 1958. The purpose of the study was to discover the effects of religion on daily life. In Lenski's (1961, 1) words:

God is concerned with the whole of man's lives: on at least this one point all churches agree. He is not merely the Lord of the Sabbath, but is equally concerned with men's activities on the other six days of the week: their work, their play, their politics, their family life.

But how does this doctrine work in practice? Does a man's religious commitment *really* influence his everyday actions, especially a man who lives in the highly secularized environment of the modern American Metropolis? Is there *really* a difference between the believer and the unbeliever in the market place or in the voting booth? Does the *type* of religious commitment make a difference: do the actions of Protestants differ from those of Catholics and Jews in the fields of politics, economics, and family life? . . .

Consistent with previous findings, Detroit Protestants were slightly better educated than Catholics. Twenty percent of each group had graduated from college, but more of the Protestants had graduated from high school (62 percent versus 55 percent). A larger percentage of the Catholics had dropped out before completing high school (25 percent versus 18 percent).

Attitudes toward work were assessed by asking respondents this question: "Some people tell us that they wouldn't be happy unless they were working at some job. But others say that they would be a lot happier if they didn't have to work and could take it easy. How do you feel about this?" The answers to this question were coded into three categories: "positive about work," "neutral," and "negative toward work." Twenty-nine percent of the Protestants gave positive responses, compared to 22 percent of the Catholics. More Catholics were neutral (58 percent versus 50 percent), and 21 percent of both groups were negative about work. Disregarding the triviality of these differences, Lenski somehow concluded that Protestantism is more conducive to hard work than Catholicism.

Self-employment was used as a measure of the entrepreneurial spirit, and the usual negligible differences were found: 10 percent of the Protestants were self-employed, and 8 percent of the Catholics were self-employed. When migration status and region of birth were controlled, the difference was enhanced to 15 percent versus 8 percent.

An important obligation imposed by the Protestant ethic is to provide one's children with opportunities for upward mobility. Lenski compared the occupational statuses of fathers and sons and discovered that 66 percent of the Protestant sons and 55 percent of the Catholic sons of lower-workingclass fathers had risen to higher occupational levels than their fathers. The difference again was very weak, but Lenski (1961, 118) concluded anyway that membership in the Catholic Church had a significant impact on occupational mobility: "At best, it [Catholic Church membership] seems to be irrelevant to mobility, and at worst, something of a hindrance."

Andrew Greeley (1964) later challenged these conclusions, contending that, when one took Lenski's data and discarded Lenski's interpretations, different conclusions emerged.

(1) Passage from working class to middle class is no more common among Protestants than among Catholics. (2) There is virtually no difference in ambitions between Protestants and Catholics. (3) Negative attitudes towards

work are no more common among Catholics than among Protestants . . . (4) There is no difference between Protestants and Catholics in the percentage of self-employed. (5) There is only a small difference (4 percent) between Catholics and Protestants in disapproval of installment buying and Catholics have a slight lead (2 percent) in keeping a budget. (6) Catholics and Protestants are equally likely to approve savings. (7) Catholics are just as likely to see God as endorsing economic efforts as Protestants (Greeley 1964, 23-24).

In addition to reviewing previous studies on the Protestant ethic theme, Greeley (1964) analyzed a national survey, which probably dated from 1962. He examined achievement values and patterns of employment and found no differences between Catholics and Protestants. Greeley insisted that nowhere in eight separate studies conducted during the previous decade could he find any support for the Protestant ethic hypothesis, and he called for a moratorium on such research.

The call fell on deaf ears. Papers on this theme continued to appear. Glenn and Hyland (1967) attempted to assess changes in the relative socioeconomic status of Protestants and Catholics by means of several national surveys done from 1943 through 1965. It seemed to them that Protestants *had* had an advantage over Catholics in education, occupational status, and income in 1943 but that the advantage had disappeared 20 years later and that a Catholic advantage in the pursuit of affluence was gradually developing. By 1967, Catholics had higher occupational statuses and larger incomes than Protestants; they had experienced considerably more upward mobility than Protestants during the postwar period, a development that Glenn and Hyland attributed to the location of the Catholic population rather than to any shifting of beliefs.

They [Catholics] are highly concentrated in the larger metropolitan areas in non-southern regions—precisely the communities with the highest average incomes, most favorable occupation distributions, and the highest average educational attainments (Glenn and Hyland 1967, 77).

In order to test the effects of regional location, Glenn and Hyland examined the achievements of young adults between 20 and 39 years old in nonsouthern metropolitan areas. In those areas, Protestants still showed a slight edge over their Catholic neighbors, but the differences were very small. Glenn and Hyland

(1967, 85) concluded that they did not offer any real support to the notion that the Protestant ethic is a source of achievement orientation:

. . . Even if there should be some small remaining difference in Protestant and Catholic achievement, much of the recent attention devoted to Protestant-Catholic differences in mobility and aspirations could more fruitfully be directed to other topics. This study shows that the effects of any Protestant-Catholic differences in influence on worldly status are small in relationship to the effects of other influences that on balance favor Catholics . . . Our analysis provides no conclusive answer to the question that has commanded so much sociological attention in recent years, but it suggests that arriving at a more nearly conclusive answer is not very important.

Subsequent investigators have continued to study the alleged effects of the Protestant ethic (among others Jackson, Fox, and Crockett 1970; Schuman 1971; Fox and Jackson 1973; Kim 1977; and Roof 1979). We will examine one more report before we bring in the data from Middletown.

Mueller (1980) criticized previous studies for using current religious affiliation as a predictor of education and focused instead on the religion in which respondents were raised. He used various national surveys done from 1973 to 1978 and made a detailed comparison of the education of cohorts of Catholics and Protestants born during five-year intervals starting with those who were born before 1908 and concluding with the cohorts born between 1949 and 1953. After adjusting for background variables, he came to the conclusion that the data showed a slight educational advantage for Catholics, but he was quick to point out that most of the differences among cohorts were statistically insignificant and that they showed no trend over time. Mueller (1980, 140) concluded that:

a detailed comparison of Protestant-Catholic differences for five-year birth cohorts beginning prior to 1908 shows no clear advantage for either, and no trend in the differences. Overall, the data indicates that during this century the net influence of religious background on educational attainment has never been very large.

Middletown's Protestant Ethic

Five different surveys collected in Middletown during 1978 were combined to determine the effects, if there were any, of religious affiliation on achievement in that community. As Table 8-6 indicates, the educational attainments of Catholics of both sexes were not significantly different than those of Protestants. What trifling differences there were favor the Catholics.

Table 8-6
Education of Catholics and Protestants, Middletown, 1978

Education	Men		Women	
	Catholics (N = 103)	Protestants (N = 628)	Catholics (N = 172)	Protestants (N = 942)
0 to 6 years	0%	2%	0%	1%
7 to 9 years	4	6	4	4
Some high school	14	15	7	13
High school graduate	28	30	31	36
Some college	19	18	26	19
College graduate	14	11	15	12
Some graduate work	6	6	7	5
Completed graduate work	16	12	11	11
Total	101%	100%	101%	101%

Sources: Middletown III men's and women's occupational surveys, religion survey, community survey, and government services survey, 1978.

We combined the results from eight national surveys conducted in 1972 through 1980 to obtain a sample with a large number of Catholics (Davis, 1980). Because of the very large sample size, some of the differences in favor of Catholics are statistically significant although substantively unimportant (Table 8-7).

Table 8-7
Education of Catholics and Protestants, United States, 1972-1980

Education	Men		Women	
	Catholics (N = 1,367)	Protestants (N = 3,394)	Catholics (N = 1,673)	Protestants (N = 4,354)
0 to 6 years	6%	8%	5%	7%
7 to 9 years	13	18	15	17
Some high school	14	12	13	16
High school graduate	31	29	43	35
Some college	19	17	15	15
College graduate	10	8	7	7
Some graduate work	5	5	2	3
Completed graduate wor	3	3	1	1
Total	101%	100%	101%	101%

Source: Davis, 1980.

The 1978 occupational distributions for Catholics and Protestants in Middletown are presented in Table 8-8. Protestant men were underrepresented in the professional occupations, and their average occupational status was significantly lower than that of Catholic men. Catholic and Protestant women had almost identical occupational distributions. The slight superiority of Catholic men in occupational status in Middletown is consistent with the national data (Table 8-9), which also show a slight Catholic superiority that is statistically significant but substantively unimportant. We can reasonably conclude that in contemporary American society the effect of religious affiliation on educational and economic achievement is negligible. From this conclusion it follows (1) that Catholics as a minority are no longer subject to any appreciable discrimination in Middletown—or in the United States—with respect to educational or occupational opportunities and (2) that Protestant religious beliefs, in their contemporary form, do not discernibly encourage hard work, personal ambition, or prudent investment of savings.

Table 8-8
Occupations of Catholics and Protestants, Middletown, 1978

	Men		Women	
Occupation	Catholics ($N = 127$)	Protestants ($N = 713$)	Catholics ($N = 154$)	Protestants ($N = 823$)
Professionals	45%	37%	44%	49%
Managers	11	15	14	9
Clericals	9	5	20	14
Sales	12	6	3	5
Craftsmen	12	14	5	6
Operatives	9	17	7	10
Laborers	0	2	1	1
Service workers	2	4	7	6
Private household worker	0	0	0	0
Farmers	0	0	0	0
Farm workers	0	0	0	0
Total	100%	100%	101%	100%

Sources: Middletown III men's and women's occupational surveys, religion survey, community survey, and government services survey, 1978.

The personal incomes of Catholics and Protestants in Middletown are shown in Table 8-10 for both men and women in the 1978 sample. The small differences in favor of Catholics are statistically significant. National data for the eight-year period 1972 to 1978 are displayed in Table 8-11. In family incomes reported by men and women, Catholic men reported a small but statistically significant income advantage; women did not. Although there may be slight differences in achievement between Catholics and Protestants in American society, they do not matter. Attention should be directed elsewhere to account for educational and occupational attainment in American society.

Table 8-9
Occupations of Catholics and Protestants, United States, 1972-80

	Men		Women	
Occupation	Catholics (N = 1,369)	Protestants (N = 3,403)	Catholics (N = 1,670)	Protestants (N = 4,363)
Professionals	17%	15%	23%	29%
Managers	13	13	4	5
Clericals	5	5	5	5
Sales	7	5	34	25
Craftsmen	24	24	2	1
Operatives	18	18	15	14
Laborers	6	7	1	1
Service workers	8	7	14	15
Private household workers	0	0	2	5
Farmers	2	5	0	0
Farm laborers	1	1	0	1
Total	101%	100%	100%	101%

Source: Davis, 1980.

Table 8-10
Incomes of Catholics and Protestants, Middletown, 1977

	Men		Women	
Income	Catholics (N = 141)	Protestants (N = 753)	Catholics (N = 111)	Protestants (N = 551)
Less than $3000	3%	2%	16%	19%
$3000 to $4999	4	3	27	25
$5000 to $7999	11	17	24	27
$8000 to $9999	6	8	6	10
$10,000 to $14,999	28	27	23	13
$15,000 to $19,999	26	22	4	5
$20,000 to $24,999	11	11	0	1
$25,000 and more	12	9	0	1
Total	101%	99%	100%	101%

Sources: Middletown III men's and women's occupational surveys, religion survey, community survey, and government services survey, 1978.

Table 8-11
Income of Catholics and Protestants, United States, 1977

	Men		Women	
Income	Catholics (N = 445)	Protestants (N = 1,150)	Catholics (N = 587)	Protestants (N = 1,559)
Less than $3000	2%	4%	4%	8%
$3000 to $4999	4	7	9	12
$5000 to $7999	11	11	13	16
$8000 to $9999	7	7	6	8
$10,000 to $14,999	19	21	17	18
$15,000 to $19,999	17	17	17	14
$20,000 to $24,999	16	15	18	10
$25,000 and more	24	19	16	14
Total	100%	101%	100%	100%

Source: Davis, 1980.

Political Behavior

Catholics have a long tradition of affiliation with the Democratic Party going back to the 19th century, when the Democrats offered haven to new immigrants faced with the antiforeign biases of the Republican Party. Catholic identification with the Democrats has held up over the years despite setbacks, such as Woodrow Wilson's apparent anti-Catholic position in the peace negotiations of 1919. The New Deal of the 1930s strengthened the bond between Catholics and the Democratic Party, as did the election of John F. Kennedy as president in 1960. During the past 50 years, Democratic presidential candidates have been able to count on at least 60 percent of the Catholic vote.

It has recently been argued that the Catholics are drifting away from the Democratic Party as they grow more affluent and move from the city to the suburbs. A study by Fee (1976) examined voters' party affiliations during three periods of time—the early 1950s, the early 1960s, and the early 1970s. In the 1950s, 42 percent of the Catholic population lived in suburbs; that had increased to 68 percent by the early 1970s. Fee noted that, despite the shift of residential location, there was virtually no change in the proportion of Catholics identifying with the Democratic Party during these 30 years. And there was virtually no difference in party affiliation between Catholics living in suburbs and those remaining in central cities.

The pattern in Middletown was consistent with these findings (Table 8-12). Almost half of the Middletown Catholics identified themselves as Democrats; most of the independents and those who did not identify themselves have voted for Democratic candidates in recent major elections. The Protestants were more evenly split between the two major parties.

Table 8-12
Political Affiliations of Protestants and Catholics, Middletown (1978)
and United States (1972-1980)

Party	Middletown		Nation	
	Catholic (N = 79)	Protestant (N = 475)	Catholic (N = 3,035)	Protestant (N = 7,731)
Republican	24%	43%	15%	27%
Democratic	48	41	49	40
Independent	17	6	35	31
Other	4	4	2	2
None	8	6	–	0
Total	101%	100%	101%	100%

Sources: Middletown III men's and women's occupational surveys, religion survey, community survey, and government services survey.

The relationship between religious affiliation and party preference is quite similar for the nation as a whole, although independents are more numerous in the nation than in Middletown. This is probably due to the National Opinion Research Center's questionnaire form which had the unintentional effect of encouraging respondents to report themselves as independents.

Political participation, as measured by voting, is nearly identical for Catholics and Protestants in Middletown. About 75 percent of both groups voted in the 1974 congressional election and 85 percent in the 1976 presidential election. The citizens of Middletown are a bit more politically active than the rest of the nation (the National Opinion Research Center's survey showed 69 percent of Catholics and 70 percent of Protestants voting in 1976) but equally unaffected by their religious affiliations when they decide to go to the polls or to stay away.

Chapter 9

Christmas and Easter

The most widely celebrated holidays in Middletown are Christmas and Easter. Although they have many similarities, their most salient point of resemblance is the fact that each has an extensive secular aspect as well as a religious one. This characteristic distinguishes them from the other festivals in the festival cycle.[1] Although the origins of Halloween and Valentine's Day as celebrated in Middletown can be traced to the Christian church calendar, no religious celebration remains as part of their observance today. Thanksgiving has religious overtones, but it is accompanied by no distinctively religious iconography, Christian or otherwise. A study of Christmas and Easter should, therefore, be most informative in considering the question of whether Middletown is indeed becoming increasingly secular.

At first glance, it seems that in these two important holidays at least secularization has made great inroads upon religion. The fear that the secular celebration of Christmas weakens the importance of the religious celebration and may eventually replace it is widespread in Middletown. If similar fears are not expressed about the secular aspect of Easter, it is probably because the secular Easter is less developed, and less obtrusive, than the secular Christmas.

There is no question that Middletown's secular Christmas celebrations require a great deal of attention, energy, and expenditure.[2] Most people begin their Christmas shopping at least a month before the day itself; they may spend about 4 percent of their annual income on gifts alone, while hospitality, travel, telephone calls, and the like increase the total spent on celebrating the secular

Christmas. Most families (83 percent) put up and decorate a tree, usually a real tree; one person in the family (most frequently the wife/mother) wraps most of the presents given within and by her family. There is intensified contact with relatives, especially primary and secondary kin, by means of gift and/or card exchange as well as through visits. Each person can expect to attend about three Christmas gatherings, at least one of which will be in his or her own home; most of these gatherings include not only the exchange of gifts but quite often a Christmas dinner as well. Although virtually everyone in Middletown participates in this celebration in some way, only 40 percent of those surveyed reported attending church at Christmas 1978. These data appear to support the view that Christmas, at any rate, is becoming increasingly secular at the expense of its religious aspect.

Easter celebrations are less secular; nevertheless, they have become more so in recent years (beginning about 1935) with the development of a secular Easter symbol, the Easter Bunny, and an increase in the exchange of Easter cards, Easter candies, and gifts such as stuffed or live animals and flowering plants. It is conceivable that Easter may eventually become as "commercialized" as Christmas is now perceived to be.

The perception is distressing to many Middletown residents, since they consider the secular and the religious aspects of these two festivals to be incompatible; where one aspect gains attention, the other must lose it. If there is an increase in the secular observance, there must be a corresponding decrease in the religious importance. The fact that the secular observance of the festivals is usually more showy than the religious observance promotes this attitude and contributes to the prevalent feeling that Middletown is becoming increasingly secular.

We have shown in other chapters that this is a mistaken conception, that, on the contrary, Middletown is a remarkably pious community. If this is demonstrable in other contexts, it would be surprising if it were not so for the celebration of Christmas and Easter. This chapter examines the secular and religious symbolism of the two festivals in order to show that these seemingly antithetical forms of celebration are, in fact, analogous, each saying the same thing in a different way.

Ritual Behavior

Before proceeding further, it is prudent to say something about the method of symbolic analysis used here: this chapter is an anthropological approach to the study of rituals. It is assumed that ritual is essentially prescribed behavior whose meaning and value are not necessarily immediately apparent to anyone belonging to a society other than that prescribing the behavior. That is, anyone from an agricultural background can recognize the planting of a crop wherever he or she travels in the world, since this activity is universally recognized as necessary to the production of cultivated food. Less easily understandable are such related practices as muttering spells over the seeds, making one's wife keep away, planting a border of red-leafed shrubs around the garden, and a host of other customs reported from various parts of the world. Such customs are comprehensible only in terms of the society in which they occur (and they are not always fully comprehended even by the members of that society); their meanings cannot be transferred from one society to another since it is commonly the case that adjacent societies attach different meanings to similar rituals.

Ritual behavior is symbolic behavior. "Symbol" can be defined as anything that stands for something else by virtue of a perceived resemblance between the entities so connected. Symbols are carriers of meaning; they acquire that meaning in part by the context in which they are found and in part by being opposed to other symbols in the same or different contexts. Symbolic behavior is not clearly separable from everyday behavior because symbolic behavior is a special case of everyday behavior. Something is deemed an appropriate symbol in a ritual context because of its significance in the less emotionally charged world of the everyday; conversely, everyday occurrences are recognized as reasonable and proper in part because the ritual context says that they are.

Our analysis of the symbolism of Christmas and Easter proceeds along these lines. These two festivals form an opposed pair, each complementing the other in both their religious and secular aspects. The secular celebration of each festival parallels the religious. We will begin this analysis with the celebration of Christmas, since it comes first in the festival cycle, and we will start with the secular aspect because its symbolism is less well understood.

Christmas

The secular celebration includes, as we have seen, gift exchange, Christmas trees, gatherings of relatives and friends, and at least one Christmas dinner eaten at such a gathering. The decorations for Christmas are more lavish than those for any other public festival; not only private houses but also public buildings and even the city itself display them, as though office workers and the entire community were representing themselves, for this season anyway, as part of a large family. And everywhere one sees representations of Santa Claus, the dominant emblem[3] of the secular Christmas. This varied collection of activities and representations can be resolved into two themes: renewing or reaffirming social ties and nurturing children. Middletown considers women to be much better than men at both of these activities, and so we can say that Christmas is also a celebration of women's special capabilities. This makes the presence of Santa Claus, a male, puzzling, but the mystery can be resolved, as we will see.

Although decorating tree and home and cooking Christmas dinner are time consuming and sometimes are mildly complained about, Middletown people grumble more about the necessity of exchanging gifts. Part of the problem is the expense involved. We have said that married couples spend an average of about 4 percent of their annual incomes on gifts; about a third of these couples find the expense burdensome. There is the additional difficulty of choosing gifts for all of one's close relatives and friends. Our survey shows that in Middletown any individual is likely to give a range of gifts to a wide circle of friends and family at Christmas. In many cases, more than one gift is given, especially to children. Moreover, it is apparently improper to give two people exactly the same things (unless there are plural gifts involved, the gift is edible, or the recipients are on the periphery of one's social world) or to give the same person the same kind of thing two years running. We must say "apparently" here because none of our informants said this in so many words, but their descriptions of the gifts they gave during 1978 showed very little duplication. Each gift given must reflect the nature of the relationship it reaffirms—whether between equals or those of unequal status, between those of the same sex or of opposite sex, between those related by blood or or friendship, between those intensely involved or only casually — as well as making reference to the recipient's interests and taste. Although it is possible to state these "rules" in this way, Middletown does not do so; evidently, overt speculation about the motivation for giving any gift or for giving gifts in general is improper.

We might explain the phenomenon by saying that people give gifts to others because they know the others will give them gifts or that people give gifts because they do not wish to be "left out." These attitudes undoubtedly account in part for the persistence of the custom, but the attitudes themselves must be accounted for. A more general explanation is that relationships between people need to be represented in some way, defined, and given some measure of objectivity. Gift giving is an important way of representing relationships; indeed, as far as we know, it is found in every human society (Mauss 1969). Conversely, the failure to give gifts, whether in reciprocation or not, implies that one has no relationships with others or no interest in maintaining relationships. Hence, Middletown at Christmas makes the effort of giving presents to a wide circle of acquaintances and of remembering an even wider circle with cards.[4]

Christmas gatherings have a similar effect. One gets a sense of one's own social group by surveying one's Christmas and thank-you lists; at the numerous parties and dinners of this season, one sees part or all of that group gathered around oneself, and one can realize not only one's relationship to the others but also their relationships to each other. The combination of gift exchanges and gatherings establishes the existence of each person's social network and affirms his or her membership in that network.[5]

Christmas custom requires not only that gifts be given but that they be wrapped. A pile of wrapped gifts is one of the emblems of Christmas: 87 percent of our survey respondents reported that all of their gifts were wrapped, and another 12 percent said that some of them were; only one person gave no wrapped presents.[6] Wrapping presents may not be as onerous as choosing or buying them, but it requires explication nonetheless since it is plainly a most important, indeed a definitive part of Christmas celebrations. Why should our presents be surprises? Why should they seem to be surprises even when they have been chosen specifically at the recipient's request? Why, if they are to surprise, may they not simply be hidden away and produced on the day of opening? Again, several answers present themselves. Surprises are, or ought to be, fun, and Christmas is a time to have fun. It is likely that for many people the act of wrapping is itself enjoyable and the finished product aesthetically satisfying. That a thing is fun or pleasurable to look at is not, however, sufficient reason for its nearly universal inclusion in a particular celebration; nor can we account for the very widespread observance of this custom by reference to its enjoyment by individuals. The explanation must be of a different kind.

One reason that wrappings are appropriate at Christmas is that they distinguish such gifts from other kinds and from the casual presentations that people make throughout the year. Giving a sweater to a child at Christmas is qualitatively different from buying the same child a sweater at another time because he or she has outgrown an old one. The difference is ceremonially marked by the wrappings as well as by the relatively formal circumstances of its presentation; the marking is important because a Christmas gift is a significant indication that there is a relationship between giver and receiver.

Another aspect of wrapping is the intent to surprise. Such giving of gifts has two stages: first the actual presentation of *a gift*, which states that a relationship is recognized, and then the discovery of what the gift is, which states what the gift giver thinks that relationship is and how well he or (more often) she thinks of the receiver. People in Middletown do not commonly expatiate verbally on the quality of personal relationships to those with whom they have those relationships (although they frequently do so to third parties, including interviewers). The gift, then, is an important way of conveying one's feelings for another person. We suggest that wrapping them heightens this effect by saying "Look at how much I love you!" The recipient is overwhelmed. True, this scenario is not always played; disappointment probably occurs as frequently as rapture; but the intention is usually there.

Among the numerous gifts given, most are for children. The relationship between parents and children in Middletown is essentially asymmetrical in that parents give their children, even when they are adults, far more than they expect or even want to get from them.[7] Christmas emphasizes the parent-child relationship above all others. The iconography is full of protective, nurturing images such as fire-lit interiors set against stark outdoor scenes— deep snow, bare trees, frozen ponds, a solitary cardinal. The Christmas tree, an evergreen, is somehow "warmer" than the deciduous trees, and its being brought inside and decorated enhances this impression. (Wrapped presents also seem "warmer" than unwrapped ones.) The secular Christmas draws a sharp contrast between the cold, harsh outdoors and the warm, protective indoors. The primary recipients of this protection are small children. Not only do they receive more gifts, but people often describe their Christmas activities as though they were almost entirely for their children's benefit.

Santa Claus, the most important Christmas emblem, exaggerates this relationship. He is a grandparental, rather than parental, figure. He is supposed to live at the North Pole, popularly imagined as a land of permanent bitter winter; Santa's house, however, is full of warmth, bustle, and cheer. This contrast is more extreme than that between indoors and outdoors in Middletown in December. Santa's gifts—almost invariably intended for children—are usually wrapped and always have the name of the recipient on the label. They are not reciprocated at all, unlike parents' presents to their children.

Santa Claus and the mythology surrounding him are in keeping with the secular Christmas themes we have so far identified. But, if, as we suggest, Christmas is primarily a celebration of feminine activities, why is the dominant emblem a male? We will propose some answers, but first it is necessary that we demonstrate more surely that this is indeed a celebration of women's work.

Christmas is child oriented, certainly; but more, it is family oriented, renewing both the solidarity of the family and its ties to other families. Christmas celebrates the family in its social network. Evidence that Christmas as a "family" holiday is abundant. The enormous amount of food needed for Christmas dinner is intended for as many of the family as can be present, as well as for persons and even families invited to share it.[8] The absence of any family member during this celebration is more keenly felt than at any other celebration.

Most significant is that, according to our survey information, Christmas trees are not merely symbols of "nurture" or "warmth";

a real, full-sized tree seems to symbolize an intact family (one that includes two parents and their children). Eighty-three percent of those surveyed put up a tree, and only 7 percent of the trees were artificial. Almost invariably the real tree is put up by an intact family; artificial trees are most commonly found in diminished families;[9] those who did not put up trees (12 percent of the sample) usually lived alone. About 80 percent of the trees put up were decorated by several family members together, and only about 16 percent were decorated by one person alone (usually, we must note, by a woman).

The tree is secondary to Santa Claus as an emblem of Christmas. Nevertheless, it is, from the perspective of this analysis, more important than Santa because it is the bridge, or link, between the secular and the religious iconographies of the festival. It is itself both secular and religious. Unlike Santa and his sleigh, it is as acceptable in a church as in a home. Only in connection with the tree is the juxtaposition of the two sets of symbols tolerated. Ornaments commonly include both secular items (small Santas, reindeer, candy canes) and religious ones; an angel or a star usually tops the tree. The scene under the tree may be either the Nativity or Santa's house. The tree not only links the sacred and the secular, it is a natural object brought indoors, and as such it links two kinds of experience that Christmas otherwise sets in opposition to each other. In symbolically bringing together otherwise disparate kinds of experience, the Christmas tree is analogous to the women of Middletown who maintain most if not all of the social ties of their families to other families and of individual family members to persons outside their family. In addition, women are more likely than men to maintain the family participation in church activities.[10] We suggest that the brilliantly decorated Christmas tree proudly dominating the house is the feminine symbol of Christmas, equivalent to the wife/mother of the household. This interpretation allows us to understand the association of the tree with the intact family; women in Middletown regard themselves as familial persons above all, and they are so regarded by men.

In spite of their increasing participation in the working world, women still dominate domestic activities (Caplow et al., 1982). Most if not all housekeeping is done by women, and Christmas celebrations represent an exaggeration of this fact. The house is not merely clean and neat but lavishly decorated, the tree being the archetypal decoration. The celebratory dinner is the most elaborate of the year. Middletown residents frequently say that women are better than men at looking after children, especially those under six years old. This attitude is probably related to the conviction that women are more emotional and therefore more understanding and sympathetic than men,[11] as well as to the fact that women choose and give more gifts than do men. As we have seen, Christmas gifts must subtly express a great deal about social relationships. Women in Middletown are much more active than their male relatives in maintaining not only their own relationships but also those of their men. But these women do not merely maintain such ties, they define and redefine them each time a gift is called for. Face-to-face interaction in Middletown is largely managed by women. This is particularly the case within the nuclear family. Although Christmas gifts may say that they are "from Mom and Dad," Dad has usually had relatively little to do with choosing them; what he has done, more often, is to provide the money for them.

This pattern is apparent in other contexts. Our Christmas survey included a few questions about the respondents' observance of Valentine's Day. People in Middletown pay relatively little attention to this festival. Among those who do, men almost always give a gift to their wives or girl friends, while women with families (that is, mothers or grandmothers) are likely to give their children or grandchildren a suitable token, such as a card or candy. Women are somewhat less likely to make gifts to husbands or lovers, although that custom is changing. Formerly, the flow of gifts was one-way, moving from man to woman and from woman to child. In day-to-day life, a similar pattern can be observed: the husband brings in an income that his wife redistributes within and outside of the family in the form of meals, cards, gifts, and parties.

We can now surmise why Santa Claus is the dominant emblem of Christmas.[12] Women, being the sympathetic and understanding sex, are supposed to be more concerned with others than with themselves (cf. Chodorow 1974). Although they do most of the work connected with Christmas, it is improper for them to allude to their labors. Women's activities are relatively private and should not be advertised. An obviously female Christmas emblem would do just that and therefore would, we suggest, be unacceptable.[13] The Christmas tree, the feminine compliment to Santa Claus, is only covertly feminine. Santa Claus is appropriate not just for this negative reason, however. As we have seen, Middletown's husbands and fathers contribute to the domestic scene by providing an income, but they do very little else. Santa Claus, who leaves gifts to be distributed by others in his absence, exaggerates the male domestic role; at the same time, he may be a kind of compensation to Middletown's family men for their limited participation at home.[14]

Having identified the important themes of the secular Christmas, we will turn next to an analysis of the religious symbolism of the Nativity. Here some of the same themes are expressed in different ways.

The church calendar and the Gospels record many events associated with the birth of Christ: the annunciation of the birth, first to Mary and then to Joseph; the visitation of Mary to her sister Elizabeth; the journey to Bethlehem; the Nativity itself; the worship of the shepherds; the circumcision of Christ; the visit of the Magi and the subsequent slaughter of the innocents and the flight into Egypt; and the purification of the Virgin Mary.

Although each of these events has been represented artistically innumerable times and each could presumably serve as a subject for a Christmas card, the religious iconography of Christmas in Middletown includes only three events: the Nativity itself, the worship of the shepherds, and the visit of the Magi; the latter two are commonly shown as occurring at the same time, although in the church calendar the Magi arrive 12 days after the Nativity. We must ask, then, why these three images, out of all the others, are selected to represent the Christian aspect of this holiday. It is not sufficient to remark that the annunciation or the visitation are inappropriate because they occur in March and May, respectively, since that supposes the logic of symbols to be far more rigorous than it is usually found to be. In any case, the slaughter of the innocents is not very distant in time from the visit of the Magi, and yet it is not figured at all in Middletown's iconography. We might attribute this lack of notice to its being excluded from Protestant observance, but we must also point out that the worship of the shepherds is not part of the church calendar but is mentioned in only one Gospel. In short, we cannot attribute Middletown's selection of these three events simply to their seasonality, to their scriptural importance, or to their inclusion in church observances. We must look instead to the present state of society in Middletown.[15]

Plainly, the three selected events stress the idea that the infant Jesus' family and life must be preserved.[16] A number of threats to both are overcome by the timely action of the divine and the human fathers. We suggest that Middletown unconsciously recognizes this latent message and its pertinence to its own anxiety about the integrity of the modern family, most especially about the welfare of the children (Caplow et al. 1982), and further that Middletown has selected these three episodes as those most clearly stating that message. Each of them presents a slightly different image of protection. Shepherds who guard their flocks by night suggest the constant vigilance of the ideal parents. The Magi come with expensive and unreciprocated gifts, also as ideal parents should. The description of the Virgin Mary's first motherly activity ("she wrapped him in swaddling clothes, and laid him in a manger" [Luke 2:7]) is preeminently protective. (Note that St. Joseph, like Middletown's fathers, has only a minor role in these proceedings.) The slaughter of the innocents, however, presents an image obviously opposed to these protective images, and it is unacceptable for that reason.

So far we have suggested that Christmas in Middletown has become a celebration of the family and its ties to other families and of the nurture of children by their parents. The secular and religious symbols both convey this idea. The secular is not, we assume, a translation of the sacred; rather, both sets of symbols have been selected and given meaning by Middletown as representations of current concerns about the family institution.

Easter

Easter is in almost every way the opposite of Christmas. Our analysis of the symbolism of this celebration follows the same form as that used for Christmas so that the contrast between them is apparent.

The secular celebration of Easter in Middletown includes the giving of various gifts, the most common being an Easter basket filled with colored eggs and candy. Flowers and young animals, especially ducklings, chicks, and bunnies, are also frequently given. The Easter-egg hunt is an important domestic ritual. Unlike Christmas dinner, Easter dinner has no prescribed menu with traditional associations. The emblem of this festival is the Easter Bunny, that enigmatic animal said to produce decorated eggs as gifts.

The secular Easter celebration includes many representations of new life, which Middletown associates with spring: pastel colors, new clothing (especially for women and children), flowers, young animals, and eggs. This sort of symbolism is fairly obvious and is, moreover, entirely consonant with the religious message of Easter. Less obvious is the significance of gift-giving patterns at this festival; least obvious, of course, is the relationship between the Easter Bunny and other secular and religious symbols. Because the meaning of this emblem is so obscure, it is much more interesting than Santa Claus, who is an obvious embodiment of the spirit of Christmas. The Easter Bunny may embody the spirit of Easter, but that spirit is not nearly so well defined as the Christmas spirit of generosity. Christmas is highly specific, but Easter is ambiguous. Its symbols and activities convey the idea that the cultural distinctions that Middletown recognizes—pet or farm animal, male or female, parent or child, life or death—need not ultimately be distinguished since all belong to the whole of Middletown's view of the world.[17] Christmas and Easter cannot be considered separately for the reason that they treat that world in opposed but complementary ways. Christmas takes the world apart and identifies each part; Easter reassembles it and refrains from identifying anything.

The gift giving associated with Easter is ambiguous; this is made clear when it is compared to the particularity of Christmas presents. Only a few kinds of things are suitable as Easter gifts, but they may be given by anyone to anyone. It is just as reasonable for a child to give a parent an Easter basket as for a parent to give one to a child (although the latter is the more common). The gift states the existence of a relationship but deliberately leaves the nature of that relationship unstated. Any social tie is taken as more or less equivalent to any other.

The custom of the Easter-egg hunt blurs or ignores conventional categories in a number of ways. The eggs themselves are, according to the mythology, of dubious origin; in fact, they represent offspring without parents since they are produced by a (male) rabbit rather than a (female) bird. As gifts they are questionable, also. The usual scenario of the hunt is that parents hide eggs for their children to find; the eggs are, in effect, gifts from parents to children, or seniors to juniors, a pattern already familiar from Halloween and Christmas. As we can see, though, Halloween giving is quite different from Christmas giving; and the giving at Easter, in the egg hunt, is different yet again. A number of adults "give" a number of eggs to a number of children but in so indirect a manner that no one establishes, or affirms, a tie with anyone else. The mechanism of hiding the eggs produces a more-or-less undifferentiated social group, divided only into hiders and seekers. Even here there is a confusion of social categories, since the adults do not automatically become hiders nor the children seekers. Except for eldest and youngest, all the participants may elect to play one role or the other (not both, however). As the usual social distinctions are ignored, each participant acts independently of the others. The Easter-egg hunt is essentially impersonal. Christmas is intensely personal: everyone knows whom each gift is from and who it is for, and the admiration and support of family and friends are part of the celebration. Halloween, too, is personal, although in a somewhat different way. The children usually know the families they accost, and the donors often try to discover who the costumed children at the door really are.

It is because rabbits are ambiguous that the emblem of the secular Easter is the Easter Bunny (Caplow and Williamson 1980). Middletown recognizes at least four classes of animal: the domestic and inedible (cats, for example), the domestic and edible (cattle), the wild and inedible (raccoons), and the wild and edible (deer). Rabbits, as a class of animal, fit into all of these categories. Any particular rabbit might be specifically defined as a pet, raised for food, snared as a pest, or trapped for food. Furthermore, rabbits are not easily distinguished according to sex or even according to age, since the mature form is not noticeably different from the juvenile form except in size. Any other animal known to Middletown is easily identified as a pet or a farm animal, as domestic or wild, as edible or inedible, as male or female, as mature or immature. Easter symbolism adds to the natural ambiguity of the rabbit the incongruity of a male mammal producing eggs and distributing them somewhat like a human giving gifts.

Additional ambiguity arises in the giving of farm animals as pets during the Easter season. Ordinary pets (kittens or puppies) are given at Christmas or on birthdays.

The religious celebration of Easter is foremost an affirmation of the Christian doctrine that death is or can be life. The events of Holy Week, above all the Crucifixion, contain many other ambiguities, however. Christ is betrayed by one disciple and denied by another. As He is dying, He commends His mother to the care of another son, the disciple John. That Christ is crucified at all is contradictory, since this was a fate reserved for criminals and He was (however mockingly) called King of the Jews.[18] His resurrection on Easter Day, which denies the existence of death, is the most extreme and important confusion of categories at Easter.

The language of the Apostles' Creed suggests that for the church Christ as the Son of God becomes an independent person at Easter, just as in another context children in Middletown become temporarily independent. The Creed, like church observance, condenses the life of Christ into His birth, death, and resurrection.[19] Significantly, the Creed puts all the events preceding the resurrection in the passive voice; the resurrection and subsequent events are described in the active voice, subtly conveying the change from protected to protector.

Conclusions

We can be satisfied that there is no substantial difference in the meanings of the secular and religious celebrations of Christmas and Easter, and we can see that the two are opposed in both their secular and religious modes. But why do the secular celebrations occur if they do no more than repeat the religious messages? Why are not the religious messages alone sufficient? We conclude by offering some suggestions on this point.

It is significant that these two festivals, and not others such as Memorial Day and Independence Day, have been selected for this sort of attention. This is related to our finding that people in Middletown regard the church and the family as similar institutions.[20]

Both are relatively feminine. Women are more likely than men to volunteer for church-sponsored activities. The comments of Middletown churchgoers indicate that they enjoy church services for much the same reasons that they enjoy their families: the sense of commonality, the feeling of peace, and the awareness of sharing with others. We regard these attitudes as relatively feminine because these respondents often mentioned also the greater emotional capacities of women, especially their ability to sympathize with others, and because women (particularly wives/mothers) promote through gift giving solicitude and the feeling of solidarity within the family. Church and family participation are relatively private, personal experiences. As such, they can be distinguished from and are even in opposition to such aspects of life as business, politics, and community activities, which are public and are considered more masculine.[21]

Unlike the church and family, none of these public institutions is felt to be endangered. The balance of importance between the public and the private spheres of life has seemed to shift strongly in recent years toward the public, with the result that the private sphere appears to be endangered not just by neglect but by certain of the public institutions themselves. The threat to the private sphere is distressing to people in Middletown because the church and the family represent for them the only sources of morality and the only means for passing on to future generations what is most desirable, as well as ultimately most necessary, in their lives today—standards of conduct, circles of acceptance, and love and friendship.

We have suggested elsewhere (Caplow et al. 1982, Chapter 10) that the secular symbolism of the entire festival cycle stresses the importance of the family, children, and women's domestic activities and that this emphasis can be traced to the perception of people in Middletown that these cherished aspects of life are threatened. Similarly, we suggest that the secular elaboration of these two religious festivals is related to Middletown's sense that religion is threatened by secular concerns, especially commercial ones. This sounds paradoxical, but in fact it is not.

The relationship of the secular to the religious is not one of simple translation: the secular is not merely the practical or everyday application of religious truths or principles. To suppose that the secular is but an extension of the religious implies that the religious form is inevitable, a permanent fixture in our society. Objectively we know that this is not true. Christianity has existed for nearly 2,000 years, but it has undergone numerous modifications during that time; in some areas it is today only a minor social force, while in others it is dominant. We cannot assume that the present importance of religion in Middletown is what is to be expected in any "right-thinking" community. Rather, we must recognize that Middletown has collectively attached importance to certain religious ideas and adherence to them.

Christmas and Easter, in their religious and secular manifestations, present the two private institutions of church and family as mutually supportive. At Christmas the Gospel message of the birth of the Son of God has become secondary to the secular theme of the preservation of the family in Middletown: the religious is subordinate to the secular, but religious iconography is used extensively to support the secular concerns of the festival. Note that the secular aspect of Christmas is not, as many allege, "materialistic"; it is devoted to the maintenance of one's social network, including the family. The parallel symbolisms of Easter reverse this relationship: the secular, heavily influenced by the religious, reflects the Easter message that human experience is ultimately an undifferentiated whole. Neither secular nor religious symbolism can properly be accorded primacy of expression: they are mutually influencing. Consequently, they produce similar messages about similar kinds of experience, and in so doing they reinforce the idea that these experiences are indeed similar.

The opposition between "religious" and "secular" that we use here obtains only in a limited sense, because the church itself tries to counteract the supposed decline of the family. It is more useful to recast the problem of the secular elaborations of religious festivals in terms of the public-private dichotomy mentioned earlier. We have said that the elaboration of religious ideas takes a secular form, but we can see now that it is more accurate to say that the elaboration of ideas about private institutions takes a public form. The relatively secular symbols that we have been analyzing—the Christmas tree, Santa Claus, the Easter Bunny—are public, standardized statements about private and personal, or individual, relationships. As such they convey to everyone, regardless of the form of his or her family or the creed of his or her church, the importance of family and church in general. The secular symbols also imply that the person using them is participating in one or both institutions, thus reaffirming on an individual basis the existence of both. These religious festivals have not become increasingly secular (or commercial) to the detriment of their religious aspects; rather, there has developed a form of public expression of certain religious attitudes that in no way diminishes their importance but, on the contrary, enhances it.

We conclude that the parallel sets of symbols express a relationship between two seemingly declining institutions, the (secular) family and the (religious) church, a relationship based on similarity of nature and mutual interest. The symbols also assert the value of each institution in itself. Together they form a defensive opposition to what are held to be encroaching public institutions, such as government and big business. It is a defense that, on the evidence, is proving successful.

Chapter 10

The Difference It Makes

Throughout the New Testament, it is taught that the Christian's life-style will set him or her apart from the nonbeliever. For example, Saint Matthew says:

> Beware of false prophets . . .
> Ye shall know them by their fruits
> Do men gather grapes of thorns, or
>   figs of thistles?
> Even so every good tree bringeth forth
> good fruit; but a corrupt tree bringeth
> forth evil fruit (Matt. 7:15-17).

Many people believe with Saint Matthew that they lead more virtuous lives with the help of religion than they could without it. Those who hold Christian principles are commonly thought in Middletown to be more honest, hardworking, sober, responsible, kind, and charitable than those without religion. All the scriptural virtues are identified by believers as good fruit that cometh forth from the good tree of Christianity.

This opinion appears in many forms in the responses of Middletown residents to several different questionnaires and interviews. For example, when married women were asked why they attended church, they gave reasons such as "keeps me pointed in the right direction," "as we go to church we try to live better lives," and "to try to make my life better." The "righteous" influence that religion was perceived to exert was also evident in responses to the question about what difference it would make to a woman if she became convinced that there was no loving God watching over her. Several of the respondents said they probably would become "meaner" if they were relieved of the commandment to love their neighbors as themselves.

You probably wouldn't care about what you did or did to other people.

I might become a mean person.

I guess, I'd be more mean. Do a lot of bad things if I didn't think someone was looking down on me.

Afraid I'd become more concerned about acquiring material things, less concerned about people and business dealings would be less according to Hoyle.

The idea that religion influences its adherents to live more virtuously appeared again in comments about premarital sex and divorce in Middletown. A supposed decline in religion was frequently cited as the reason for premarital sex and divorce: "lack of religion," "lowered moral values," "a turning away from God." The connection between religion and family stability was conceived as obvious.

I think people aren't given the spiritual information they need to make their lives work. They don't really understand enough to make a lifetime commitment.

A lot of young people aren't being raised in the church. They don't know what marriage really is.

In other contexts, survey respondents in Middletown took it for granted that church members are less likely to divorce, to beat their children, to steal from their neighbors, to cheat their employers, or to abuse alcohol and drugs. Kindness and personal responsibility, family solidarity, charitable contributions, service in the PTA, and a general pattern of good citizenship are associated with the practice of religion in the minds of most Middletown people.

A change of life-style is expected to follow a conversion or a new religious commitment; indeed, it is the sign that validates the experience. The following story appeared in a newspaper column; similar episodes are often described in sermons.

Here was a young sailor who manned a gun on a battleship in the midst of one of the biggest sea battles in the Pacific during WWII. He prayed, (you and I would have too in his shoes) if God would spare his life, he would live for Him. The young man was sincere and conscientious and eventually returned home when the war ended.

Three weeks later he stood at the altar of his home town church and took the vows of membership by professing his faith in Jesus Christ. He married, opened a business and started to raise a family.

Today, he is a highly respected member of the community and a faithful hard-working member of his church. His influence is wide-spread and it all began with a vow made to God during a crisis in his life (Middletown's evening newspaper, October 25, 1980).

Aside from such success stories, righteousness is thought to be its own reward, and a life based on religious principles is assumed to be intrinsically happier than one without God. That trials can be endured and sorrow overcome by faith and prayer is a prime article of Middletown's religion. The most common reaction when people were asked to imagine themselves losing their faith in God was that they would be "depressed." Some said that life would become so meaningless that death would be a welcomed escape.

The supposed relationship between religious affiliation and good behavior has not been much investigated. A Jewish rabbi, writing 20 years ago, referred to:

. . . the disquieting paradox we cannot escape. On the one hand, heartening evidence that more and more Americans are formally associating themselves with the agencies of religion; on the other, appalling reason to fear that the ideal goals of religion may be farther from our grasp than ever (Gittelsohn 1961, 23).

He proposed that one reason for this paradox ". . . is that even those who retain a formal affiliation with religion find their professions of faith more and more divorced from life itself" (Gittelsohn 1961, 24).

This chapter will examine the relationship among religion, socially approved behavior, and personal happiness by comparing the background characteristics, life-styles, and self-reported happiness of persons with and without religious affiliations and of persons who attend church with varying degrees of assiduity. This was the strategy of most of the previous research on this topic, and its limitations will be obvious before we begin. If we do find an association between happiness and church attendance, we will have no way of telling whether people go to church because they are happy or are happy because they go to church or whether some other variable happens to influence both happiness and church attendance in the same direction. Presumably, all of these effects account for the correlation, *if* there is a correlation.

Two further cautions are required before we proceed. First, our reading of the trend from 1924 to the present must be highly speculative since the Lynds did not directly address the relationship between religion and behavior. Second, for the reasons noted in the preceding paragraph, we cannot argue that observed differences in life-style are attributable to the influence of religion. We must be content to describe the differences between the religious and the nonreligious and leave the problem of explaining them to future research.

Economic Success

Max Weber in his classic work *The Protestant Ethic and the Spirit of Capitalism* ([1904] 1958) proposed that Protestantism had encouraged the historic development of capitalism because Protestant beliefs about work, saving, competition, and acquisition of wealth had encouraged the Protestants' educational and occupational achievements. Early Protestantism, in most of its branches, put its hope of salvation in God's election, not in good works, but it interpreted worldly prosperity as a sign of God's favor while rebuking extravagant expenditures. This combination of beliefs gave religious legitimation to the pursuit of wealth; in the extreme, it made the accumulation of wealth a religious duty. Although there continues to be academic controversy about whether a Protestant ethic still exists and whether it contributes to educational and occupational achievement, the belief that religion encourages ambition and hard work is certainly alive and well in Middletown.

The Lynds obtained rather complete information on the church attendance of business-class and working-class families from their housewives' survey of 1924 and retrospective information about the church attendance of their respondents' parents around 1890, which can be used to estimate the association of economic success and church attendance at those two earlier points in time. The grouping of families into business-class and working-class is a rather crude measure of economic success, but not a meaningless one. Business-class men worked with their minds or tongues by providing professional services, managing factories and businesses, or selling ideas and products. Working-class men worked with their hands in factories and shops. According to the Lynds (1929, 23-24):

The mere fact of being born upon one or the other side of the watershed roughly formed by these two groups is the most significant single cultural factor tending to influence what one does all day long throughout one's life; whom one marries; when one gets up in the morning; whether one belongs to the Holy Roller or Presbyterian church; or drives a Ford or a Buick; whether or not one's daughter makes the desirable high school Violet Club; or one's wife meets with the Sew We Do Club or with the Art Student's League; whether one belongs to the Odd Fellows or to the Masonic Shrine; whether one sits about evenings with one's necktie off; and so on indefinitely throughout the daily comings and goings of a Middletown man, woman or child.

If housewives' memories of how often their parents attended church were reasonably accurate and if the housewives were truthful about their own church participation, then business-class families were somewhat overrepresented among those who were active in religion in 1890 and 1924. Seventy-six percent of the parents of business-class wives had attended Sunday morning services at least once a month in 1890, compared with 61 percent of the parents of working-class wives. We surmise that many more of the latter group lived in rural areas in 1890. This difference between business-class and working-class families in 1924 was in the same direction but much greater. Seventy-four percent of the business-class families but only 31 percent of the working-class families attended Sunday morning service at least once a month. The correlation between religiosity and economic success suggested by the 1890 figures is unmistakable in 1924.

Business-class respondents also reported more attendance at evening services and Sunday school, with two exceptions. First, in 1890 the working class reported slightly higher attendance at Sunday school. Second, only 9 percent of the business-class families attended evening services once a month or more in 1924, compared to 30 percent of the working class.

We have no information about the relationship between religiosity and economic success in Middletown during the long interval from 1924 to 1978, but we do have some studies of other communities. Cantril (1943) combined three national surveys administered in 1939 and 1940 in order to test the relationship of religious affiliation to education and economic status. He was primarily interested in differences between Catholics and Protestants, but he included information about the nonaffiliated population as well. The Protestants in his sample reported more education and higher economic status than the Catholics or the nonaffiliated, who were very similar to each other. For example, 15 percent of the Protestants had a college education, compared to 9 percent of the Catholics and 10 percent of the nonaffiliated.

Similar findings were reported in Bultena's 1944 study of Madison, Wisconsin (Bultena 1949). In a sample of 25,000 Madison residents, the Protestants showed a somewhat higher level of educational and occupational status than the Catholics, and the nonaffiliated respondents were closer to the Protestants. The average educational attainment was 12.1 years for Protestants, 11.2 years for Catholics, and 11.8 for the nonaffiliated. Seventeen percent of the Protestants worked in professional occupations, compared to 16 percent of the nonaffiliated and 9 percent of the Catholics. The differences between church members and nonmembers were so trivial that Bultena (1949, 386) concluded ". . . that the no-church people are about equally represented in every social class as determined by occupational, educational and economic indexes." It seems he did not consider as a biasing factor the presence in Madison of a university community with a large proportion of religiously indifferent professionals.

Other studies followed thick and fast. Reviewing the research relating church membership and attendance to social and economic status up to the middle 1960s, Dillingham (1965, 416) concluded that "social status is *positively* related to *membership* in a Protestant denomination," but he found the relationship between *attendance* and social status to be more complex. Dillingham's reanalysis of data from four major studies indicated that *within* any of these denominations church attendance was correlated with social status. Moreover, the difference in social status between regular and occasional church attenders was increased when nonmembers, who infrequently or never attended, were added to the sample (Dillingham 1967, 110).

Glenn and Hyland (1967) combined four Gallup polls collected in 1963 through 1965 to create a national sample of more than

12,000 individuals. They found that nonchurch members had higher educational levels (12.2 years versus 11.2 years), higher occupational statuses (46 points on the Duncan Socioeconomic Index as compared to 37 points), and higher incomes ($6,118 versus $5,763) than church members.

The observed superiority of the unaffiliated in the 1960s is small, like the earlier superiority reported for Protestants. Glenn and Hyland (1967, 82), unable to resolve the apparent contradiction between their study and previous studies, cheerfully decided that they did not really care: "Our analysis provides no conclusive answer to the question [Catholic-Protestant differences] that has commanded so much sociological attention in recent years, but it suggests that arriving at a more nearly conclusive answer is not very important."

An innovative test of the Protestant ethic was conducted by Kim (1977), who explored the relationship between Protestant values and beliefs (instead of the usual church affiliation) and occupational status. A random sample of 252 adult males was interviewed in a small midwestern city. The men were asked whether they thought that hard work is a virtue, that worldly success is God's reward, and that people should save even when it required some sacrifice. Kim found that Protestants and Catholics had very similar work values and that these were significantly stronger than those of unaffiliated respondents. Individual acceptance of the work ethic was signifantly related to occupational status; 68 percent of those who gave strong verbal support to the work ethic were in nonmanual (the Lynds' business-class) occupations. Although Kim (1977, 261) proposed "that any study of behavioral correlates of religion should abandon the use of religious affiliation as a measure of the Protestant Ethic," his data showed the work ethic to be strongly associated with church membership.

Mueller (1980) combined five national samples collected from 1973 to 1978 and examined the relationship between the religion respondents were raised in (rather than their current affiliation) and the educational level they had achieved. Respondents were divided into three birth cohorts (one born before 1920, one born between 1920 and 1937, and one born between 1938 and 1953), and each of these cohorts was further divided by six.

The focus was again on Catholic-Protestant and denominational differences, but the unaffiliated were included, also. Church members had a slight educational advantage over nonmembers in four of the six cohorts, but the differences were trivial; for the sample, as a whole, church members averaged 11.78 years of education and nonmembers, 11.81. Mueller (1980, 150) warned that:

> . . . we must conclude, based on the data currently available, that the influence religious background has on educational achievement has never been large in this century and discourses invoking "religious achievements subculture" and/or "discrimination" explanations to account for the small differences should be avoided because they only serve to perpetuate misconceptions and stereotypes.

Because of the inconsistent findings of these previous studies, we did not expect to find much difference in educational and occupational achievement between church members and nonmembers in Middletown. On the other hand, it was difficult to deny all credence to the widely held local opinion that connects religiosity with worldly success.

After combining information about religious affiliation and educational achievement collected in several different surveys, we found that church members in Middletown (excluding non-Christians) are a shade better educated than nonmembers (Table 10-1). The tiny difference between members and nonmembers is not statistically significant. The larger advantage of high attenders over low attenders is significant; only 38 percent of those with a grade school education were high attenders, compared to 59 percent of those with graduate training. Thirty-six percent of the high attenders had graduated from college compared to only 27 percent of the low attenders. In other words, church membership alone has no discernible association with educational achievement, but active church members are somewhat better educated than inactive members and nonmembers.

The distribution of high attenders and low attenders in the eight major occupational categories is shown in Table 10-2. Church membership and occupational level are not significantly related, but church attendance is moderately correlated with occupational status; 49 percent of high attenders were in the professional or managerial occupations, but only 34 percent of low attenders. The pattern is similar to what we found for educational achievement.

Table 10-1
Education and Religiosity in Middletown, 1978

Religiosity	Total	Education					
		0-9 Years	Some High School	High School Graduate	Some College	College Graduate	Graduate Training
Religious Preference:							
Denominational Preference	88%	83%	87%	89%	87%	91%	87%
No preference	12	17	13	11	13	9	13
Total	100%	100%	100%	100%	100%	100%	100%
# of cases (N)	(1,397)	(59)	(142)	(471)	(295)	(189)	(255)
Attendance:							
High	50%	38%	40%	48%	50%	56%	59%
Low	50	63	60	52	50	44	41
Total	100%	101%	100%	100%	100%	100%	100%
(N)	(1,204)	(48)	(120)	(403)	(253)	(163)	(217)

Sources: Middletown III men's and women's occupational surveys, religion survey, community survey, and government services survey, 1978.

Given the somewhat higher educational and occupational status of regular church attenders in Middletown, we anticipated that they would have somewhat larger family incomes, and so they did, as Table 10-3 shows. The differences between church members and nonmembers and between high attenders and low attenders are both statistically significant. The median family income of

Table 10-2
Occupational Level and Church Attendance, Middletown, 1978

Occupational Group	High Church Attendance	Low Church Attendance
Professionals	33%	22%
Managers	16	12
Sales workers	5	7
Clerical workers	19	19
Craftsmen	9	12
Operators	11	17
Laborers	1	2
Service workers	6	9
Total	100%	100%
(N)	(505)	(529)

Sources: Middletown III men's and women's occupational surveys, religion survey, community survey, and government services survey, 1978.

Table 10-3
Family Income and Church Attendance, Middletown, 1978

Income	High Church Attendance	Low Church Attendance
Less than $5,000	5%	8%
$5,000 to $9,999	10	13
$10,000 to $14,999	15	18
$15,000 to $19,999	18	22
$20,000 to $24,999	17	17
$25,000 to $29,999	6	7
$30,000 and over	28	15
Total	99%	100%
(N)	(501)	(446)

Sources: Middletown III men's and women's occupational surveys, religion survey, community survey, and government services survey, 1978.

church members was $19,000; that of nonmembers was under $16,000. Thirty-four percent of the high attenders had incomes over $25,000, compared to only 22 percent of the low attenders.

These results agree with previous studies that found the differences between church members and nonmembers to be small and not particularly useful for interpreting educational and occupational achievement. But active church members in contemporary Middletown display better-than-average educational levels, occupational statuses, and incomes.

Attitudes toward jobs and toward work in general were examined for evidence of a work ethic among the religious. There were no significant differences between church members and nonmembers; 61 percent of both groups disagreed with the statement "To me, my work is just a way of making money." Neither was there a significant difference between high and low attenders. The responses to a dozen such items suggested that the association of the work ethic with religious activity in contemporary Middletown is too weak to explain the superior occuaptional status and higher incomes of active church members.

To see whether the positive relationship between religion and worldly success observed in Middletown is characteristic of the entire country, we examined eight national surveys conducted by the National Opinion Research Center from 1972 through 1980. The eight independent samples were combined into a single large sample of about 12,000 respondents (National Research Center 1980).

The categories church membership, church attendance, education, and occupation (the same ones were part of the Middletown analysis) were used to analyze the national data. The only variation was that the Midletown income scale had an extra category, "$30,000 and more," while the top category in the national income scale was "$25,000 and more."

The national data are presented in Table 10-4. High attenders and low attenders have virtually identical distributions in educational achievement. The positive correlation between education and church attendance that we found in Middletown is not evident in the national sample.

At the risk of seeming to dismiss findings that happen to be inconsistent with our own, we are inclined to attribute this finding to a sampling bias that somehow evaded the National Opinion

Table 10-4
Education and Church Attendance, United States, 1972-1980

Education	High Church Attendance	Low Church Attendance
0 to 9 years	21%	23%
Some high school	15	13
High school graduate	33	34
Some college	17	16
College graduate	8	9
Graduate training	6	5
Total	100%	100%
(N)	(6,641)	(5,386)

Source: Davis, 1980.

Research Center's meticulous sampling procedures. Ninety-three percent of the national respondents gave their religious preference as Christian, and only 7 percent admitted to having no preference. This seems highly implausible; we must conclude that the center's procedures somehow oversampled Christians or somehow led respondents with no religious preference to identify themselves as Christians.

Occupational data from the same series of eight national surveys lead us to the same conclusion. There are no important differences between the occupational distributions of those who attended church regularly and of those who attended infrequently or never (Table 10-5). Income data from the same source tell us

Table 10-5
Occupation and Church Attendance, United States, 1972-1980

Occupation	High Church Attendance	Low Church Attendance
Professionals	14%	17%
Managers	10	9
Sales workers	6	6
Clerical workers	18	22
Craftsmen	15	10
Operatives	17	16
Laborers	4	3
Farmers	2	2
Farm laborers	1	1
Service workers	13	12
Household workers	1	3
Total	101%	101%
(N)	(6,080)	(4,871)

Source: Davis, 1980.

Table 10-6
Family Income and Church Attendance, United States, 1972-1980

Income	High Church Attendance	Low Church Attendance
Under $5,000	18%	18%
$5,000 to $9,999	23	23
$10,000 to $14,999	22	21
$15,000 to $19,999	15	14
$20,000 to $24,999	10	11
$25,000 and over	13	13
Total	101%	100%
(N)	(5,464)	(4,250)

Source: Davis, 1980.

the same thing. The income differences between high and low attenders are negligible (Table 10-6).

In the association between church attendance and secular achievement as reflected by education, occupation, and income, Middletown is slightly out of step with the rest of the nation. In Middletown, churchgoers, especially those who attend church frequently, are somewhat more educated and have more prestigious occupations and larger incomes than those who stay away from church. However, it must be stressed that even in Middletown the association between religion and secular achievement is weak.

Political Participation

The relationship between religion and political participation in the United States has been extensively discussed, and it is generally agreed that most denominations have a conservative orientation in politics to the extent that they hold any political views at all (Glock and Stark 1965). The Unitarian-Universalists; Quakers; and some factions among Catholics, Episcopalians, Congregationalists, and Presbyterians, however, constitute abundant exceptions. The latent connection between right-wing Republicanism and Protestant fundamentalism surfaces from time to time under the aegis of religious entrepreneurs, currently exemplified by Jerry Falwell and the Moral Majority and at times in the past by much less savory characters such as Gerald L. K. Smith.

One explanation proposed for the allegedly inherent conservatism of organized religion is the familiar Marxist axiom that "religion is the opiate of the people" (curiously echoed by Emile Durkheim, the cofounder of modern sociology, in the famous passage we quoted in Chapter 1) that is, that religion quiets the resistance of the disadvantaged to exploitation by promising them heavenly rewards to compensate for their earthly deprivations. Social psychologists call this "deprivation theory."

Glock and Stark (1965) reviewed the considerable evidence testing deprivation theory in the American setting and brought in a verdict of not proven. They discovered, as we did in Middletown, that one of the basic premises of the theory is mistaken; the working class is no more religious than the business class, and each has many alternative reactions to deprivation, such as alcohol abuse, drug use, suicide, crime, insanity, television watching, and adult education.

On the basis of previous studies, we did not expect to find any strong relationship between religious participation and political participation in Middletown. The data surprised us (Table 10-7). The relationship between church attendance and political affiliation is statistically significant, although not very strong. High attenders are overrepresented in the Republican Party and low attenders among the Democrats. Religious people in Middletown are both more conservative and more active in politics than those who keep their distance from the church.

Eighty-six percent of the church members in our sample voted

Table 10-7
Political Party Preference and Church Attendance, Middletown, 1978

Party Preference	High Church Attendance	Low Church Attendance
Republican	46%	28%
Democrat	38	48
Independent	6	8
Other	4	4
None	6	12
Total	100%	100%
(N)	(289)	(403)

Sources: Middletown III men's and women's occupational surveys, religion survey, community survey, government services survey, 1978.

in the 1976 presidential election, compared to 69 percent of the nonmembers; 89 percent of the high attenders voted, compared to 79 percent of the low attenders.

In our survey of working men, we asked respondents about their choice for president in the 1976 election, and some rather interesting relationships appeared. Church members split their votes equally between Ford and Carter. Church members who classified themselves as independents voted for the two major candidates in about equal numbers. On the other hand, 90 percent of those without a religious affiliation and 100 percent of the independents without a religious affiliation voted for the Democratic candidate. Fifty-five percent of the high attenders voted for Ford, but only 35 percent of the low attenders. These differences are statistically significant and indicate again that religiously active persons in Middletown are more conservative and more politically active than their nonreligious neighbors.

In order to compare Middletown with the country as a whole, we turned again to the National Opinion Research Center data. The nation as a whole gave a little more support to Carter than did Middletown, but no relationship between church attendance and voting in the 1976 election could be discerned. The information collected by the center in 1977, 1978, and 1979 from about 3,500 respondents showed that high attenders and low attenders had identical voting patterns and nearly identical patterns of political affiliation. The relationship we found in Middletown between religious and political participation may be a local or regional peculiarity.

Family Life

Every Christian denomination has doctrines about marriage and divorce. At the one extreme is the Catholic Church with its insistence on indissoluble marriage. At the other are liberal Protestant churches that favor premarital experimentation, family planning, and "rational" divorce. But even the most liberal denominations are in favor of marital stability and family harmony. Therefore, we expected some differences in marital status between those who were religiously active and those who were not.

As anticipated, churchgoers in Middletown reported more marriage and less divorce (Table 10-8). Significantly more high attenders were in their first marriages. Low attenders had a higher percentage in every other category except widowed. These differences between high and low attenders were not large but still showed a significant relationship between church attendance and the disposition to marry and to stay married.

Table 10-8
Marital Status and Church Attendance, Middletown, 1978

Marital Status	High Church Attendance	Low Church Attendance
Single — never married	10%	14%
Married — first marriage	77	60
Remarried — following divorce	3	8
Divorced or separated	4	12
Widowed	6	6
Total	100%	100%
(N)	(398)	(473)

Sources: Middletown III men's and women's occupational surveys, religion survey, community survey, and government services survey, 1978.

Not only are religiously active Middletowners more likely to be married, they are also more likely to describe their marriages as very happy and less likely to describe them as unhappy to any degree. We asked three different questions about marital happiness, marital satisfaction, and willingness to marry the same person again. The responses to the three questions were very similar and can be represented by the responses to the question about marital happiness (Table 10-9). Whatever the reason, there is a significant relationship between churchgoing and marital happiness in Middletown.

Table 10-9
Marital Happiness and Church Attendance, Middletown, 1978

Marital Happiness	High Church Attendance	Low Church Attendance
Very happy	64%	53%
Pretty happy	33	36
Not too happy	2	7
Pretty or very unhappy	1	4
Total	100%	100%
(N)	(236)	(277)

Sources: Middletown III men's and women's occupational surveys, religion survey, community survey, and government services survey, 1978.

Another difference between the religious and the nonreligious is in the number of children. High attenders had significantly fewer childless marriages and more children (Table 10-10).

Table 10-10
Number of Children and Church Attendance, Middletown, 1978

Number of Children	High Church Attendance	Low Church Attendance
None	27%	38%
One	10	16
Two	22	19
Three	18	14
Four or more	23	13
Total	100%	100%
(N)	(397)	(472)

Sources: Middletown III men's and women's occupational surveys, religion survey, community survey, and government services survey, 1978.

A comparison of the Middletown data with the National Opinion Research Center's findings reveals that the relationship of religion to family life in the rest of the country is the same as it is in Middletown. In the United States as a whole, high attenders have relatively more marriages and fewer divorces, report more marital happiness, and have fewer childless marriages and more families of four or more children. The only differences are that a smaller proportion of the national sample described their marriage as very happy and that there were fewer childless marriages in the national sample among both high and low church attenders.

Because of the Christian values supporting traditional family life, we anticipated that religiously active Middletowners would be somewhat more familistic, but we were surprised at the strength of the relationship. The high attenders were more likely to be married, to be very happy in their marriages, to remain married, and to have larger families. The observed association is not unique to Middletown; national data reveal a similar pattern. It is not, of course, legitimate to claim that religion *caused* the observed differences in family life; the relationship presumably works both ways. It is easier for successful families to participate in organized religion and easier for religiously active families to be successful (with "success" defined in terms of values that are traditional but by no means outmoded in Middletown and the United States as a whole).

General Happiness

The last question we asked about the difference religion makes was whether it leads to happiness. It can be argued that being religious, being saved, turning to Jesus, or giving one's life to God engenders feelings of peace, contentment, and happiness. On the other hand, the renunciation of certain pleasures and the expenditure of time, energy, and money on religious activity might conceivably detract from personal happiness.

Respondents in a number of our surveys were asked, "Taking all things together, how would you say things are these days: would you say you are . . .?" The results presented in Table 10-11 reveal that high attenders reported themselves to be somewhat happier than low attenders. Twice as many high attenders

Table 10-11
Personal Happiness and Church Attendance, Middletown, 1978

Level of Happiness	High Church Attendance	Low Church Attendance
Very happy	37%	18%
Pretty happy	52	65
Not too happy	9	13
Pretty or very unhappy	2	4
Total	100%	100%
(N)	(397)	(472)

Sources: Middletown III men's and women's occupational surveys, religion survey, community survey, and government services survey, 1978.

described themselves as very happy, more low attenders described themselves as unhappy to some degree.

The same question was asked of the National Opinion Research Center's national samples, with results consistent with those from Middletown. Churchgoers were considerably happier, or at least more likely to describe themselves as so, than those who infrequently or never attended religious services. The association between religion and happiness in the national samples was not quite as dramatic as in the Middletown sample, but it was there (Table 10-12). Whether religious activity leads to happiness or happiness leads to religious activity remains undetermined, but the correlation is unmistakable.

Table 10-12
Personal Happiness and Church Attendance, United States, 1972-1980

Level of Happiness	High Church Attendance	Low Church Attendance
Very happy	40%	29%
Pretty happy	49	56
Not too happy	11	15
Total	100%	100%
(N)	(5,385)	(6,641)

Source: Davis, 1980.

Chapter 11

Youth and the Church

Middletown was portrayed by the Lynds as a religious community buffeted by a rising wind of secularization. In religious matters, the world view of Middletown's people was that of conservative Protestants; and, if the city was more secular than it had been in 1890, still it was taken for granted that one belonged to a Christian faith, and professed doubters were not quite respectable (Lynd and Lynd 1929, 315-16).

The intrusions of secularization were seen in the disappearance of the "family altar," an apparent decline in attendance at church services, the redefinition of the Christian Sabbath as a day of recreation, a narrowing of the purview of organized religion, the sponsorship of a growing array of secular activities by the churches, and the declining role of the ministry as "interpreters of the Permanent to a world of Change" or as sources of information and inspiration (Lynd and Lynd 1929, 337-38, 339-43, 359, 401; 1937, 306-7, 318). Secularization was said to affect certain types of people more than others, so that men were more secularized than women, young people more than older people, and the business class more than the working class (Lynd and Lynd 1929, 329, 342-43, 359, 396).

The theme that organized religion was losing its attraction to young people appeared in *Middletown* but was more salient in *Middletown in Transition*, which emphasized the small percentage of churchgoers under age 30 and quoted local observers who said that "children are growing farther and farther from religion" and

217

"so far as youth is concerned, we may as well admit that any formalism in religion is out of the picture" (Lynd and Lynd 1937, 297-98, 304-5). Raymond Fuller (1937, 89-113), who studied Middletown's youth the year after Robert Lynd and his students collected data for *Middletown in Transition*, devoted a special survey to clergymen's views on the status of religion and young people. He corroborated the finding that Middletown's clergy were having difficulty reaching the city's young people.

That religion was losing its influence over the city's young people was what local experts *thought* was happening. The observations should not be taken at face value as accurate descriptions of what in fact was happening among the young people. The basis for comparison is usually ambiguous—sometimes an observer referred to his own youth and sometimes to former attendance patterns in his own church; sometimes there was no reference point at all anchoring the perceived trend. The only reliable statistical data come from the Lynds' 1924 high school survey, which were presented in a chapter whose overriding theme was the *pervasiveness* of five dominant Christian beliefs and the atypicality of skepticism.

Dominant Beliefs

The Lynds' (1927) chapter entitled "Dominant Religious Beliefs" identified five commonly held beliefs: the all sufficiency of Christianity as the one true religion, the sacredness of the Bible, the divinity of Jesus, the reality of life after death, and the respect for organized religion. For each of these dominant beliefs except respect for organized religion, there was a single item on the high school questionnaire.[1] Evidence for the importance of organized religion was drawn from high school students' designation of "being an active church member" as one of the qualities "most desirable" in fathers and mothers. There was also an item on the theory of evolution versus the literal biblical account of the origin of humankind that served to illustrate "the degree of dominance of religious ways of thinking at the end of ten or twelve years of education" in the chapter on "The Things Children Learn" (Lynd and Lynd 1929, 204-5). Finally, an item on Sunday attendance at movies provided evidence of the apparent secularization of the Christian Sabbath.

We have described elsewhere (Caplow and Bahr 1979, 4-7) how an item-by-item comparison of the attitudes of Middletown high school students in 1925 with those of students in 1977 suggests that many of the dominant beliefs have persisted with remarkable tenacity. That comparison used an adjusted sample of the 1977 students from which ninth-graders and blacks were deleted so that it matched the 1924 students sample.[2] The comparison revealed statistically significant declines in the apparent ortholdoxy of the students, but the declines were much less than we had anticipated. (See Appendix Table 11-1.)

The 1977 students were almost twice as likely to prefer evolutionary theory to the biblical account of the creation (28 percent in 1924 versus about 50 percent in 1977), but even so *half* of them still clung to the Bible story. About two-thirds of the 1977 sample, compared to 83 percent in 1924, agreed that "Jesus was different from every other man who ever lived in being entirely perfect," a significant decline but hardly evidence for 50 years of rampant secularization. The most dramatic changes were a virtual disappearance of opposition to move going on Sunday (only 6 percent said it was wrong in 1977, compared to 33 percent in 1924) and a sharp decline in support for the statement that "Christianity is the one true religion and all peoples should be converted to it" (94 percent in 1924, 38 percent in 1977). The boys and girls of Middletown in 1977 were overwhelmingly Christian, and they subscribed to most of the "dominant beliefs" listed by the Lynds; however, they were much less willing to assert that all other people should believe as they did. They were less likely to view the Bible as an all-sufficient guide to life's problems (50 percent, compared to 74 percent in 1924) but essentially no different from the young people of their grandparents' generation in defining the purpose of religion as preparation for a future life (53 percent, compared to 60 percent in 1924).

Among the beliefs represented in Appendix Table 11-1, the most universal (affirmed by two out of three students) is the idea that Jesus was a perfect being. The Lynds (1929, 319) interpreted the statement "The purpose of religion is to prepare people for the hereafter" as "extreme form" of a generally held belief in a life after death. We would hesitate to label the statement "extreme." It certainly is not extreme in Middletown, where well over half of the students agreed with it. Moreover, to disagree with this definition of the objective of religion is not necessarily to rule out a belief in life after death, and it is probably best to limit interpretation to the manifest meaning of the statement. Also endorsed by over half of the students was the orthodox view of the sufficiency of the Bible as a guide to life's problems.

The doctrinal belief receiving the least support among the 1977 students was one we have called "evangelicalism," as expressed in the statement "Christianity is the one true religion and all peoples should be converted to it."[3] Virtually all of Middletown was evangelical in 1924: 94 percent of the respondents agreed with the statement. In 1977, less than 40 percent of Middletown students gave the evangelical response.

Observe (Appendix Table 11-1) that in 1977 orthodoxy varied by sex; girls were more likely to believe that Jesus was perfect and to reject evolution in favor of creation. However, there were no differences by sex with regard to evangelicalism, Sunday activities, the purpose of religion, or the acceptance of the Bible as a guide to life's problems. If, as the Lynds suggested, the boys were more secularized in 1924, the girls seem to have "caught up" by the late 1970s. We have elsewhere reported a similar decline in male-female differences in various family-related attitudes (Bahr 1980). The largest differences between girls and boys reported in Appendix Table 11-1 have to do with the social utility of religion.

Most young people agreed with the statement that churchgoers are usually bored, but they seemed to think that Sunday-school lessons may be useful and that ministers can be helpful with everyday problems, girls significantly more than boys.

In their attitudes toward religion, high school students whose fathers worked in white-collar occupations did not differ much from students whose fathers followed blue-collar occupations. As can be seen in Appendix Table 11-2, significant differences by social class showed up for only two of the nine religious attitudes. Business-class students were a little more apt to define churchgoers as bored but dutiful and a little less likely to define Sunday movie going as wrong. In contemporary Middletown, the religious values of the business class and the working class seem to be nearly identical.

We have shown that the Christian attitudes and beliefs reflected in the nine items from the Lynds' high school questionnaire do not differ systematically by gender or social class. The significant differences, it turns out, are between people who attend church and those who do not, or between those who have a religious preference and those who do not. Indeed, it would be surprising if those who identify with and attend the churches were not more orthodox, more sure of the social utility of religion, and more confident that religion would prepare them for the hereafter than those who do not attend church or have a denominational preference.

What is noteworthy is the sizable percentage of no-preference and nonchurchgoing students who were orthodox in their views (Appendix Table 11-3). Of course, they were less orthodox than the churchgoing students, and, therefore, most of the differences shown in the table are statistically significant. But it is a testimony to the pervasiveness of Christian belief in Middletown that more than half of the students who *never* attended church said that Jesus was perfect and that counseling by ministers and priests is worthwhile. Almost half of them agreed that the purpose of religion is preparation for the hereafter, and a fourth accepted Christianity as the one true religion to which everyone should be converted.

Some denominational differences turned up, also. Protestants were more supportive of Sunday school than Catholics, and they were also (1) more likely to see religion as a way to prepare for the hereafter, (2) more reliant on the Bible as a guide to life and faith, and (3) more evangelical.

Church Attendance

Today, most of Middletown's young people attend church. About one in three reported attending church at least weekly, and another one in three reported frequent (at least once a month) or occasional (several times a year) attendance. Thus, the population of young people may be viewed in thirds, with one-third attending religious services weekly, another third attending frequently or occasionally, and the final third attending on special occasions or not at all.

In line with a pattern well established in national surveys, the high school boys did not attend church as often as the girls did. Thirty-five percent of the girls reported weekly attendance, compared to 27 percent of the boys. And boys were significantly more likely to avoid churchgoing entirely: 25 percent marked "not at all," compared to 14 percent of the girls. In light of these differences, it is not surprising to find that the boys were less apt to claim a religious preference: 33 percent said they had no religious preference, compared to 25 percent of the girls.

Comparisons of the church attendance of Middletown students with that reported in national samples (Appendix Table 11-4) suggest that the Middletown levels are fairly typical. The percentage of senior high school students who reported regular weekly attendance (36 percent) is about the same as for high school seniors nationwide in 1977 (40 percent). The corresponding national figure for adults in the same year was 36 percent.

As in Middletown 50 years ago, business-class people in Middletown today attend church more often than do working-class people. Thirty-nine percent of the students whose fathers had business-class occupations said they went to church weekly, compared to 28 percent of working-class students.

Thus far, the findings are predictable and unexciting. They are almost sociological clichés: girls go to church more than boys, and higher-status persons attend more frequently than lower-status persons. However, a closer look at the combined effects of class, sex, and denominational preference reveals that these accepted patterns do not hold for some subgroups of the Middletown population.

Do girls attend church more regularly than boys? As the percentages in Appendix Table 11-5 show, the answer depends upon their denominational identity and class. Among Catholics, being business-class or working-class makes a big difference in church attendance. When Catholic boys and girls of the same class are compared, girls show more church attendance than boys by about 10 percentage points. But business-class Catholic boys are *more* likely to attend church regularly than working-class Catholic girls. Among Protestants, sex and class do not make much difference;

Protestant boys attend church about as often as Protestant girls, and working-class Protestant children about as often as their business-class counterparts.

Middletown students showed no decline in church attendance as they moved through adolescence. At each age between 14 and 18, about one-third of the students said they attended regularly and about one-fifth said they never attended.

There is a strong relationship between academic achievement and churchgoing. Among students who said they received "A's or mostly A's" on their last report cards, 41 percent attended regularly. The percentage attending regularly dropped consistently with reported grades. Only 19 percent of those receiving "C's and D's" were regular church attenders and in the lowest grade category, grades of "mostly D's or below," only 12 percent attended regularly.

Orthodoxy, Attendance, and Denominational Identity

We have said that the business and working classes do not differ much in their acceptance of the dominant Christian beliefs but that they do differ substantially in church attendance. The religious beliefs of working-class students are similar to those of business-class students, but the latter are far more likely to claim a denominational preference and to attend church. It follows that there are many "believing" boys and girls in working-class families who do not attend church.

To clarify the relationship between religious belief and church attendance, we combined three indicators of "orthodoxy" (items 1, 2, and 3 in Appendix Table 11-1) into a composite "orthodoxy index" and then compared students' orthodoxy scores to their church attendance. The index was calculated by simple addition, with one point given for each "orthodox" answer; the range is from zero to three. However, because at least two of the items—the all sufficiency of biblical guidance and the literal interpretation of the early chapters of Genesis—may reflect denominational differences as much as Christian orthodoxy, we consider index scores of two or three as high.

Here is the distribution of index scores for the 950 students answering the questionnaire form including the orthodoxy items:

High orthodoxy (scores two and three)	57%
Moderate orthodoxy (score one)	28
Low orthodoxy (score zero)	15
	100%

Both attending church and having a religious preference were positively associated with orthodoxy (Appendix Table 11-6). When the threshold for high orthodoxy is set at two, the distribution of orthodoxy is the same for Catholics and Protestants, with about 60 percent classified as high orthodox and fewer than 15 percent as low orthodox. Even among students with no religious preference, 43 percent qualified as highly orthodox.

Sunday Activity: No Longer a Battleground

Middletown in 1924 was torn, wrote the Lynds (1929, 339), by "the battle raging for the possession of the stronghold of religious tradition—the Christian Sabbath." A generation earlier, they said, all manner of recreational activities, let alone work, had been either illegal or strongly discouraged. Sunday had been reserved for prayer, churchgoing, scripture reading, and little else. A strict observance of Sunday in the 1890s was described this way: "We weren't allowed to play games or even to crack nuts or make candy on Sunday. Father would never take pictures on Sunday. We couldn't read a newspaper or any weekday reading, but only things like our Sunday School papers" (Lynd and Lynd 1929, 339-40).

By 1924, although some ministers still proclaimed that "the Christian Sabbath belongs to the Lord . . . if it is His day, then He has a right to say how we shall spend it," that was a minority opinion. Parks, golf courses, and movie houses were full; and fewer than a third of the high school students said it was wrong to go to the movies on Sunday (Lynd and Lynd 1929, 341-43).

A decade later, the Lynds (1937, 306-7) saw the forces of secularization winning the "battle." The municipal swimming pool was open and crowded on Sundays; horse shows were held on that day; popular tunes had displaced religious music on Sunday afternoon broadcasts; and Sunday driving, "starting before morning church and coming home too late for the evening service," was common.

From the perspective of the late 1970s and early 1980s, it appears that the forces of secularization won the battle but lost the war. Church attendance is not lower now than it was in the 1920s and 1930s, although there are even more competitive alternatives for Sunday time than there were then. The battle lines marked by the Lynds have been made irrelevant as the churches have adopted more tolerant views of proper Sunday behavior. Christian ministers today shy away rom listing 'dos" and "don'ts." Instead, they claim that they stress principles and let the people decide the specifics. Most denominations have redefined appropriate Sunday activity to include all licit forms of entertainment and recreation.

During 17 in-depth interviews with Middletown ministers in 1981, we asked for their views on "Sabbath observance." The consensus was that people should worship on Sunday, that is, that they should attend at least one church meeting, and beyond that freely do whatever they liked. The majority of the ministers we interviewed held that the only activities inappropriate for Sunday were activities that are inappropriate at any time. One Protestant minister, asked what we would encourage his parishioners to do on Sundays, replied:

My approach to the Sabbath is that it is a day of rest, a day that should be dedicated first and foremost to your spiritual nourishment but it is also a day when you should be involved, perhaps, in those things which you cannot be involved in other times because you work, or whatever. I see nothing inconsistent with the Sabbath being the day of the Lord, let's say, and a husband and his family going out for a picnic or going to the beach or something like that, or spending time together as a family. I think the problem is this, where I have to try and educate the members of my congregation, the problem is not going out had having a picnic or going out and playing tennis or golf, the problem is going out and leaving God home . . . If a man and his wife and children decided they want to go out and have a picnic Sunday afternoon, I think that's great. Take your Bible along; when you get there, before you leave have a prayer, maybe read a little passage of scripture to let your children know, as well as yourself, that this is the Lord's day . . . I think as long as God is brought in to whatever it is you are doing on the Sabbath, that's fine.

Sometimes a minister made a distinction between his personal views and what he expected, or prescribed, for the people. "Sunday should be a day of recreation, you know, the true sense of re-creation," reported one. He said that his church expected people to worship, "to express their adoration of God," but apart from that, "hopefully it's a day of rest for them, and not just sitting around doing nothing, but a day of re-creating." In his opinion, shopping on Sunday was wrong, but he said that he did not make a major point of that with his congregation.

I take, personally, a very strong stand against shopping on Sunday, even though I don't think we can force our values in that way on others. I think that just because stores are open, that that's no reason that I have to do my shopping on Sunday. I think there's a social pressure that has built up in business, and stores stay open because people do shop. I don't think we should, simply because you are keeping other people working who would like to be with their families.

A more direct attempt to influence the Sunday activities of young people is the sponsorship of sports or social events by churches. A youth minister explained.

During the summertime, every Sunday afternoon, the youth group gets together and we play softball as a group. They're not all off doing their own thing. It's not a mandatory thing, but you give them an opportunity of recreation and fun, then you're keeping them from doing something that maybe would alter their belief or maybe even compromise what they feel they ought to be doing.

The minister of one of the more conservative Middletown denominations answered the question, "What do your members do on a Sunday?" this way:

We teach that the first day of the week is the Lord's day. It's to be used for worship. If during the other hours, other than the times we are assembled for worship, there's a baseball game, or there's activities our members are a part of, want to be a part of, I can see no particular objections. If they want to go hoe in the garden, that's okay too, but I think they would be expected by God to worship at the worship hours on the first day of the week.

The interviewer probed, "I just wondered about movies and boating and picnics." The minister answered, "I wouldn't have any objection to that, and I don't believe the Bible would."

Thus, the formula for Sunday observance today is worship *and* recreation. Ministers' attitudes are flexible. "We don't try to put out people in a mold," said the minister of a south-side church.

I tell people that I don't think they should go out of their way to work on Sunday. If it's a necessity, we're not against that. If it's something that would just continually keep them out of church, then we would be against that. Here again, we don't really hammer something like that, we would encourage people as much as possible, try to relax on Sunday. Be in church on Sunday morning, be in church Sunday evening, and just try to relax.

The minister of one of the city's largest north-side churches also stressed flexibility and made a bigger point of variety. According to him, Sunday's enrichment potential is, in part, a result of "doing something different" on that day:

A good Sunday activity is to get up, have yourself a nice breakfast, and meet with your worshipping community. Then, depending on your personal schedule and cycle and so forth, whether you work six days or five days, to don't do anything you would do any other day. Sometimes we have tried to encourage people to develop a unique Sunday life-style, something like a Sabbath, like, here's the day where you go out and visit your grandmother or visit your sick friend in a hospital or take your kid out for a walk, and if one doesn't have any other time to spend with family, that certainly is the time to spend with them. But we haven't emphasized that too much because people's lives are quite complex and it's hard to lay a strict rule down . . . But I don't have the slightest inhibition against somebody going to a movie on Sunday afternoon, or to a play. If it's a bad movie they shouldn't go any time.

Some ideas about what families actually do on Sundays were gained from the high school questionnaire, which asked young people how they had spent the previous Sunday. The Lynds' 1924 questionnaire had included this item: "List what you did between breakfast and bed-time the last two Sundays." The item was followed by a blank section headed "Last Sunday" divided into thirds by the headings "Morning," "Afternoon," and "Evening" and a smiliar section headed "Sunday before last." For some reason, the data generated by these queries were not published in *Middletown* in any identifiable form. Even though the comparative data from the previous use of the item were unavailable, we went ahead and included a similar question in the 1977 questionnaire: "Please list what you did between breakfast and bedtime last Sunday." There followed a 12-line space where the boys and girls could summarize their Sunday. Following the Lynds' pattern, the space was divided into thirds by the headings "Last Sunday morning," "Last Sunday afternoon," and "Last Sunday evening."

For this question, and several other open-ended items in the questionnaire, we analyzed a random subsample amounting to approximately half (N = 767) of the questionnaire in the high school survey. Each student's description of the previous Sunday was tabulated according to the kinds of activities mentioned.

Many students (29 percent of the boys and 15 percent of the girls) did not take the time to write in the details of their Sundays. Those who did mentioned from 1 to 10 kinds of activities. Table 11-7 lists the activities mentioned most often.

Table 11-7
Activities Reported for "Last Sunday," Middletown High School Students, 1977
(in percentages)

Activity	Boys (N = 258)	Girls (N = 337)
Watching television	48	44
Attending church	31	35
Resting, sleeping	30	24
Participating in sports	22	8
Visiting friends	21	24
Doing homework	20	19
Working	15	13
Cleaning	2	15
Eating out	7	13
Shopping	5	21

Source: Middletown III high school survey, 1977.

What do Middletown's young people do on Sunday? Above all else, as these percentages suggest, they watch television. Nearly half of the boys and almost that many girls watched enough television to mention it as one of the dominant activities of the day. Churchgoing and napping were the next most popular Sunday activities. About one student in seven had a job that required Sunday work, and one girl in seven spent part of Sunday housecleaning. Other popular Sunday activities not making the "top ten" were going to parties or picnics, going to movies, reading, listening to tapes and records or to the radio, and playing cards and other indoor games.

One may be able to get a better idea of the students' Sunday activities by reading some of their responses verbatim. Church attendance was noted in each of these cases:

Got ready for church, ate, just messed around, went to church, and did homework [girl, regular churchgoer] .

Ate, went to church, cleaned room, ate, played tennis, did art, ate, read, watched movie [girl, regular churchgoer] .

Have breakfast, go to church, have lunch, go bowling with church group, dinner, read and watch TV [girl, attends weekly] .

Went to church, went to our lake cottage, watched TV [boy, regular churchgoer] .

Slept until 10:30 A.M., got ready for and went to noon mass, went bowling with friends, played a few games of chess, ate out, played cards and ping pong with friends who stayed overnight [boy, regular churchgoer] .

Made cookies, did homework, worked at movie theater [girl, intermittent churchgoer] .

Stayed in bed, went to the river on motorcycles, at home doing chores [boy, intermittent churchgoer] .

Church, ate, drove around, watched TV, homework, ate, read a book, homework [boy, attends at least monthly] .

Slept until 12:00, went to work, went out with my boyfriend [girl, attends several times a year] .

Took shower, painted fingernails, went to the store, laid down for a nap, I didn't feel well, went with my boyfriend to a dance, before dance we went out to eat [girl, attends several times a year] .

Got up at 7:00, watched TV to 12:00, after watching TV ate lunch, went out, came home, watched TV, ate supper, went to bed 10:00 [boy, attends several times a year] .

Got up, listened to some music and worked on car, went to my girl friend's, watched a basketball game [boy, attends several times a year] .

Ate and did dishes, parents went to store, had to watch kids, went out to eat with boyfriend [girl, attends once or twice a year] .

I slept until 12:30, listened to the radio, took my cousin home, went shopping, went over to a friend's house, came home, watched TV, talked on the phone, went to bed [girl, attends once or twice a year] .

Paper route, played basketball, homework, played baseball, lunch, homework, played tennis, homework [boy, attends once or twice a year] .

I watched TV all day, had some cigarettes and went to bed, got hungry and ate and that's all I did, I watched TV [boy, attends once or twice a year] .

Woke up, got dressed, ate breakfast, played ping pong, listened to some music, ate lunch, worked on my car, studied homework, listened to music, read my *Time* magazine [boy, attends once or twice a year] .

Fixed breakfast, cleaned house and bathed, watched TV and partied, ate supper and went to bed [girl, never attends] .

I slept in, read, did homework and went shopping, did homework, watched TV [girl, never attends] .

Went over to a friend's house, played pool, played pinball, and walked around at the Mall, rode around in my brother's car [boy, never attends] .

Suggestions for Change

The best material illustrating young people's attitudes toward organized religion is drawn from their answers to the question "What change or changes should the churches make to suit you and your friends better?" The material is *illustrative* only, since there was no systematic effort to cover the entire range of their attitudes or to find out how strongly they felt about the suggestions they made.

One student in three did not answer the question at all. Of those who did answer, almost half said "none" or commented that they were happy with the church as it was or would make no changes.

There were a few hostile remarks—that church buildings should be torn down, that nothing would bring them to church, that organized religion is irrelevant—but they were rare. Most of the boys and girls who answered the question either said they had no suggestions for change or pointed to ways that the church could meet their spiritual needs more effectively. Overall, the nature of the suggestions and their implicit context showed the same respect for the church we encountered among adults in Middletown.

In a recent volume based on data from Gallup polls about religion in America, George Gallup, Jr., and David Poling (1980, 15-18) reported that young people in America are vitally concerned with religion in their lives, although most believe that one can be a good Christian even without attending church. Despite their deep concern and enthusiastic commitment to religion, however, many young people are disillusioned and critical of the established churches. Five major criticisms revealed by one Gallup poll were: (1) the churches' failure to reach and genuinely to serve the common people, (2) church members' superficiality and misplaced emphasis on nonessentials, (3) the unappealing "packaging" of the Christian message, (4) an apparent lack of excitement and personal support in fellowship, and (5) negative models presented by members of the clergy. All these points were made in response to the Middletown questionnaires, but points three and four were most emphasized.

Presentation of the Christian Message

Gallup and Poling (1980, 18) described the churches' difficulty in presenting the Christian gospel in ways acceptable and meaningful to young Americans as "the inability of congregations to deal with the basics of faith and appeal to youth on a solid spiritual basis." To Middletown's youth, this inability boils down to a perception that church meetings are too boring, too formal, too lengthy, and too often devoted to topics that seem out-of-date. The youth plead for services that command their attention and speak in language they understand.

"I think the service could be less formal and the minister could try and use language easier to understand," said one girl; another echoed, "Make the sermons easier to understand, have it more exciting." Some variations of the same message by students who said they attended church regularly or frequently were:

They are fairly OK, but they should preach at a more teen level to the teens.

Not make services so long; separate the congregation into groups and preach to the different age levels. The understanding and attendance would improve.

They are going to have to get a more modern service if they want to keep a lot of the younger generation in the church.

Similar statements were made by students who attended less often or never. "They need to make it more interesting, it is so boring," wrote a girl who said she never went to church anymore. Another nonattender said the ministers should "talk in a language which we can understand more fully; I don't mean slang words, but just saying things so that we can understand easier."

There were many complaints about the apparent irrelevance or outdatedness of church services and church activities. "I'm not sure I want a change in the church, except that it should try more modern ideas," said a boy who regularly attended church. A girl who attended at least monthly said the church would be improved "if they would preach new stuff." Another girl with comparable church attendance suggested that church services would be improved if there were more music, less formality, and a sermon concerned with "everyday, common happenings."

Church should be interesting, even fun, argued the young people who said they attended church only on special occasions (once or twice a year) or occasionally (several times a year). For example:

Be brought up to date, let young children be a little more free, let them do things they like to do.

Be more interesting, go places; God made the outside world too.

Make the lessons more fun, have more special activities.

Become more modern and never try and bribe people to go, because they won't come; be more like a school and have a discussion break. Church sometimes gets boring.

I think churches should try to come up with something a little different for the young people. It is the same every week. I have the whole service memorized and it just seems ridiculous.

They should explain what they are saying in a more modern way, and not always ask for money.

An elegant description of the kind of church service that appeals to many young people was the statement "I like a church when it's not like a church."

In response to the statement "Most people are bored by going to church but go because they think it is a duty," 65 percent of the students marked "agree" or "strongly agree." In fact, the rate of agreement with the "church is boring" item was on a par with that for the item on the divinity of Jesus. Moreoever, most of the characteristics of the students that affected other aspects of religiosity had no influence on the attitude that church is boring. Judging by their responses to this item, freshmen are as bored as the seniors, girls as bored as the boys, Catholics as bored as Protestants. Even church attendance makes no difference: students who attended regularly were as bored as those who attended rarely or not at all. There *was* a slight but significant difference by social class: students from business-class families were more likely than working-class students to think that most churchgoers are bored but dutiful (72 percent to 64 percent). The same difference appeared when parents' education was used as the measure of social class.

Lack of Excitement and Personal Support in Fellowship

This perceived deficiency was most plainly seen in suggestions that more attention be given to the special needs of adolescents. Some churches had too few active adolescents to maintain a special program, and others gave young people little opportunity to express themsevles. Some of the Middletown churches have successful youth programs, and perhaps that majority who said they liked things as they were or had no suggestions were being served effectively. Nevertheless, the number of complaints about the narrow range of youth activities and their limited appeal suggests that, even though many churches have special youth programs, they are often perceived as ineffective and inappropriate by the intended audience.

The churches need to "make it so it won't be so dull," said one girl, "the choirs are the best things in the church, so they have to be good." Said another, "They should let us participate in church sports, such as a baseball or bowling team." The suggestions for a more vital fellowship often took the form of wishing for more "opportunities," coupled with criticism of church formalism, the minister, or sermons generally. For example:

Don't preach and yell so much, just sing.

Have a less boring minister and more opportunities for people my age.

Include more teenagers into things. And stop asking them if they have made up their mind in which church they're going to. Stop pursuing.

[The church members should be] trying to understand kids' feelings today and not when they were kids.

More youth-oriented programs, group sessions in which many aspects of life are discussed.

Some of the students who attended regularly said they wished their church would do more to attract other young people. One boy said that his church "should design a youth group that is fun and attracts new members from the community," and another sought "shorter sermons, better acquaintance with young people."

Superficiality and the Failure to Serve the Needy

Our Middletown teenage students, unlike the young adults inter-viwed by Gallup, were not able to articulate completely their feeling that their own and other people's spiritual needs were not being met. But they showed no hesitancy about attacking what they saw as a churchly overemphasis on appearances and the material side of things, on externalities and the outer person rather than the essential spiritual core. Their brief and sometimes biting comments had a central message: the organized church as we know it is too concerned with appearances. Here, for instance, are complaints about "high-status" churches from girls who said they attended church once or twice a year:

[The church ought] not to be such a status symbol. You go to our church just to say you go there. I don't like this. A church is a place to be humble.

The churches today are stuck up. They only want you in if you're important or have money.

I consider church a place to come to be judged by the people in your community as to how you dress, act, or how much money you have. Church is too social.

Far more common than criticisms of church membership as a status symbol were complaints about hair and dress standards and about how churchgoers looked down on persons who did not dress well. A boy who attended regularly said he wished that the church would "become less strict on the modern customs of dress at church," and a girl who attended only once or twice a year explained that "the church people always treat you snobbish if you're not dressed as good as they are." A girl who attended several times a year added that churches "should not put so much stress on what you wear or look like and emphasize how you think, feel, and believe." A girl who attended regularly saw the externalities as harsh rules illegitimately grafted onto the gospel by ministers and church members: "They set too many rules, and God made the church for those who need it, not to set rules to go by. People go on their own free will. They shouldn't be so harsh with rules they make."

The frequent failure of the organized churches "genuinely to serve those whom Christ loved and sought and reclaimed" was summarized by Gallup and Poling (1980, 19):

. . . The young people in this Ohio study indicate strong attraction for volunteer work and a high consideration for social work as a career option. Their humanitarian impulse appears to be fueled by their valuing a Christian orientation which they believe their church to have neglected or given a rather low priority.

Judging from their comments on things they would like changed, Middletown's youth are more disturbed by dress and grooming standards that they consider irrelevant than by any failure of local churches to serve the needy and the poor in spirit. However, some students did criticize the churches for not doing enough for the poor, and there were numerous complaints that the churches were too commercial, too preoccupied with money, too proud, or too "stuck up." Some students said they felt rejected by the church. One girl, who said she never went to church, explained: "I don't think they should be as strict as they are. I don't think they ought to look down their noses at us because they think they are closer to God than we are." And a nonattending boy said, "They force stuff on you and make you feel inferior." Variations on the theme that some of the churches ignore the poor or, by their attitudes, add to the burdens of the poor were voiced by students who said the churches should:

Associate with everyone, not just talk to certain people.

Do more things with children, and earn money for people who need it.

Quit snubbing people because of being poor.

. . . Make you feel wanted. I often feel left out in churches.

. . . Not be so greedy, and spend some of its money to help out the young people in their plans.

Negative Views of the Clergy

A few students criticized ministers and priests in their suggestions for change. Apart from the charge that services are boring, ministers were criticized for being hypocritical, too involved in money-raising activities, and too old. "Get younger ministers," said one boy. "Have younger priests, and more recreational activities," said another. A few students called for "a different preacher" or said things like "the ministry at our church is not to our liking" without giving any reasons for their feelings.

The charge of hypocrisy was leveled against church members at least as often as against the ministry.

They should change the way that they do, not act like certain ones seen at the church. Because it is God's, not theirs. The preachers should practice what they preach, not preach to us and go out and do it themselves.

Not to be so hypocritical. They think they are the only ones who are living in God's way because they go to church. They won't really look out into the world.

The image of the clergy as being money hungry was reflected in comments such as these:

Stop taking people's money and buying those big cars.

Don't sell things.

Quit being so preoccupied with money.

Not so much emphasis on giving money to the church.

Not to be so boring and not always be after money. They sent me a bill once when I forgot to pay my pledge for four months.

Not to become a racket where the only thing they want from you is your money.

Cut down the offering to once instead of three times.

Perhaps the saddest statement about youth and the clergy was this boy's lament: "I know a priest who was kicked out because he was too liberal, but everybody, especially me, liked him better than any."

Affirmation and Approval

Having reviewed the students' criticisms of organized religion in Middletown, we will return to the point that most students either made no suggestions or said they liked things as they were. The most common response was a simple "none." Sometimes the satisfaction with the status quo was elaborated in statements such as "They suit me fine" and "None, I like my church the way it is organized." A few students gave a theological reason for not wanting change.

None, if any changes should be made, they should be made for God, not for man [girl, attends weekly].

None, I like my church because it's the truth [boy, attends weekly].

None, because it's the Lord's church and if He wanted it changed He would have done it [boy, attends weekly].

They should not change to suit the whims of me or my friends. They are governed by the Lord and His rule. He set it down and it is our choice to believe or not. We must conform [boy, attends weekly].

Others said they wanted no changes because their needs were already being met.

Nothing, my spirit is getting fed greatly. I am now able to walk in a truer faith, praise the Lord [girl, attends weekly].

None, I think it's fine now. I love church, I am very involved [girl, attends weekly].

Students who attended church often were less likely to be critical than were others less regular in attendance, but many of the latter also said they were satisfied or at least that they had no suggestions for change.

Really none at all, the services are just great [girl, attends several times a year].

No changes, it is a very good church, it seems to me it's perfect [girl, attends once or twice a year].

None, I don't attend, and they suit my friends very well [girl, never attends].

None, I just don't want to go [boy, never attends].

None whatsoever, our church is in perfect agreement, with young people and old people alike [girl, attends monthly].

I can think of no conceivable changes; I am simply not interested. Nor do I believe in religion [girl, never attends].

Before concluding this discussion of young people's ideas for making the churches more responsive to their needs, we should note that, in contrast to the vast majority who wanted the churches to become more youth oriented, informal, or in tune with modern language and dress, there were a few who called for a return to the traditional ways they saw as being eroded. "None, it's changed too much already. Ought to change back to more formality, there's not enough anymore in my church" (girl, attends monthly).

Religion should be interesting and immediate and helpful, Middletown's youth said again and again; it should be concerned with the inner, not the outer, person, with hearts and minds, and not complexions and clothes. Even the words "church" and "religious" had negative connotations to many. One girl's pithy suggestion about what would improve churches was "Not be so churchy." And we imagine that to many Midletown Christians the following statements echo as a haunting indictment of the image, if not the reality, of church life in Middletown.

Not to be so prejudiced. Let anyone come who wants to.

Not to dress so fancy, God doesn't look on the outside of you, he looks on the inside.

Quit snubbing people because of being poor.

Youth as Seen by the Ministry

We have considered what Middletown's youth say about the churches and how they would like to see the churches changed. Now let us look at the subject from another perspective, that of the clergy.

The 1920s and 1930s were not times of religious optimism in Middletown. Local observers thought young people were losing interest in organized religion. The growing power of secularism was evident, said the Lynds in 1935, for the "unalert acceptance and lethargy" that had characterized the city's religious life in 1925 had become more ervasive. The Great Depression had not brought new vitality, there seemed fewer young people in the churches than before, and the secularization of the Christian Sabbath had apparently continued (Lynd and Lynd 1937, 295-97, 301-7).

The impression that young people were turning away from the churches in the 1930s was neither confirmed nor refuted by the report on the needs of Middletown's youth prepared by Raymond Fuller in 1936 and 1937. His research included a mail survey of the city's ministers on the topic of youth and the church. The ministers were asked about changes in young people's attitudes. Most of the ministers responding said there had been recent changes: of the 29 whose answers to the attendance question were reproduced in Fuller's report, 11 said there had been a decline in attendance and an equal number said there had been an increase. In attitudes about religion, 20 of the 21 recorded responses noted change, with a slight majority (11 of the 20) defining the change as decline or loss (Fuller 1937, 92-96).

In contrast to the pessimism and mixed optimism of the earlier era, Middletown's ministers in the late 1970s and early 1980s were remarkably hopeful about the faith of their young people. They recognized that the young people have special problems, but they attributed them to the various social pressures that young people face, rather than to their weakness, rebelliousness, faithlessness, or sunfulness. One minister had this to say about community responsibility:

. . . The illnesses of individuals tell us a great deal about the communities in which these individuals live. This is easy to accept when we speak of drug addictions, alcoholism, juvenile delinquency, and crime. However, we must extend this list to include mental and physical illnesses. The prevailing value system in any given community will many times determine the health or illness of individuals in that community (Newby 1980, 6).

The concerns of ministers about young people were, for the most part, centered on family and social contexts:

Our young people have many problems. They have problems in their schools facing a culture that does not represent the sort of thing they have been told in their homes and their Sunday Schools. They have been taught to be very tolerant but sometimes the tolerance breaks down. The peer group pressures are very great here in Middletown; to withstand those pressures as a Christian young person is very difficult. There are drugs in the schools, there's cheating, there's sex. And the traditional values that you don't have sex until you're married, you certainly don't use drugs, you certainly don't cheat on a test, these things are very bothersome . . . I think young people go through a phase of throwing it all over . . . I have found over the years that most young people will hang on to their religious heritage. The few we've had problems with have become the stronger because of it.

The ministers did recognize challenges in reaching today's young people. Some ministers lamented the changing family standards and their effects on people of all ages.

A problem of family life, and associated with that, dirorce. The increasing number of singles, so that we now have a singles group. The youth always presents a challenge to the church, and I see the breakdown of family life, and permissiveness of society, the low moral atmosphere, which is a part of our culture affects church families just as much as it affects non-church families . . . There's always been that sort of thing going on. But it seems to be on a much wider scale today. You have only to pick up the newspaper and look at marriage applications there, and discover, as I have done over a period of weeks, the number of people applying for marriage licenses who give the same address. I think that probably is different from what it was a generation ago. Maybe they were living together a generation ago, but they gave different addresses when they went to apply for a license.

Another minister said that many young people had trouble finding his messages compatible with their life-styles: "I would say that [on account of] the new moral issues that are so commonly practiced among youth, that they resent the minister to preach on a general [antisexual sin approach]. Some of them do resent that." Asked whether he did much counseling of young people in matters related to personal morality, he answered, "Used to, but it seems like a lot of them, they're bored with it; they don't say anything." He continued with an illustration.

I talked this week with a young lady who's got a young child and she was going to commit suicide and I was asked to go out and see her. She was living with a fellow and decided that he didn't want her anymore. This broke her heart. She didn't flinch in any way in saying that "we lived together" and that he just recently got a divorce and was going to marry her. So now he got his divorce but doesn't want her. That morality in some way has slipped.

Even while describing these problems, however, he referred to other young people in his congregation in whom he had great faith.

Actually, it's not all young people, it's the middle-aged people, too. However, we have some youth that are as straight as a button, you know . . . They get together and they have a youth leader and they have a great time. They worship, they talk about life, and I really think they are trying to do what is right . . . A lot of those young people are just the opposite of what I've been talking about, they're good. You know what I mean. It isn't all of them.

Several ministers said that the problems of the young people could be traced to inadequate training in the home. Here is a minister's indictment of parental instruction:

I have a difficult time with that because a lot of our young people that come to us, they come out of colleges or they're in college where they're being taught by professors who share the new approach, let us say, and they teach these young people as if what they're teaching them is absolute fact. And then they [the young people] come into church and they hear something else and they say, "Wait a minute, this is confusing to me." So yes, there's a difficult time with young people who get exposed to this ["new morality"] and then they come into church and find out that other people really have a different set of values. One of the problems we're faced with, and I can honestly say this is very definitely the case in Middletown as well as everyplace else, is that children, generally speaking, are not receiving proper guidance from their parents. In the sense that many parents are not guiding their children at all . . . It never ceases to amaze me that parents will take two-thirds of their child—the physical and mental part—and they will spend an exorbitant amount of time, money, and energy developing those two-thirds . . . But yet when it comes to their spiritual development they just, you know, plop, let it fall flat. So these children grow up and they go to college and then in college they start getting all of these moral values—or I think in today's society a *lack* of moral values—thrown at them, and then they come to church and all of a sudden this is what becomes traumatic for them. All of a sudden, at 20 years old, they hear somebody say adultery is wrong, fornication is wrong, homosexuality, alcoholism, drug addiction, these are wrong, and it just blows their mind. And so this is something that, when it comes to the young people, that really has to be dealt with with kid gloves. You can't go in and beat them over the head with it because they will totally rebel and have to understand where they're coming from and the lack of any kind of education they have, some of them.

Another minister told us that the defection of a certain proportion of young people from the church was part of the normal process of growing up: "In our churches, sad to say, there is a loss of a good percentage of the young people, say, when they get to be age 14. It is not necessarily increasing, and it is a general experience [in his church and others] ."

Generally, Middletown's ministers do not define today's youth as being misguided, as rejecting the church, or as being alienated through a widening generation gap. In contrast to the apprehensions recorded by the Lynds and by Fuller two generations ago, their outlook for the rising generation is distinctly positive. For example:

I find that youth in our church right now, the youth and children, are just easier to work with than any time I've ever experienced. I think that real young parents right now are doing a good job with their children.

I'm real encouraged, real optimistic. I see with the last year and a half, last two years, especially with the young people. We train them for marriage and I can see there a much more healthy sense of commitment to marriage, which if it's true, that's where the future lies . . . I'm real optimistic.

I feel very positive about young people today and I see them as having a deep faith, a deep Christian faith. Some of it is expressed in, or rather seeks to be fulfilled in some rather fundamentalistic ways, but nevertheless it reflects a deep search for my students, I've never found the spiritual atmosphere as fertile as it is today.

That's the problem with a lot of the churches, they don't give their people enough to do or they don't give their young people enough to do. And I'm not saying I run the legs off these young people [laughter] . Well, yes I do. But I give them things to do because I feel that we've got to give them an alternative. There are so many young people that have come into this youth group that said, "I can't believe the fun that you as a youth group have; I can't believe you still clown around and you still joke and you still tease and you still cut up, but when it comes time to worship, there's tears flowing out of the eyes of these kids because they've really got a special relationship with Christ.

Conclusion

The Middletown ministers' optimistic attitudes about the future may reflect an occupational worldview as biased as that held by Middletown preachers described by the Lynds. However, there is other evidence for their faith in the continued vitality of organized religion. In previous chapters, we have reported comparisons between the Lynds' findings and our own that reveal that today's Middletowners are more likely to attend church, to donate larger fractions of their incomes to churches, and to manifest a heightened religious fervency, at least in the business class. The 50-year contrasts seem to show that Middletown people today are more zealous in religious observance than were the townspeople of their grandparents' generation, and yet contemporary Middletown is also much more tolerant of religious and other life-style diversities.

Chapter 12

Middletown's Clergy

This chapter describes the members of Middletown's clergy and explores the religious life of Middletown people as they experience it. It is based on responses from the 112 ministers who participated in our 1978 mail survey, and the 17 ministers whom we interviewed at length during the summer of 1981[1] as well as on the experiences and impressions of the Middletown project investigators who attended services and meetings in many of Middletown's churches.

At the end of each of these . . . religious groups is the man who gets his living by "ministering to" that particular group . . . He is first and foremost expected to be a good talker . . . He is also expected to be a "sympathetic pastor," a "good fellow among the men," and to "draw the young people" (Lynd and Lynd 1929, 344).

The ministers are themselves harried, overworked, perplexed that religion has not vindicated itself more in the depression (Lynd and Lynd 1937, 308).

[We] must now begin to challenge our most able young leadership to look upon the . . . pastorate as one of the highest callings a person can receive . . . No amount of gimmickry or religious faddishness can take the place of a "beloved community" which has [as] the basis of their fellowship together a regular, well prepared vocal ministry, a creative program of Christian education, and trained pastoral help for persons in need of counseling (Newby 1980, xiv).

According to the Lynds, the successful Middletown preacher was a "good talker." In large measure, his livelihood depended on his ability to attract people to church through his sermons. Eloquence continues to be a characteristic trait of successful ministers in Middletown today. Respondents in the 1978 housewives' survey, when asked why they did or did not attend church, often referred to the quality of the minister's sermon.

I enjoy the music, a peaceful feeling, and the minister gives interesting talks [Regularly attending business-class wife].

To feed my spirit. My husband goes for that reason. Our minister is a good speaker. [Regularly attending business-class wife].

It depends on who is speaking. If it's interesting, we go [Occasionally attending working-class wife].

Boring sermons [Nonattending working-class wife].

I belong to and support the church financially. However, I have lost the habit of going to church because the minister is an ineffective speaker [Nonattending working-class wife].

Besides providing a successful "vocal ministry," the contemporary Middletown pastor is expected to listen sympathetically and to counsel wisely. "They still come to us for consolation," a leading clergyman said half a century ago (Lynd and Lynd 1937, 318), and the role of the minister as an "emotionally stabilizing agent" is as important today as it was in earlier generations. Most Middletown ministers spend many hours each week dispensing spiritual and personal guidance to individual members of their flocks. Most of them do not have provessional training in counseling, although a few said they had taken classes or seminars in order to improve their counseling skills. Church members in several surveys noted that their ministers had helped them cope with such personal problems as marital conflict, quarrels with children, and dissatisfaction at work and with feelings of depression, rejection, and worthlessness.

Although successful ministers of the 1920s got along with the young people in their congregations and were able to attract them to services, their attention was directed principally to the women in their congregation, by whom, said the Lynds, they were "more highly esteemed" (Lynd and Lynd 1929, 347). Many of today's ministers have resolved this point of strain by employing an assistant with special responsibility for young people. Although the assistant pastor often has other duties, typically the youth ministry is part of his responsibilities.

The low esteem accorded to the ministry by the men of the community in the 1920s was reflected in conversations like this one recorded by the Lynds (1929, 348):

A group of half-a-dozen influential business men, all college graduates, were discussing the ministry: "I'd never advise a boy to go into it," said one emphatically. "I never heard a preacher yet," added another, "who didn't make me mad by standing up there where he knows you can't talk back and saying things he doesn't really believe and he knows he can't prove." The general opinion of the group was that the ministry is "played out."

Such feelings were not confined to the business class (Lynd and Lynd 1929, 348).

"What's a minister without his salary, anyway?" asked a labor union man of a group sitting about talking before a labor meeting. "You take away his salary and he's nothin'! When he gets a chance to make more money at another place he calls it a call from God!"

Except in a few of the largest churches, clergymen earned meager incomes and their families lived in near poverty at the time the Lynds studied Middletown. Today, full-time ministers, although not paid as well as comparably educated persons in other professions, have incomes above the median level. Salaries for ministers in well-established churches around 1980 typically fell between $18,000 and $25,000 and were supplemented by free housing and transportation and allowances for travel, entertainment, and other expenses.

In the marginal churches, most ministers work at other jobs. In 1978, 56 percent of the ministers reponding to the survey said they received all their support from the church; 12 percent gained a "significant" part of their livelihood from the church; 24 percent received only "nominal" support; and 8 percent received "none" of their livelihood from the church. Those in the latter three categories worked at least part-time in factories, supermarkets, banks, and schools to maintain their families; one was a veterinarian. The ministry is unpaid as a matter of principle in a handful of churches, whose religious leaders work full-time at other occupations, but these instances are exceptional. Most of the part-time ministers were interviewed presided over new congregations and anticipated that the membership would eventually increase to the point at which they could be supported full-time. One minister who was working "sixteen hours a day" for a part-time salary said he depending on savings he accumulated during a business career before his ordination to the ministry. He was confident that the church would be able to support him before his personal resources were exhausted.

The Lynds did not systematically record the educational qualifications of Middletown's ministers, but they described the training of the ministers of the six leading churches. Four of the six had worked at other occupations before being called to the ministry; five of the six were college graduates trained for other professions. All had prepared themselves for the pulpit by attending a divinity school, and three had graduated. But these six were surely better educated than the average clergyman of the 1920s.

In 1978, 86 percent of Middletown's ministers had graduated from college. Most had received additional training for the ministry: 62 percent of the college graduates had attended a seminary and 23 percent, a Bible college. The great majority of contemporary ministers are fully trained professionals.

About one-third of Middletown's full-time ministers at one time had held a position with a new congregation that required them to work part-time outside the ministry to support their families. Either the congregation had then grown capable of providing full support, or the minister had obtained sufficient experience to move to a larger church.

Ministerial Duties

The denominations differ in what they expect of their pastors, but most expect leadership in church worship and in other organized programs and expertise in the interpretation of scripture and church doctrines and policies. Beyond that, there is great variation. The ministers of some of the larger churches are much like corporate executives. Backed by the church equivalents of junior executives, administrative assistants, and secretaries, they oversee and orchestrate a multitude of religious, educational, recreational, welfare, and fund-raising activities. They are also deeply involved in matters of church governance, interacting with committees, boards, associations, and other constituencies in their church communities. In many denominations, the minister is also responsible to higher church officials, "superiors" in the church hierarchy whose wishes and interests must be taken into account.

"The purpose of the church is to turn the people to the Lord," said the minister of an Evangelical Protestant church. In many Middletown churches, the multiple expectations associated with the role of minister complicate the pursuit of that objective. Of course, some ministers work less hard than others, and a few enjoy a fairly relaxed life-style, but as a group Middletown's ministers seem to put in longer workweeks than most other professionals. A minister who had been in Middletown less than a year explained that he had not joined the local ministerial association because he was just too busy: "The first six months of any ministry is like pulling your hair out; you are going 24 hours a day, and I don't really have the time to get involved." One minister nearing retirement answered the question about occupational stress this way:

There are times when I am literally pumping from a dry well. You know, that I go and go, and give of myself, without having equal time to back off and be refilled. One of the advantages of vacation is to back away from things. The problem is, for me to get started afterwards, to get really turned back on and get up to snuff. It takes me a week or more to get back in the swing. Yes, the demands of this church are too great for one man. One pastoral man. And that's why we're going after the second one now. To see if we can't alleviate some of that. However, my enjoyment of my work makes it so that I would do it anyway. I don't know of anything that I would rather do.

Other examples of the strain of ministerial duties were drawn from the lives of ministers our respondents had known. An assistant who was temporarily serving as minister because the minister had suddenly died recounted how, after he had noticed the work load his predecessor carried, he had asked him whether there was any way that he could take some of the load from him. He had urged the pastor to take a few days off or at least to take off the one day a week he was supposed to have for himself. The other had replied, "You will not ever feel the total burden of this church until you pastor totally this church." Now, with his predecessor released by death, the young assistant said he was feeling the burden.

Another minister explained how stress and its consequences seemed to catch ministers unaware. "Is it a hard life?" he was asked.

Well, it is in many ways. I know I feel the need maybe to kind of slow down just a little bit. It's not physically, you're not digging ditches, you're not laying bricks. And yet I was talking to a pastor friend in Fort Wayne, and he recently had a heart attack. He's doing fine now, but this is due to stress and sometimes you don't even realize it. Sometimes you're not aware of it.

Sometimes you're not aware of it. Something happens and you realize you need to kind of slow the pace down a little bit and kind of take things in stride. A lot of times when you begin to feel the needs and the hurts of other people, whether you realize it or not, it can have an effect on you.

The unexpected events that continually upset a minister's work schedule were singled out as special sources of strain. A pastor who said he spent most of his time in "active ministry" and that perhaps his job was stressful because he let it be that way.

[The minister's life] is what you make it. It is [stressful], I think I make it that. Most of us who do have a church even this size, sometimes you don't plan what you do—you do what they call you to do and what you have to do and have to go. Like this morning I had a funeral. Yesterday afternoon we had a picnic. Coming home I had to go to the hospital. I had to go to the funeral home. And this morning a funeral and this afternoon I need to see a member in a mental ward in the hospital. It's that kind of thing.

One way to relive the pressure is to refer problems to other experts or agencies. The Middletown Ministerial Association sponsors a counseling service, and many of the ministers reduce their counseling load by sending people with serious problems to professional counselors. The pastor quoted just above said:

I counsel only when I have to. Because any minister, I suppose, could spend all of his time counseling. He could spend 25 hours a day because there is always someone who wants to sit down and talk to him and bring him problems. And there's plenty of problems, too. We try to refer the ones that we think are serious. We do have a counseling service in Middletown promoted by the Ministerial Association, and we send some to the Family Counseling and some to the state university counselors . . . Anything that's very serious, I try to refer it as best I can so far as counseling goes. Unless it's just a minor problem of the members. But for the main part we try as much as possible to refer. I think that's not only good for them maybe, but it relieves us . . .

But most ministers spend a great deal of time listening and counseling: "[We do] counseling, quite a bit of counseling, almost daily. People with situations, and problems that we try to help them in. That's about it, really, other than hospital visiting . . . so it's a daily thing."

Some pastors take a very limited role in community concerns beyond the activities of their own congregation. Others are busy in civic and regional activities. Let us highlight the range of social activism exhibited by Middletown ministers by describing the extremes. Here are statements by two ministers who define their community roles narrowly:

I feel that my prime importance or my prime function is to carefully and correctly study the Bible and to teach it in classes, publicly in sermons, in writing, privately in counseling sessions, or whatever. Or wherever I can help people to understand what the Bible says. That's what I view as my primary function.

I simply am what you definitely label a Bible preacher in trying to translate the principles taught in that book into everyday life that lie within the reach of man . . . I do not believe that this world is ever going to become a utopia. History has taught us that man just makes a mess out of everything. Especially if he is divorced from God. And therefore, we simply teach and believe that, when people get right in their relationship with God, they will consequently have a right relationship with their fellow man, in their families, with their spouses, and children, etc. . . .

In sharp contrast are the ministers who find civic responsibilities and the "social gospel" taking up most of their time. "I have to balance activity in social concerns with my pastoral duty," said one such minister. Another activist pastor described his efforts on behalf of the Association of Migrant Opportunity Service, the State Office of Campus Ministry, the Middletown County Council of the Arts, the State Renaissance Fair, the annual city art shows, the Aquarius House program for people with drug problems, and assorted welfare and educational programs. His activism led to occasional conflicts with people holding opposite views, he said, but he respected people who worked in the community and got things done even when their values differed from his. An instance was his opposition to abortion.

I certainly am very much opposed to abortion and that's not just a church stand, it is a personal stand, and I've run in head-on with people from Planned Parenthood and the NOW group from time to time. I have no problem with the NOW group except when they take this very militant stand on abortion, and we do have problems with that. I have to respect Planned Parenthood because there is a real problem with sexuality and teenagers in the community, and at least they are taking a positive stance, they are doing something.

The differences in role definitions show up in the minister's day-to-day work within the congregation as well as in activities in the wider community. A few of Middletown's ministers virtually limit their jobs to the leadership of church services. One said that not proselytizing was a matter of principle with him.

We advertise through the radio, not extensively, one program a week. I do not urge anybody to come to this church. I specifically state I simply want to share with you what's happening here. That is my conviction, my approach. We run an ad in the paper each week, and that's it. We do not get—and maybe this is a weakness—but we do not get out and knock on doors, we do not get out and urge people, we don't beg people to come, they just simply come. We don't, we can't, there's no way we can visit the people who visit this church.

He went on to say that only occasionally did he visit people at home, only "when we are specifically invited." He felt free to make such visits, he said, but did not because "time does not permit me."

This concept of limited ministerial roles is not held by the majority. Most ministers are involved with innumerable persons and groups outside of their formal worship services.

Some insights into how Middletown's ministers fulfill their callings can be derived from their accounts of how they spend their time. Here is an example:

A normal week? Well, usually I try to reserve Mondays for a rest day. I'm usually pretty well worn out after Sunday, so Monday is my Sunday, as far as activity goes. On Tuesdays I try to spend my morning studying, and sometimes in the afternoon I do things like visit the hospital, or sometimes if I know there are members who will not be working, I'll visit. Like in the afternoons, and this could be true of any afternoon. And of course, sometimes in the evening there are other churches in the immediate area that have activites, and I go visit them, learning of their activities, encourage them, etc. . . . So some of the evenings are taken up with that. I try to visit for the purpose of encouraging, at least one family a week sometime—it might be in the afternoon, evening, or whatever and usually that takes an hour or two when you do it. Like, here, which took about two hours. I'd say I'd average about one of those a week . . . I spend a good bit of time on teaching, my classes. See, I teach two classes every week, plus two sermons every week. This week I've got an extra sermon, because I'm going to [nearby town] to preach on Tuesday evening at a special gathering, so I have an extra one this week . . . There's always that kind of thing. And I do spend probably about three hours a week on just reading things like journals, various bulletins from other churches that I get. Of course, this is where I get all my sermon ideas, and where my own personal growth comes, out of reading this type of material.

Middletown as a Context for the Ministry

None of the ministers we interviewed were native to Middletown! A few of them had lived in the city for two decades or more, but they were still "outsiders" in the sense that they had come to Middletown as home; two who had taken pastoral assignments elsewhere after an initial appointment in Middletown subsequently returned to the community. But the fact that none of them is native lends an aura of objectivity to their observations about the community.

Several of the ministers referred to the conservatism of Middletown as an obstacle to their ministry. Others found the world views of Middletown's people more rural than urban.

For me it's rather enjoyable, it's somewhat easygoing. To me Middletown is not an industrial town. When I lived in Dayton, Ohio, I lived in what I call an industrial town. Middletown is not that. It is still a country town to me. It's a big one, but it's still a country town.

The pastor of one of the city's larger churches regards the local form of religion as "strange."

I kind of felt like it was a strange form of religion. I don't know whether other men have found this or not, but it seems like it's kind of apple pie and patriotism and that sort of thing rather than—well maybe I don't know if I want to say *rather than*, but, *maybe* rather than—a real commitment to the person of Jesus Christ and the ministries that flow from that kind of commitment. I don't think it's that they are non-Christian. I think Christianity has been affected so much by their conservatism, if it is conservatism. But it's kind of different from other places that I've been, let's put it that way . . . Many times [they belong to] no church. Not involved in a church particularly, but consider themselves Christian because they do Christian things. That's been an interesting thing for me. Our own church finds itself many time in that kind of a stance . . . We'll have some people who are committed generally to Christianity, but as far as ministries, that would be coming out of that commitment, and they simply do not get involved. They'll come to church quite regularly, but they will not get involved.

Other pastors were not sure the spirit of noninvolvement or complacency they encountered was any different in Middletown than elsewhere.

This may be true anywhere, but is what seems to me to be at least a more and more prevalent problem with a lackadaisical [attitude] or a spirit of not

really caring about a lot of different things. It wouldn't just be for one particular area. I see it . . . in regards to the way in which we should be reaching
out to other folks. It seems as though it is more a spirit of selfishness or concern about me, personally, and not too much worry about my neighbor. And,
like I say, this may be true everywhere. I'm not sure.

I like Middletown. There are some cities, without naming any, that you hear
preachers say, "Boy, that's a hard city." Or certain denominations are a little
hard. . . . Dallas, Texas, for example—there's a church on every corner,
just about. There just seems to be different parts of the country where there
are a lot of churches, a lot of spirituality, where other cities, not quite so
much. I say Middletown would probably be average.

The ministers had quite different perceptions of the people's
faith and commitment. Several referred to an old survey of church
membership that had shown the county's percentage of affiliated
Christians to be far below the state average.

For instance, in somewhere, in about 1960 there was a survey taken by the
Indiana Council of Churches and I've forgotten the exact date but there was
something like 32 or 33 percent of the people in the county who were associated with churches. Now it was almost twice that in the state, it was something like 60 percent in the state. And why so low in here? . . . Some said
it was because there were so many southerners here that had not said they
were affiliated with churches—they were still members of the churches back
home—like Kentucky and Tennessee. I don't know how much that is—that's
anybody's guess—I suppose. I suppose it had its impact but I do think that
it's on the upswing now.

Another view of Middletown as unusual stressed the cultural
opportunities and the challenges created by the mixture of traditional and evangelical churches in the city.

So I find Middletown as sort of an unusual combination of the traditional,
the Methodist, Presbyterians, the Lutherans, along with all of these other
independent movements, independent churches, so that the atmosphere here
is sort of a mixed bag. And our own congregation is made up of both kinds,
too, you see. So it's interesting to learn how to live with and seek to influence
it. . . . I think it is an evangelical atmosphere. I regard myself as a liberal
evangelical and some people regard it as a contradiction in terms. I do not
think it is so at all. The gospel is unashamedly evangelical, and I think the
liberal interpretation of the gospel makes the most sense.

Even those pastors who think the community as a whole is
irreligious or complacent are likely to describe their own members

as exceptions to these tendencies. When we asked them what religion means to their congregation, their responses were, for the most part, enthusiastic.

It would be very much tied in with their values, life, and also the attitudes they have toward us [ministers]. They see religion as giving a sense of purpose and direction in their present life leading them to eternal purpose. . . . I find more integration, you might say, of their religion into their business and professional life here in Middletown than in some of the other parishes. . . . I know this is especially true of the men. I guess maybe you kind of expect women to be more religious. I see in the men that integration.

Basically, the ultimate for the Christian, I think, is Christ-likeness, in attitudes, and thus that would come forth in daily life-style. And so I think that if most of our members were asked that question: What's your concept of religion? I believe they would probably answer that it is a Christ-likeness in their daily living and that would come forth in their caring and sharing with other folks, other people, in whatever capacity they might find themselves. I think that's probably the way they would answer.

Religious to our people is quite a lot of service. When we began our church, we were the second church to begin in Middletown. And the first church at that time was quite a wealthy church and had good worship programs and this other thing, and we felt that another church if it began out to be a service-minded kind of church. So we opened our building to all kinds of community programs and this sort of thing, simply because that's the approach that we took. And we have an emergency fund in which we help people that other agencies don't particularly help. So, religion to them means a commitment to humanity. There's the worship part, too.

The Sabbath

On the basis of their observations of Middletown's Sunday activities in 1924-1925 and again in 1935, the Lynds claimed that Sunday as a Sabbath day was rapidly being replaced by Sunday as a holiday. They saw Middletown's churches fighting a losing battle against recreational pursuits, and they implied that the struggle would end with the churches empty. As we noted in the chapter on church attendance, this prophecy has not yet come to pass. Middletown's houses of worship are more crowded today than they were two generations ago; however, relatively high rates of church attendance do not mean that Sunday recreation has diminished. Rather, a comfortable compromise has been worked out between religion and recreation. In contemporary Middletown, the church member attends a 60- or 90-minute service Sunday morning and then is free to spend the rest of the day resting and playing.

When asked what they teach their members about proper Sunday activities, the ministers we interviewed stressed the importance of some formal worship.

I can tell you how I would like an ideal Sunday. I would like, first of all, the opportunity to worship. And I think for me once a Sunday would be sufficient.

We teach that the first day of the week is the Lord's day. It is to be used for worship.

A good Sunday is to get up, have yourself a nice breakfast and meet with your worshiping community. . . .

Most ministers hold that after their people have fulfilled the obligation to worship they are free to spend the rest of the Sabbath as they wish. "Fun after church" was not grudgingly acknowledged by ministers as the prevailing practice; rather, they affirmed that it is appropriate behavior. For the ministers as much as their parishioners, that part of Sunday that follows church services is valued for leisure and entertainment.

The term that I always use is that Sunday should be a day for recreation, you know the true sense of re-creation. We expect them to assist at Mass, in a public way express their adoration of God. Hopefully, it's a day of rest for them, not just sitting around doing nothing. But again, recreation, re-creating.

We teach that the first day of the week is the Lord's day. It's to be used for worship. If during the other hours, other than times we are assembled for worship, there's a baseball game or there's activities our members are a part of, want to be a part of, I can see no particular objection. If they want to hoe in the garden that's okay, too. But they would be expected by God to worship at the worship hour on the first day of the week. [What about movies, boating, picnics, etc.?] I would have no objections to that, and I don't believe the Bible would.

Not only do none of the ministers we interviewed object to recreation on the Sabbath, several of them have organized Sunday recreation for members of their congregations. One described a picnic his church had sponsored the previous Sunday at a local lakeside park as an example of what he feels religious people should do on a Sunday. A youth minister proudly described his

Sunday athletic program for young people as an activity that "keeps them off the streets and out of trouble on Sunday."

A few respondents referred to quiet, reflective, and virtuous Sunday activities but without much insistence.

. . . Sometimes we have tried to encourage people to develop a unique Sunday life-style, something Sabbath-like. Here's a day where you go out and visit your grandmother, or visit your sick friend in a hospital or take your kids out for a walk. If one doesn't have any other time to spend with family, this certainly is the time to be with them.

This same minister made it clear that he did not disapprove of other forms of Sunday recreation.

We don't emphasize that [unique Sunday life-style] too much because people's lives are quite complex and it's hard to lay a strict rule down. . . . I don't have the slightest inhibition against somebody going to a movie on Sunday afternoon or to a play. If it's a crappy movie, they shouldn't go any time.

Another respondent suggested a compromise between Sunday religion and Sunday recreation.

My approach to the Sabbath is that it is a day of rest, and a day that should be dedicated first and foremost to your spiritual nourishment. But it is also a day when you should be involved perhaps in those things which you cannot be involved in other times because you work or whatever. I see nothing inconsistent with the Sabbath being the day of the Lord [and] let's say a husband and his family going out for a picnic or going to the beach or something like that or spending time together as a family. I think the problem is (this is where I try to educate members of my congregation) not going out and having a picnic or going out and playing golf or tennis. The problem is going out and leaving God home.

In contemporary Middletown, where the family is almost as sacred as the church, even the direct encroachment of Sunday recreation on Sunday religion is viewed indulgently when the activity is done in the name of family solidarity.

In the summertime, unfortunately, I think they sometimes misrepresent family as religion. People who drop out of church do so because they become inactive. About 75 to 80 percent of the inactive members have resorted to a "close family" reason. They buy a cottage and they think, boy, they must leave work every week on Friday afternoon and get up there in some kind of little haven. . . . Now who can say that this isn't good—in other words, they're covering themselves—who can say that it isn't good to be together as a family.

In sum, the conflict over Sabbath activities observed by the Lynds has been resolved to veryone's satisfaction. Church members are expected to attend one relatively brief worship service on Sunday; they are not only allowed but encouraged to devote the rest of the day to secular entertainments. Many churches continue to offer both morning and evening services, but attendance at both is not often expected. One minister lamented the fact that his congregation insists on a Sunday-evening service despite his own conviction that one Sunday service would be sufficient.

Thus, the "battle for the Sabbath" is no longer a significant problem. Middletown's churches are well attended on a typical Sunday, and so are its parks, lakes, tennis courts, theaters, and golf courses.

Contributing Money

Middletown's economic well-being depends heavily on the automotive industry; the slump in that industry at the time we conducted this inquiry had meant financial hardship for many local families. Unemployment levels were high, and among the employed earnings had not kept pace with inflation. Even so, in various surveys, Middletown people claimed to be supporting their churches generously. We were curious to see whether the ministers would confirm this contention. Almost without exception, they did. Despite inflation and recession, financial support of the churches had not declined.

I will share with you that in our particular church, if inflation is having an effect, we don't feel it in the collection plate. I guess that's the best way to put it. I feel that the level of giving on the part of these people for an 3-M church is very good.

Maybe we're odd people. Our budget has grown every year since I've been here. When I came here it was like around $100,000, and we're up to about $175,000 a year. We have added a new staff member and are about to add another at the end of this year. Our giving is good. Our people are generous, especially if the needs are demonstrated. I have absolutely no worry. A short time ago we needed to get a typewriter for the campus minister. I called a half dozen people and we had a typewriter. This is besides their regular giving.

Each year the overall finances have steadily grown. I'm sure that there is a financial crunch, but to be very honest with you, I haven't seen a drop in finances but a steady climb. We don't believe in pressuring people along that line.

We have grown each year in our total giving and once again I say this is to the Glory of the Lord. We have no bazaars, we have no suppers, we don't get involved in any of the money-making schemes because we believe and teach that the Bible tells how to support the Lord.

After hearing the same positive answer repeated several times, we began to think that the ministers might be misunderstanding the question. We wanted to verify that larger budgets were the result of increasing per capita contributions and not of mere congregational growth. So in the next interview we probed harder.

INTERVIEWER: How are members' financial commitment to the church, given inflation and other economic hardships?

MINISTER: They are exceeding inflation slightly.

INTERVIEWER: You're staying ahead of inflation?

MINISTER: Yes, slightly.

INTERVIEWER: Now that's not just because you've got more members? . . . the individual member has increased his giving?

MINISTER: That's correct. Yes.

Only 2 of the 17 ministers we interviewed said that their budgets had not quite kept up with inflation, but even in those two instances there had been no appreciable decline in the church's budgetary situation.

The prosperity of Middletown's churches is apparent in the appearance of their buildings and in the programs they operate. Most church structures are attractive and well cared for. The wood exteriors are neatly painted, and the rock and brick exteriors are regularly cleaned. The yards are tidy, with flower beds, carefully groomed lawns, and trimmed shrubs. Most of the interiors have polished pews, unworn carpets, and elaborate sound systems.

The number and variety of the special programs sponsored by Middletown churches are another sign of their prosperity. Most have special youth ministries, often directed by an assistant pastor. Theses youth programs require athletic equipment, transportation, dining and camping facilities, and so forth. The larger churches have programs for elderly members that include weekly or monthly breakfasts or dinners, bus transportation to church services,

and special home visits. Some congregations support foreign missionary programs. Such endeavors require resources, and, despite
the somewhat depressed economic climate of Middletown around
1980, they were being amply supported by the faithful. With
few exceptions, the principle of tithing is proclaimed by Middletown's churches and quite often practiced as well.

I teach tithing. I teach that a very simple Biblical tithing is 10 percent. I
practice it and the congregation knows it. Every year we have an annual meeting. . . . I stand up and just go through about a 15-minute little speech,
right out of the Bible, on what tithing is. You can play games with it. Is it
before or after taxes and all the rest of this stuff, but basically, it's just whatever you get, 10 percent of it is returned to the Lord.

We really believe tithing is a scriptural command from God. All through the
Old Testament you read different examples of how, like Abraham saying,
"I'm giving up my 10 percent to the Lord." And here at the church we do
share with them the area of tithing. I believe I heard, just before the pastor
passed away, I heard him say that in nine years, he's preached on tithing
twice, because the people of the church have understood the importance of
tithing so they don't have to be preached at about it. They just do it.

We stress tithing. We don't ride it hard. We hold it as the Christian standard
and invite people to it. If they feel that they can't reach that standard, then
at least to give a certain proportion of their income.

Only 4 of the 17 ministers we interviewed did not maintain tithing as a doctrine. Two of these taught "representative" or "proportionate" giving, which is not very different.

We have gone to the concept that our gift to the church should be a representative gift. It should represent our dedication to God. It should represent a
balance of our expenditure like for instance if you own a cottage and a home,
then you should give in proportion to how you actually are financially. We
feel that it's an individual decision, you have to decide for yourself. But we
do push people to give a representative gift, a responsible gift. In other words,
we don't ask for a tithe. I drop very subtle hints frequently about the tithe
and proportionate giving but the stewardship committee has taken the stand
only on the responsible gift.

We don't teach a tithe, or a 10 percent. I don't think a tithe, or a 10 percent,
has any biblical basis to it. But we do try to talk about proportionate giving,
saying that when one is serious about funding the church or the Kingdom of
God, that one might well make some comparisons about how much he used
on the Kingdom versus how much he spends on his dinners out every week
or how much he spends on cocktails or how much he's putting into his

cottage. We suggest that one could make some interesting parallels and not simply say, "the church gets what's left" because these days there's not much left.

The other two ministers who did not teach tithing were Catholic priests, and their official position was that practicing Catholics in Middletown should give 5 percent to the church and 5 percent to community charities. According to them, their parishioners understood the "five and five" standard, and they seldom discussed it from the pulpit.

Most of the ministers did not know exactly what percentage of their congregations were tithers because fund raising was handled by a lay committee or official. For the "integrity of their ministry" they considered it important not to know who contributed what, but most of them had a rough notion about the prevalence of tithe paying among their people. One minister said that nearly *every* family in his congregation gave the full 10 percent.

We feel that just about all our people pay a tithing. Basically speaking, the general nucleus of our church membership are tithers. To be a church official, to be a youth leader, it is a necessity that they be tithers. If needs be, we would feel free to approach them about it. That's part of the Christian stewardship.

In most churches, however, tithing remains voluntary but is not rare, with anywhere from a tenth to two-thirds of member families giving the full tithe, most of the remainder contributing substantially, and an appreciable minority giving little or nothing probably under no penalty.

The fund-raising strategy mentioned most frequently was the teaching of principle of tithing (or proportionate or representative giving) once or twice a year. Some churches send out a yearly letter reminding members of their obligations and inviting formal pledges or commitments. In the ministers' view, there is rarely any pressure applied, but individual parishioners said that they sometimes felt pressured. The churches have fund-raising projects—bazaars, dinners, programs, candy sales, book sales, and so on—but such activties typically are used to raise money for special projects or programs (for example, a new organ, a trip for the Sunday school, or a new classroom). The bulk of the financial support for Middletown's churches comes from regular contributions quietly offered during the Sunday collection or mailed at regular intervals.

Middletown's generosity to organized religion is illustrated by one incident that occurred while we were there. When the downtown Methodist church was nearly destroyed by a natural gas explosion in January 1978, the congregation met in a high school auditorium to decide whether to tear down the existing shell and start again or to restore the original building. The session was dramatically emotional, and the decision was for restoration. An insurance company advanced $2.5 million to start construction, but by August it was apparent the money would be gone by the first of November, with the project only two-thirds completed. Members were asked to contribute cash immediately, and over a half million dollars was raised by October 1.

The goal was to hold the first service in the restored church on December 16 and to raise more than a million dollars in contributions by that time. A series of dinners was held after Sunday services in a temporary location at which people were told how much money was needed to complete the project. On December 16, 25 church officials with calculators totaled the gifts brought to the front of the chapel and reported to the congregation that the target had been exceeded.

The minister recounted how retired couples had come to the church and had given him $500 checks, which in relation to their capacity were equal he said, to gifts of $50,000 from others. He said he had been tempted to refuse those gifts but then questioned his right to deny the donors the opportunity to sacrifice. "I wasn't about to say to them, you can't do this. I couldn't deny them this blessing." He told of a woman who brought her diamonds and told him to "get them appraised fast and sell them before I change my mind." Several families borrowed money in order to give it to the church. The campaign seems to have revitalized the church.

Trends in Religion

The ministers' opinions about how religion in Middletown is changing were not uniform and were not necessarily accurate. Each of them had a personal and a denominational perspective. Some had extensive local experience; others compared the trends they thought they saw in Middletown with changes in the Midwest or in the big cities or in the nation as a whole. We tried to discover what standards of comparison they were using, but that was not always possible.

Despite their differences of perspective, our respondents agreed remarkably well about recent trends in Middletown's religion; nearly all of them shared three prevailing impressions. First, things are better than they were. If anything, there have been modest increases in religious activity and doctrinal zeal. Second, the future of religion is bright. Third, there have always been problems. The spiritual, emotional, and social problems of Middletown's families, although serious and real, are probably no more severe than those of prior generations. In the main, they are problems of human life generally, not indicators of a decadent society or collapsing morality.

A dissenting point of view was voiced by a minority of the ministers, who saw a process of "family collapse" and "social deterioration" under way. Sometimes this "decline-and-fall" scenario was tied to a belief in the imminence of the Second Coming of Christ. We do not know exactly how many of the city's ministers share this perspective; we do know that most of the ministers from the city's largest churches do not subscribe to it but rather view the immediate future much more positively.

Things Are Better Than They Were

Often, a minister's opinion that things are better than they were reflected his personal experience. A minister whose church served one of the north-side subdivisions had seen a long, steady growth in attendance fostered in part by his own pastoral activity: "We've had to make a go. When you start from nothing, you have to keep them going." His church had a very successful youth program, and he attributed its success to a conscious strategy.

You have to work hard with them. The main thing is to interest the right people, the right youth. There are leaders just like in anything else, and you have to try to motivate those leaders to bring the other youth in, you can't do it by yourself. [Our attendance has increased] . . . partly because more people are living in the area and partly we happen to have the leaders of a couple of schools in our church now, and they [the young people] follow the leaders.

The minister of one of the city's largest churches visualized its situation 15 or 20 years ago as "kind of, maybe, drifting along";

it was an old church, set in its ways. He began a program of "community outreach," and by 1980 the church was enjoying rapid growth and unprecedented community support. As an example of how innovative programs have flourished, he described a special ministry to the divorced: "We had been doing just a little ministry with divorced people, with about maybe a dozen people. That thing just took over, and right now we have 75 people coming every week at one stage of divorce or another."

Asked what he did in 1981 that was different than in previous years, the minister of another successful and growing church explained how he had tempered fundamentalism to the times.

I think one of the big things that I see is trying to maintain a reasonable fundamentalism in the midst of such an open society in which we live and still have the feeling that we are not compromising important issues. . . . Some churches say you can't go to the movies, you can't dance. . . . I even knew [people], say 20 years ago, in churches where I pastored that thought that television was kind of "the work of the devil" as they put it. But now I think most everybody accepts that you can be selective, especially for children, but that you can still have it as part of life and live a reasonably fundamental way of life in Christ and not feel guilty or not have the Lord come down on you. I think the Lord means for us to enjoy life, to have a good time, to live it to the fullest. . . .

Another minister who perceived a general upswing in church attendance said that the 1960s and early 1970s had been hard for many Middletown churches, although his own church had held its own during the difficult times.

We didn't grow a great deal . . . but there were few churches in town generally speaking that grew a great deal, with the exception of _____ and _____. So those two are the ones that grew. But some of the rest held their own. But now I feel like it's up. Of course, this had been true of all lodges and civic organizations, it somewhat swings together. And I feel like there is a little life going on now and it's maybe going to get better.

Ministers of mainline denominations observe the substantial growth of fundamentalist churches with mixed feelings. They see people discovering what seems to be valid religious experiences, but, at the same time, they question the fundamentalists' narrow and rigid approach to life, society, and Christian living. Asked whether he thought Middletown was becoming a more Christian community than it used to be, one of them said, "Well, I see tremendous advancement of the fundamentalist sects." When the interviewer asked, "Does that bother you, or do you welcome it?" he replied:

Well, Jesus once said that if they are not against us they are for us, and they still are Christian, but I have a little bit of a problem with some of their theology and especially their mode of operating. It gets down to a very literal interpretation of scripture and trying to impose it on other people—the Moral Majority kind of thing.

Some respondents perceived the growing popularity of the fundamentalist churches as a national trend and attributed it to factors outside the local community. One "liberal" minister interpreted it as a shift away from individual responsibility.

I think there's a shift, just like in every place else, from the mainline denominations to more what we call fundamental kinds of religions. And I think it's basically because many people are uncertain about things and they want someone to tell them what to do and what to think. And I'm not saying this is bad. I'm not criticizing, but that's just the way that I see it.

Such concerns, however, are not worrisome. Looking at their own churches, the ministers saw few serious problems even though some of them, faced with neighborhood changes and congregations of shifting composition, defined success as maintaining, not expanding, an existing program.

The Future Is Bright

There is optimism about the future among the members of Middletown's clergy. Protestants and Catholics, conservatives and liberals, pragmatists and millennialists, all anticipate religious growth in the decade of the 1980s, whether growth for them means drawing more of the elect from a doomed and sinful world or building a more efficient bureaucracy.

The general optimism even extends to family life and other matters peripheral to religion. In an earlier chapter, we reported the observation of one minister that young people seemed more committed to marriage than they had been formerly: "We train them for marriage and I can see there a much more healthy sense of commitment to marriage, which if it's true, that's where the future lies—in the families."

The minister of a strongly evangelical Mideletown church described the 1980s as a "decade of destiny."

I think the church overall is going to see great growth. I just looked at the headlines of the paper this morning and it said, "The Church is alive and well in China." I've heard reports from people who have been to China since the doors have been opened, and they say it is phenomenal and communism there is about 30 years old, roughly. And they say a great majority of the Christians, born-again Christians, in China are 25 and under, so that tells me something. Not only in America, but worldwide I think there's been tremendous growth in the church, in the spiritual world, and so, I see a lot of great things for the 80's.

Another placed his hopes closer to home.

Well, I'm not a doomsday man. I really believe that the churches can stand. And we have some realness to share with people. Our church is right at the rebirth place, and I don't know when or how it's going to come about, but surely as shootin', in a short time, we'll have a burst of newness. I may not be permitted to see it, you know. It may not be in my tenure here, but it'll be relatively soon, in the next five or six years, or earlier, maybe in the next year. The new man who comes, may be the spark or whatever that will ignite it. We're just on the verge of it.

In the Evangelical denominations, it is taken for granted that their growth will be greater than that of mainline denominations. The pastor of a large Evangelical church spoke of the future with entrepreneurial confidence.

But practically all the churches that I'm aware of that are evangelical, that have services that are uplifting, and on the up and up, what I mean, they are "up" services, and relate to people's needs, real needs, and preaching that Bible in the context of the current needs of people, those churches I think have a galaxy of hope for the future. And for this church, we're being urged to draw plans for a 1,000-seating auditorium, a senior auditorium in which I am wholly involved. . . . It [the expense] puts the brakes on a bit, but we're practically debt free, and will be very shortly. We'll be able to do it, I suppose we will have to do it. As far as I am concerned, the future is tremendously exciting.

There Have Always Been Problems

For some of the respondents, the question about whether things were getting better seemed inappropriate. As an article of faith, they denied the possibility of secular progress. According to their view of history, secular change does not matter since the basic elements of the human situation remain fairly constant. Adding that there have always been sin and trouble, they saw nothing unique or especially disturbing in the contemporary world. This view, in context, is optimistic rather than fatalistic. Even if the present is no better than the past, it is certainly no worse. This religious conservatism counters the stereotypes of moral decay associated with liberalism. Thus:

I do not believe that the world is probably any worse now than it was when Jesus Christ was here. I don't believe personally that there is any more sin. I believe that there has always been temptation around and there's always been sin. So I don't view us in a crisis. I really don't. I believe that it is my duty to encourage people to examine the Bible, live by the Bible, and be optimistic. I don't paint a doomsday picture. I try not to, anyway.

Expressions of discouragement and concern were frequently heard during the interviews of Middletown's ministers, as well as complaints about the strain of a 60- or 70-hour workweek, but the respondents did not attribute the stresses of their occupation to any social crises, large or small. Social and personal problems represented business as usual for them.

All of them without exception, however, made doleful comments about the breakdown of the family and the personal costs associated with it. All of them said that they attempted to help their people cope with the temptations of sexuality and hedonism. Indeed, the use of the word "hedonism" reflects a curiously neutral and sociological attitude toward what used to be called sin.

We don't believe in doing your own thing. We do not believe in a hedonistic-type approach. There are two reasons we don't. One is because our foundation is the Bible, and we make no apologies for it, we just sit back and say, there it is. Secondly, from a psychological standpoint, from a historical standpoint, not only in this country, but as you look around the world various societies who have gone through these kinds of sexual revolutions, sexual freedoms, hedonism, and things like this. The end result has never been good. It has always been a degradation of the society, it's always been a breaking up of the family unit. And I think we're seeing that in this country. And we take a very strong position on it. I particularly take a strong position on it because I firmly believe that as the family unit breaks up in the United States of America, so does the United States of America weaken.

To the extent that some of Middletown's fundamentalist ministers do perceive the contemporary world in terms of crisis and breakdown, they expected the consequences to be favorable for religion. Even though they did not rejoice over the state of the contemporary world, they found the spectacle more elating than discouraging.

The developments of things in the world in general are becoming more of an evident testimony to people that the coming of the Lord is near. There is, irregardless of their response, an acknowledgment in their hearts, an increased God-consciousness, that the coming of the Lord is near. As people are seeing the breakdown in society, in marriage and family life, in school systems, in governments, there is a need to turn somewhere. The drug culture and so on, they learn, is not the answer.

Chapter 13

Cooperation Among the
Churches of Middletown

Robert and Helen Lynd had little to say about cooperation among the churches of Middletown in 1924-1925 (Lynd and Lynd 1929). On the contrary, in the report of their 1925 study they reported an increase in subtle church rivalry (1929, 333) and a decline of "interdenominational mingling" at services (1929, 333), and they made much of the refusal of one large downtown church to allow a struggling sister congregation to use its kitchen for fund-raising events (1929, 334, n.4). Only in the ministerial association was there any provision for ongoing religious cooperation as the members of the clergy attempted collectively to raise the moral tone of the community (1929, 351) or to bring the churches of Middletown together for evangelistic crusades and for religious education (1929, 352).

Middletown was probably not much different from many other communities of its generation. The word "ecumenical" had not yet been introduced as a label for church unity. There were no national or international bodies trying to unite the various Christian traditions. In the Protestant sector, the fundamentalist movement was at its peak, frequently dividing denominations over doctrinal issues and stimulating distrust among them.

Since then, however, our nation has seen some new trends in church cooperation. The World Council of Churches came into being in 1948 and has encouraged a unified global vision among those Protestant denominations that, despite their continued commitment to individual traditions, agreed to acknowledge their essential unity with other believers around the world. Most of the so-called "mainline" denominations in the United States hold membership in the World Council of Churches and contribute, through their national organizations, to its annual support.

The National Council of Churches was created in 1950 in order to foster mutual understanding among the various Protestant denominations and to allow them to speak with something approaching a unified voice on social and political issues. It, too, claims most of the mainline denominations in its membership and benefits from their support. One achievement of the National Council is the now familiar and widely used revised standard version of the Bible.

The movement toward denominational mergers that began soon after World War II was part of the same impetus that created the World Council of Churches and the National Council of Churches. Congregationalists joined with the Christian Church and then later with the Evangelical and Reformed Church to form the United Church of Christ. Methodists joined with the Evangelical United Brethren to become United Methodists. Two branches of the divided Presbyterian family joined forces to become the United Presbyterian Church in the United States of America, with a future prospect of merging with the Presbyterian Church, United States, which is centered in the southern states. No fewer than 12 Protestant denominations have been in negotiation since 1960 to explore the dream of a Church of Christ Uniting that would bring them together in a supermerger.

Another avenue of cooperation that had never been dreamed of opened up during the 1960s between Roman Catholics and Protestants following Vatican II, the great reforming council called by Pope John XXIII. The attitudes of mutual suspicion that separated *all* Protestant and Catholic churches before that council have largely disappeared.

In short, the national climate is much more favorable to cooperation among churches now than it was when the Lynds made their studies. How is this reflected in the religious landscape of Middletown?

Middletown's Varied Church Patterns

The church pages in Middletown's Saturday newspapers reveal a great deal about the city's churches in the paid advertisements that announce the sermon topics and schedules of services for the following day. Some of the larger advertisements display the smiling face of a minister or a view of the church building. They cover a wide range of denominations and offer the prospective churchgoer a considerable number of alternatives from which to choose.

The paid announcements, however, do not begin to cover *all* of Middletown's churches. Many of the smaller churches ignore this form of publicity either because they cannot afford it or because they think it is unproductive. The three large Roman Catholic churches along with a large, independent Baptist church were notable examples.

By a recent count, Middletown has 165 churches[1] ranging in size from several with more than 1,000 members each to tiny storefront congregations of fewer than 50 souls. Although Middletown's churches are scattered throughout the city, it is not unusual to find two or three of them in close proximity, sometimes on adjacent corners. Only three sizable churches remain in the central business district; all the rest are located in outlying neighborhoods.

Well over a hundred churches would identify themselves as "fundamentalist" in doctrine and practice, while most of the remainder would regard themselves as "conservative", there are scarcely half a dozen that would be comfortable with the label "liberal" or "progressive."

Located in the Bible Belt, Middletown has a predominance of conservative and fundamentalist churches. The majority of them are unaffiliated with any larger church organization or conference. All of the mainline denominations are represented, too, as Table 13-1 shows.[2]

Middletown's "Council of Churches"

The official organ of cooperation among the churches of Middletown is called Christian Ministries of Middletown's county; it was founded in 1945 and involves both the clergy and the laity. The purpose of Christian Ministries is to draw the churches of Middletown into cooperative activities in spite of their differences in theology and liturgical style.

Table 13-1
Church Denominations Represented in Middletown

Denominations	Number of Churches
American Baptist	3
Episcopal	1
Lutheran	6
Methodist	14
Presbyterian	3
Quaker	1
Roman Catholic	3
United Church of Christ	2
Unitarian-Universalist	1
Other denominations or independents	131
Total	165

Source: Christian Ministries of Middletown's county.

At the time of its founding, the organization was called the Middletown County Council of Churches, following a pattern common in most medium- or large-sized American communities. By 1973, however, a number of its members had decided that the name of the organization was a roadblock to its success in a community where, both in the churches and in the press, considerable hostility was expressed toward the National Council of Churches and the World Council of Churches for their unpopular stands on social and political issues. They hoped that changing the name to Christian Ministries of Middletown's county would make the organization more attractive to nonparticipating churches.

This effort was not conspicuously successful. Of Middletown's 165 churches, only 35 (14 of them Methodist) along with a few service clubs contributed to the organization in 1980. None of the Roman Catholic churches and none of the fundamentalist and/or independent churches were contributors. In effect, this cooperative effort has been limited to the established Protestant denominations.

The council has a part-time executive director and a board composed of representatives from the contributing churches. In 1980, it had an annual budget of about $10,000, and it supported several modest programs addressed to the religious, charitable, and educational problems that seemed to require cooperative action by churches.

In education, the organization has gained considerable publicity through its Good News Caravan, a traveling summer theater company of clowns, puppeteers, mimes, and musicians that operates out of the back of a brightly decorated trailer and is designed to reach out to Middletown's children. The council also sponsors a religious education class for the mentally handicapped and, from time to time, workshops for Sunday school teachers.

The council's other programs include a ministry to the migrant farm workers who come into the area with their families during the summer, a weekly service of worship and Bible study at the Juvenile Detention Center, and a program designed to improve infant nutrition in lower-income families by soliciting individuals and churches to "feed" a baby during the first year of its life through extrabudget contributions.

A church festivals committee of the Christian Ministries sponsors several annual events that attempt to bring the churches of Middletown together in acts of celebration. Noonday services involving the participation of clergy members and laypeople are held during the Lenten season and are followed by a sacrificial meal in a parish hall. A service for Christian unity is held annually in January, and the festivals committee sponsors an annual Pentecost breakfast.

The Pentecost breakfast is held on a Saturday morning as close as possible to the Sunday in late spring when liturgically oriented churches celebrate the coming of the Holy Spirit as described in the New Testament book of Acts (Acts 2:1ff.). As many as 200 persons from a wide spectrum of churches have gathered for that event, expressing a solidarity that extends beyond the limited pattern of cooperation that is normal in Middletown's churches.

During the 1960s and 1970s, before it was renamed, the Council of Churches took aggressive social action. The council's positions responded to the racial unrest of the 1960s that was evident in Middletown as it was in other parts of the nation with "living-room dialogues" designed to foster interracial communication and to build bridges of friendship between whites and blacks. It was able to get 22 of Middletown's churches to sign "covenants of open membership," subsequently published in the local press, in which they indicated their willingness to welcome persons of any race into their membership. The council formed a fair-housing group and conducted a workshop on housing issues out of which evolved the Mayor's Human Rights Commission, an entity that still hears complaints about racial and economic discrimination and attempts to resolve them peacefully.

The agenda of Christian Ministries of Middletown's county in 1980 showed no trace of the social activism that characterized it earlier. Although some of Middletown's mainline churches included individuals, both from the clergy and the laity, who were still social activists, the consensus was that the structure of church cooperation was too fragile to absorb the stress of controversy at that time.

The Ministerial Association

Those who might be expected to rock the boat or still the trouble, waters, depending on one's outlook, would, of course, be the members of Middletown's clergy. There are approximately 250 of them (counting those who serve churches in the rural area and those who are retired or inactive). They represent every element of the social, political, and theological spectrum, although they are concentrated at the conservative end of each.

The Ministerial Association of Middletown's county has been in continuous existence since before the time of the Lynd studies. It gives the clergy of Middletown an opportunity for fellowship in what is sometimes described as a lonely occupation. On the first Wednesday of each month except during the summer, 25 or 30 ministers (a fairly small number out of those eligible to attend) gather for a luncheon meeting at a local cafeteria. For several years, the meetings were held in local churches on a rotating basis in the hope that more members of the clergy would be attracted out of curiosity, but the experiment was not successful.

Once an all-male enclave, the Ministerial Association now includes two or three women pastors. Its overall representation is somewhat broader than that of Christian Ministries. Perhaps this reflects the ministers' need for some social experience away from the members of their respective congregations. The association seems to provide such experience in a limited way.

The black members of Middletown's clergy are represented in the association, although there are proportionately fewer of them than the number (25 or so) of black churches would indicate.

A number of those churches have part-time pastors who sustain themselves by other employment that discourages their attendance at a meeting held during working hours. But the limited attendance of the black clergy at these luncheons also reflects the complaint often expressed by one of their representatives that the other members are not moved by their concerns.[3]

Missing entirely from the Ministerial Association are the priests who serve the three Catholic parishes in Middletown.[4] Although they are officially invited to share in the ministerial fellowship, the priests' absence is taken for granted by their Protestant colleagues.[5]

The custom of the Ministerial Association, established by common consent, is to avoid any discussion of potentially divisive issues at its meetings, especially theological and political issues, that it feels would destroy the association's precarious unity. Sitting side by side over their soup and hamburger plates at the monthly luncheon meetings can be found the pastor of the Unitarian-Universalist Church and the pastor of the Church of the Nazarene. Presbyterian ministers exchange pleasantries with the pastors of the Church of God.

The programs of the Ministerial Association, which attract at least a sizable minority of Middletown's clergy, are informative but not controversial; they deal in the generalities of clerical concern. All the participants are happy to hear about new efforts to cope with juvenile delinquency and pornography, but they would not hold still for discussions of nuclear safety, world hunger, welfare cheating, or similar issues whose very labels imply political orientations.

A conspicuous exception to the avoidance of social issues occurred in the summer of 1980 after the home of a black family who had moved into a middle-class white neighborhood on the south side of town was bombed by anonymous assailants. A petition of protest initiated in the Ministerial Association was circulated among the churches and later published in the press. The momentum of that event induced the association to sponsor an all-day workshop on the causes of racism, for which it obtained the services of an interfaith agency from a larger metropolitan area. About 20 ministers attended the workshop.

The association's longest-standing project has been an attempt to persuade Middletown's hospital to add a paid Protestant chaplain to its staff. The association has long maintained an arrangement whereby part-time women volunteers notify the appropriate minister when patients identify themselves as members of a particular church or as wanting pastoral services from a particular church. The board of trustees, however, has resisted for a decade the effort to establish a formal connection between the hospital and the churches. Nevertheless, the hospital recently put into place a hospice program for terminally ill patients that allows them to spend as many of their final days as possible at home. An ordained clergyman has been employed to manage the program, an action noted with approval by the Ministerial Association.

Ad Hoc Efforts at Cooperation

Cooperation among the churches of Middletown, though it is ever so partial in terms of the number who actually cooperate and the scope of their cooperation, does not end with the two organizations just described. Indeed, it can be argued that the most significant cooperation takes place through ad hoc efforts that lack any official approval of either Christian Ministries or the Ministerial Association. In a community with such a diversity of churches, it is unlikely that any organization could properly represent *all* of them or speak in a single voice on their behalf. What happens instead is that those churches of Middletown that have similar styles band together from time to time to work toward common objectives.

At the initiative of several of the more liberal members of the clergy, a pastoral care and counseling center was established several years ago to provide professional counseling at a depth beyond the training of most ministers. Operating as a branch of a larger counseling center in a nearby metropolitan area, the center has its own board of directors drawn from the membership of the 16 supporting churches that make an annual contribution to its support. The center employs a full-time minister trained and accredited in psychotherapy. It is housed in a Methodist church building, and patients are either referred there by ministers or go there on their own. The task of providing competent psychological counseling to people from the wide variety of religious traditions found in Middletown without challenging their established values has proven to be a continuing problem, but the program remains in place and continues to gain the support of those churches that value this type of activity, still, however, by no means *all* the churches of Middletown.

Other ad hoc cooperative efforts are Good Friday and Thanksgiving services initiated by the clergy of the larger churches. Attendance at these events is seldom heavy, however.

One particular episode of cooperation among Middletown churches deserves extended comment, for it highlights the difficulties encountered by those who would like to see the Protestant churches join in any kind of united effort. At the request of a local evangelistic association, members of Middletown's clergy were polled in the spring of 1979 to see whether their churches might join together and sponsor a "crusade" led by a representative of Billy Graham's organization. The response was mixed and cautious. Some ministers were ready to get on the bandwagon immediately. Others were interested but wanted to defer any decision until they had more information. Still others expressed no interest whatever. Eventually, with the support of a few enthusiasts, a steering committee was formed, a date was set, and an evangelist was contacted for the eight-day event to be held at a large public arena in Middletown during the week after Easter of the following year.

Repeated efforts were made to involve all the members of the clergy and their churches in planning the crusade, but fewer than a third of Middletown's churches actually gave it any real support or sought funds for it from their members. The Episcopalians, Presbyterians, Lutherans, Unitarian-Universalists, and Quakers refused to participate at all, presumably because the style of the event was too conservative and they sensed that it would give little attention to the moral and social issues of the day.[6] Many of the fundamentalist churches also refused to participate, not trusting the relatively "liberal" theology of Graham's organization! The largest Methodist church in town, along with some of its sister churches, pursued an evangelistic plan of its own.

In the end, the crusade that was to have represented, the vast majority, if not all, of the churches in Middletown gained the support of only a limited number of the more conservative congregations. The Ministerial Association declined to give its official blessing, and Christian Ministries included notice of the event in its publicity but carefully avoided giving it an official endorsement. Thus, the churches of Middletown found it quite impossible to come together in a united effort.

The crusade was held on schedule, and 2,000 to 4,000 people attended nightly for the gospel singing, the testimonials, and the visiting evangelist's preaching. But the churches of Middletown could hardly claim to have celebrated their unity of mission and purpose. It remains doubtful whether any religious figure or organization or program could gain the approval of all or of even a majority of Middletown's Protestants, so great is the difference between the liberal churches and the fundamentalist churches in their view of the world around them.

The Charismatic Movement in Middletown

Below the level of formal interchurch cooperation in Middletown, there is a substructure to the community's religion that displays much more unity than its official programs. Like other communities during the past two decades, Middletown has experienced the impact of the charismatic movement. Reaching across all denominational lines and including Roman Catholics, there has been a "stirring of the Spirit" among those who are dissatisfied with the ritual of organized worship and seek a new dimension to their religious lives.

Fired by the conviction that the presence of the divine in one's life can be a personal, highly charged, emotional experience, those who are attracted to the movement look for the gifts (Greek: *charismata*) of the Holy Spirit to empower them with a new religious vitality. The gift that is most highly regarded (which, indeed, has become the touchstone of the charismatic movement) is "speaking in tongues," the ability to burst forth in a setting of worship with an unrecognizable torrent of soft vocal sounds that are identified as a message from God intended to encourage and to strengthen the believer.

The charismatic movement is alive and well in Middletown. There is no public listening of the neighborhood groups who met in living rooms all over town to seek the new experience, but those who are interested discover a network that takes them in promptly.

Middletown has two religious organizations that foster the experience and that regularly stage large assemblies for singing and "witnessing." Aglow attracts housewives and women employed outside the home who seek to be "aglow with the Spirit," an attitude that the Bible records the Apostle Paul commending to the first-century Christians of Rome (Rom. 12:11). The Full Gospel Business Men's Fellowship is a local chapter of an international organization founded by a Greek immigrant in California during the 1960s. Members from a variety of church backgrounds gather twice a month to reinforce their faith in the "power of the Spirit." Although their number is small, members of this group believe that their influence has been spreading throughout the business community.

There are several churches in Middletown that can identify with the charismatic movement as a reflection of their own style of worship and theological understanding. For the rest, the movement lies somewhat outside the framework of organized religion, heralded by some, deplored by others, and largely ignored by church leaders.

There is a prominent exception to this pattern. One of the three Catholic churches gives its full sanction to a charismatic group composed of some of its own communications who meet regularly in the parish hall. Included in the group are a number of Protestants who find spiritual renewal in the charismatic experience at the same time they remain loyal to their own congregations.

The charismatic movement must be seen as a significant force in the religion of Middletown, though one whose credentials have not yet been validated.

Conclusions

What then can we conclude about cooperation among the churches of varying traditions and brought them together for common goals? Or has the community settled for something less?

As noted earlier, there are forms of cooperation among some of the churches that would have been unthinkable half a century ago. There is a sense of mutual appreciation between some Catholics and some Protestants that was never known before. The structures are in place, both officially, and unofficially, for furthering cooperation among those of like spirit.

But in 1980 those structures showed little promise of attracting interest from any more than a minority of Middletown's churches. In 1945, the community was one of the first to form a council of churches, but there were never more than 48 churches, including some in nearby rural areas, supporting that organization. By 1980, the number of participating churches had dwindled to about 25, while the number of churches in the community had increased from fewer than 100 to 165.

The strategy of adopting a new name to free the organization from any implication that it might follow the agenda of the National Council of Churches or the World Council of Churches did not prove successful for the county Council of Churches. To the majority of the members of Middletown's clergy, Christian Ministries was still a council of churches, and they would have nothing to do with it. That the renamed organization avoided controversial social concerns has not changed matters; ecumenicism itself is still controversial to many of the independent churches. The organization's record of mild activism in the 1960s has not been forgotten, not to mention its occasional use of the World Council's emblem during those same years.

The Ministerial Association, an older institution, is still unable to attract more than a fraction of Middletown's clergy. The differences in style and understanding between the ministers of the mainline Protestant churches and the ministers of the independent, fundamentalist churches constitute a gulf that has not been bridged.

The churches of Middletown seem to cherish independence far more than they do cooperation. As noted earlier, only the ad hoc communication of kindred spirits (the Billy Graham Crusade) or the gathering of individuals from many churches for a common purpose (the charismatic movement) have the flavor of successful cooperation.

It must be added that, as most of the churches in Middletown perceive their task, there is little *need* for cooperation. Each has its own programs of worship and fellowship. Each is faithful to the Bible as interpreted in its own religious traditions. There is no need for cooperation on political or social issues, for that is not considered the task of the faithful. The concept of the church as "one body" remains somewhat foreign to Middletown's understanding of divine purpose. To move in that direction would be to approach Catholicism. The independent, uncooperative style of Middletown's organized clergy is closer to the spirit of the Protestant Reformation as they understand it.

As this chapter was being written, Chrisitian Ministries made a new effort to reach out to the hundred or more churches that officially ignore its existence. A breakfast event for all the members of Middletown's clergy, to which each received a personal invitation by telephone, brought out almost 70 ministers. A multimedia presentation describing the purpose and program of the organization was put before the assembled group. It received polite attention.

Chapter 14

The Future of
Middletown's Religion

What then can we say about the future of religion in Middletown? The methods available to sociology for peering into the future are not very powerful, and, to speak candidly, they have not worked very well even in the hands of the masters of our discipline. Until quite recently, the predicted scenario was some version of social evolution—"The advance from the simple to the complex, through a process of successive differentiation," as Herbert Spencer put it in 1857 (1915, 35). When it comes to predicting the future course of Middletown's religion, social science provides us very little help, because its most reliable device, the extrapolation of existing trends, is not applicable. As we have shown in this volume, the trend of Middletown's religion in the past century has been inconclusive: the general level of religious belief and practice is not very different today from what it was a century ago, and the leading tenets of popular theology have remained virtually the same during the past half-century. Organizationally, the Protestant churches have grown a little stronger and the Catholic Church a little weaker. There is much more tolerance among churches and a good deal of ecumenical good will that was formerly lacking but no more cooperation than before toward common goals. The denominations of Middletown are perhaps more significant as sources of personal identity today than they were two generations ago, but the difference is small and is counterbalanced by a modest decline in religious endogamy. The Reverend Rip van Winkle, Methodist minister, awakening in Middletown after a 60-year sleep, would hardly know he had been away.

Two Generations of Change in Middletown's Religion

We say "two generations" because it is difficult to fix the exact length of the interval through which these changes occurred. The Lynds observed the religious practices of Middletown in 1924-1925 and again in 1935; the Middletown III team's examination of the same topic extended from 1977 to 1981. When we matched the data from comparable surveys, periods ranging from 52 to 56 years were spanned, but some of the informal observations compared in the preceding chapters were only 42 years apart and a few comparisons, based on the retrospective information the Lynds gathered about church attendance in the 1890s, covered a period of more than 80 years. However, most of the Lynds' data was gathered in 1924-1925 and most of ours in 1977-1978, and "two generations" is a fair description of that interval. The average age of the high school students who filled out the Lynds' questionnaire on attitudes and values in the fall of 1924 was 16 years. In 1978, when we asked Middletown's high school students to respond to a very similar questionnaire, those of their predecessors who were still alive were 69 years old on the average, the right age to be the grandparents of the second set of subjects; a good number of them actually were their grandparents. We estimate that more than a quarter of the high school students who responded to our 1977 questionnaire had one or more grandparents who had responded to the Lynds' questionnaire in 1924.

It is not a great lapse of time as history goes, even the short history of a prairie state, but it is long enough for appreciable changes to have occurred. Middletown celebrated the sesquicentennial of its founding without much fanfare in 1977, the same year our high school survey was conducted. Thus, we were examining about a third of the communitie's history.

In Dwight Hoover's review of the history of Middletown's churches (Chapter 2), we read that the impetus to form new churches, to find permanent homes for them, and eventually to relocate them in grander structures has not flagged at any time in Middletown's history. Indeed, the two grandest churches were constructed in the depths of the Great Depression when other construction, public and private, had been virtually halted.

The proliferation of churches in Middletown has had almost

the character of a biological process. Each new denomination is established by a small group of enthusiastic laypeople meeting in somebody's home and served first by amateur or visiting ministers. As the congregation grows, it rents or borrows a hall for its meetings. Then, it buys a cast-off church building. Later, it builds a finer one and begins to establish satellite churches of the same denomination in other neighborhoods. By this process, the number of denominations increases continually. The number of congregations in growing denominations also increases continually, but the number of congregations in shrinking denominations shows little tendency to decline. The largest congregations never grow beyond a manageable size, and every residential suburb is furnished with a full complement of churches as soon as it is settled. The competition for religious audiences in Middletown is less regulated and restricted than the competition among the commercial media for entertainment audiences. Consequently, a much wider range of tastes can be satisfied, with much less institutional friction.

The situation does entail some economic inefficiencies, however. Over the course of time, as new churches appear and old ones refuse to disappear, there seems to be a steady rise in excess capacity and a hidden increase in the overhead costs of the community's religious sector taken as a whole. Middletown's churchgoers have been willing to pay the price by contributing larger shares of their incomes.

Most of the changes we recorded in the religious habits of this community over the past half-century favor freedom of choice. Most churches have a roughly designated territory and several denominations have precisely demarcated parish boundaries, but parishioners are free to cross them when they wish. Nowhere, not even in the Catholic churches, are worshipers turned away or made to feel unwelcome because they come from outside a designated territory, and no Middletown church today pretends to have any authority to compel the attendance of reluctant members. The boundaries between Protestant denominations have become so permeable that husband and wife may belong to churches of different denominations without inviting censure in either place. Many people who belong to a church of one denomination regularly attend services at a church of another denomination and contribute to its support. The transfer of a member from one church to another of the same denomination elicits hardly any comment. Transfers between Protestant denominations are viewed with almost the same equanimity. Every Catholic church has a few ex-Protestants, and all the large Protestant churches have a few ex-Catholics whose presence is taken for granted.

With so few restraints on mobility it might be expected that the churches would be very responsive to consumer preferences, and indeed they are. The battle between clergy and laity for the possession of the Sabbath that the Lynds described in such detail has been agreeably settled by reserving Sunday morning for religious services and Sunday afternoon for secular recreation. The revivals, although more numerous than ever, have been shortened in recognition of the participants' other interests and obligations. The onerous parts of religious observance—long sermons, afternoon services, compulsory fasts—have been mostly abandoned.

Sin is still regularly denounced from the pulpits, but sinners are treated with consideration. Divorced persons are admitted to communion; suicides are buried in consecreated ground; wayward youths are counseled, not excommunicated.

In every measurable way, Middletown's religion has become less puritanical in the past two generations, that is, less conscience stricken about faults, less censorious about shortcomings, less emphatic about rewards and punishments, and less preoccupied with sex. The theological implications of these changes are not easy to decipher. It might be argued that the importance of religion has been diminished by the relaxation of the moral criteria that formerly separated saints from sinners. On the other hand, the attitudes toward personal conduct that prevail today in most of Middletown's churches are much more compatible with the doctrine of original sin than the former emphasis on moral perfectability. In the fundamentalist churches, this leads to a view of the world as hopelessly corrupt and unimprovable; the goal of the believer is to stop taking the world seriously. In the mainline denominations, it encourages a type of humility that withholds condemnation of even the most heinous personal acts, with blame reserved for political and economic "systems." No sentence in the New Testament is more widely known or more often quoted in today's Middletown than "Let him who is without sin cast the first stone."

The responsiveness of the churches to their audience is mirrored by the enthusiastic response of the audience to the churches. When we first discovered the pattern that Bruce Chadwick described in Chapter 3, a sharp decline of church attendance from 1890 to 1924 followed by a sharp increase from 1924 to 1978, we were skeptical about it and looked for some statistical accident that might explain the reversal. We shared with the Lynds and with our 1978 respondents the impression that religious faith and practice had declined over the past two generations.

There *is* one serious flaw in our statistical data on Middletown's church attendance, but it affects the figures for 1890, not 1924. The Lynds asked the housewives they interviewed in 1924 to estimate the church attendance of their parents around 1890. These estimates were given unhesitatingly and in full detail, but they cannot be taken as equivalent to a survey of church attendance in Middletown in 1890 for three excellent reasons: (1) some undetermined but sizable proportion of that earlier sample lived somewhere other than Middletown; (2) the retrospective reports of the parents' church attendance given by their daughters 35 years later could not have been as accurate as the contemporary reports of the daughters' own attendance; and (3) people labeled business-class and working-class in 1890 may not have been correctly classified; they are merely assumed to have been in the same class in 1890 as their daughters were in 1924. Thus, we must view with caution the Lynds' conclusion—and our own—that church attendance in Middletown declined significantly from 1890 to 1924. We have no reliable contemporary survey of church attendance in 1890 for Middletown, or for anywhere else in the United States as far as we have been able to determine.

Much more confidence can be placed on the finding that church attendance increased spectacularly from 1924 to 1978, the proportion of married women in Middletown samples who attended regularly rising from 23 percent to 48 percent and the proportion who never attended falling from 53 percent to 17 percent. As Bruce Chadwick pointed out, this does not tell the whole story since Sunday-school attendance and attendance at evening and weekday services have followed somewhat different trends, but the general conclusion that religious participation has increased in Middletown over the past two generations is unmistakable. The downward trend we seem to see from the 1890s to the 1920s as well as the upward trend from the 1920s to the 1970s are supported by the one available fragment of public, verifiable information that bears directly on the point: the proportion of local marriages performed by members of the clergy declined from 85 percent in 1890 to 63 percent in 1924 but rose again to 79 percent by 1975.

Similarly tending to support the overall growth of religious zeal is the evidence that shows that the sharp differences between the church attendance of men and the attendance of women (the Lynds estimated church attendance to be about two-thirds female) has declined to the point that the preponderance of females is barely noticeable and the age differential, although still evident, has been so much reduced that 76 percent of the young adults in our sample attend church at least occasionally and about a third of them attend at least once a week. The predominantly elderly and female congregations observed by the Lynds have given way to a broad cross section of the population.

Changes in the religious participation of business-class and working-class families have been a little more complex. The working-class people of 1924 expressed abundant faith but reported very little church attendance, apparently because they lacked the means to make a respectable display. Two-thirds of them never went to church at all, although most of the non-attenders sent their children to Sunday school more or less regularly. Today, as in many other respects, working-class families in Middletown do not differ very much from business-class families in religious participation. When we examine the data more carefully, however, we discover that there has been a dramatic decline in agnosticism among white-collar people and a dramatic increase in church participation among blue-collar people.

There is no reason to think that this reinforcement of organized religion has been balanced out by subjective secularization. On the contrary, the conventional forms of Christian piety—prayer, fasting, meditation, alms giving—all flourish in contemporary Middletown. What was supposed to be an age of skepticism has turned out to be an age of faith, closer perhaps to medieval Europe than to modern Europe in its spiritual climate.

The religious beliefs that prevail in Middletown have not changed appreciably over the past two generations. For this sector of the local culture, time has stood still. The words and the turns of phrase that people use now to describe their inner religious experience are so close to the language of their grandparents that we cannot tell them apart. The continuum of belief that the Lynds discovered in 1924 is still intact, running from people who put their total trust in themselves, to those who rely on themselves and their families, to those who trust in their families and in God, to those who trust in God alone. There are more people now at the pious end of the continuum. Moreover, the differences in devotion between women and men and between the working class and the business class that the Lynds described have all but disappeared. The theological differences among denominations, relatively unimportant to the laity in the 1920s, are now for the most part ignored by the clergy, too, so that mainline and fundamentalist pastors differ more in style than in substance on religious issues, although they differ profoundly in their social and political attitudes.

The elements of Middletown's shared Christian creed — God, Jesus, the Bible, church, heaven, morality — are not very differently perceived by Nazarenes, Baptists, Methodists, Presbyterians, Episcopalians, or Lutherans, and only some differences of emphasis separate these from Unitarians or Roman Catholics. Seventh-Day Adventists, Quakers, Mormons, Christian Scientists, and Jehovah's Witnesses do subscribe to some important doctrinal differences, but even these inconsistencies with the majority creed are subdued in the ecumenical atmosphere of contemporary Middletown. With respect to the doctrinal differences that ostensibly account for the existence of so many Protestant denominations (disagreement about episcopal authority, free will and predestination, the efficacy of sacraments, infant or adult baptism, original sin, revelation and the interpretation of scripture) we could not find a flicker of interest among laypeople, who for the most part were unaware of the beliefs they were supposed to hold on these contentious points. And, although members of the clergy are aware of the finer theological points, they seem even less inclined to argue them with the representatives of other denominations.

As we demonstrated in Chapter 4, the same harmonious spirit that suppresses theological arguments before they begin inhibits censure of other people's behavior. There is plenty of preaching against classes of sinners in Middletown's churches (profligates, gamblers, irresponsible parents") but virtually none against individual sinners. Divorce, suicide, bankruptcy, and unmarried pregnancies are treated as disasters, not as crimes, by Middletown's ministers and churchgoers, and the victims are much more likely to be consoled than to be ostracized. Hester Prynne would be welcomed at a church supper nowadays and, after a little discreet whispering, would even be treated with a special kindness.

The new tolerance is the most striking change in Middletown's religion in the past half-century; indeed, it represents a signal departure from Christian practice throughout history. Not only do Protestants speak well of each other and benignly of Catholics, they abstain from condemnation of the heathen and favor teaching about Buddhism in the public schools. There is no longer any preaching against the pope at revival meetings. There are no more diatribes against the Jews in Easter sermons. The rise of Islamic fundamentalism in the late 1970s and the anti-American vituperation of Moslem mobs during the Iranian hostage crisis did not provoke any discernible anti-Moslem reaction in Middletown's churches. The attack on the pope by a Moslem assassin in 1981 did not make Middletown's Catholics hostile toward Islam. Religion of any kind is no longer perceived as a legitimate object of aggression. The wrath of the godly is now reserved for such secular targets as bureaucrats, abortionists, and pornographers.

Although Middletown's churches support more foreign missionary activity now than in 1924, those efforts are construed to be directed against poverty, hunger, and social injustice, never against alien religions.

Ecumenicism in Middletown still stops far short of the blurring of denominational boundaries. Mergers and schisms have occurred periodically, mostly in response to national initiatives, and the distribution of churches in Middletown has been fairly volatile from decade to decade, with a long-term increase in the proportion of Pentecostal-Evangelical churches. These figures, although accurate, can easily be misinterpreted. Denominational preferences have shifted much less than a count of church buildings would suggest. A closer look at Howard Bahr's admirable tables for Chapter 5 shows that three denominations—Methodist, Baptist, and Roman Catholic—still account for more than half of all the reported denominational affiliations of Middletown adults of both sexes, as well as their parents and their children; that Methodists predominate by a considerable margin among adults but not among adolescents; and that the three leading denominations do not differ dramatically in their ability to hold members from one generation to the next, although the Catholics have a little more holding power than the Methodists and the Methodists a little more than the Baptists. More than two-thirds of all marriages are denominationally endogamous (more than three-quarters among Methodists and special-creed Christians), although the incidence of intermarriage has been rising in every denomination.

Even though the denominations represented in Middletown (excluding the predominantly black churches) do not display the strong ethnic character that some of them show elsewhere in the country, church membership is still largely inherited and denominations are still rather sharply distinguished by the education, income, occupation, and other social characteristics of their members. For example, the percentage of college graduates varies from 8 percent of the Pentecostal-Evangelicals in our sample to 67 percent of the Universalist-Unitarians, and the percentage of men in white-collar occupations varies from 30 percent among the Baptists to 78 percent in the Lutheran/Church of Christ/Brethren group. Catholics still have a few more children than Protestants, and Baptists report a little more divorce than Methodists. All these differences, however, are probably diminishing in the long run, an and none of them is dramatic. There are no longer any business-class churches in Middletown as there were during the Lynds' time; every church with a preponderance of members in white-collar occupations has a substantial proportion of blue-collar members. There are no sizable working-class churches either, although a few of the storefront congregations, composed for the most part of recent migrants from Kentucky and Tennessee, come close to being segregated by social class. All of Middletown's churches are predominantly black or predominantly white, although no white church is segregated in principle and nearly every church has some token representation of the other race.

Among the predominantly white churches, neither ethnicity nor class consciousness accounts for denominational preference in contemporary Middletown. Residential location, however is a factor; other things being equal, people are likely to attend the nearest church of their own denomination. Casual attenders often go to the nearest church without considering its denomination, but distance is not a crucial element. The overwhelming majority of churchgoers travel by automobile, and there is no one in Middletown who does not have at least a dozen churches within convenient driving distance.

Aside from the inertia that keeps people in a denomination until they have some motive to change, the binding force that holds a denomination together is the preference for one style of ritual over another. As Joseph Tamney showed in Chapter 6, there are not only two main styles of ritual, the solemn ritual illustrated by the Catholic mass ("a stylized performance by persons in uniform manipulating sacred objects") and the holiness ritual (which attempts to "give participants a direct experience of their mutual solidarity"). These types are not mutually exclusive, of course. There are some elements of the holiness ritual in the Catholic mass, particularly in the contemporary vernacular mass, and some elements of solemnity in a Pentecostal revival. With the passage of time, the attractiveness of a given ritual style is enhanced by habit and familiarity. In an established denomination, the immediate effect of liturgical change is likely to be a loss of attendance or membership, as happened in the Roman Catholic Church when the Latin mass was abandoned and in the Episcopal Church during the long, controversial introduction of a new prayer book. Meanwhile, expanding denominations like the Nazarenes and the Southern Baptists were vigorously promoting new styles of prayer and public celebration that had the common purpose of encouraging enthusiasm. If solemnity and holiness are the opposite poles of religious ritual, then it might be said that the ministers of nearly all Christian denominations have recently eschewed solemnity and cultivated holiness and that these initiatives have been more favorably received by the laity in denominations that were already inclined toward holiness than in those that were accustomed to solemnity.

Meanwhile, many new styles of religious observance have developed outside the customary framework of church worship: televised services, gospel music concerts, home prayer groups, coffeehouse ministries, retreat centers, and charismatic conferences. Most of these new rituals were designed for the cultivation of holiness rather than the enactment of solemnity, but even so more than a third of the Catholics and mainline Protestants participated in them along with more than two-thirds of the Baptists, Nazarenes, and Pentecostals.

We cannot go very far back with this analysis because we do not know whether there has been a long-term drift toward religious solemnity that has recently been checked by liturgical reform and charismatic innovation or whether, on the contrary, solemnity has been waning for a long time. The Lynds thought they saw a trend toward solemnity in the decline of the revival movement from 1890 to 1924, but, as Chapters 2 and 6 have shown, that decline was illusory. The trend in revivals since 1924 is equally inconclusive. There were 106 revivals in Middletown in 1980 compared to 33 in 1924, an increase that more than kept pace with the growth of the population, but the 1980 revivals were shorter and involved a smaller proportion of the local churches.

The Methodists, who had originally invented the revival as a device for countering the solemnity of established Anglicanism, had almost ceased to participate in revivals by 1980 and were moving slowly but steadily toward the solemn end of the spectrum. Solemnity may be losing ground, but by no means has it been abandoned. A national survey of Episcopalian laity and clergy conducted by the Gallup organization in 1980 for a group of dissident Episcopalians revealed that a three-to-one majority of the clergy favored the newly revised prayerbook with its infusion of holiness, while a three-to-one majority of the laity preferred the old Book of Common Prayer with all its 16th-century solemnity. The long-term trend continues to elude us, but that may be because it is not a very clear trend.

A denomination's position on the continuum from holiness to solemnity has a curious relationship to the ingenious devotional index developed by Howard Bahr. Devotion is not significantly related to gender, education, social class, occupation, or family income in Middletown today. Contrary to our expectations, the women in our samples were not more devout than the men, and uneducated people were not more devout than the well educated. Devotion *does* increase with age, although we cannot be sure how much of this is a historical effect, that is, how much is a difference between generations and how much is the effect of advancing age on individuals.

Denominational preference is the other factor that has a powerfull effect on devotion, but it is not the effect we would have predicted. The most devout laypeople are found among the Catholics and the Pentecostal-Evangelicals, that is, at the extreme ends of the continuum from solemnity to holiness. The Methodists, in the middle of the continuum, are the least devout of Middletown Christians by a fair margin. Other denominations distribute themselves appropriately. Both the holiness style and the solemn style of public worship seem to lead their followers to private worship and to religiously centered lives, but the blending of these styles in public worship seems to discourage private devotions.

Devotion seems to act as a reinforcement for other religious practices and beliefs. Many of the people who attend church regularly are not devout, but most devout people attend church, spend much more time in church activities, and contribute a much higher proportion of their incomes to organized religion. Not all believers are devout, but virtually all devout persons in Middletown accept the main tenets of Christian belief. Those who are devout subjectively connect their religion with their choice of friends and leisure activities, with their job performance, and with their family relationships, although they are not conspicuously happier than their fellow citizens.

There is an apparent inconsistency between Bahr's finding that the devotional index has only a slight correlation with personal happiness and Bruce Chadwick's finding in Chapter 10 that church attendance is significantly related to personal and marital happiness, a finding also reported in recent national surveys. The inconsistency is more apparent than real, however, because of the effect of age as an intervening variable. In general, but with numerous exceptions, devotion increases with age and happiness decreases. When we substitute church attendance for devotion as a measure of religiosity, there is a significant although not overwhelming relationship between happiness and churchgoing or at least between respondents' reports of their churchgoing and estimates of their happiness, both in Middletown and national samples. There is an intrinsic difficulty in eliciting differences of this kind because about a third of the population describe themselves as "very happy" in such surveys and more than half as "pretty happy," leaving only a small minority to acknowledge lives of quiet despair. This heavily skewed distribution makes it difficult to tease out differences, and we have, of course, no way of knowing whether churchgoers report themselves as happy because they are happy (whatever that means) or because they lean toward conventionality and think it fitting and proper to describe themselves as happy in the same way that it is fitting and proper to go to church.

We stand on somewhat more solid ground when we examine the relationship of church attendance with the primary indicators of socioeconomic status' education, occupation, and income. Church attendance in Middletown is positively and significantly correlated with education, occupational level, and income, so that the majority of persons with less than a high school education do not attend church regularly while the majority of college graduates do. The majority of persons in professional and managerial occupations attend church regularly, while the majority of those in semi-skilled and service occupations do not. The majority of our respondents who had high family incomes (over $30,000) attended church regularly; the majority of those with low family incomes (under $20,000) did not; and those with intermediate incomes were evenly divided.

These Middletown results have not been confirmed by the eight national surveys conducted by the National Opinion Research Center from 1972 through 1980. The national surveys found no significant differences in education, occupation, and income between those who attend church regularly and those who do not.

The discrepancy is disturbing and cannot be readily explained, although Chadwick has made a brave attempt to do so. There is no reason why Middletown must mirror the nation as a whole, but in the course of the Middletown III project we have become accustomed to finding social indicators for Middletown close to national averages. In fact, much of the value we attribute to the study of Middletown as a specimen community derives from the expectation that it is, in the words of a local poet, "Normal City." The relationship we have found between church attendance and socioeconomic status is clearly abnormal, however, and the abnormality is aggravated by another set of figures that shows that

Republicans in Middletown are much more likely to attend church than Democrats. We have no satisfactory explanation to propose for this anomaly. It may be due to some hidden flaw in the sampling procedure of the national surveys or in our own. It may be an emergent local peculiarity related in some way to the two features that impair Middletown's image a typical American community: the virtual absence of persons of foreign birth or foreign parentage and the presence of a large but locally oriented university. It may be an emerging pattern that has arrived a little earlier on the banks of the White River than in the country as a whole.

In the wider perspective, it does not matter so much whether we find a moderate positive correlation between religiosity and social status as in Middletown or no relationship at all as in the National Opinion Research Center surveys. What matters more is that we can find no trace of the inverse relationship between income, education, and other measures of achievement that was anticipated by the theory that secularization accompanies modernization and continues inexorably until traditional religion disappears. The Lynds, like most of their intellectual contemporaries, took this proposition for granted and were not surprised to discover that women were more religious than men and that the working class was more religious than the business class. They wrote that "in many activities, as has been repeatedly pointed out, the working class today employs the habits of the business class of roughly a generation ago" (Lynd and Lynd 1929, 496), an observation not to be faulted with respect to household equipment but highly suspect when applied to religious or political behavior.

Just as the working-class family was thought to resemble the business-class family at an earlier stage of development, so rural families were used to represent the urban families of an earlier era and differences between rural and urban habits were interpreted as social trends. That method was used by Ogburn and Tibbitts in a famous essay, "The Family and Its Functions," they published in 1933. They purported to demonstrate the loss of the family's religious functions by showing that grace before meals and family prayers were more commonly recited in country homes than in city homes around 1920 (Ogburn and Tibbitts 1933, 634). The method is outrageous, of course, and the Lynds, who were never deficient in common sense, were quick to point out that "the direction of change is highly erratic" (Lynd and Lynd 1929, 498). But for all that, they never questioned the inevitability of secularization, and, though they considered at length the possible ways in which religion might adapt to the changing times, they never envisioned the possibility that traditional religion would persist in the face of technological progress. Of that persistence there can be no serious doubt. There are more churches in Middletown today in relation to the population than there were in 1924 and more people who attend them regularly. More people contribute to churches now than then, and they give larger proportions of their incomes. There is about as much piety in the working class as there used to be, and there is considerably more in the business class. The mutual dependence of the family and church is closer than ever, as the discussion of the symbolic devices that link the celebration of family solidarity to the high points of the Christian liturgy in Chapter 9 shows. And the prestige and influence of the clergy have not declined.

In Chapter 1, we listed 11 trends that ought to accompany secularization over an appreciable period of time, such as the interval between 1924 and 1978, and 4 additional trends that might be looked for if a special definition of secularization were adopted. It is time now to see how many of these trends were discovered in Middletown.

1. EXPECTED TREND: A decline in the number of churches per capita of the population.

ACTUAL TREND: The number of churches increased from 0.0013 per capita in 1931 to 0.0020 in 1977.

2. EXPECTED TREND: A decline in the proportion of the population attending church services.

ACTUAL TREND: For married women in Middletown, the proportion attending church regularly increased from 23 percent in 1924 to 48 percent in 1978. The attendance of married men, estimated from the reports of their wives, increased correspondingly.

3. EXPECTED TREND: A decline in the number of rites of

passage held under religious auspices.

ACTUAL TREND: The proportion of Middletown's marriages performed by ministers or priests increased from 63 percent in 1924 to 79 percent in 1979. The proportion of burials at which ministers or priests officiated is not known for 1924; it was 99 percent in 1979.

4. *EXPECTED TREND: A decline in religious endogamy.*

ACTUAL TREND: Twenty-four percent of married couples reported interdenominational marriages in 1977, compared to 12 percent of their parents—a significant increase.

5. *EXPECTED TREND: A decline in the proportion of the labor force engaged in religious activity.*

ACTUAL TREND: The proportion of Middletown's labor force engaged in religious activity increased between 1920 and 1980.

6. *EXPECTED TREND: A decline in the proportion of income devoted to the support of religion.*

ACTUAL TREND: The proportion of family income contributed to churches by a sample of working-class families in 1924 was 1.6 percent, and the proportion contributed by a comparable sample in 1978 was 3.3 percent. We do not have any 1924 figures for business-class families.

7. *EXPECTED TREND: A decline in the ratio of religious to nonreligious literature.*

ACTUAL TREND: No figures are available for Middletown.

8. *EXPECTED TREND: A decline in the attention given to religion in the mass media.*

ACTUAL TREND: The proportion of space given to religious announcements and activities in Middletown's local newspapers has remained relatively constant since 1924. The proportion of broadcasting time occupied by religious services has increased.

9. *EXPECTED TREND: A drift toward less emotional forms of participation in religious services.*

ACTUAL TREND: As previously noted, the long-term trend is difficult to decipher, but within the past two decades there has been a drift toward more emotional forms of participation.

10. EXPECTED TREND: A dwindling of new sects and of new movements in existing churches.

ACTUAL TREND: Appendix Table 5-1 tells the opposite story. Most of Middletown's new sects can be described as Pentecostal-Evangelical. In 1931, 17 out of 61 churches fell into that category; in 1977, the proportion was 61 out of 160, an appreciable increase. Such national sects as the Moonies, the Hare Krishna, and the Black Muslims are also known in Middletown. As to new movements in existing churches, the charismatic movement alone loomed larger in the existing churches during the 1970s than any new movement during the 1920s. There were other movements as well, including social activism, liturgical reform, ecumenicism, ordination of women, congregational democracy, and innumerable innovations in "outreach" and "stewardship."

11. EXPECTED TREND: Increased attention to secular issues in sermons and liturgy.

ACTUAL TREND: Of the 102 sermons we sampled at random in Middletown's churches in 1978, only 2 dealt with secular issues, and those not closely.

So much for secularization in the ordinary sense. What about secularization in the special sense proposed by Jeffrey Hadden—a break in the connection between church and state? The expected trends were these four.

12. EXPECTED TREND: A declining level of political activity by organized religious groups.

ACTUAL TREND: There was no political action among Middletown's churches in the 1920s and none in the 1930s, according to the Lynds, except for the solitary minister who urged his congregation to vote for Roosevelt and who was soundly censured for doing so. During the 1960s and 1970s, the Middletown Council of Churches experimented gingerly with social activism, but that movement, as Laurence Martin explained in Chapter 13, has now subsided. A small minority of Middletown people contri-

bute to the Moral Majority and other national lobbies that have grown out of the Electronic Church. There was nothing like this in the 1920s, unless we count the Ku Klux Klan, but the radio campaigns of Father Charles Coughlin and Gerald L. K. Smith in the 1930s bear some resemblance to the recent right-wing activities of television preachers.

13. EXPECTED TREND: Diminished interest in the religious credentials of candidates and officeholders.

ACTUAL TREND: This seems to have occurred in Middletown. The Democratic candidate for mayor in 1979 was a Catholic. Although he was defeated, his religion, according to local observers, was not an important factor, as it presumably would have been for a Catholic candidate in the 1920s.

14. EXPECTED TREND: Less regulation of religious organizations by government.

ACTUAL TREND: There is not much direct governmental regulation of churches today, but church schools are extensively regulated by various federal agencies as are religiously sponsored colleges, orphanages, rest homes, camps, and social agencies. The resulting litigation is voluminous. There was no regulation of this kind in the 1920s.

15. EXPECTED TREND: The removal of religious symbols from the ceremonies and insignia of the state and of patriotic symbols from the ceremonies and insignia of the church.

ACTUAL TREND: There has been no discernible change since the 1920s except for the abolition of prayer in the public schools by the federal courts and the addition of the phrase "under God" to the pledge of allegiance by an act of Congress.

There is no more evidence for secularization in this special sense than there is for secularization in the conventional sense. The overall tendency, such as it is, looks more like scaralization.

To sociologists of religion, we may seem to be beating a dead horse. All of them are familiar with the long-term increase of church affiliation and the long-term growth in the volume and importance of church-sponsored activities in the United States. Serious students of religious behavior are no longer likely to rely very much on secularization as an explanatory concept, but the idea lingers on.

Of course, we cannot assume that the religious trends in Middletown are the same as the trends in the entire country. As we noted in earlier chapters, Middletown's denominational distribution is different from the country's as a whole; it has too many Methodists and too few Catholics, and it lacks many of the religious types that create such a stir in metropolitan cities: the worker priests, women rabbis, reforming theologians, national fund raisers, and moral entrepreneurs. There are few opinion makers and style setters in Middletown.

Yet, it would be inaccurate to characterize the place as a museum of old-time religion. Pious as Middletown is, the survey evidence seems to tell us that it is rather less pious than the country as a whole. Comparing our 1977-1978 surveys of Middletown with the 1979-1980 national surveys carried out by the Princeton Religious Research Center, we find that 16 percent of Middletown adults reported "no religious preference" compared to 8 percent of the national sample. Twenty-nine percent of Middletown adolescents said they had no religious preference, compared to 11 percent of the corresponding national sample. Thirty-two percent of Middletown adults attended church weekly, compared to 41 percent of the national sample. Sixteen percent of Middletown people said they never prayed, compared to 11 percent of the national sample. Although the differences are not huge and may be at least partially procedural, they are statistically significant and there are no offsetting differences in the other direction.

The public perception of trends in religion has been much more volatile than religion itself. In response to the question "At the present time, do you think religion as a whole is increasing its influence on American life or losing its influence?" the ratio of respondents perceiving religious progress to respondents perceiving religious decay ranged in successive Gallup surveys from 4.9:1.0 in 1957 to 0.2:1.0 in 1970 to 0.8:1.0 in 1980. The opinions of scholars have been even more volatile. Secularization was much in vogue in the 1960s (Schneider 1967; Berger 1967). It is presently less fashionable but still taken for granted in many sociological writings.

The continued vitality of traditional religion in America is something of a puzzle, because religion has recently been declining in all of the other advanced industrial nations. The hypothesis that modernization leads inevitably to secularization would be moderately plausible were it not for the American case, although it would still have to be admitted that secularization did not appear until modernization had been under way for many generations. In France, where public and parochial records are good enough to permit the construction of very long time series describing religious observance (Boulard 1971, 61-98), the 19th century and the first half of the 20th century showed numerous fluctuations in religious practice but no long-term trend. The appearance in metropolitan cities of a sector of the population completely detached from organized religion seems to have been compensated by increased religiosity in other sectors. After 1960, however, there were some sharp declines in religious practice (Isambert 1980, 219-45). In the nine years from 1966 to 1975, the proportion of the French population regularly attending Sunday mass decreased from 23 percent to 13 percent. Between 1958 and 1971, the proportion of infants baptized decreased from 92 percent to 74 percent. By 1974, the proportion of the population confessing monthly was down to 1 percent. Between 1965 and 1975, the number of priests decreased from 41,000 to 36,000; the number resigning from the priesthood annually rose from around 50 to around 200; and the number of new recruits, which had oscillated between 700 and 1700 a year for about 150 years, dropped to less than 200.

In England, the proportion of Easter communicants in the Church of England, expressed as a percentage of the population over the age of 15, declined from more than 9 percent in 1900 to under 5 percent in 1970 despite some intermediate fluctuations. Sunday school attendance declined by about two-thirds over the same interval (Argyle and Beit-Hallahmi 1975, 8-12).

Gallup's 1980 cross-national study shows the near disappearance of religious practice among young adults (18 to 24 years old) in France, the United Kingdom, Sweden, West Germany, Switzerland, and Japan, all among the world's most modernized countries. The proportions of young adults in these countries who think that religion should be very important in life range from 7 percent in France to 11 percent in Sweden, compared to 41 percent in the United

States. Answers to other questions about religious activities and attitudes were consistent: if the trends of the past two decades were to continue, organized religion would become a negligible force in those national societies, but there would be no real change in the situation of American religion.

In another report based on the Middletown III project, we confronted the myth of the declining family, showed how it arose and what purposes it served, and suggested that, despite certain structural and demographic weaknesses, the pattern of family life that is central to Middletown's culture is likely to persist without drastic change during the foreseeable future (Caplow et al. 1982, Chapter 13). Predicting the future of religion is a parallel but not an identical problem. Although there is a myth of declining religion that has some currency in Middletown, it is not as widely believed and it has recently been losing ground. The Lynds careful but exhaustive description of Middletown's culture in the 1920s enables us to assert with confidence in the face of both myths that religion and the family in Middletown have not changed greatly in the past two generations despite continued technological progress, continued economic development, the massive intrusion of the federal government and of network television into local life, and the great events that reverberate endlessly through the outside world—the Great Depression, World War II, the Cold War, the civil rights movement, the ideological turmoil of the 1960s, the inflation of the 1970s, and the foreign policy crises of the 1980s. Contrary to most expectations, these events have had little visible effect in Middletown on the two institutions that are outside the sphere of bureaucratic control and ostensibly rational manipulation. But predicting the future of religion is more difficult than predicting the future of the family. Although the family persists in an essentially traditional form in all advanced industrial societies, including the People's Republics, religion has been virtually abolished by the state in the Soviet Union and some other countries with Marxist regimes and has declined spectacularly in countries such as Sweden and West Germany, where the state exerts no pressure at all against it. This seems to tell us, on the incontrovertible basis of experience, that large-scale organized religion is not a necessary component of a modern mass society. Its removal does not make a society unworkable. Unlike the persistence of the family, the persistence of religion in Middletown and in the United States cannot be taken for granted. It needs to be explained.

A full explanation would take us far afield, but there are certain obvious differences between the situation of religion in the United States, where 41 percent of the young adults think that religion should be very important in life, and in the Western European countries, where fewer than 10 percent of the young adults think so. In each of the Western European countries, organized religion is an aspect of the national state, even where it is not fully established, while in the United States, with its "multitude of sects," the churches, for all their formal patriotism, are not only independent of the state but quietly antithetical to it. The state is universal, the denomination is particular; the state is founded on compulsion, the denomination is founded on voluntarism; the state gradually curtails other forms of local autonomy, but autonomy, in most American denominations, extends down to individual churches. As the relationship between the individual and the polity becomes more encompassing, more uncertain, the more antagonistic, the refuge offered by the churches against the insatiable demands of the state seems to become more attractive. It is conceivable that major changes might occur in Middletown's religion—a widespread loss of faith, a wave of denominational mergers, some new messianic movement—but it is unlikely that such changes will occur without a prior transformation of the political and economic arrangements of the national society. Until that happens, Middletown's future religion will probably continue to resemble Middletown's present religion, archaic, fragmented, and wonderfully untroubled.

APPENDIX: TABLES

Table 1-1
The Religious Preferences of Middletown Adults, 1976-1977, and U.S. Adults, 1972-1980

Religion	Middletown		United States	
	Number	Percentage	Number	Percentage
Methodist	254	20.4	1520	12.5
Baptist	164	13.2	2524	20.8
Roman Catholic	127	10.2	3049	25.2
Protestant	121	9.7	469	3.9
Presbyterian/Christian/Episcopal	115	(9.2)	–	–
Presbyterian	59	4.7	572	4.7
Christian, Congregational	44	3.5	263	2.2
Episcopal	12	1.0	322	2.6
Pentecostal-Evangelical	126	(10.1)	–	–
Pentecostal Holiness	34	2.7	195	1.6
Nazarene	32	2.6	46	0.4
Church of God	31	2.5	108	0.9
Assembly of God	13	1.0	72	0.6
Apostolic Pentecostal	5	0.4	17	0.1
Other (Christian Pilgrim, Bible-Believing, Missionary Alliance, Full Gospel, God's Free-Will Tabernacle, Salvation Army, etc.)	8	0.6	89	0.7
Spiritualist	3	0.2	1	–
Lutheran/Church of Christ/Brethren	70	(5.6)	–	–
Church of Christ	28	2.2	267	2.2
Lutheran	25	2.0	962	7.9
Disciples of Christ	8	0.6	28	0.2
Church of the Brethren	9	0.7	36	0.3
Special-Creed Christians	46	(3.7)	–	–
Quakers	24	1.9	7	–
Latter-Day Saints	10	0.8	100	0.8
Seventh-Day Adventist	6	0.5	55	0.4
Jehovah's Witnesses	5	0.4	67	0.6
Christian Science	1	0.1	34	0.3
Mennonite	–	–	9	0.1
Universalist-Unitarian	20	1.6	26	0.2
Jews	2	0.2	286	2.4
Other	9	0.7	137	1.1
No Religious Preference	192	(15.4)	–	–
No preference	184	14.8	824	6.8
Agnostic	8	0.6	–	–
No Answer	–	–	28	0.2
Total	1246	99.8	12,113	99.7

Sources: Middletown composite sample, kinship, family role, and neighboring surveys, 1978. African Methodist Episcopal (two cases) excluded because sampling of Middletown's black churches was minimal in these surveys. United States, 1972-1980, Cumulative Sample, National Opinion Research Center, *General Social Surveys, 1972-1980: Cumulative Codebook,* Storrs, Conn.: Roper Public Opinion Research Center, July 1980, pp. 89, 301.

Table 3-1
Church Attendance of Married Couples in Middletown, by Social Class, 1890 and 1924

	Business-Class Husbands			Working-Class Husbands		
Church Attendance	1890 (N = 39)	1924 (N = 40)	Difference	1890 (N = 101)	1924 (N = 163)	Difference
Regular	69%	40%	−29%	44%	21%	−23%
Intermittent	3	35	+32%	15	8	−7%
Occasional	0	0	0%	1	2	+1%
Never	28	25	−3%	40	69	+29%
Total	100%	100%		100%	100%	
	Business-Class Wives			Working-Class Wives		
Church Attendance	1890 (N = 40)	1924 (N = 40)	Difference	1890 (N = 119)	1924 (N = 123)	Difference
Regular	78%	40%	−38%	53%	20%	−33%
Intermittent	2	33	+31%	11	14	+3%
Occasional	0	0	0%	3	2	−1%
Never	20	27	+7%	33	65	+32%
Total	100%	100%		100%	101%	

Source: Lynd and Lynd 1929, Table XXI.

Note: Difference between business-class husbands in 1890 and in 1924 is significant at the .001 level, χ^2 = 14.1. Difference between working-class husbands in 1890 and in 1924 is significant at the .001 level, χ^2 = 24.8. Difference between business-class wives in 1890 and in 1924 is significant at the .001 level, χ^2 = 15.3. Difference between working class wives in 1890 and in 1924 is significant at the .001 level, χ^2 = 31.7. Difference between business- and working-class husbands in 1890 is significant at .05 level, χ^2 = 8.0; difference in 1924 is also significant at .001 level, χ^2 = 32.9. Difference between business- and working-class wives in 1890 is significant at .05, χ^2 = 7.1; difference in 1924 is significant .001 level, χ^2 = 18.2.

Table 3-2
Church Attendance of Married Women in Middletown, 1890, 1924, 1978

Church Attendance	1890 (N = 159)	1924 (N = 173)	1978 (N = 333)	Difference 1890-1978	Difference 1924-1978
Regular	59%	23%	48%	−11%	+25%
Intermittent	9	23	14	+5%	−9%
Occasional	2	1	20	+18%	+19%
Never	30	53	17	−13%	−36%
Total	100%	100%	99%		

Sources: Lynd and Lynd 1929, Table XXI; Middletown III housewives' survey, 1978.

Note: Difference between 1924 and 1978 is significant at .001 level, χ^2 = 104.9. Difference between 1890 and 1978 is significant at .001 level, χ^2 = 38.8.

Table 3-3
Church Attendance of Middletown Adults by Social Class,
1977-1978

Church Attendance	Business Class (N = 766)	Working Class (N = 628)	Difference
Regular	38%	26%	-12%
Intermittent	13	7	-6%
Occasional	32	37	+5%
Never	17	29	+12%
Total	100%	99%	

Sources: Middletown III women's and men's occupational surveys, family role survey, kinship survey, and religion survey, 1977 and 1978.

Note: Difference is significant at .001 level, χ^2 = 49.9.

Table 3-4
Church Attendance of Middletown Adults, by Sex,
1977-1978

Church Attendance	Women (N = 1,196)	Men (N = 664)	Difference
Regular	33%	28%	-5%
Intermittent	10	8	-2%
Occasional	35	35	0%
Never	22	29	+7%
Total	100%	100%	

Sources: Middletown III men's occupational survey, women's occupational survey, religion survey, family role survey, and kinship survey, 1977 and 1978.

Note: Difference is significant at .01 level, χ^2 = 13.9.

Table 3-5
Church Attendance of Middletown Adults, by Age, 1977-1978

Church Attendance	15-29 Years (N = 226)	30-39 Years (N = 194)	40-49 Years (N = 146)	50-65 Years (N = 220)	Over 65 Years (N = 76)
Regular	24%	33%	38%	40%	49%
Intermittent	10	8	8	14	18
Occasional	42	35	32	30	21
Never	24	24	22	16	12
Total	100%	100%	100%	100%	100%

Sources: Middletown III men's and women's occupational surveys and religion survey, 1978.

Note: Difference is significant at .001 level, χ^2 = 41.5.

Table 3-6

Reasons Given by Middletown Women for Attending Church,
1924 and 1978

Reason	1924 (N = 62)	1978 (N = 230)	Difference
Habit	44%	15%	−29%
Enjoyment	35	65	+30%
Benefits to children	8	13	+5%
Other	13	7	−6%
Total	100%	100%	

Sources: Lynd and Lynd 1929, 360-61, 366-67; Middletown III housewives' survey, 1978.

Note: Difference is significant at the .001 level, χ^2 = 29.2.

Table 3-7

Reasons Given by Middletown Women for Not Attending Church,
1924 and 1978

Reason	1924 (N = 83)	1978 (N = 115)	Difference
Work or fatigue	27%	19%	−8%
Lack of habit	27	21	−6%
Dislike of service	23	31	+8%
Competing activities	10	9	−1%
Cost	7	7	0%
Ideological reasons	6	13	+7%
Total	100%	100%	

Sources: Lynd and Lynd 1929, 362-68; Middletown III housewives' survey, 1978.

Note: Difference is not statistically significant.

Table 3-8
Outside Religious Activities of Middletown Adults, 1978

Activity	Percentage Participating (N = 170)
Televised church at home	25
Home Bible study	18
Gospel music concert	18
Home prayer group	13
Retreat centers	12
House church	4
Coffeehouse ministry	3
Religious communes	3
None	50

Source: Middletown III religion survey, 1978.

Note: Percentages total more than 100 because some respondents engaged in more than one activity.

Table 3-9
Organizational Memberships of Married Women and Men,
Middletown, 1978 (in percentages)

Organization	Women (N = 330)		Men (N = 330)	
	Belong	Active	Belong	Active
Church	74	59	61	43
Social clubs	60	55	37	32
Lodges	15	9	29	15
Unions	11	9	45	37
Other	32	26	24	23

Source: Middletown III housewives' survey, 1978.

Note: Percentages total over 100 percent because some respondents belonged to more than one organization.

Table 3-10
Percentage of Family Income Contributed to Churches and
Secular Charities by Working-class Families in Middletown,
1924 and 1978
(in percentages)

Contribution	1924 (N = 100)	1978 (N = 140)
Churches	1.6	3.3
Secular charities	0.7	0.8

Sources: Lynd and Lynd 1929, 514-17; Middletown III housewives' survey, 1978.

Table 5-1

Number of Churches in Middletown City Directories, by Denominational Category, 1931-1977

Denominational Category	1931-1932	1936-1937	1952	1960	1970	1977
Methodist	11	12	11	14	19	22
Baptist	8	7	9	16	27	38
Presbyterian/Christian/Episcopalian	7	6	6	7	6	8
Pentecostal-Evangelical	17	20	45	62	66	61
Lutheran/Church of Christ/Brethren	9	11	13	16	18	18
Special-creed Christian	4	3	5	6	6	8
Universalist-Unitarian[a]	2	1	1	1	1	1
Catholic	2	2	2	2	2	3
Jewish	1	1	1	1	1	1
Total	61	63	93	125	146	160
Middletown population[b]	46,548	47,000	58,479	68,603	69,082	79,932
Population per church	763	746	629	549	473	500

Sources: For 1931-1932 and 1936-1937, Emerson's Directory and County Gazeteer (Cincinnati: Williams Directory Company) for those years; for 1952, 1960, 1970, and 1977, Polk's City Directory (Cincinnati: R. L. Polk, 1952 and 1960; Detroit: R. L. Polk, 1970; Taylor, Mich.: R. L. Polk, 1977).

a. The Universalist-Unitarian congregation unaccountably was not listed in the Polk directories for these years, but the congregation was in existence. In this instance only, we have adjusted the directory listings.

b. These are U.S. census figures for 1930, 1950, 1960, and 1970; the figure used for 1936-1937 is the 1935 estimate of the Lynds (1939, 517); and the 1977 figure is an estimate computed by the Middletown III project.

Table 5-2

Denominational Preferences of Middletown Adults, Their Parents, and Their Children, by Sex, 1977

Denominational Category	Males			Females		
	First Generation	Second Generation	Third Generation*	First Generation	Second Generation	Third Generation*
Methodist	21%	20%	12%	24%	23%	14%
Baptist	13	12	10	15	11	13
Roman Catholic	10	11	16	10	11	15
Protestant (unspecified)	9	11	8	11	8	6
Presbyterian/Christian/Episcopalian	9	6	6	12	12	9
Pentecostal-Evangelical	4	7	6	7	10	9
Lutheran/Church of Christ/Brethren	8	5	4	8	7	4
Special-creed Christian	4	4	1	5	4	2
Universalist-Unitarian	1	1	0	1	2	1
Non-Christian	1	2	3	0	0	3
No preference	21	21	33	8	12	25
Total	101%	100%	99%	101%	100%	101%
Number of cases (N)	(448)	(361)	(631)	(457)	(506)	(664)

Sources: Middletown III kinship survey, family role survey, and high school survey, 1977.

*High school students, white only.

Table 5-4

The Religious Preferences of Middletown Adults, Their Parents, High School Students (1977), and Young Adults (1937)

Religious Preference	Adults, 1977	High School Students, 1977[a]	Recent High School Students and Dropouts, 1937[b]	Adults' Parents, 1977[c]
Methodist	20%	13%	12%	22%
Baptist	13	11	11	14
Roman Catholic	10	15	9	10
Protestant (unspecified)	10	7	26	10
Presbyterian/Christian/Episcopalian	9	8	26	11
Pentecostal-Evangelical	10	8	1	5
Lutheran/Church of Christ/Brethren	6	4	11	8
Special-creed Christian	4	2	5	4
Universalist-Unitarian	2	0	0	1
Non-Christians	1	3	0	1
No religious preference	15	29	3	14
Total	100%	100%	104%	100%
Number of cases (N)	(1,246)	(1,295)	(1,080)	(905)

Sources: Adults' parents: Middletown III kinship survey, 1977; adults: Middletown III kinship survey, family role survey, and neighboring survey, 1977; students: Middletown III high school survey, 1977; recent high school graduates and dropouts: Fuller 1937, Append. B, xvii, xxxii.

a. Whites only; only a handful of blacks responded to the mail surveys, and so the appropriate group for generational comparisons is white students. These are not the literal children of the adults represented in column 1, but rather a representative sample of the high school population.

b. Whites only; includes graduates and dropouts from the classes of 1930, 1933, and 1936.

c. Of course, not all of these parents of contemporary Middletown adults were themselves ever residents of Middletown or its environs, but most were. Sixty-percent of the kinship survey respondents with living parents said that their parents lived in Middletown or within 50 miles.

Table 5-5

Denominational Preferences of Middletown Young People, 1937 and 1977

Religious Preference	High School Students, 1977[a]	Recent High School Students and Dropouts, 1937[b]
Methodist	13%	12%
Baptist	11	11
Roman Catholic	15	9
Protestant (unspecified)	7	21
Presbyterian/Christian/Episcopalian	8	26
Pentecostal-Evangelical	8	1
Lutheran/Church of Christ/Brethren	4	11
Special-creed Christian	2	5
Universalist-Unitarian	0	0
Non-Christians	3	0
No preference	29	3
Total	100%	99%
Number of cases (N)	(1,295)	(1,080)

Sources: For 1937: Fuller 1937, Append. B, pp. xvii, xxxii. For 1977 Middletown III high school survey, 1977. The questionnaire was administered to the entire high school population (N = 3,257 [completed instruments from an estimated total enrollment of 4,000]) but only a random sample were tabulated, and for comparability only whites (N = 1,080) are included here.

a. Whites only; blacks were omitted from this tabulation to improve comparison with the 1937 study, which had virtually no black respondents.

b. Whites only; includes graduates and dropouts from classes of 1930, 1933, and 1936.

Table 5-6

Intergenerational Religious Mobility Reported by Middletown Respondents, 1977

Religious Preference	Total Number	Percentage of Stayers	Percentage of Switchers	Net Change	
				Number	Percentage
Father's:					
Catholic	44	68	32	3	7
Methodist	93	67	33	6	6
Baptist	56	54	46	-2	-4
Protestant (unspecified)	40	28	72	-16	-40
Presbyterian/Christian/Episcopalian	41	51	49	7	17
Pentecostal-Evangelical	18	72	28	20	111
Lutheran/Church of Christ/Brethren	35	57	43	-2	-6
Special-creed Christians	16	81	19	7	44
Universalist-Unitarian	5	*	*	3	*
Non-Christian	4	*	*	-2	*
No preference	92	34	66	-24	-26
Total number or average percentage	444	52	48	—	—

Table 5-6 (continued)

Religious Preference	Total Number	Percentage of Stayers	Percentage of Switchers	Net Change	
				Number	Percentage
Mother's:					
Catholic	46	78	22	1	2
Methodist	108	65	35	-9	-8
Baptist	67	55	45	-11	-16
Protestant (unspecified)	49	33	67	-23	-47
Presbyterian/Christian/Episcopalian	57	54	46	-9	-16
Pentecostal-Evangelical	29	55	45	13	45
Lutheran/Church of Christ/Brethren	36	53	47	-2	-6
Special-creed Christian	21	67	33	2	10
Universalist-Unitarian	4	*	*	4	*
Non-Christian	2	*	*	0	*
No preference	35	63	37	34	97
Total number or average percentage	454	58	42	—	—

Source: Middletown III kinship survey, 1977.

*Percentages were not computed when base is less than 10.

Table 5-7
Denominational Preferences of Married People in Middletown, 1977

Husband's Preference	Wife's Preference											
	Catholic	Methodist	Baptist	Protestant (unspecified)	Presbyterian/Christian/Episcopalian	Pentecostal-Evangelical	Lutheran/Church of Christ/Brethren	Special-Creed Christian	Universalist-Unitarian	Non-Christian	No Preference	Total
Catholic	35	4	1	1	1	—	—	2	—	—	3	47
Methodist	1	84	7	3	2	4	3	—	1	—	3	108
Baptist	2	6	44	2	4	1	2	—	—	—	2	63
Protestant (unspecified)	2	8	—	25	6	5	5	—	—	—	5	56
Presbyterian/Christian/Episcopalian	2	5	2	—	36	—	1	1	—	—	—	47
Pentecostal-Evangelical	1	—	—	1	1	33	—	—	—	—	1	37
Lutheran/Church of Christ/Brethren	1	2	—	—	4	3	21	—	—	—	—	31
Special-Creed Christian	—	3	—	—	—	1	—	15	—	—	1	20
Universalist-Unitarian	—	—	—	—	—	—	1	—	6	—	1	8
Non-Christian	—	—	—	—	1	1	—	—	—	2	—	4
No preference	10	8	10	4	4	8	6	4	2	—	48	104
Total	54	120	64	36	59	56	39	22	9	2	64	525

Sources: Middletown III kinship survey (328 reported their own and their spouse's religious preference), and family role survey (197 matched couples each reported their own religious preference), 1977.

Table 5-8

Denominational Preferences of the Parents of Married People, Middletown, 1977

Husband's Preference	Wife's Preference											
	Catholic	Methodist	Baptist	Protestant (unspecified)	Presbyterian/Christian/Episcopalian	Pentecostal-Evangelical	Lutheran/Church of Christ/Brethren	Special-Creed Christian	Universalist-Unitarian	Non-Christian	No Preference	Total
Catholic	35	1	—	3	3	1	1	—	—	—	1	44
Methodist	2	84	4	—	1	—	1	—	—	—	1	93
Baptist	1	—	47	—	3	—	1	1	—	—	1	54
Protestant (unspecified)	1	—	2	32	3	1	1	—	—	—	—	40
Presbyterian/Christian/Episcopalian	1	1	1	—	39	—	—	—	—	—	—	42
Pentecostal-Evangelical	—	—	—	—	1	17	—	—	—	—	—	18
Lutheran/Church of Christ/Brethren	1	1	1	1	—	—	29	2	—	—	—	35
Special-Creed Christian	—	—	—	—	—	—	—	16	—	—	—	16
Universalist-Unitarian	—	—	—	—	1	—	—	—	4	—	—	5
Non-Christian	1	1	—	—	—	—	—	—	—	2	—	4
No preference	4	18	10	9	6	8	4	2	—	—	32	93
Total	46	106	65	45	57	27	36	21	4	2	35	444

Source: Middletown III kinship survey, 1977.

Table 5-9

Mixed Marriages of Middletown Respondents and Their Parents, 1977

Denominational Preference	Married Respondents (N)	Percentage of Mixed Marriages	Parents of Respondents (N)	Percentage of Mixed Marriages
Catholic	101	30	90	22
Methodist	228	26	199	16
Baptist	127	31	119	21
Protestant (unspecified)	92	46	85	25
Presbyterian/Christian/Episcopalian	106	32	99	21
Pentecostal-Evangelical	93	29	45	24
Lutheran/Church of Christ/Brethren	70	40	71	18
Special-creed Christian	42	29	37	14
Universalist-Unitarian	17	29	9	*
Non-Christian	2	*	6	*
No preference	168	43	128	50
Total	1,046	335	888	211

Source: Middletown III kinship survey, 1977.

*Percentages were not computed when base is fewer than 10 cases.

Table 5-10
Divorce Experience by Religious Preference, Middletown, 1977

Denomination	Total (N)	Ever Divorced Number	Ever Divorced Percentage
Catholic	92	13	14
Methodist	190	28	15
Baptist	109	26	24
Protestant (unspecified)	85	22	26
Presbyterian/Christian/Episcopalian	88	11	12
Pentecostal-Evangelical	80	11	14
Lutheran/Church of Christ/Brethren	51	9	18
Special-creed Christian	37	5	14
Universalist-Unitarian	14	0	0
No preference	124	33	27
Total or average percentage	870*	158	18

Sources: Middletown III kindship survey (N = 405) and family role survey (N = 465), 1977.

*Does not include five non-Christians.

Table 5-11
Religious Preference by Selected Indicators of Social Class, Middletown, 1977

Denominational Preference	Percentage College Graduates	Percentage with $20,000+ Family Income	Percentage in White-collar Professions Men	Percentage in White-collar Professions Women
Catholic	36	30	72	85
Methodist	34	36	65	82
Baptist	11	24	30	64
Protestant (unspecified)	15	27	44	61
Presbyterian/Christian/Episcopalian	45	45	57	88
Pentecostal-Evangelical	8	17	31	58
Lutheran/Church of Christ/Brethren	30	25	78	69
Special-creed Christian	27	26	47	84
Universalist-Unitarian	67	47	*	100
No preference	18	15	37	54
Total	26	31	51	74

Sources: Middletown III kinship and family role surveys, (N = 940 for education, N = 893 for income, N = 837 for occupation), 1977.

*Percentages were not given when base is fewer than 10 cases.

Table 6-1

Church Attendance and Participation in Nonchurch Rituals, Middletown, 1978

Church Attendance	Percentage Participating in Nonchurch Rituals
More than once a week	92
Once a week	54
At least once a month	33
Once/several times a week	34
Never	27
Tau b	-.36

Source: Middletown III religion survey, 1978.

Table 6-2

Church Attendance and Participation in Particular Nonchurch Rituals,
Middletown, 1978
(in percentages)

Church Attendance	Home Services	Gospel Concerts	Electronic Church	Retreat Centers
More than once a week	63	46	25	21
Once a week	22	13	36	22
Less than once a week	7	12	19	3
Tau b	.40	.22	NS	.24

Source: Middletown III religion survey, 1978.

Note: NS means not significant at the .05 level.

Table 6-3

Religious Orientation and Participation in Nonchurch Rituals, Middletown, 1978

(in percentages)

Religious Orientation	(Number)	Home Religious Activities[a]	Gospel-Music Concerts	Electronic Church	Retreat Centers	No Services Outside Church
Catholic	(25)	9	9	13	13	65
Mainline Protestant[b]	(23)	10	11	27	9	61
Lower-class Protestant[c]	(71)	28	20	28	12	32
Pentecostal/other[d]	(31)	48	32	29	19	29
Chi-square		.001	.04	NS	NS	.003

Source: Middletown III religion survey, 1978.

a. This refers to either a home prayer group or a home Bible study group or a house church.

b. This refers to members of the Church of Christ or Disciples, Episcopalians, Lutherans, Methodists, and Presbyterians.

c. This refers to members of the Nazarene and Baptist churches.

d. These are the categories chosen by respondents.

Table 6-4
Education and Participation in Nonchurch Rituals, Middletown, 1978

Educational Achievement	Percentage with No Participation	(Number)
Less than high school	50	(14)
High school graduate	43	(47)
Some college	46	(35)
College graduate	57	(21)
Some graduate education	60	(45)
Tau b	.11*	

Source: Middletown III religion survey, 1978.

*Significant at .06 level.

Table 6-5
Viewing of Televised Services by Sex and Age, Middletown, 1978
(in percentages)

Age	Male (Number)	Female (Number)
17-49 years	11 (29)	28 (75)
50-59 years	15 (13)	39 (18)
60 years and above	17 (6)	55 (11)

Source: Middletown III religion survey, 1978.

Table 6-6
Viewing of Televised Services among women, Employment Type and attitude toward
Women's liberation, Middletown, 1978
(in percentages)

Employment Type	Unfavorable Attitude (Number)	Favorable Attitude (Number)
Unpaid	56 (18)	31 (16)
Paid	43 (21)	21 (48)

Source: Middletown III religion survey, 1978.

Table 6-9
Sermon Content Evaluated by Respondents, Middletown, 1978
(in percentages)

How Often Sermons Refer to Heaven/Hell	Comments Made on Public Issues	
	Yes	No
More than half	15	24
About half	10	7
Less than half	22	22

Source: Survey of Middletown residents, 1972.

Table 6-10
Education and Recall of Sermon Topic, Middletown, 1978

Educational Achievement	(Number)	More than Half Refer to Heaven/Hell	Comments on Public Issues
Elementary school	(10)	70	46
Some/completed high school	(44)	46	48
Some college	(15)	33	20
Four years or more of college	(24)	21	63
Tau b		-.29	NS*

Source: Survey of Middletown residents, 1972.

*For the relation between education and public issues chi-square was significant at the .08 level.

Table 6-11
Distribution of Denominations and Clergy Responding to 1978 Survey

Religious Group	Number of Churches in Middletown's County	Percentage Responding
Apostolic	6	0
Baptist	40	35
Brethren	5	40
Catholic	3	100
Christian	15	47
Church of Christ	15	40
Church of God	13	54
Church of God in Christ	7	0
Jehovah's Witness	2	0
Lutheran	4	75
Methodist	29	54
Mormon	1	0
Nazarene	17	35
Presbyterian	3	100
Seventh-Day Adventist	3	67
United Brethren	2	50
Wesleyan	5	20
Other	47	47
Total number or average percentage	217	45*

Source: Survey of Middletown's county clergy, 1978.

*This figure is lower than the percentage of churches for which we have data because we were unable to identify 14 returned questionnaires; therefore, these response cases are not included in the above table.

Table 6-12
Tau bs for Relations among Statements Forming Solemn-Holiness Dimension,
Middletown, 1978

Descriptive Statements	2	3	4	5	6	7	8
1. Leader wears special clothes	.41	.39	.33	-.39	-.31	-.39	-.35
2. Service follows predetermined order		.45	NS*	-.35	-.23	-.40	-.26
3. People assigned tasks ahead of time			.22	-.37	-.32	-.33	-.29
4. There is a printed Bulletin				-.32	-.23	-.31	-.30
5. People speak when spirit moves them					.56	.52	.44
6. People speak out approval of what is said						.54	.41
7. People testify							.37
8. People move about room during service							

Source: Survey of Middletown's county clergy, 1978.

*Tau b not significant at .05 level.

Table 6-13
Frequency Distribution of Sunday Services along Solemn-holiness dimension,
Middletown, 1978

Dimension Score	Percentage of Services
8 (solemn style)	16
9	21
10	6
11	16
12	12
13	9
14	9
15	9
16 (holiness style)	4

Source: Survey of Middletown's county clergy, 1978.

Note: Number of respondents was 82.

Table 7-3

Themes Mentioned by Middletown Housewives as Providing "Courage to Go On," by Social Class, 1978

Themes	Business Class		Working Class	
	Percentage of Respondents (N = 188)	Percentage of Mentions (N = 305)	Percentage of Respondents (N = 142)	Percentage of Mentions (N = 207)
Religious:				
Religious belief (faith, knowledge of God, of Christ)	21%	13%	23%	16%
Prayer	3	2	4	3
Scripture reading	6	4	1	1
Meditation	2	1	1	—
Other religious themes[a]	9	6	10	7
Family:				
Husband or wife	10	6	6	4
Children	18	11	19	13
Parents, other relatives	2	1	3	2
Family and home[b]	15	10	13	9
Other:				
General optimism (hoping for the best, things get better)	15	9	15	10
Keep trying (must go on, can't stop)	3	2	3	2
Self-reliance (set goals, feelings of security, autonomy, inner strength)	11	7	10	7

Table 7-3 (continued)

Themes	Business Class		Working Class	
	Percentage of Respondents (N = 188)	Percentage of Mentions (N = 305)	Percentage of Respondents (N = 142)	Percentage of Mentions (N = 207)
Reliance on others (I am not alone, others have similar problems, look to friends, exemplars)	7	5	6	4
Conscious gratitude (count your blessings, remember it could be worse, compare situation to others' problems)	6	4	6	4
Time (change will come, bring better things, look to the future)	13	8	8	5
Acceptance (life goes on, that's the way things are, we have no choice, make the best of it)	11	7	8	6
Other (patriotism, curiosity, view life as challenge, personal thought control, other responses)	10	6	11	8
Total[c]	*	102%	*	101%

Source: Middletown III housewives' survey, 1978.

a. Includes counseling by clergy, confession, prayer meetings; reading religious materials other than the Bible; fasting, reference to other world or afterlife; general reference to faith or love or living a good life; and other general references to religion.

b. Includes use of the words "family" and "home" but not references to specific family members.

c. Percentages marked with asterisks are nonadditive.

Table 7-4

Frequency of Private Prayer in Middletown in 1978, by Education and Social Class

Response	Education					Social Class (Self-Defined)		
	Some High School (N = 29)	High School Graduate (N = 65)	Some College (N = 48)	College Graduate (N = 39)	Advanced Degree (N = 39)	Working[a] (N = 65)	Lower Middle (N = 63)	Upper Middle[b] (N = 88)
Never Pray	14%	8%	12%	16%	21%	11%	16%	14%
Pray only on very special occasions	21	21	23	13	18	20	22	17
Pray quite often/but not at regular times	52	46	31	44	28	46	27	44
Pray regularly, at least once a week	14	25	33	28	33	23	35	25
Total	101%	100%	99%	101%	100%	100%	100%	100%

Source: Middletown III religion survey, 1978.

Question: Do you ever pray privately?

a. Includes three respondents who called themselves "lower class."

b. Includes three respondents who called themselves "upper class."

Table 7-5
Frequency of Prayer and Devotional Index in Middletown, by Family Income, 1978

Frequency/Devotional Index	$9,999 and less	$10,000 to $19,999	$20,000 to $29,999	$30,000+
Frequency of Prayer:				
Never	11%	18%	9%	12%
Very special occasions	18	17	25	24
Quite often	45	32	39	52
Regularly	27	32	27	12
Total	101%	99%	100%	100%
Number of cases (N)	(83)	(71)	(44)	(25)
Devotional Index Score:				
0, 1	33%	34%	39%	36%
2	29	34	25	28
3, 4	38	32	36	36
Total	100%	100%	100%	100%
Number of cases (N)	(89)	(71)	(44)	(25)

Source: Middletown III religion survey, 1978.

Note: The questionnaire asked for respondent's income and spouse's income, with standard categorical responses (e.g., under $3,000, $3,000-$4,999, $5,000-$6,999, and so on). "Family income" was approximated by taking the midpoints of the categories and summing husband's and wife's incomes. Devotional index scores ranged from 0 (low) through 4 (very high).

Question: Do you ever pray privately?

Table 7-9

Devotional Index Scores by Respondent Characteristics, Middletown, 1978

(in percentages)

Characteristics	(Number)	Devotional Index Score			
		Low (0, 1)	Moderate (2)	High (3, 4)	Total Total
Sex:					
Male	(74)	42	30	28	100
Female	(155)	31	30	39	100
Education:					
Less than 12 years	(31)	42	23	35	100
High school graduate	(65)	29	32	38	99
Some college	(48)	31	25	44	100
College graduate	(42)	40	21	38	99
Professional degree	(40)	32	48	20	100
Age:					
Under 30 years	(62)	39	34	27	100
30-39 years	(54)	44	22	33	99
40-54 years	(64)	31	31	38	100
55 years and over	(46)	20	33	48	101
Occupational Class:[a]					
Business	(108)	34	31	35	100
Working	(84)	36	30	34	100
Social Class (Self-Defined):					
Working	(67)	39	30	31	100
Lower middle	(63)	33	30	37	100
Upper middle	(92)	32	29	39	100
Denominational Background:[b]					
Catholic	(26)	23	23	54	100
Lutheran/Church of Christ	(16)	31	31	38	100
Presbyterian/Episcopal	(15)	20	60	20	100
Baptist	(27)	33	22	44	99
Methodist	(64)	42	34	23	99
Pentecostal/Nazarene	(22)	23	32	45	100
Other Christian	(30)	23	30	47	100
Other religions, non-Christian	(15)	60	7	33	100
No religious background or preference	(10)	80	20	0	100

Source: Middletown III religion survey, 1978.

a. Married women were assigned husbands' occupational classes.

b. The item read: "If a Christian: which would you describe your background as?" followed by 10 options: Baptist, Catholic, Church of Christ or Disciples, Episcopalian, Lutheran, Methodist, Nazarene, Pentecostal, Presbyterian, and Other (please specify).

Table 7-10

Devotional Index by Religious Beliefs and Church Activities, Middletown, 1978

	Devotional Index Score		
	Low (0, 1) (*N* = 77)	Moderate (2) (*N* = 69)	High (3, 4) (*N* = 80)
Religious Beliefs			
God:			
I know God really exists.	35%	68%	91%
While I have doubts, I feel that I do believe in God.	23	15	5
Sporadic belief, agnosticism, unbelief[a]	42	17	4
Total	100%	100%	100%
Jesus:			
Jesus is the Divine Son of God and I have no doubts about it.	36%	63%	88%
While I have some doubts, I feel basically that Jesus is Divine.	22	21	5
Other.[b]	42	16	7
Total	100%	100%	100%
The Bible			
The Bible is the word of God and all it says is true.	16%	44%	60%
The Bible was written by men inspired by God, but it contains some human errors.	59	46	39
Other.[c]	24	10	1
Total	99%	100%	100%
Church Activities			
Attended Church in Past Year			
Yes	40%	72%	91%
No	60	28	9
Total	100%	100%	100%
Frequency of Church Attendance[d]			
More than once a week	0%	15%	34%
Once a week	13	42	42
Less than once a week, more than once a year	30	27	23
Once or twice a year or never	57	15	1
Total	100%	99%	100%

Table 7-10 (continued)

	Devotional Index Score		
	Low (0, 1) (N = 77)	Moderate (2) (N = 69)	High (3, 4) (N = 80)
Hours per Week Usually Spent in Church Activities: d			
0	86%	49%	23%
1 to 2	9	24	24
3 to 4	3	15	23
5+	2	12	30
Total	100%	100%	100%
Gave Money to Church in Past Year: d			
No	40%	15%	9%
Yes	60	85	91
Total	100%	100%	100%
Percent of Income Donated to Church: e			
Less than 2%	77%	38%	27%
3% to 5%	23	28	14
6% to 9%	0	18	11
10%+	0	18	48
Total	100%	102%	100%

Source: Middletown III religion survey, 1978.

a. Includes "I find myself believing in God some of the time but not at other times," "I don't believe in a personal God, but I do believe in a higher power of some kind," "I don't know whether there is a God and I don't believe there is any way to find out," "I don't believe in God," and "None of the above represents what I believe. . . ."

b. Includes belief that Jesus was a great man but not divine, doubts about historical validity of Jesus, and "none of the above. . . ."

c. Includes idea that Bible is "a good book written by men," "obsolete," "an uneven collection," and so on.

d. Only asked of persons identified with a particular denomination.

e. Only asked of those who had given regularly to a church during the past year.

Table 7-11
Devotional Index and Religious Influence, Middletown, 1978

Area Influenced	Devotional Index Score		
	Low (0, 1) (N = 37)	Moderate (2) (N = 49)	High (3, 4) (N = 68)
The Friends I Have:			
No influence	66%	35%	10%
Some influence	29	39	32
Great influence	5	26	57
Total	100%	100%	99%
The Political Candidates I Vote For:			
No influence	84%	72%	44%
Some influence	16	24	27
Great influence	0	4	29
Total	100%	100%	100%
What I Do in My Leisure Time:			
No influence	70%	37%	13%
Some influence	27	41	38
Great influence	3	22	49
Total	100%	100%	100%
How I Treat My Family:			
No influence	37%	10%	3%
Some influence	39	31	19
Great influence	24	59	78
Total	100%	100%	100%
How I Perform My Job:			
No influence	57%	22%	6%
Some influence	32	45	27
Great influence	11	33	67
Total	100%	100%	100%

Source: Middletown III religion survey, 1978.

Question: How much have the following activities been influenced by your religious faith?

Note: The numbers (Ns) given are the modal values. The number of cases varies from item to item because of missing data. The questions were only asked of persons claiming identification with a denomination or church; hence, these Ns do not represent the entire sample.

Table 11-1

Percentages of Middletown High School Students Agreeing with Selected Indicators
of Religious Attitudes, 1977

Topic and Item	Males	Females
Orthodoxy:		
1. Jesus Christ was different from every other man who ever lived in being entirely perfect.	64 (269)	72 (295)
2. The Bible is a sufficient guide to all the problems of modern life.	49 (266)	51 (295)
3. The theory of evolution offers a more accurate account of the original history of mankind than that offered by a literal interpretation of the first chapters of the Bible.	55 (253)	45 (275)
Social Utility of Organized Religion:		
4. Sunday School pupils get nothing practical that they can use in everyday life from their Sunday School lessons.	25 (145)	14 (169)
5. Most people are bored by going to church but go because they think it is a duty.	66 (274)	69 (307)
6. Ministers and priests should be consulted about religious problems but it is of very little use to consult them about the practical problems of everyday life.	42 (257)	25 (297)
Evangelicalism:		
7. Christianity is the one true religion and all peoples should be converted to it.	38 (411)	39 (475)
Sunday Activity:		
8. It is wrong to go to the movies on Sunday.	7 (281)	6 (313)
Religion's Objective:		
9. The purpose of religion is to prepare people for the hereafter.	54 (271)	53 (310)

Source: Middletown III high school survey, 1977.

Notes: Underscored pairs of percentages differ at the .05 level of significance. The responses of black students and ninth-graders are not included in the data shown in this table. Figures in parentheses are percentage bases (*N*s).

Table 11-2
Percentages of Middletown High School Students Agreeing with Selected Indicators
of Religious Attitudes by Father's Occupational Class, 1977

Topic and Item	Business Class	Working Class
Orthodoxy:		
1. Jesus Christ was different from every other man who ever lived in being entirely perfect.	69 (344)	67 (446)
2. The Bible is a sufficient guide to all the problems of modern life.	50 (345)	53 (438)
3. The theory of evolution offers a more accurate account of the original history of mankind than that offered by a literal interpretation of the first chapters of the Bible.	50 (326)	50 (408)
Social Utility of Organized Religion:		
4. Sunday School pupils get nothing practical that they can use in everyday life from their Sunday School lessons.	22 (192)	18 (247)
5. Most people are bored by going to church but go because they think it is a duty.	<u>72</u> (353)	<u>64</u> (458)
6. Ministers and priests should be consulted about religious problems but it is of very little use to consult them about the practical problems of everyday life.	<u>28</u> (339)	<u>39</u> (433)
Evangelicalism:		
7. Christianity is the one true religion and all peoples should be converted to it.	41 (551)	42 (700)
Sunday Activity:		
8. It is wrong to go to the movies on Sunday.	5 (363)	8 (469)
Religion's Objective:		
9. The purpose of religion is to prepare people for the hereafter.	<u>51</u> (355)	<u>58</u> (453)

Source: Middletown III high school survey, 1977.

Notes: Underscored pairs of percentages differ at the .05 level of significance. The responses of black students and ninth-graders are not included in the data shown in this table. Figures in parentheses are percentage bases (*N*s).

Table 11-3

Percentages of Middletown High School Students Agreeing with Selected Indicators of Religious Attitudes by Religious Preference and Church Attendance, 1977

Topic and Item	Religious Preference			Church Attendance		
	Catholic	Protestant	None	Regularly (Weekly)	Frequently or Occasionally	Rarely or Never
Orthodoxy:						
1. Jesus Christ was different from every other man who ever lived in being entirely perfect.	71 (121)	74 (461)	54 (231)	80 (281)	69 (274)	54 (328)
2. The Bible is a sufficient guide to all the problems of modern life.	50 (123)	63 (456)	37 (230)	71 (281)	53 (271)	38 (326)
3. The theory of evolution offers a more accurate account of the original history of mankind than that offered by a literal interpretation of the first chapters of the Bible.	50 (118)	48 (430)	52 (211)	37 (264)	51 (256)	59 (299)
Social Utility of Organized Religion:						
4. Sunday School pupils get nothing practical that they can use in everyday life from their Sunday School lessons	31 (68)	12 (249)	29 (129)	16 (153)	14 (156)	30 (178)
5. Most people are bored by going to church but go because they think it is a duty	69 (127)	67 (471)	65 (243)	64 (285)	68 (284)	67 (345)
6. Ministers and priests should be consulted about religious problems but it is of very little use to consult them about the practical problems of everyday life.	32 (120)	30 (452)	46 (224)	23 (276)	36 (275)	46 (313)

Table 11-3 (continued)

Topic and Item	Religious Preference			Church Attendance		
	Catholic	Protestant	None	Regularly (Weekly)	Frequently or Occasionally	Rarely or Never
Evangelicalism:						
7. Christianity is the one true religion and all peoples should be converted to it.	40 (196)	49 (720)	24 (377)	61 (435)	41 (436)	23 (516)
Sunday Activity:						
8. It is wrong to go to the movies on Sunday.	5 (128)	10 (487)	6 (247)	14 (286)	5 (300)	5 (350)
Religion's Objective:						
9. The purpose of religion is to prepare people for the hereafter.	49 (118)	62 (477)	49 (237)	61 (280)	62 (290)	47 (336)

Source: Middletown III high school survey, 1977.

Notes: Underscoring denotes statistical significance at the .05 level based on the volume of chi-square computed for the two-by-three contingency tables from which the above percentages were taken. The responses of black students and ninth-graders are not included in the data shown in this table. Figures in parentheses are percentage bases (Ns).

Table 11-4
Church Attendance of Middletown High School Students, and of
Two National Samples, 1977

| Response Category | Middletown High Schools | | United States | |
	All Students	Seniors	High School Seniors	Adults
Regular attendance (weekly)	31%	36%	40%	36%
Frequent Attendance (at least monthly)	13	9	17	17
Occasional Attendance (several times a year	18	15		12
Attendance only on special occasions (once or twice a year)	19	19	33	13
Not at all	19	21	10	22
Total	100%	100%	100%	100%
Number of cases (N)	(1,601)	(288)	(15,285)	(1,521)

Sources: Johnston, Bachman, and O'Malley 1980, 18; National Opinion Research Center 1977, 86; Middletown III high school survey, 1977.

Note: The item read "How frequently [national surveys: how often] do you attend religious services?" The questionnaire for the national sample of high school seniors had only four response categories: never, rarely, once or twice a month, and about once a week or more. The National Opinion Research Center's national survey had nine categories, which were combined as follows to match the categories in the Middletown survey: several times a week, every week, and nearly every week = weekly; two to three times a month and about once a month = at least monthly; several times a year = several times a year; about once a year = once or twice a year; and less than once a year or never = not at all.

Table 11-5

Church Attendance by Sex and Father's Occupational Class for Catholic, Protestant, and No-Preference Middletown High School Students, 1977

Church Attendance	Catholic				Protestant				No Preference			
	Business Class		Working Class		Business Class		Working Class		Business Class		Working Class	
	Males	Females	Males	Females	Males	Females	Males	Females	Males	Females	Males	Females
High (weekly)	64%	73%	38%	48%	39%	43%	39%	43%	2%	2%	4%	8%
Moderate (at least monthly or several times a year)	17	21	38	38	39	39	33	37	16	30	17	26
Low (once or twice a year or not at all)	20	6	24	14	22	18	28	20	82	68	79	66
Total	101%	100%	100%	100%	100%	100%	100%	100%	100%	100%	100%	100%
Number of cases (N)	(66)	(52)	(29)	(42)	(163)	(178)	(157)	(234)	(50)	(47)	(142)	(113)

Source: Middletown III high school survey, 1977.

Table 11-6

Middletown High School Students Orthodoxy Index Scores, by Religious Preference
and Church Attendance, 1977

	Religious Preference			Church Attendance		
Orthodoxy Index	Catholic	Protestant	None	Regular (Weekly)	Frequently or Occasionally	Rarely or Never
3 ⎱ High	22%	37%	17%	45%	26%	16%
2 ⎰	38	27	26	30	32	24
1 Moderate	26	24	35	17	28	37
0 Low	14	12	22	7	14	23
Total	100%	100%	100%	99%	100%	100%
Number of cases (N)	(127)	(481)	(245)	(289)	(291)	(346)

Source: Middletown III high school survey, 1977.

NOTES

Notes

Chapter 1

1. This research project was supported by the National Science Foundation, grant number SOC 75-13580. The investigators were Theodore Caplow, Howard M. Bahr, and Bruce A. Chadwick.

2. The chapter was not without satiric intent. Compare it to the similar litany included in Sinclair Lewis's novel *Babbitt* — George Babbitt's after-dinner speech at the Get Together Fest of the Zenith Real Estate Board.

3. Including Anderson 1923, Mowrer, 1927, Thrasher 1927, Wirth 1928, and Zorbaugh 1929.

4. As of 1982, we estimate that less than 1 percent of the empirical studies in sociology carried out so far have seriously replicated earlier studies.

5. Warner and Lunt (1941) is the principal report, but the publication of findings extended through a number of volumes until the appearance of Warner's *The Living and the Dead* (1959) more than 25 years after the completion of the fieldwork.

6. For example, Marks 1967, Hirsch and Stark 1964, and Allport and Ross 1967.

7. Since brought up-to-date by *Religion in America 1979-80*, Gallup Opinion Index, 1981.

8. It is unlikely that the 4 percent advantage of the middle year represents a meaningful fluctuation. A question like this is particularly susceptible to various contextual effects.

Chapter 2

1. Richard Jensen, oddly enough, in "The Lynds Revisited" (1979, 315) said that Lynd was a graduate of Princeton Seminary. Lynd was a Presbyterian much influenced by the Social Gospel movement and sympathetic to the modernist side in the modernist/fundamentalist debate of the 1920s.

2. This, of course, is Ernst Troeltsch's classic definition of a sect.

3. Taken from Alexander M. Bracken, Jr., 1978, 52.

4. These churches are all listed in *Emerson's Directory, 1889* (1889, 273-75). The dates of the founding of all the churches save those with no date are from *Churches of Delaware County, 1976* (1976).

5. In his dissertation "Middletown as a pioneer Community" (1978), Alexander M. Bracken, Jr., has argued that Middletown had become a modern industrial community by 1880.

6. *Emerson's Directory, 1899-1900* listed Eighth Street, but Dr. G. W. H. Kemper (*A Twentieth Century History of Delaware County* [1908]) did not.

7. In 1890, there were 14 churches for a population of 11,345; in 1925, there were 52 churches for a population of 41,536. This works out to one for each 810 persons in 1890 and one for each 798 persons in 1925.

8. By 1950, the ratio of churches to population was one to each 899 persons.

9. *Polk's City Directory, 1977* listed only 115 churches. This number, however, had been reported since 1974 and was only one more than had been reported in 1970, so it is questionable, in our opinion.

10. Mitchell, in his *History of the First Universalist Church* (1974), discusses the repercussions of a statement made by a former pastor of the church to the effect that Middletown "society was full of Ingersollism" when his appeared in the *Star Covenant* (a local paper) in 1880. Though Ingersollism may have been acceptable in Universalist practice, it was not acceptable to say so in the newspaper.

Chapter 5

1. The percentages expressive "no preference" on the Middletown surveys were much higher than the national percentages cited in the text. Presumably, some of the difference stems from different wording; the Gallup questionnaire did not include "no preference" as an explicit option, but the Middletown questionnaires did.

2. Another indication of more marginal denominational identity among males is their higher representation in the "Protestant (unspecified)" category among both adults and young people.

3. See the discussion of the "feminization" of Middletown in Theodore Caplow et al. 1982, Chapter 2.

4. Before commenting on the differences between this distribution and that for the Middletown high school students who completed questionnaires in 1977, let us note that the two populations are not precisely comparable. The former students studied in 1936-1937 were interviewed individually; the 1977 students completed questionnaires. Also, the 1936-1937 respondents were high school graduates or dropouts whose ages ranged from 16 years through 27 years, with a median age of 21. (See Raymond G. Fuller 1937, 171, 173, Appendix B, xvii, xxxii.)

5. The item "What is your religious preference? Is it Protestant, Catholic, Jewish, some other religion, or no religion?" was followed by a probe for specific denomination if "protestant" was the reply. The item "in what religion were you raised?" was also followed by a probe for specific denomination. (See National Opinion Research Center 1977, 85, 87.)

6. According to Samuel A. Mueller (1971, 80); the data derive from items on the respondent's religious preference and that of his or her father. The option "no preference" is not included as a category in the published mobility matrix, and consequently the rates refer only to interfaith mobility, that is, they do not include switchers to and from "no preference" and therefore probably understate intergenerational switching.

7. Stark and Glock and Mueller used father's preference as the point of departure for the measurement of intergenerational mobility; we have been unable to locate studies that use mother's preference as the reference point. As noted earlier, "religion in which raised" is sometimes used; but, as a comparison point for measuring intergenerational mobility, it is also ambiguous. Technically, "religion in which raised" is a proper initial reference point for studying *intra*generational mobility since it is assumed that the respondent did, in fact, once belong to that religion or maintain it as a preference. As an example of the ambiguity inherent in its use in *inter*generational comparisons, imagine

a child whose parents are of different religions and who compromise by agreeing to raise the child in a "neutral" third faith. In this case, the "religion in which raised" is that of neither parent. On the other hand, knowing that one's father or mother held a particular preference does not mean that the child was necessarily raised to share that preference. Nevertheless, the study of intergenerational religious mobility does not require the assumption that children are raised to follow parental religious preferences, although typically that is what happens. Rather the straightforward question is how does a person's religious preference differ from that of his or her parents? For this question, referring to the person whose religious preference differs from his or her mother or father's as a "switcher" may also be inaccurate in that one cannot switch from a religious preference one never held. However, if the "switch" is interpreted to mean a change across generations—the adoption of a different preference from one's parent—then the term is appropriate. It does not mean, as we have used it, that one has switched religious preferences in his or her own personal history. That is the topic of *intra*generational mobility. Rather, it means that he or she has played a part in a *generational* switch, that one's present religion, whatever it may or may not have been during childhood, differs from that of one's parent. Additional ambiguity derives from possible changes in one's parents' religious preferences. Conceivably, they may have switched faiths during or after the time when they were raising their children. The question in the kinship survey on parents' religious preferences did not take the possible intragenerational mobility of the parents into account by specifying a particular reference point in time. As a result, it is possible that some of the apparent intergenerational religious mobility we identify is really parental intragenerational mobility, that is, that it represents instances in which an adult respondent has maintained the same religious preference once held by a parent while that parent has switched to a different denomination.

8. The net intergenerational gains in the "no preference" category that appear in the bottom half of Appendix 5-6 reflect the low percentage of mothers of Middletown adults who had no preference rather than any sizable tendency toward secularization. This conclusion is supported by the absence of any such gain—instead, there is a sizable loss—in the "no preference" category when father's religion is the reference point.

9. In this case, "interdenominational" refers to marriages that cut across any of nine summary categories, including Catholic, Jewish, no religion, other, and five categories of Protestants (Baptists, Lutherans, Methodists, Presbyterians, and other Protestants). Monahan warned that the census figures underestimate the extent of religious intermarriage because (1) they refer to current religion, not religion at the time of marriage, and many couples who were once religiously mixed will have become homogamous by one or both spouses switching faiths; and (2) they apply only to presently married couples, and there is much evidence that religously mixed marriages are less stable than homogamous ones. Accordingly, the "survivors" who remain married at the time of a particular survey are more homogamous than was the total cohort of married couples before the divorcing pairs selected themselves out of the married population. (See Monahan 1971, 87.)

10. Defined as someone in another of three major denominational categories: Protestant, Catholic, or Jewish. Thus, a marriage between persons of different Protestant affiliation was not counted as an interfaith marriage.

11. Incidentally, in Middletown at least, use of the 11 denominational categories captures most of the interfaith mobility. A count of same-faith marriages using the most detailed denominational categories yielded only a handful of additional instances of interfaith marriage. In our 11-category list, 33.5 percent of the couples had interfaith marriages; when the more detailed list with over 50 categories was used, the percentage of interfaith marriages increased only to 34.5 percent.

12. To facilitate the intergenerational comparisons, consult Appendix Table 5-8, which shows the percentage of persons in each denominational category married to someone in a different category.

13. Congruent with the Middletown findings are the results of a 1976 survey of the ever married in eight mountain states in which the percentage ever divorced varied by denominational category as follows: Catholics, 13 percent; Jews, 14 percent; Mormons, 14 percent; Protestants, 19 percent; others, 22 percent; and no-preference respondents, 29 percent. (see Bahr 1980.)

14. See, for example, Smith and Zopf 1970, 351-52; Westoff et al. 1961, 183-84; and Vernon 1962, 366-69.

15. The eight denominations were Baptist, Lutheran, Methodist (including Evangelical and United Brethren), Presbyterian (including Reformed Church of America), Episcopalian, Congregational (including Evangelical Reformed United Church of Christ), Christian (including Disciples of Christ), and all others combined (Westoff and Potvin 1967, 33-40).

16. The seven Protestant groups were Baptists; Episcopalians; Lutherans; Methodists; Presbyterians; a category including Unitarians, Congregationalists, and Evangelical sects; and a residual category containing all other Protestants.

17. These means are based on a total of 334 women aged 35 and over (combined kinship and family role surveys).

18. See, for example, Schneider 1967, 229, 231; Lazerwitz 1964, 428-29; Underwood 1957, 400-401; Cooley 1976, 33-43; and Greeley 1977, 54-58.

19. We have noted elsewhere that, although two-thirds of the Middletown high school students of 1977 said that they believed in the divinity of Jesus, only 38 percent were willing to affirm that "Christianity is the one true religion and all peoples should be converted to it." The comparable percentages among high school students in 1924 were 83 and 94 percent, respectively. In matters of religious faith, Middletown's Christians today are much more willing to live and let live than were their grandparents. (See Caplow and Bahr 1979.)

Chapter 6

1. Given that our sample is biased toward women, their greater interest in the Electronic Church helps account for the relative popularity of this item among our selected non-church activities.

2. They were given 10 categories from which to choose: Catholic, Church of Christ or Disciples, Episcopal, Lutheran, Methodist, Presbyterian, Nazarene, Baptist, Pentecostal, and other.

3. We may be wrong in emphasizing sex roles. Watching televised services, for instance, was also related to being in favor of allowing teachers to lead children in prayer in public schools. Those watching television may be seeking to legitimate a broad, traditional ideology.

4. The 37 churches, however, held only 38 events specifically called "revivals"; 1 was a joint event.

5. A further problem involved two churches, both with primarily black congregations, that held services every evening but Friday—the Apostolic Faith Assembly and the Triumph Church (which met even on Friday). These churches at times called their services revivals, but one wonders whether there was anything truly special about those so designated. In 1924, church services were announced on Saturday in two separate columns, "Sunday Services in Churches" and "In Colored Circles." The latter contained news about church services and church social news. For whites, social news appeared in another column

entitled "Church Social News." The two columns about church services usually appeared on different pages but in no set order. For several Saturdays, however, I could not find "In Colored Circles."

6. For three Saturdays we also examined Middletown's Evening Paper. Nothing was found that was not contained in the morning paper as well.

7. The total sample for the survey conducted by Joseph Tamney was 220, but 31 claimed no religious identity. In addition, 74 respondents were eliminated because they did not attend a specific church. We then discarded responses from nonwhites and from Christians who either never attended church or were "not sure" about the nature of sermons in their churches.

8. In their later work, the Lynds (1937, 11) noted that the Episcopalian Church also is less dependent on sermons.

9. We perceive holiness rituals as approximations of *communitas* because of the importance of spontaneity in them. Although holiness rituals usually include personal confessions, the confessions are too stylized to express the individuality of those who testify.

10. Two churches with which clergy were affiliated were outside Middletown's county. However, we left them in the study, assuming their presence in the directory was meaningful.

11. Responses to the question "What is this service called?" were as follows: worship, 84 percent; service, 7 percent; mass, liturgy, or eucharist, 4 percent; feast or celebration, 2 percent; holiness or evangelistic meeting, 2 percent; prayer meeting, 1 percent; Bible class, 1 percent.

12. The questionnaire was critiqued at an informal seminar on the sociology of religion at Ball State University. The members were Ronald Burton, Bruce Chadwick, Brad Chappell, John Hopkins, George Jones, and Joseph Tamney.

Chapter 7

1. As we explained in an earlier chapter, the three other dimensions in the most frequently used typology of religiosity are belief, knowledge, and ritual practice. (See Stark and Glock 1968.) In their earlier work, Glock and Stark had combined ritual practice and devotional practice into a single ritualistic dimension. Even in their introduction to *American Piety* (1968, 14-16), the "religious practice" dimension included both formal ritual and private devotion, and there was another dimension of religious commitment, the consequential ("the effects of religious belief, practice, experience, and knowledge in persons' day-to-day lives") that was explicitly mentioned but then set aside as qualitatively different from the other four dimensions. Then, in the body of the book, there were separate chapters on five dimensions of commitment: religious belief, religious practice—ritual, religious practice—devotional, religious experience, and religious knowledge. Thus, private devotion differs from a related dimension of religious commitment—the experiential—which refers to occasions when the worshiper believes that he or she has experienced some kind of contact with the supernatural.

2. Of the 223 persons sampled in the religion survey who answered the question "How do you feel about the Bible?" 40 percent agreed that "the Bible is the word of God and all it says is true"; 48 percent said that "the Bible was written by men inspired by God, but it contains some human errors." An additional 7 percent agreed with the statement "the Bible is a good book because it was written by wise men, but God had nothing to do with it," and 5 percent said that the Bible had little relevance for the present or that they did not know what it was.

3. Stark and Glock's "devotional index" was based entirely on two items about prayer, namely, "How often do you pray privately?" and "How important is prayer in your

life?" People who said that they thought prayer was "extremely important" and that they prayed privately at least once a week, were considered "high" in devotionalism. (See Stark and Glock 1968, 121.) Other studies using the same definition of devotionalism include Nelson 1974, Finney 1978, and O'Connell 1975.

4. The religion survey contained several measures of social class, including these items: "To what social class do you feel your family presently belongs?" "How far did you go in school?" and "How much income did you earn at your job last year?" Married respondents were also asked for an estimate of their husband's or wife's annual income, and our approximation of family income was obtained by summing the respondent's income and his or her spouse's income.

5. Unlike the percentages for the items on meditation and fasting, the percentages for this item do not add to 100 percent because the respondents had the option of checking as many of the activities listed as applied to them. Thus, 14 percent said they meditated; many of these meditators may also have said that they prayed (56 percent of the sample said they did), and so on.

6. It will be recalled that two-thirds of the sample occupied the two "high-frequency" categories on the prayer item, whereas on the devotional index there was an even distribution, with about one-third in the "none" and "low-devotional" categories, one-third "moderate-devotional," and one-third "high-devotional" and "very high-devotional."

7. The item read, "If a Christian: Which would you describe your background as?" and provided 10 options: "Baptist, Catholic, Church of Christ or Disciple, Episcopalian, Lutheran, Methodist, Nazarene, Pentecostal, Presbyterian, and Other (Please specify) ." It was possible to divide the "others" into persons with no religious background or preference and those preferring a denomination not included in the list. However, the structure of the item prevented detailed analysis by denominational group along the lines of the denominational analysis in Chapter 5.

8. Details of the relationship between devotion and three indicators of religious belief appear in Appendix Table 7-10.

9. The question on membership in organizations was worded so as to exclude religious organizations. It read, "Not counting religious organizations, about how many clubs, service organizations, unions, school organizations or lodges do you *belong* to?"

10. The correlation coefficient (r) summarizes the relationship between two variables in a single number and so is much more efficient at quickly communicating the strength of a relationship than are percentage tables. The larger the coefficient, the stronger the relationship between the variables in question. The relationship may be either positive, in which an increase in one variable is matched by a corresponding increase in the other, or negative, in which an increase in one is matched by a corresponding decrease in the other.

11. Cohen (1977, 287) defined "Holiness" as "a divine quality of life which is attributed to man and which man progresses toward experientially as he participates as an individual member with the Body of Christ." Thus, Holiness may embrace all of the dimensions of religiosity previously noted; it certainly includes the devotional and experiential dimensions. Holiness should not be confused with the "holiness rituals" described in Chapter 6.

Chapter 9

1. The Festival Cycle is what we call the series of celebrations beginning with Halloween and running throughout the year. It includes Halloween, Thanksgiving, Christmas, New Year's Day, Valentine's Day, Washington's Birthday, Easter, Mother's Day, Memorial Day, Father's Day, Independence Day, Labor Day, and Columbus Day. The significance

of this cycle in Middletown is discussed more fully elsewhere (Caplow et al. 1982, Chapter 10).

2. Information about Christmas observances in Middletown is derived from the Middletown Christmas survey, supported by National Science Foundation grant number SOC 75-13580. The number of respondents was 110.

3. "An emblem is a type of symbol that represents a complex but bounded social or cultural phenomenon by means of an easily recognized picture or design which has no morphological relationship to the thing represented" (Caplow and Williamson 1980, fn. 3).

4. Presents are given on many occasions, of course, including birthdays, weddings, anniversaries, Valentine's Day, Easter, Mother's Day and Father's Day and even in a perverted way at Halloween. (See Caplow et al. 1982, Chapter 10, for elaboration of this point.) Only at Christmas, however, is it mandatory to remember with a present everyone with whom one has an informal, affectionate relationship. There is probably a hierarchy among all these occasions. For example, one must give a Christmas present to someone to whom one gives a birthday present, but the reverse is not true; and the giving of wedding presents is not predictably related to the giving of presents on other occasions. The details of these relationships, however, have not yet been worked out.

5. Or so we interpret Christmas secular symbols. At the same time, we know that Christmas is frequently reported to be a depressing and even suicidal season, presumably because many people feel especially isolated at this time. We think, however, that this supports rather than undermines our interpretation. Although the relationship between collective behavior and individual emotion is too complex to be described in detail here, we can suggest that the increased depression reported for this season is due to the symbols of Christmas being almost too effective (or affective) in conveying the messages of unity, fellow feeling, and so on; those who recognize the messages but not a corresponding lightening of heart within themselves (and suppose themselves to be unique in this regard) become depressed as a result. They do not live up to expectations about Christmas.

6. Women are far more active than men in wrapping gifts. Men usually have someone else wrap their gifts (shop clerks or wives), while women usually wrap their own as well as their husbands'.

7. This is more thoroughly discussed in Caplow et al. 1982, Chapter 10.

8. We have discussed elsewhere (Caplow et al. 1982, Chapter 10) the significance of serving turkey at Thanksgiving, which also celebrates family solidarity. Its frequent inclusion on the Christmas dinner menu is probably for the same reasons: it is large, it is undivided before its distribution among those present, and it is "American."

9. They are found also in offices, where the assumption of a familial relationship is merely an assumption and where any appropriate sentiments are probably seasonal. The office party is, of course, an entirely adult affair.

10. This matter is considered more fully in Caplow et al. 1982, Chapter 10.

11. The association of children of either sex with women is very common if not universal; examples from other cultures abound in the anthropological literature. Frequently, though not invariably, this attitude is associated with elaborate initiation rituals for adolescent boys, rituals designed to remove the boys formally from the female sphere of life and incorporate them into the male world. Middletown, of course, has no such rituals for either boys or girls, unless we recognize a man's first job as such (cf. Chodorow 1974).

12. We reject as an explanation the "historical" fact that Santa Claus has always been associated with the holiday. As Barnett's study shows, Santa Claus has been variously associated with December 6, 25, and 30; and even in the United States his appearance,

mode of travel, and gifts have varied from generation to generation and place to place (Barnett 1954). We must distinguish a true history, based on documents, from a made-up history (or myth) generated collectively to account for the presence of some otherwise inexplicable behavior. Middletown justifies its Christmas behavior in "historical" terms by saying that Santa is traditional and that gift giving was instituted by the Magi. Both statements have some truth, but we argue that neither Santa nor gift giving would occur in Middletown today if they seemed inappropriate in the modern context. For this reason, we do not find it necessary to allude to the history of these customs in order to explain them. Rather, since the "historical" explanation offered by Middletown is a product of the present state of its society, it also is a social fact deserving analysis. Such an exercise is, however, beyond the scope of the present investigation.

13. We may mention in this connection the fact that all of Middletown's festival emblems, the Halloween witch excepted, are male: the Valentine cupid, the Easter Bunny, and even the Thanksgiving turkey.

14. This raises questions about the control that each sex exercises in making cultural (rather than individual) decisions. This is a topic with far-reaching implications, and consequently it is not one to be dealt with summarily. We will state here for elucidatory purposes that we reject the idea that culture, or society, is invented and directed solely by men; on the other hand, we cannot accept the opposing view that it is invented solely by women. Our assumption is that it is a human invention and that questions of gender are irrelevant.

15. Warner's 1961 study of religion in Yankee City attempts something similar to what is presented here, namely, relating religious ideas to social forms, in particular, the Holy Family and the human family.

16. Since this is so, we wonder whether the state of the family was of equal concern to the writers of the Gospels and their contemporaries.

17. Feeley-Harnik (1981), in her recently published study of the eucharist in the early Christian church, made a similar statement about early Christianity as a whole. She pointed out that contemporary Judaism was producing ever more refined and narrow categories (of persons, food, activities, and so on), while the Christians denied the usefulness or indeed the validity of these categories and insisted on the unity of everything. A well-known example of the Christians' attitude toward Jewish categories of food is St. Peter's vision of the laden sheet or tablecloth (Acts 10:9-16).

18. Beheading was appropriate to kings during that period. This was the fate of St. John the Baptist, who never claimed to be king (another contradiction).

19. The Gospels concentrate on Christ's ministry to a far greater extent than does church observance. The life of Christ was that of an independent man, without question. The point we wish to emphasize here is that the church regards Christmas and Easter as celebrating the two most significant aspects of His life and that it opposes those aspects not just as life versus death (which is also life) but as dependent versus independent.

20. These points are considered more fully in Caplow et al. 1982, Chapter 10.

21. For an anthropological discussion of the public/private and male/female poles of social organization, see Rosaldo 1974.

Chapter 11

1. The Lynds' true-false questionnaire, which they gave to junior and senior high school students, included 10 items on religion. For some reason, they did not report the responses to 4 of these, all of which dealt with attitudes toward ministers and organized religion in Middletown.

2. It also involved recalculation of the percentages reported in *Middletown* and used a percentage base from which "uncertain" responses had been removed.

3. This one-item definition is much broader than the Gallup organization's definition of evangelicals as Christians who describe themselves as "born again," who have encouraged other people to believe in Christ, and who say they believe in a literal interpretation of the Bible. According to recent polls, by this definition about one-fifth of the adult population of the United States is evangelical (Gallup Opinion Index 1981, 57).

Chapter 12

1. In the spring of 1978, a mail questionnaire was sent to the 217 ministers listed in the Christian Ministries of Middletown's county. By the time the three follow-up mailings had been completed, 112 ministers had responded, for a response rate of 52 percent. The respondents represented a wide range of Christian denominations and an adequate sample of Middletown's ministry. The in-depth interviews with pastors were conducted during the summer of 1981, when two of the investigators spent a week in Middletown collecting additional material on local churches and interviewing ministers. The 17 ministers interviewed at length were chosen as representatives of the range of local denominations and included ministers from the city's largest churches.

Chapter 13

1. A half-century ago, the Lynds identified only 42 churches, and, although their count did not include the black congregations, it is evident that the density of churches for a community whose population was slightly over 35,000 was considerably less than it was in 1980. The trend is examined in detail elsewhere in this volume.

2. Not included in Table 13-1 is a tiny but active Reform Jewish synagogue that has no resident rabbi but draws upon a rabbinic school a hundred miles away to supply a student to lead Sabbath services.

3. There is no evidence that members of the black clergy and/or the churches they serve display any greater degree of cooperation toward one another than they display toward the established structures in the religious community as a whole. This can be partially explained by the fact that most of the black churches, with the prominent exception of a very activist black Methodist congregation, are fundamentalist and independent in spirit, with little, if any, official concern about social change.

4. One of the three Catholic parishes was organized to serve the students at Middletown's state university and has a reputation for intellectual stimulation and creative worship. In addition to a large student following, it commands the loyalty of a number of liberal Catholics who prefer it to their own parish churches.

5. Although not affiliating with the Ministerial Association or with Christian Ministries, in recent years individual Catholic priests have, from time to time, cooperated with the latter group to plan special events of celebration, notably the Pentecost breakfast.

6. History seems to repeat itself. The Lynds noted in the Middletown of 1925 that ministers of several leading churches opposed revival-type services — their reason was that the effects of a revival were soon spent (Lynd and Lynd 1929, 381).

BIBLIOGRAPHY
AND PUBLISHED
MIDDLETOWN PAPERS

Bibliography

Allport, Gordon W., and J. Michael Ross. "Personal Religious Orientation and Prejudice," *Journal of Personal and Social Psychology* 5 (1967), 432-43.

Anderson, Nels. *The Hobo*. Chicago: University of Chicago Press, 1923.

Argyle, Michael, and Benjamin Beit-Hallahmi. *The Social Psychology of Religion*. London: Routledge and Kegan Paul, 1975.

Backman, Milton V., Jr. *Christian Churches of America: Origins and Beliefs*. Provo, Utah: Brigham Young University Press, 1976.

Bahr, Howard M. "Religion and Divorce," in Stan L. Albrecht. *Divorce*. Unpublished manuscript, 1980.

Bahr, Howard M., Theodore Caplow, and Geoffrey K. Leigh. "The Slowing of Modernization in Middletown," pp. 219-32 in Louis Kriesberg (ed.). *Research in Social Movements, Conflicts and Change* (vol. 3). Greenwich, Conn.: JAI Press, 1980.

Barnett, James H. *The American Christmas: A Study in National Culture*. New York: Macmillan, 1954.

Bell, Daniel. *The Coming of Post-Industrial Society*. New York: Basic Books, 1973.

Bellah, Robert. "Civil Religion in America," *Daedalus* 96 (1967), 1-21.

Berger, Peter L. *The Sacred Canopy: Elements of the Sociological Theory of Religion*. Garden City, N.Y.: Doubleday, 1967.

——————. *A Rumor of Angels: Modern Society in the Rediscovery of the Supernatural*. Garden City, N.Y.: Doubleday, 1970.

Boelen, W. A. Marianne. "Street Corner Society Revisited." Unpublished paper, 1970.

Bohlander, Bruce A. "A Look at the Parish Family of Grace Church (Episcopal) and Its Impact on Muncie in the Last Half of the Nineteenth Century." Unpublished seminar paper. Muncie, Ind.: Ball State University, 1979.

Boling, T. Edwin. "Sectarian Protestants, Churchly Protestants and Roman Catholics: A Comparison in a Mid-American City," *Review of Religious Research* 14 (Spring 1973), 159-68.

Boulard, Fernand. *La Déchristianisation de Paris* (vol. 31). Paris: Archives de Sociologie des Religion, 1971.

Bracken, Alexander M., Jr. "Middletown as a Pioneer Community." Ph.D. dissertation, Ball State University, 1978.

Bultena, Louis. "Church Membership and Church Attendance in Madison, Wisconsin," *American Sociological Review* 14 (1949), 384-89.

Bumpass, Larry. "The Trend of Interfaith Marriage in the United States," *Social Biology* 17 (December 1970), 253-59.

Bumpass, Larry, and J. Sweet. "Differentials in Marital Instability: 1970," *American Sociological Review* 37 (1972), 754-66.

Burch, Thomas K. "The Fertility of North American Catholics: A Comparative Overview," *Demography* 3 (1966), 174-87.

Cady, John F. *The Origin and Development of the Missionary Baptist Church in Indiana.* Franklin, Ind.: Franklin College, 1942.

Campbell, Thomas C., and Yoshio Fukuyama. *The Fragmented Layman: An Empirical Study of Lay Attitudes.* Philadelphia: Pilgrim Press, 1970.

Cantril, Hadley. "Educational and Economic Composition of Religious Groups: An Analysis of Poll Data," *American Journal of Sociology* 48 (1943), 574-79.

————. (ed.). *Public Opinion, 1935-1945.* Princeton, N.J.: Princeton University Press, 1951.

Caplow, Theodore, and Howard M. Bahr. "Half a Century of Change in Adolescent Attitudes: Replication of a Middletown Survey by the Lynds," *Public Opinion Quarterly* 43 (Winter 1979), 1-17.

Caplow, Theodore, Howard M. Bahr, and Bruce A. Chadwick. "Piety in Middletown," *Transaction* 18 (January/February 1981), 34-37.

Caplow, Theodore, Howard M. Bahr, Bruce A. Chadwick, Reuben Hill, and Margaret Holmes Williamson. *Middletown Families: Fifty Years of Change and Continuity.* Minneapolis: University of Minnesota Press, 1982.

Caplow, Theodore, and Margaret Holmes Williamson. "Decoding Middletown's Easter Bunny: A Study in American Iconography," *Semiotica* 32 (1980), 221-32.

Chodorow, Nancy. "Family Structure and Feminine Personality," pp. 43-66 in M. Rosaldo and L. Lamphere (eds.). *Woman, Culture and Society.* Stanford, Calif.: Stanford University Press, 1974.

Churches of Delaware County, 1976. Muncie, Ind.: Christian Ministries of Delaware County, 1976.

Cohen, Eric J. "Holiness and Health: An Examination of the Relationship between Christian Holiness and Mental Health," *Journal of Psychology and Theology* 5 (Fall 1977), 285-91.

Coldwater, Charles F. *The Ghost of Gas Boom Past and Other Poems.* Muncie, Ind.: Phil Ball, 1980.

Cooley, Michael F. "Socioeconomic Correlates of Religious Mobility among Seattle Residents." M.A. thesis, Brigham Young University, 1976.

Davis, James Allan. *General Social Surveys, 1972-1980: Cumulative Data.* Chicago: National Opinion Research Center, 1980.

Demerath, N. J., III. *Social Class in American Protestantism.* Chicago: Rand McNally, 1965.

Dillingham, Harry C. "Protestant Religion and Social Status," *American Journal of Sociology* 70 (1965), 416-22.

————. "Rejoinder to Social Class and Church Participation," *American Journal of Sociology* 73 (1967), 110-14.

Ducey, Michael H. *Sunday Morning.* New York: Free Press, 1977.

Dufus, R. L. *New York Times Book Review,* April 25, 1937.

Durkheim, Emile. *Le Suicide.* Paris: University of France Press, 1930.

————. *The Division of Labor in Society* (G. Simpson, trans.). New York: Macmillan, 1933. (Originally published in 1893.)

————. *Suicide: A Study in Sociology.* New York: Free Press, 1951. (Originally published in 1897.)

————. *The Elementary Forms of Religious Life* (Joseph Swain, trans.). New York: Free Press, 1965. (Originally published in 1915.)

Earle, John R., Dean D. Knudsen, and Donald W. Shriver, Jr. *Spindles and Spires: A Restudy of Religion and Social Change in Gastonia.* Atlanta: John Knox Press, 1976.

Ellul, Jacques. *The Technological Society.* New York: Alfred Knopf, 1964.

Emerson's Muncie Directory and Delaware County Gazeteer. Cincinnati, Ohio: Williams Directory Company, 1880 to 1937.

Fee, Joan. "Political Continuity and Change," pp. 76-102, in Andrew M. Greeley, William C. McCready, and Kathleen McCourt. *Catholic Schools in a Declining Church.* Kansas City, Mo.: Sheed and Ward, 1976.

Feeley-Harnik, Gillian. *The Lord's Table: Eucharist and Passover in Early Christianity.* Philadelphia: University of Pennsylvania Press, 1981.

Finney, John M. "A Theory of Religious Commitment," *Sociological Analysis* 39 (1978), 19-34.

Fox, William S., and Elton F. Jackson. "Protestant-Catholic Differences in Educational Achievement and Persistence in School," *Journal for the Scientific Study of Religion* 12 (March 1973), 65-84.

Fukuyama, Yoshio. "The Major Dimensions of Church Membership," *Review of Religious Research* 2 (1961), 154-61.

Fuller, Raymond G. *A Study of Youth Needs and Services in Middletown.* Washington, D.C.: American Youth Commission, American Council on Education, 1937.

Gallup, George H. *The Gallup Poll: Public Opinion 1935-1971.* New York: Random House, 1972.

Gallup, George, Jr., and David Poling. *The Search for America's Faith.* Nashville, Tenn.: Abingdon Press, 1980.

Gallup Opinion Index. *Religion in America.* Princeton, N.J.: American Institute of Public Opinion, 1976, 1977-1978, 1978-1980, 1979-1980, and 1981.

Garrison, Winfred Ernest, and Alfred T. De Groot. *The Disciples of Christ: A History.* St. Louis: Bethany Press, 1948.

Gittelsohn, Roland B. "Have We Outgrown God?" *Saturday Review* 16 (September 1961), 23-25.

Glenn, Norval D., and Ruth Hyland. "Religious Preference and Worldly Success: Some Evidence from National Surveys," *American Sociological Review* 32 (February 1967), 73-85.

Glock, Charles Y., Benjamin B. Ringer, and Earl R. Babbie. *To Comfort and to Challenge.* Berkeley, Calif.: University of California Press, 1967.

Glock, Charles Y., and Rodney Stark. *Religion and Society in Tension.* Chicago: Rand McNally, 1965.

————. *Christian Beliefs and Anti-Semitism.* New York: Harper and Row, 1966.

Goldstein, Sidney. "Socioeconomic Differentials among Religious Groups in the United States," *American Journal of Sociology* 74 (1969), 612-31.

Goode, William J. *Women in Divorce.* New York: Free Press, 1956.

Greeley, Andrew M. "The Protestant Ethic: Time for a Moratorium," *Sociological Analysis* 25 (1964), 22-33.

————. "Religious Intermarriage in a Denominational Society," *American Journal of Sociology* 75 (May 1970), 949-52.

————. *The Denominational Society: A Sociological Approach to Religion in America.* Glenview, Ill.: Scott, Foresman, 1972a.

————. *Unsecular Man: The Persistence of Religion.* New York: Schocken Books, 1972b.

————. *The American Catholic.* New York: Basic Books, 1977.

————. "The Sociology of American Catholics," *Annual Review of Sociology* 5 (1979), 91-111.

Hadden, Jeffrey K. "Religion and the Construction of Social Problems," *Sociological Analysis* 41 (1980), 99-108.

Haimbaugh, Frank D. (ed.). *History of Delaware County, Indiana.* Indianapolis, Ind.: Historical Publishing, 1924.

Handy, Robert T. *A History of the Churches in the United States and Canada.* New York: Oxford University Press, 1977.

Helm, Thomas B. *History of Delaware County, Indiana.* Chicago: Kingman Brothers, 1881.

Herrick, Horace N., and William Warren Sweet. *A History of the North Indiana Conference of the Methodist Episcopal Church.* Indianapolis, Ind.: W. K. Stewart, 1917.

Hewitt, John D., and Dwight W. Hoover. "Social Order in Middletown: 1845-1975." Paper presented at the Social Science History Association Meeting, Rochester, New York, November 8, 1980.

High Street Church History. Unpublished manuscript. Muncie, Ind.: High Street Church, no date.

Hirsch, Travis, and Rodney Stark. "Hellfire and Delinquency," *Social Problems* 17 (1964), 203-13.

Hollingshead, A. B. *Elmtown's Youth.* New York: John Wiley and Sons, 1961.

—————. *Elmtown's Youth and Elmtown Revisited.* New York: John Wiley and Sons, 1975.

Hudson, Winthrop S. *Religion in America* (2nd ed.). New York: Charles Scribner's Sons, 1973.

Isambert, Francios A. "Le Sociologue, le prêtreaet le fidèle," pp. 219-45 in Henri Mendras (ed.). *La Sagesse et le désordre.* Paris: Editions Gallimard, 1980.

Jackson, Elton F., William S. Fox, and Harry J. Crockett, Jr. "Religion and Occupational Achievement," *American Sociological Review* 35 (1970), 48-63.

Jensen, Richard. "The Lynds Revisited," *Indiana Magazine of History* 75 (December 1979), 303-19.

Johnston, Lloyd D., Jerald G. Bachman, and Patrick M. O'Malley. *Monitoring the Future: Questionnaire Responses from the Nation's High School Seniors: 1977.* Ann Arbor, Mich.: Institute for Social Research, University of Michigan, 1980.

Jones, Carmel L. "Migration, Religion, and Occupational Mobility of Southern Appalachians in Munci, Indiana." Ed.D. dissertation, Ball State University, 1978.

Kemper, G. W. H. (M.D.). *A Twentieth Century History of Delaware County* (vol. 1). Chicago: Lewis Publishing, 1908.

Kim, Hei C. "The Relationship of Protestant Ethic Beliefs and Values to Achievement," *Journal for the Scientific Study of Religion* 16 (1977), 255-62.

King, Michael L. "Sermons and Sorcery: Churches Use Magic to Lure Parishioners," *Wall Street Journal* (5 August 1980), pp. 25.

Kirsten, Lawrence K. *The Lutheran Ethic: The Impact of Religion on Laymen and Clergy.* Detroit: Wayne State University Press, 1970.

Larsen, John A. "Self-Actualization as Related to Frequency, Range, and Pattern of Religious Experience," *Journal of Psychology and Theology* 7 (Spring 1979), pp. 39-47.

Lazerwitz, Bernard. "Religion and Social Structure in the United States," pp. 426-39 in Louis Schneider (ed.). *Religion, Culture, and Society.* New York: John Wiley and Sons, 1964.

Lenski, Gerhard. *The Religious Factor: A Sociological Study of Religious Impact on Politics, Economics, and Family Life.* Garden City, N.Y.: Doubleday, 1961.

Lewis, Sinclair. *Babbitt.* New York: Harcourt and Brace, 1922.

Liu, William T., and Nathaniel J. Pallone. *Catholic/USA.* New York: John Wiley and Sons, 1970.

Lynd, Helen. "Middletown." Speech at the American Sociological Association. *Community Section Newsletter* 10 (Fall 1980).

Lynd, Robert S., and Helen Merrell Lynd. *Middletown: A Study in American Culture.* New York: Harcourt and Brace, 1929.

—————. *Middletown in Transition: A Study in Cultural Conflicts.* New York: Harcourt and Brace, 1937.

McCready, William C., and Andrew M. Greeley. *The Ultimate Values of the American Population.* Beverly Hills, Calif.: Sage Publications, 1976.

McLaughlin, William G. *Revivals, Awakenings, and Reform.* Chicago: University of Chicago Press, 1978.

Martin, Bernice. "The Sacralization of Disorder: Symbolism in Rock Music," *Sociological Analysis* 40 (Summer 1979), 87-124.

Marty, Martin E. "Interpreting American Pluralism," pp. 78-90 in Jackson W. Carroll, Douglas W. Johnson, and Martin E. Marty. *Religion in America: 1950 to the Present.* San Francisco: Harper and Row, 1979.

Marks, Gary. "Religion: Opiate of Inspiration of Civil Rights Militancy among Negroes?" *American Sociological Review* 32 (1967), 64-72.

Marx, Karl *Das Kapital* (Samuel Moore and Edward Aveling, trans.). Chicago: Encyclopaedia Britannica Great Books Edition, 1952.

Mauss, Marcel. *The Gift: Forms and Functions of Exchange in Archaic Societies* (Ian Cunnison, trans.). London: Cohen and West, 1969.

Mayer, Albert J., and Harry Sharp. "Religious Preference and Worldly Success," *American Sociological Review* 27 (April 1962), 218-27.

Mitchell, William R. *History of the First Universalist Church.* Unpublished manuscript. Muncie, Ind.: First Universalist Church, 1974.

Miyakawa, T. Scott. *Protestants and Pioneers: Individualism and Conformity on the American Frontier.* Chicago: University of Chicago Press, 1964.

Monahan, Thomas P. "The Extent of Interdenominational Marriage in the United States," *Journal for the Scientific Study of Religion* 10 (Summer 1971), 85-92.

Mowrer, Ernest. *Family Disorganization.* Chicago: University of Chicago Press, 1927.

Mueller, Charles W. "Evidence on the Relationship between Religion and Educational Attainment," *Sociology of Education* 53 (July 1980), 140-52.

Mueller, Samuel A. "Dimensions of Interdenominational Mobility in the United States," *Journal for the Scientific Study of Religion* 10 (Summer 1971), 76-84.

Myerhoff, Barbara G. "Organization and Ecstasy: Deliberate and Accidental Communitas among Huichol Indians and American Youth," pp. 33-67 in Sally Falk Moore and Barbara G. Myerhoff (eds.). *Symbol and Politics in Communal Ideology.* Ithaca, N.Y.: Cornell University Press, 1975.

Nash, Roderick. *The Nervous Generation: American Thought, 1917-1930.* Chicago: Rand McNally, 1970.

National Opinion Research Center. *Cumulative Codebook for the 1971-1977 General Social Surveys.* Chicago: University of Chicago, 1977.

—————. *Cumulative Codebook for the 1972-1980 General Social Surveys.* Chicago: University of Chicago, 1980.

Nelson, L. D. "Functions and Dimensions of Religion," *Sociological Analysis* 35 (1974), 263-72.

Newby, Richard P. *Life Is to Be Celebrated and Other Messages.* Dublin, Ind.: Prinit Press, 1980.

Niebuhr, H. Richard. *The Social Sources of Denominationalism.* Cleveland: World Publishing, 1968. (Originally published in 1929.)

Norwood, Frederick A. *History of the North Indiana Conference, 1917-1956.* Winona Lake, Ind.: Light and Life Press, 1957.

O'Connell, Brian J. "Dimensions of Religiosity among Catholics," *Review of Religious Research* 16 (Spring 1975), 198-207.

Ogburn, William F. (with the assistance of Clark Tibbitts). "The Family and Its Functions," pp. 661-708 in *Recent Social Trends in the United States.* New York: McGraw-Hill, 1933.

Polk's Muncie City Directory. Taylor, Mich.: R. L. Polk, 1938 on.

Pope, Liston. *Millhands and Preachers: A Study of Gastonia.* New Haven, Conn.: Yale University Press, 1942.

Redfield, Robert. *The Folk Culture of Yucatan.* Chicago: University of Chicago Press, 1941.

Roof, Wade Clark. "Socioeconomic Differentials among White Socioreligious Groups in the United States," *Social Forces* 58 (1979), 280-89.

Roof, Wade Clark, and Christopher Kirk Hadaway. "Shifts in Religious Preference: The Mid-Seventies," *Journal for the Scientific Study of Religion* 16 (1977), 409-12.

Rosaldo, Michelle Z. "Woman, Culture, and Society: A Theoretical Overview," pp. 17-42 in M. Z. Rosaldo and L. Lamphere (eds.). *Woman, Culture, and Society.* Stanford, Calif.: Stanford University Press, 1974.

Rudolph, L. C. *Hoosier Zion: The Presbyterians in Early Indiana.* New Haven, Conn.: Yale University Press, 1963.

Sandeen, Ernest R. *The Roots of Fundamentalism: British and American Millenarianism, 1800-1930.* Chicago: University of Chicago Press, 1970.

Schneider, Herbert Wallace. *Religion in Twentieth Century America.* Cambridge, Mass.: Harvard University Press, 1967. (Originally published in 1952.)

Schroeder, W. Widick, and Victor Obenhaus. *Religion in American Culture: Unity and Diversity in a Midwestern County.* New York: Free Press, 1964.

Schuman, H. "The Religious Factor in Detroit: Review, Replication, and Reanalysis," *American Sociological Review* 36 (1971), 30-48.

Shoman, J. Frank. "Does Religion Have a Future?" *The Torch* 53 (Spring 1980), 28-29.

Smith, T. Lynn, and Paul E. Zopf, Jr. *Demography: Principles and Methods.* Philadelphia: F. A. Davis, 1970.

Spencer, Herbert. "Progress: Its Law and Cause," pp. 8-62 in *Essays: Scientific, Political, and Speculative (vol. 1).* New York: Appleton, 1915. (Originally published in 1857.)

Stark, Rodney, Bruce D. Foster, Charles Y. Glock, and Harold E. Quinley. *Wayward Shepherds: Prejudice and the Protestant Clergy.* New York: Harper and Row, 1971.

Stark, Rodney, and Charles Y. Glock. *American Piety: The Nature of Religious Commitment.* Berkeley, Calif.: University of California Press, 1968.

Strommen, Merton P., Milo L. Brekke, Ralph C. Underwager, and Arthur L. Johnson. *A Study of Generations.* Minneapolis: Augsburg Publishing, 1972.

Swanson, Guy A. "Modern Secularity," pp. 801-34 in Donald R. Cuttler (ed.). *The Religious Situation: 1968.* Boston: Beacon Press, 1968.

Tamney, Joseph. "The Prediction of Religious Change," *Sociological Analysis* 26 (Summer 1965), 72-81.

Thernstrom, Steven. *Poverty and Progress: Social Mobility in a 19th Century City.* Cambridge, Mass.: Harvard University Press, 1964.

Thomas, Belle. *The First One Hundred Years.* Muncie, Ind.: The Women's Auxiliary and the Flower Mission of the First Presbyterian Church, 1938.

Thomas, John L. *Religion and the American People.* Westminster, Md.: Newman Press, 1963.

Thomas, William I., and Florian W. Znaniecki. *The Polish Peasant in Europe and America.* New York: Dover Publications, 1958. (Originally published in 1918.)

Thornes, Barbara, and Jean Collard. *Who Divorces?* London: Routledge and Kegan Paul, 1979.

Thrasher, Frederic M. *The Gang.* Chicago: University of Chicago Press, 1927.

Tocqueville, Alexis de. *Democracy in America.* Garden City, N.Y.: Mayer Edition, Doubleday, 1969. (Originally published in 1835.)

Tönnies, Ferdinand. *Community and Society (Gemeinschaft and Gesellschaft)* (C. P. Loomis, trans.). East Lansing, Mich.: Michigan State University Press, 1957. (Originally published in 1887.)

Troeltsch, Ernst. *The Social Teachings of the Christian Churches.* New York: Macmillan, 1932.

Tuchman, Barbara. *The Proud Tower.* New York: Macmillan, 1966.

Turner, Victor, and Edith Turner. *Image and Pilgrimage in Christian Culture.* New York: Columbia University Press, 1978.

Underwood, Kenneth Wilson. *Protestant and Catholic.* Boston: Beacon Press, 1957.

United States House of Representatives. Fifty-Second Congress, First Session, House Miscellaneous Document 340, Part 17, Eleventh Census, *Churches,* 1891.

United States Bureau of the Census. *Statistics of the United States in 1860.* Washington, D.C.: U.S. Government Printing Office, 1866.

————. *Eleventh Census, 1890, Indiana.* Washington, D.C.: U.S. Government Printing Office.

————. *Twelfth Census, 1900, Indiana.* Washington, D.C.: U.S. Government Printing Office.

Van Meter, Lorna. "High Street Methodist Church, Muncie, Indiana, and the Social Gospel, 1890-1910." Unpublished seminar paper. Muncie, Ind.: Ball State University, 1979.

Vernon, Glen M. *Sociology of Religion.* New York: McGraw-Hill, 1962.

Von Hildebrand, Dietrich. *Liturgy and Personality.* New York: Longmans, Green, 1943.

Warner, W. Lloyd. *The Living and the Dead.* New Haven, Conn.: Yale University Press, 1959.

————. *The Family of God.* New Haven, Conn.: Yale University Press, 1961.

Warner, W. Lloyd, and Paul S. Lunt. *The Social Life of a Modern Community.* New Haven, Conn.: Yale University Press, 1941.

Weber, Max. *The Protestant Ethic and the Spirit of Capitalism* (Talcott Parsons, trans.). New York: Charles Scribner's Sons, 1958. (Originally published in 1904.)

————. *The Sociology of Religion.* Boston: Beacon Press, 1963. (Originally published in 1922.)

Westoff, Charles F., Robert G. Potter, Jr., Philip C. Sagi, and Elliot G. Mischler. *Family Growth in Metropolitan America.* Princeton, N.J.: Princeton University Press, 1961.

Westoff, Charles F., and Raymond H. Potvin. *College Women and Fertility Values.* Princeton, N.J.: Princeton University Press, 1967.

Westoff, Charles F., and Norman B. Ryder. *The Contraceptive Revolution.* Princeton, N.J.: Princeton University Press, 1977.

Whyte, William Foote. *Street Corner Society: The Social Structure of an Italian Slum.* Chicago: University of Chicago Press, 1943. (Enlarged edition, 1955.)

Wilmore, August Cleland. *History of the White River Conference of the Church of the United Brethren in Christ.* Dayton, Ohio: United Brethren Publishing House, 1925.

Wirth, Louis. *The Ghetto.* Chicago: University of Chicago Press, 1928.

Yearbook of American Churches, 1933 (Herman Weber, ed.). New York: Round Table Press, 1933.

Yearbook of American and Canadian Churches, 1976 (Constant H. Jacquet, Jr., ed.). Nashville, Tenn.: Abingdon Press, 1976.

Yearbook of American and Canadian Churches, 1979 (Constant H. Jackquet, Jr., ed.). Nashville, Tenn.: Abingdon Press, 1979.

Zorbaugh, Harvey W. *The Gold Coast and the Slum.* Chicago: University of Chicago Press, 1929.

Published
Middletown Papers

Austin, Penelope C. "The Federal Presence in Middletown, 1937-1977," *Tocqueville Review* II (Spring/Summer 1980), 92-107.

Bahr, Howard M. "Changes in Family Life in Middletown, 1924-77," *Public Opinion Quarterly* 44 (Fall 1980), 35-52.

————. "The Perrigo Paper: A Local Influence Upon *Middletown in Transition*," *Indiana Magazine of History* LXXVIII (March 1982), 1-25.

————. "Shifts in the Denominational Demography of Middletown, 1924-1977," *Journal for the Scientific Study of Religion*, forthcoming.

Bahr, Howard M., Theodore Caplow, and Geoffrey K. Leigh. "The Slowing of Modernization in Middletown," pp. 219-32 in Louis Kriesberg (ed.). *Research in Social Movements, Conflicts and Change* (vol. 3). Greenwich, Conn.: JAI Press, 1980.

Caplow, Theodore, "The Gradual Progress of Equality in Middletown: A Tocquevillean Theme Re-examined," *Tocqueville Review* I (Fall 1979), 114-26.

————. "The Measurement of Social Change in Middletown," *Indiana Magazine of History* LXXV (December 1979), 344-57.

————. "The Changing Middletown Family," *Journal of the History of Sociology* II (Fall-Winter 1979-80), 66-98.

————. "Middletown Fifty Years After," *Contemporary Sociology* 9 (January 1980), 46-50.

————. "Evaluation des changements sociaux à Middletown," pp. 49-60 in R. Boudon, F. Bourricaud, and A. Girard (eds.). *Science et théorie de l'opinion publique*. Paris: Retz, 1981.

————. "Christmas Gifts and Kin Networks," *American Sociological Review* 47 (June 1982), forthcoming.

————. "Religion in Middletown," *The Public Interest*, forthcoming.

Caplow, Theodore, and Howard M. Bahr. "Half a Century of Change in Adolescent Attitudes: Replication of a Middletown Survey by the Lunds," *Public Opinion Quarterly* 43 (Spring 1979), 1-17.

Caplow, Theodore, Howard M. Bahr, and Bruce A. Chadwick. "Piety in Middletown," *Transaction* 18 (January/February 1981), 34-37.

Caplow, Theodore, and Bruce A. Chadwick. "Inequality and Life Styles in Middletown, 1920-1978," *Social Science Quarterly* 60 (December 1979), 367-86.

Caplow, Theodore, and Margaret Holmes Williamson. "Decoding Middletown's Easter Bunny: A Study in American Iconography," *Semiotica* 32 (1980), 221-32.

Chadwick, Bruce A., and C. Bradford Campbell. "Change in the Two-Income Family Middletown USA from 1924 to 1978," pp. 27-42 in Stephen J. Bahr (ed.). *Economics and the Family.* Lexington, Mass.: Lexington Books, forthcoming.

Guterbock, Thomas M. "Social Class and Voting Choices in Middletown," *Social Forces* 58 (June 1980), 1044-56.

Hewitt, John D., and William S. Johnson. "Dropping Out in 'Middletown'," *The High School Journal* 62 (March 1979), 252-56.

Leigh, Geoffrey K. "Kinship Interaction over the Family Life Span," *Journal of Marriage and the Family* 44 (February 1982), 197-208.

Margolick, David M. "Law in 'Middletown'," *National Law Journal,* (August 20, 1979), 1, 14-17.

INDEXES

Author Index

Subject Index

Abortion, 9

Academic achievement, and adolescent church attendance, 223

Achievement, effect of religious affiliation on, 176-77

Adolescent church attendance, 77-78, 220-21; Catholic, 222; nationwide, 222; and social class, 222; sex differences in, 222; Protestant, 222-23; and academic achievement, 223

Adolescents: religious beliefs of, 93-94, 95, 219-20; religious attitudes of, 97-98, 149, 220-21; religious preferences of, 113-35; importance of organized religion to, 218; influence of religion on, 218; Sunday activities of, 226, 227-30

Adventists, participation in public events, 9

Afterlife, belief in, 92

Age: and church attendance, 77; and participation in nonchurch rituals, 131; and devotional index, 155

Aglow, and charismatic movement, 277

Agnosticism: decline of, 285; and social class, 285

Alms giving, 285

Anglicans, fertility rate of, 122

Anti-Catholic prejudice, 166-69

Antireligion sociologists, 30-31

Anti-Semitic attitudes: of Christians, 23; in theological doctrine, 23; secular, 23-24; difference between clergy and laity, 25

Apostles' Creed, 195

Assemblies of God, participation in public events, 9

Atheism, 102

Attendance, church. See Church attendance

Baptist church: distribution of, 11-12, 13; founding of, 43-44, 46, 48, 50; relative size of, 110-11; membership in, 287-88

Baptists: retention rate of, 117; interdenominational marriage of, 118; divorce rate of, 120; fertility rate of, 123; education of, 125; social class of, 125; and revivals, 136; devotional index of, 155; participation in new rituals, 290

Baptists, southern, participation in public events, 9

Belief, and religious commitment, 147

Belief system, 91-95, 164-66, 221

Bias in sociology of religion, 30-32

Bible: and acts of private devotion, 146; as word of God, 165

Bible Belt, 269

Bible reading: as devotional act, 146; decline of in family, 148

Billy Graham Crusade, 275-76

Billy Sunday Crusade, 58

Black Muslims, 296

Blacks, in population, 4

Blessing of food, verbal, decline of, 148

Brethren Church: relative size of, 110-11; as denominational preference, 112,

❊ ❊ ❊

All Faithful People is the second of several studies to be based on the research of the Middletown III Project, undertaken by a group of social scientists in the 1970s to replicate the Middletown (Muncie, Indiana) studies of Robert and Helen Lynd in the 1920s and 1930s. Theodore Caplow, Howard M. Bahr, and Bruce A. Chadwick are the principal investigators in the Project and senior authors of *All Faithful People* and of *Middletown Families*, published by the University of Minnesota Press in 1982.

Theodore Caplow, Commonwealth Professor of Sociology at the University of Virginia, is the author of *The Sociology of Work*, *Two Against One: Coalitions in Triads*, *Toward Social Hope*, *The Academic Marketplace*, and many other books and articles.

Howard M. Bahr is professor of sociology and director of the Family and Demographic Research Institute at Brigham Young University. He is the author of *Skid Row: An Introduction to Disaffiliation* and co-author of *Old Men Drunk and Sober*, *Women Alone*, *Sunshine Widows: Adapting to Sudden Bereavement*, and *Life in Large Families*.

Bruce A. Chadwick, professor and chairman of the department of sociology at Brigham Young, has published widely in the areas of ethnic relations and social psychology. He is co-author of *American Ethnicity* and co-editor of *Native Americans Today* and *Population, Resources, and the Future*.

Dwight W. Hoover, Lawrence A. Martin, Joseph B. Tamney, and Margaret Holmes Williamson are contributing authors of *All Faithful People*.

Dwight W. Hoover is professor of history and director of the Center for Middletown Studies at Ball State University, where he has taught since 1959. His chief research interest is American social and intellectual history; he is the author of *Henry James, Sr., and the Religion of Community, The Red and the Black,* and other books and articles. Hoover served as a consultant to the Middletown Film Project and the Middletown III Project.

Lawrence A. Martin has been pastor of the First Presbyterian Church in Muncie, Indiana, since 1973. He is active in inter-denominational church affairs and has served as moderator of the Whitewater Valley Presbytery in central Indiana. In addition to a special interest in sociology and religion, he claims some expertise in the Hebrew Bible.

Joseph B. Tamney, professor of sociology at Ball State University, is the author of *Solidarity in a Slum* and many articles in his principal fields of interest, community life and religion from a cross-cultural perspective.

Margaret Holmes Williamson is associate professor of anthropology and chairs the department of sociology and anthropology at Mary Washington College. She acted as consulting anthropologist for the Middletown III Project and was a contributing author of *Middletown Families*.